REDUNDANT SPACES
IN CITIES AND REGIONS?

REDUNDANT SPACES IN CITIES AND REGIONS?

STUDIES IN INDUSTRIAL DECLINE AND SOCIAL CHANGE

INSTITUTE OF BRITISH GEOGRAPHERS
SPECIAL PUBLICATION, NO. 15

Edited by

J. ANDERSON

S. DUNCAN

R. HUDSON

1983

ACADEMIC PRESS

A Subsidiary of Harcourt Brace Jovanovich, Publishers

London · New York · Paris · San Diego · San Francisco
São Paulo · Sydney · Tokyo · Toronto

ACADEMIC PRESS INC. (LONDON) LTD.
24/28 Oval Road,
London NW1

United States Edition published by
ACADEMIC PRESS INC.
111 Fifth Avenue
New York, New York 10003

British Library Cataloguing in Publication Data

Redundant spaces in cities and regions? – (Institute of
  British Geographers Special Publication,
  ISSN 0073-9006; no. 15)
  1. City planning – Great Britain   2. Open spaces
  – Great Britain
  I. Anderson, J.   II. Duncan, S.   III. Hudson, R.
  IV. Series
  33.7'8   HT169.G7

  ISBN 0-12-058480-8

  LCCCN 83-070171

Text set in 11/13 Plantin
by Oxford Verbatim Limited
Printed in Great Britain by
Galliard (Printers) Ltd, Great Yarmouth

CONTRIBUTORS

JAMES ANDERSON, Department of Geography, The Open University, Milton Keynes, UK

JAMES BROWN, working as a civil servant, correspondence c/o Peter Smith

DAVE BYRNE, Department of Sociology and Social Policy, Durham University, UK

ALLAN COCHRANE, Faculty of Social Sciences, The Open University, Milton Keynes, UK

JOE DOHERTY, Department of Geography, St. Andrews University, Fife, Scotland, UK

SIMON DUNCAN, Department of Geography, London School of Economics and Urban and Regional Studies Division, Sussex University, Falmer, Brighton, UK

ANDY FRIEDMAN, Department of Economics, University of Bristol, UK

RAY HUDSON, Department of Geography, Durham University, UK

KEVIN MORGAN, School of Social Sciences, Sussex University, Falmer, Brighton, UK

LINDA MURGATROYD, Lancaster Regionalism Group, Department of Sociology, University of Lancaster, UK

SUZANNE MACKENZIE, Department of Geography, Queens University, Ontario, Canada

DON PARSON, School of Architecture and Urban Planning, University College Los Angeles, California, USA

FRED ROBINSON, Centre for Urban and Regional Development Studies, University of Newcastle, UK

NICK ROGERS, Centre for Urban and Regional Studies, University of Birmingham, UK

DAMARIS ROSE, Department of Geography, McGill University, Québec, Canada

ANDREW SAYER, Urban and Regional Studies Division, Sussex University, Falmer, Brighton, UK

PETER SMITH, Trade Union Research Centre, Glasgow College of Technology, Scotland, UK

JOHN URRY, Department of Sociology, Lancaster University, UK

PREFACE

This collection of essays focusses on British cities and regions during periods of crisis, periods when some parts of the country apparently become "redundant" to society's needs. To explore such situations, and indeed to question what "redundant" means in different circumstances, the essays cover a range of related economic, social and political issues in the context of changing geography. The chapters address questions of uneven development in capitalism and its local effects, worker-management relations and the creation of areas of social deprivation, the management of surplus labour in space, the links between home life and urban development, racial conflict and nationalism in the context of economic change, and finally state "spatial" policy in the cases of a new town, local economic strategy and enterprise zones.

It is because of changes in such activities and processes that cities and regions change in character, and perhaps become redundant. But, at the same time, particular social processes are shaped by the character of the cities and regions in which they take place, and hence a full understanding of the crisis requires an analysis at the level of the city or region as well as at the national or international level. The different types of processes covered in the book are all interrelated and the focus on one country, Britain, helps to bring out some of their more important interrelationships.

The collection was developed from some discussion papers given to the Social Geography Study Group of the Institute of British Geographers. As well as thanking the contributing authors, we would like to thank all those, both in the IBG and outside it, who helped in making the collection of essays into a book.

London
July 1983

J. Anderson
S. Duncan
R. Hudson

CONTENTS

ONE

Uneven development, redundant spaces?: an introduction

J. ANDERSON, S. DUNCAN and R. HUDSON

(August 1982)

Redundant spaces? To whom are they redundant and why? Perhaps to the industries which have pulled out or closed down – but what about new industries to replace them, what about the people left behind? Why has "de-industrialization" affected some areas more than others, and how has it affected the people in them? What have governments been doing – what can they do – about the economic, social and political problems of the "industrial graveyards"? How does uneven geographical development relate to the accelerated processes of social change in a period of crisis?

This collection of essays provides some answers to these questions. It started as a number of discussion papers in the Institute of British Geographers Social Geography Group, but to attempt to answer such inter-related questions it was clear that we had to expand our concerns beyond Social Geography's traditional focus on "social" issues. The social problems of the "industrial graveyards" are certainly related to economic and political problems, even if sometimes the nature of the interrelationships is by no means obvious. The different problems are interwoven in a complex web of causes and effects, and they compound one another partly through sharing the same geographical spaces – a situation summed up in the popular terminology of the so-called "inner-city problem" and the "regional problem". The question is how to unravel the web of problems, to uncover the interrelationships between different processes. How, to start with, should we relate the "social" to the "economic"?

1. The "social" and the "economic"

Social problems are often seen simply as the result of economic problems: social deprivation and alienation, and associated political conflicts, are seen as deeply influenced, if not caused, by the collapse of employment in many industrial areas. However, the "economic" and the "social" are much more deeply integrated than this conventional cause-and-effect view would suggest. Indeed this simple linear linkage depends on a rather shallow understanding of the concepts "social" and "economic". In this view, they are seen as autonomous. It would be possible to examine first economic changes and then, separately, the social problems which result. This reflects a conventional assumption – that economic and social change are essentially separate – an assumption which underlies much of the traditional organization of the Social Sciences, very much split into Economics-based and Sociology-based specializations. Even Geography, which has a tradition of claiming to act as a synthesizing discipline, reflects this. The split between Economic Geography and Social Geography reaches far into teaching and research.

But if we look rather more deeply at the "economic" and "social", we find that the economic is also social. This is not just a matter of effects, but also of causes. Indeed, the very foundation of economic change lies in social change. For instance, economic change also means changes in the social organization and methods of working, in mechanisms of work discipline and control: the social relations of the factory lie directly behind its economic behaviour. In like manner, these workplace relations, and changes in them, are deeply affected by social relations outside the workplace such as those of the family, or between different sections of the working class, or the wider relations of power and control between classes. For example, how would a modern city function without a mass of unpaid domestic labourers (male as well as female); how different would industrial relations be without large pools of unemployed labour either *in situ* or available through migration; would not industrial relations have developed differently in Britain without the political weight exercised by large landowners or the City of London?

Finally, the economic is deeply influenced by the actions of the state. Capitalist states attempt to manage these social relations both at work and outside, as well as pursuing direct economic policies. Not surprisingly, several chapters of this book explore these themes.

However, the social and the political are also economic. Partly, this follows as simple inversion. Family relations, or state action, are now seen to be directly involved in production and are not things that merely follow after. Modern capitalist production is itself, above all, a social activity. But also, and crucially, social and political relations are partly determined by economic change. An economic structure which produces concentrations of proletarians working in the same industry and in the same way (as in the coalfield areas in Britain) is likely to lead to social and political behaviour far different from that likely in an area of small firms, family farms and the self-employed – as in much of Cornwall and Devon, for instance. This relationship between work patterns and behaviour outside work is never simple: for instance, collective political action by coalminers in Britain is encouraged by egalitarian working practices just as the tradition of hierarchically-organized work gangs common in much of the steel industry militates against it; furthermore, gender role divisions may intervene, and indeed the political culture of coal in Britain seems overwhelmingly male-dominated. These links between work and social activity outside work are important, though complex. This completes the circle, for people's behaviour has to be understood in terms of this uneven development of social relations; economic development will take place in a specific way and political relations will constrain the economic actions or policies which may, or may not, be achieved. Again, some of the chapters in this book pursue these links. But certainly, if Social Science (including Human Geography) is about understanding change with a view to controlling or even changing change, it does not help at all to assume that the economic and the social are separate and autonomous realms.

2. The "social and the "spatial"

As may be clear from the discussion so far, it is difficult to conceive of these integrated social and economic processes in non-spatial terms, even if much of current Sociology and Economics has a good (in fact, bad) try. The advanced division of labour characteristic of contemporary British society simultaneously gives rise to spatial concentrations of both highly skilled and de-skilled workers. Their differing workplace relations affect, and are affected by, relations outside the workplace. These also vary in different places, and their geographical unevenness in turn effects whether particular types of economic and social development take place, or fail to take place. This is the other major theme of the collection: the necessity to integrate the "social" (now including "the economic") with the "spatial". Very often these are also seen as separate or autonomous to the detriment of our understanding of the social world. How, then, should we relate them?

Again the relationship can be conceived in a simple linear "cause and effect" fashion. Social change occurs and its effect varies in different places because the things which are changing have particular geographical locations. The steel industry declines, for example, and areas with steel plants are clearly those most affected. The social division of labour is also a spatial division of labour: change in the former produces change in the latter. In essence, spatial change is "read-off" from social change.

However, this initial view is inadequate. Social change is not, as it were, being mapped for the first time, on a clean slate. Social relations are *already* unevenly developed over space as a result of previous social developments *before* any particular current round of social changes occur. This pre-existing uneven development actively shapes the processes of change. Space is a *formative* element in social change, not simply an effect of it. People use space, respond to it, imbue it with meaning, and act within it. It is, for instance, an integral part of the process of industrial and technological change: plant relocation is one way of achieving change in work practices, of pruning workforces, or of obtaining different sorts of labour. Such action will again change the character of particular areas, changing, for example, the type of labour and the way it works, or the level of physical infrastructure. The creation of uneven development is a cumulative process.

As these examples show, "spatial processes" (such as plant relocation) are not in any sense independent of, or separate from, social processes. Indeed, rather than thinking in terms of "spatial processes", it is more illuminating to think of the "uneven development of social processes". Seeing social processes and problems in primarily geographical terms leads easily to an analytical distortion which obscures their *social* causes. It makes for "fetishism of space" (Anderson, 1973); relationships between people are formulated as relationships between geographical areas, and social problems *in* particular areas are posed as problems *of* those areas, rather than as spatially-differentiated problems of the social system. The so-called "inner city problem" and "regional problem" are cases in point. It is not, for example, an inner city location which produces the problems, nor are solutions to be found within these areas as if they were somehow isolated, or separable, from wider social processes, such as the general economic crisis, the changing world division of labour, the political situation in Britain, and so on. Conversely, the harmful effects of these wider processes are not confined to inner city locations: for instance the "inner city problem" is also found in "industrial graveyards" which do not occupy an inner city location.

The problems are spatially-differentiated, geographically uneven in their occurrence, but their causes are *social*. Hence the explanatory futility of much of "spatial analysis" which abstracted "spatial processes" from their social contexts, or emphasized spatial *form* at the expense of social *content*. This point is now widely accepted within Geography and congruent "spatial" disciplines such as Urban Sociology. However, the "spatial fetishism" or spatial determinism of earlier work did produce, as an over-reaction, a tendency to see the problems of particular areas simply as the imprint of wider national and international processes, forgetting that these processes operate in a situation of already existing uneven development, and denying the importance of more localized processes and responses to change. It is therefore important to reiterate that spatial unevenness and variation is a *formative* component in social change. Having thrown out the bath water, we should take care to save the baby.

3. Britain's economic decline

"De-industrialization" and its spatially-differentiated implications in Britain have to be seen in the context of the country's long-term decline as an industrial power. This wider national and international context is of course by no means the whole story as the chapters in this book make clear, but it is important in setting the scene for their more detailed analyses. So a few simple facts.

In 1870 Britain was the world's leading industrial country, accounting for nearly a third of world manufacturing production. But as a *producer*, it was overtaken by the USA in the 1880s and by Germany in the early 1900s, although it continued to be the world's leading country in terms of international *trade* well into the twentieth century (Rostow, 1978). Even as recently as 1950, it accounted for 25% of the world's exports in manufactured goods. Since then, *relative* decline has been precipitous. By the late 1970s, Britain's share of world manufacturing exports had fallen below 10% and this reflected more than simply faster industrial growth in other countries: by the end of 1981, Britain's manufacturing output in *absolute* terms had fallen below its 1967 level. By 1982 (for the first time since the relevant statistics were first collected), Britain was importing more manufactured goods than it exported. The decline in industrial *employment* has been even more marked. Even where output does expand, it no longer necessarily means an increase in terms of employment. Indeed, "jobless growth" is now the most common type of growth in many industrial sectors. For example, in the chemical industry, investment in plant increased by over 70% between 1964 and 1973, but employment *decreased* by over 8%. Given that many manufacturing firms have not even experienced "jobless growth", more like job-shedding decline, the effect on employment in manufacturing has been spectacular. In 1951, manufacturing accounted for 35% of jobs in Britain; by 1981, this figure had shrunk to 27%. In absolute terms, this was a decline from more than 8 million to 5·8 million jobs. Many workers were absorbed by the expansion of the service industries, especially in the 1960s, but, as manufacturing continued to decline, the growth in service employment did not keep pace, and indeed it has itself more recently been subject to decline. About 600 000 jobs disappeared in the service sector between mid 1979 and 1982 and the loss seems to be increasing: as many as 70 000 disappeared in the second quarter of 1982 alone. Added to the dramatic decline in manufacturing jobs, employment (the number of jobs in the economy) has declined even faster than unemployment has increased. Between mid 1979 and mid 1982, 2·3 million jobs (10½%) have been lost, well above the 1·9 million increase in unemployment; as many as 182 000 jobs vanished in the second quarter of 1982.

Moreover, in many cases a transfer from manufacturing to service employment has brought a drop in wages and, together with the rise in unemployment in both sectors, this has simultaneously meant cuts in working-class living standards and a reduction in effective demand for industry's products. Economic decline and social deprivation have been part of the same downward spiral.

Behind the decline in manufacturing output and employment has been a decline in investment and rates of profit. Industrial investment in Britain per head of population was as much as 60% *below* West German and Japanese rates in the 1960s. Since then, it has shrunk even further. In 1978, manufacturing output per employee in West Germany was 33% greater than in the UK. Net investment in British manufacturing industry (i.e. new investment net of capital consumption) fell from £2101 million in 1970 to an abysmal £154 m. in 1981; that is a decline of 93% (measured in constant 1975 prices). Not surprisingly, gross profit rates in manufacturing fell from some 20% of income in 1966 to less than 4% in 1974, and the decline has continued despite the fact that wage levels are now among the lowest in the EEC. Nor are the lower investment levels in the UK limited to direct manufacturing investment. In education, to take one crucial example, 90% of 16 to 19-year-olds in West Germany experienced some form of higher education, but only 40% of those in the UK were as lucky (Prais, 1982).

The comparative EEC figures for Gross Domestic Product (which include service as well as industrial production) show Britain's economic decline in stark terms (even allowing for variations in national accounting methods). In total GDP, the UK in 1978 not only lagged behind both France and Germany, but its GDP was *less than half* that of Germany's; and its *per capita* GDP was half that of Denmark's with only Italy, Ireland and Greece being lower.

The decline in particular industries and regions of Britain has been, if anything, even more dramatic. For example, Scotland accounted for some 12% of world shipbuilding output in the early 1950s. By the 1970s this figure was little more than 1%, while in terms of employment another traditional British industry, coalmining, has seen its workforce reduced from over 800 000 to less than 300 000 in the last thirty years. Nor is such decline confined to what were the staple industries of the nineteenth century. The car industry, symbol of post-war affluence, has suffered drastic cut-backs and Coventry, a showcase and producer of this affluence, has, like areas of older industry, begun to resemble a relic feature of a bygone age. Registered unemployment there rose from under 4% in 1971 to nearly 17% by 1981, and in some inner areas of Coventry it was estimated to be at least 30%. Moreover, branch plants established in development areas in the 1960s to replace old industries which had declined have increasingly been closing down or shedding labour.

Of course, there has been growth of output in some sectors of manufacturing (e.g. chemicals) and some, but much less, growth in certain types of employment (e.g. in research and development). Some areas of Britain reflect this: Aberdeen for instance enjoyed an oil-related boom, and the "M4 corridor" from London Airport to Bristol has a smattering of research establishments and information processing industries. But if Silicon Valley is the symbol of new industry in the 1980s, it is not to be found in England's green and pleasant land. Some private service industries, the City of London, and, especially, the banks have continued to maintain relatively high profit rates, but even in these sectors, overall employment has not grown significantly in recent years. Moreover, it is estimated that word processors may reduce office employment by over 15% by 1990. In the public sector only defence, law and order, and services devoted to managing unemployment seem bouyant, which in itself tells much about the current state of British society. In the first half of 1982, there were 5500 bankruptcies in Britain: a 75% increase on 1981. During the three months of the Falklands/ Malvinas War, as Britain displayed its military prowess to the world, the economic reality back home was that some 226 companies went into liquidation every week, and capital continues to cascade out into overseas investment (Guardian, 6 July 1982). In 1981 alone, there was over £8 billion *net* capital outflow, of which over £4 billion was direct investment. This was "an unprecedented defecit of direct investment" (Barclays Review, August 1982). Many City of London financial institutions, such as unit trust or investment companies, now hardly bother to invest at all in British manufacturing industries.

The most dramatic, and often traumatic, effect of "de-industrialization" has been the rise in unemployment: from a post-war low of 260 000 *registered* unemployed in 1955 to over 3 400 000, or more than 14% of the workforce, by late 1982. In fact, the official figure systematically *under*-enumerates the true level by as much as 30% (Walker, 1981). The level of real unemployment (e.g. including married women who wish to work but do not register because they do not qualify for financial benefit) was probably well over the 4 000 000 mark.

But even the official unemployment statistics bring out sharply the unevenness of economic decline and its differential effects on particular areas and particular social groups. Whereas the South-East experienced official unemployment rates of only 0·7% in 1955, at the other end of the regional spectrum, 6·8% were registered as jobless in Northern Ireland. By September 1982, these figures were 10·5% in the South East (still, at a time of unprecedented unemployment, only 3·7% above Northern Ireland's post-war low), and 22·3% in Northern Ireland, although in some small localities of chronic long-term unemployment the figure was nearer 50%. With the crisis in the vehicle industries, the West Midlands showed the most spectacular change, with unemployment rising from 0·5% in 1955 to 16·9% in September 1982. Within regions, the decline of manufacturing has been mainly concentrated in inner city and in industrial villages and towns where older plants were located, though newer branch plants have often been equally insecure. In some of these localities, unemployment is far higher than the national or even regional averages. For example, in September 1982, 32% of male workers were registered as unemployed in Poplar and Stepney (part of London's ex-docklands), over 40% in inner-city Liverpool and more than 50% in some localities in Northern Ireland. Unemployment is also strongly differentiated among social groups. The risk of an unskilled manual worker becoming unemployed is six times as high as that for a non-manual worker and part-time workers (mainly women); older workers, school leavers and black people are also particularly vulnerable (Walker, 1981). By 1982, unemployment among 16 to 24-year-olds was more than twice the national average for unemployment among all groups. Nor should we forget that unemployment is one (particularly measured) part of a continuum. De-industrialization often also means lower real wages, worse working conditions or more boring work for those who keep jobs.

Furthermore, just as unemployment increases and real wages fall, so state spending on housing, health, education and social welfare also falls, just when it is needed most. (Spending on unemployment has, we should mention, risen hugely over the last five years, although only as a function of the rising numbers of unemployed.) This feeds back into unemployment. Particular areas (especially inner cities) are more vulnerable to public sector employment cuts. The public sector is the largest employer in Inner London, for example.

If we add together unemployment benefit, extra social security payments, expenditure on special job schemes, losses in government revenue through unemployment (chiefly direct and indirect taxes), extra health service and policing costs, etc., this amounts to £12 000 m. expended on unemployment in 1981/82 (James and Lister, 1981). This is greater than all the government revenue from North Sea Oil (around £8000 m. in 1980/81). That is one measure of Britain's economic decline, a decline that would be even more catastrophic if it had not been partially cushioned by the "windfall" from the North Sea.

4. Redundant spaces?

Sections 1–3 set the scene for the more detailed analysis in the following chapters of the relations between the "social" and the "spatial", and the role of geographical unevenness as an active component of change in a period of crisis. "De-industrialization" has been very uneven in its effects on different social groups and on different parts of the country. For millions of people, workers and dependants, it has meant redundancy with all that this implies for their living conditions and life-styles, their hopes and morale, and while redundancies have been widespread there are marked sectoral and spatial concentrations of unemployment; whole communities are dominated by it. While Britain as a whole has declined as a centre of industrial production, there are "industrial graveyards" in many of the older industrial areas (and some not so old) where industrial production has virtually ceased. Areas of redundant fixed capital, in the form of abandoned machinery and empty workplaces, where capital has been written off on a massive scale; areas of redundant workers and redundant skills – from East London to Invergordon, from Liverpool to Peterlee New Town – where a wealth of human experience and abilities have also been written off on a large scale.

However, for the people trapped in such areas (and, even assuming they wish to move, they usually *are* trapped because of the unavailability of housing, to say nothing of jobs, in other areas), these are hardly redundant spaces. They have to continue to live in them. As a result, there are increasing pressures brought to bear on their respective local authorities to attempt to fill the vacuum left by industrial collapse, yet these authorities lack the resources to achieve solutions in any way commensurate with the problems.

However, neither are they redundant spaces for some employers. Far from seeing these areas as redundant, they are strongly attracted to them. For, as we have already suggested, relations inside the workplace can be crucially conditioned by social conditions outside it, and these areas contain large reserves of unemployed labour. People are desperate for jobs and can be more easily persuaded to accept low pay, new work practices and poor conditions of employment. Indeed some of the firms moving into these areas are "sweatshops" or "backstreet factories" attracted by cheap premises and the possibility of employing non-unionized labour at low wages. History seems to be repeating itself: and as tragedy for people in run-down areas. One effect of the Great Depression in the late nineteenth century was to accentuate and entrench the archaic production methods of "sweatshops" and "homeworking" in London's East End; today "homeworking", which has affinities with the pre-Industrial Revolution "putting-out" system, is again on the increase in this and other areas. It has again become a source of profit. (Anderson *et al.*, 1982). Nor is this attraction felt only by "backstreet" firms; multinational firms often relocate production plant to find cheap, pliant labour and research has shown that many "backstreet" firms are in fact owned by multi-national corporations.

Redundant spaces like redundant workers may not remain redundant, but through being redundant they are vulnerable to transformations which are not necessarily to their advantage. It is perhaps more accurate to talk about *transformed* space, rather than redundant space.

5. Unity in diversity

In the discussion so far, some of our examples have been taken from individual chapters in the book, but before outlining their specific contents, a word about their general methodology. In their analysis of uneven development they cover a diverse range of topics and, like any collection of essays by different writers, they vary in style and approach. Nevertheless they are unified in two important ways.

First, they attempt to integrate the social, the economic and the spatial, for the reasons we have outlined: such an integrated approach is necessary if we are to begin to understand the complexities of industrial decline and social change in cities and regions. Second, they share the view that the interrelationships between Britain's economic decline and the various types of change in cities and regions are based on, and have to be understood in terms of, the dynamics of capitalist production and reproduction.

The central dynamic of the capitalist system is the competitive drive for profits in the sphere of production: if firms do not make adequate profits they cannot invest adequately, they fall behind their competitors, and get taken over or go bankrupt, which is what we have seen has happened to numerous firms in Britain. The competetive dynamic compels capitalist enterprises to invest and accumulate profits. As Karl Marx (1970, p. 592) put it:

> ... that which in the miser is a mere idiosyncrasy, is, in the capitalist the effect of the social mechanism, of which he is but one of the wheels ... competition makes the immanent laws of capitalist production to be felt by each individual capitalist as external coercive laws. It compels him to keep constantly extending his capital, in order to preserve it, but extend it he cannot, except by means of progressive accumulation.

Continued profit-making also depends on a labour force which has to be continually reproduced, and not just in a biological or generational sense but in a day by day, year by year, *social* sense. It has to be housed and fed, educated in particular skills, persuaded to accept its position as wage labour, provided with health and welfare facilities, the means of getting to and from work, and so forth. Some of these tasks are performed by unpaid labour in the home and family, some have been taken on by the state, and some the state is currently endeavouring to return to the realm of the family, or the market. But all, in one way or another, have connections with the sphere of production. For example, the better performance of the West German economy is not simply due to greater investment in industry, though that is very important (much less is it due simply to the oft-repeated and exaggerated reason that Germans have a propensity for hard work); it is also related to the greater investment in education which, as we have noted, is markedly higher than in Britain.

Furthermore, continued profit-making depends too on the social system *as a whole* being reproduced. People must also be willing, or at least give some measure of assent, for society to be run in this way. For both these reasons the conflicts which arise in the sphere of production ("industrial relations"), and over issues such as housing, health, education or other social welfare "cuts", have to be contained by political, ideological and other means, and by the physical force of the state.

Thus the system of social relations, itself, contains an inherent unity of eocnomic production, social consumption, welfare and political control. Recognizing this, and making it explicit, helps to unify the analysis of a diversity of topics and problems which would otherwise seem unrelated.

However, this unity of the social system, far from being a smoothly-functioning whole, is a contradictory unity. Problems and conflicts may not be successfully contained, the attempted resolutions may fail, or they may even go too far and prejudice some basic features of the social system. Very often, the attempt to solve one difficulty, often mistakenly seen as an autonomous, almost technical matter, will work through to other parts of the social system and reappear in a problematical form. Quite often, different problem-solving strategies are in direct conflict with one another. Above all, and fundamentally, the unity of the social system is driven by conflicts between classes and groups with different, often contradictory interests.

This becomes most obvious in periods of general crisis when the contradictions appear in sharpened form. For example, we have seen that profit-making depends on social welfare provision, yet social welfare spending (e.g. on education, health and housing) has been *reduced* as part of government's attempts to raise the sagging profitability and investment levels in British industry. Building workers remain on the dole despite the need for more and better houses; factories lie empty despite the need for the products which they could produce. But then, in a capitalist system, what is produced, or not produced, is determined by profitability criteria, not by human needs (and this also applies to a *state* capitalist system of production – such as Poland's – and in Britain to the nationalized industries). Similarly, monetarism (one attempted resolution at the present time) may fail even as a narrow economic policy and may produce such social pressures as to be quite counter-productive.

The basic contradiction of the system, and the one which generates a host of secondary contradictions and conflicts, lies within its central profit-making dynamic: the mutual dependence, yet contradictory, interests of capital and labour. Capital (private and state) exploits labour in the sense that what labour receives in wages or salaries is *less* than the value of what it produces and the *surplus* which is appropriated by capital takes the form of profits and other "unearned incomes". If labour received in wages the full value of what it produced, there would be no profits, no point in capital organizing production, no future for the enterprise except eventual bankruptcy. So the characteristic form which the basic contradiction takes is the conflict over wage and salary levels, or more precisely, the conflict between the major social forces representing earned and "unearned" incomes.

However, the ramifications of this basic contradiction permeate all aspects of capitalist society in one form or another; as we have seen, the economic is also social and political, and all three are spatial. Therefore, to be properly understood, industrial and social change in cities and regions has to be seen in terms of this basic contradiction and the variety of conflicts and problems which it generates.

Nonetheless, this relationship is neither simple nor undifferentiated. Very different responses are produced by people acting in different situations. And, as well as understanding basic causes, this book is, of necessity, interested in understanding such varied mechanisms of change and their specific results. Nor is this contradiction, the question of class, the only structuring feature in society. For instance, gender relations, so that we may speak about patriarchal society as well as capitalist society, are also important. It is rather that the features of capitalist production and reproduction distinguish a certain sort of society, and it is within this society that the book's problems and analyses are set. So while the immediate cause of many changes may be much narrower than society-wide structuring features like gender and class, it is hardly possible that the development of these changes can escape their influence. And, more importantly, where do such immediate causes come from? In most cases, their context and origins lie in gender and class relations. If it is misleading to try and simply reduce complex and uneven outcomes to one major cause, however fundamental, it is equally unhelpful to refuse to try and explain these outcomes. General causes must be related to particular events by the discovery of specific mechanisms of change. This is what the following chapters of the book attempt to do for the uneven development of cities and regions.

6. The following chapters

The succeeding substantive chapters, broadly speaking, focus in turn on production, reproduction and political conflict. This is a matter of the main emphasis of the chapters only, reflecting *what* is to be explained; it is *not* a question of the economic, social and political aspects of uneven development being treated separately from one another. The latter is a matter of *how* to explain and, as we have seen, such a separation would not be useful.

In Chapters 2 to 5, the main emphasis is on industrial production, state policy for industry, social relations in the workplace and the impact of industrial decline on local economies. Chapters 6 and 7 switch the main focus on to the labour force, the role of home life in production, and the management of the "reserve army" of unemployed workers. The main emphasis in Chapters 8 and 9 is on social and political conflict, in particular the increase in racial conflict, and the resurgence of nationalism in Scotland, both of which are seen as related to, if not caused by, the onset of general economic crisis. The last three chapters, 10 to 12, also have an essentially political emphasis, taking three state policy responses to industrial decline: a new town in a depressed area; attempts by local authorities, including authorities of a Left labour complexion, to regenerate industry in their localities; and the Conservative Government's Enterprise Zone experiment for run-down industrial areas.

In *Chapter 2*, Kevin Morgan and Andrew Sayer begin by problematizing the process of uneven development as deriving from specific characteristics of capitalism. They relate the process to the British economy and its regional development and look in detail at the steel crisis and its effects on South Wales.

Andy Friedman, in *Chapter 3*, looks at one particular aspect of uneven development: the relations in the workplace between managements and workforces. In using various strategies to sectionalize and control labour, managements effectively help create social deprivation. In treating certain workers, often already socially deprived, as "peripheral labour" to be used in particular jobs and managed in particular ways, managers compound pre-existing deprivation and create it anew. Thus, Coventry had (and required) a deprived and "peripheral" inner-city population when it was one of the country's most prosperous cities situated at the centre of a booming motorcar industry.

"Centrality" and "periphery" are common terms in the study of uneven development. In *Chapter 4*, Linda Murgatroyd and John Urry show that they *change* their locations over time, however, and that different firms and sectors also become more or less central to an industry or a whole economy. Lancaster's industrial structure and "rurality" might have been expected to lead to an expanding industrial future, but they show why this did not happen, why, instead, the area was "de-industrialized". The chapter force-fully demonstrates that, in order to understand industrial change, it is necessary to uncover the overlapping mechanisms and processes of spatial restructuring by which this occurs. Only then, is there much real prospect of changing change.

Industrial restructuring has been dramatic over the last decade but, of course, it is nothing new. Nick Rogers in *Chapter 5* develops this theme in the context of Birmingham in the Great Depression of the 1870s and 1880s. One result of the Depression was a major restructuring of production tech-nology. Small workshops in inner Birmingham, with a finely graded, dif-ferentiated and highly skilled workforce were replaced by factory-based mechanized production on greenfield sites, using semi-skilled labour and producing in different sectors from those previously dominant. This economic and social restructuring had important consequent effects on the development of the urban built form, and, as in Lancaster, on the social and political behaviour of the local labour force.

Switching the main focus to the labour force, Dave Byrne and Don Parson in *Chapter 6* look at the management in space of one result of the processes of uneven development: the creation of a surplus population of peripheral workers and the unemployed. This section of the working class may be "peripheral", or "surplus", but it is nonetheless crucial for production, for both economic and political reasons. Yet its management and control can be problematical. One response to this problem is to use housing provision and administration to create spatially segregated "reserve areas", and the authors detail this for housing areas in North-East England.

Production, as we have already suggested, does not live by the workplace alone. In *Chapter 7* Suzanne Mackenzie and Damaris Rose show how the main activities that go on in the home are related to those in the workplace. The domestic economy and home life developed in relation to the develop-ment of specifically capitalist ways of organizing production. It is not possi-ble to adequately understand one without the other, and the chapter situates these historical processes within the developing geography of the city. It is women who most obviously bridge "home" and "workplace" and the changing relations between the two have a major impact on their lives in particular.

Chapter 8 switches the focus directly on to social and political conflict. One of the most dramatic and well-publicized responses so far to the crisis in Britain has been the rioting in some inner city and other rundown areas. Not a new response (Britain's cities have a long history of rioting in periods of severe crisis), but this time black people played a predominant role, though whites were also involved. In Chapter 8 Joe Doherty looks at the post-war history of black immigration to Britain, in relation to the need for extra labour in a period of economic boom; at the racism black immigrants and their children faced; and at state policies intended to control racial conflict, including "law and order" or physical force.

The resurgence of nationalism in Scotland was another sort of response to the decline of the British economy, though it was also fuelled by what was seen as the promise for Scotland of North Sea Oil. "It's Scotland's oil" said the Scottish National Party, and in *Chapter 9* Peter Smith and Peter Brown relate its electoral rise in the early 1970s to post-war industrial change in Scotland. Socio-economic changes connected with the decline of Scotland's basic industry weakened the social bases for Labour and Conservative support. Old urban working-class communities were broken up, both at home and in the factory, and the economic power and organizational base of the labour movement was weakened. Similar shifts affected Conservative support, while the actions of both Labour and Conservative governments after 1970 did little to cement the cracks. For the period between 1974 and 1979, the SNP was successful in capturing the mantle of Scottishness for large sections of erstwhile Labour and Conservative voters. The chapter analyses this relationship between changing political geographies and industrial structure.

In *Chapter 10*, Fred Robinson examines the changing course and effects of direct intervention, by the central state, in local spatial change. Peterlee New Town started as a response to the local labour movement's demands for better living conditions and secure employment. Central government, justifying its actions in the name of "the national interest", replaced local government and effectively saw Peterlee as a way of ensuring the maintenance and reproduction of a labour force for mining coal. Other industries employing male workers were not to be introduced, and even the town's physical development was phased in accordance with the demands of coal-mining. Subsequently, coal mining collapsed – as had often been predicted but, equally often, these predictions had been ignored by central government. Peterlee now became a spatial concentration of cheap "peripheral" labour to be used in low-paid and insecure assembly jobs. Nor was the new town a success in terms of the housing it provided (high rents for low quality) while it was detrimental to development in the rest of the sub-region. Furthermore, not only was the state intervention seen to fail, but it had effectively lost the mantle of legitimacy that local electoral government can confer.

With industrial closures and unemployment hitting all parts of the country (albeit much more severely in some areas than others), most local authorities have developed some policy for attracting investment and jobs. In *Chapter 11* Allan Cochrane looks at attempts by local government to direct and plan industry at a local level. He questions the extent to which such attempts can be successful, particularly in view of the limited amount of investment capital for which the local authorities are competing with each other, and he explores in particular the potential of "socialist" local policies which attempt to go beyond the immediate constraints of "the market".

In contrast, the Conservative Government elected in 1979 had a strong commitment to "the market" and a widely-expressed opposition to state planning and controls on private industry. One of the fruits of this *laissez-faire* ideology was the Enterprise Zone experiment which Sir Geoffrey Howe introduced in 1980. In *Chapter 12* James Anderson analyses the history of the idea, in the context of the ineffectiveness of the British state in responding to post-war industrial decline, and the uses of the experiment in the politics of crisis. He discusses its ideological and political objectives; the likely effects on the run-down areas in which the zones are located; and the contrast between their reality and the rhetoric surrounding them.

After the chapter was written, the Government announced that another 11 zones were to be added to the 11 already in operation, and Sir Geoffrey Howe suggested that the "free for all" principles of the Enterprise Zone experiment had "potential application throughout the country" (*The Guardian*, 5 July 1982). Redundant spaces also have ideological uses.

References

Anderson, J. (1973). Ideology in geography, *Antipode*, 5, 3, 1–6.

Anderson, J., Mayo, M. and Newman, I. (1982). "Social Change, Geography and Policy: A Geographical Case Study", Block 6, Units 23–26, D102 Social Sciences: a foundation course. The Open University Press, Milton Keynes.

James, C. and Lister, R. (1981). The costs of unemployment, *in* L. Burgess and R. Lister (eds), "Unemployment: who pays the price?", Child Poverty Action Group, Poverty Pamphlet 23.

Marx, K. (1970). "Capital", Laurence & Wishart, London.

Prais, S. J. (1982). "Productivity and Industrial Structure: a statistical study of manufacturing industry in Britain, Germany and the USA", Oxford University Press, London.

Rostow, W. W. (1978). "The World Economy: history and prospect", Macmillan, London.

Walker, A. (1981). The level and distribution of unemployment, *in* L. Burgess and R. Lister (eds), "Unemployment: who pays the price?", Child Poverty Action Group, Poverty Pamphlet 23.

TWO

Regional inequality and the state in Britain

K. MORGAN and A. SAYER

(September 1981)

1. Introduction

In this chapter we shall look at the process of uneven development and its geographical implications in the context of recent British regional development, and in particular in terms of the steel crisis in South Wales. Our account is radically opposed to conventional views of the regional problem, and it may help to anticipate some of the more unorthodox claims that will be defended:

  (i) that the problems of uneven spatial development are inherent structural consequences of capitalist development;

 (ii) that the capitalist state can do little but reproduce uneven development or facilitate its continuation in forms congenial to capital;

(iii) that regional policy is not a welfare measure but increasingly a subsidy to capital. As such it is primarily a disguised response to national economic problems and has little to do with direct employment creation;

(iv) that the state affects regional development in many other ways besides through regional policy, and that these different forms of state intervention are normally mutually incompatible. This point is illustrated particularly clearly by the South Wales case study.

We shall introduce and apply some elements from marxist theory at several points in the discussion, but one concept is perhaps in need of a few prefatory remarks. In referring to "uneven development", we mean far more than the simple fact that the types and quantities of economic activities vary from area to area, or that there is some kind of "imbalance" or disequilibrium between regions. Geographical variations characterize any kind of society, but "uneven development" is used here primarily to refer to the uneven *process* of development which derives from the particular character of capitalism.

Traditionally, regional problems are often seen as "imbalance" or "disequilibrium" in an economy which, fundamentally, does lead to balanced development; such problems become merely a temporary aberration caused by overdependence on "old" industries which are still shedding labour. Writing in 1969, a standard text on regional policy claimed that:

> . . . as time goes on, the structure of the problem regions is gradually becoming more favourable; the declining industries cannot decline for ever, and new industries are playing a larger part in the regional economies. As this process continues the problem should get easier" (McCrone, 1969, pp. 165–6)

The experience of recession since that time has shown this to be utterly mistaken, for the new industries have reproduced the same problems in new forms. Both the emergence of the inner city as a problem area, and the spread of employment decline in manufacturing to virtually the whole country but for rural and outer metropolitan areas, show that the uneven spatial pattern which results from the uneven process of capitalist development changes as capitalism changes. Yet in a longer historical perspective such geographical shifts would not surprise us; after all, seventy years ago, much of the South-East was backward relative to what are now the Development Areas!

Capitalist development is inevitably an uneven process for several reasons. There is an unevenness in economic power which derives from the concentration of control and ownership of the means of production into the hands of a minority and the consequent class nature of society. The relationship between the market signals (especially profit rates) which guide capital, and social needs for goods and services is also highly uneven, such that needs are met only in the most approximate fashion and in terms which suit capital. Competition between firms often forces them to reduce their workforces, and although new plants and even new industries may start up, there is no mechanism in a capitalist economy to ensure that they come in the right amounts and at the times and places where they are most needed. The continual flux of capital from parts of the economy where profit rates are low to parts where they are high can create sudden reversals in development, and as firms increase in size, the resulting upheavals become greater. Moreover, the fragmented nature of a capitalist economy, with a multitude of separately owned and controlled firms each making its own individual plans, also means that disproportionalities between sectors of production are the norm rather than the exception.

We shall enlarge on these points in the course of our substantive analysis of regional development in Britain and then South Wales, but at both levels of focus it will be necessary to look outside the area of interest in order to understand what is going on inside it. For example, changes in British regional development are related to changes in the international economy; the latter cannot be taken as a passive backcloth. Similarly, state intervention in a region such as South Wales has to be seen in relation to attempts to revive the national economy in its international context. We therefore make no apology for going beyond the traditional scope of regional analysis.

2. British capitalism, the state and regional development

The major official review of regional development policy in Britain (*Regional Development Incentives*, HMSO, 1973) resigned itself to the conclusion that:

> . . . the geographical pattern of greater and less employment has not vastly changed over the years[1]

Although the assessment of the actual impact of regional policy is controversial (cf. Keeble, 1980; Moore and Rhodes, 1973, 1976; Massey, 1979; Hudson, 1977), the conclusion of the official review as to the general level of regional uneven development is hardly contestable.

What is less commonly recognized, and what we shall argue, is that the "regional problem" is a *structural* aspect of capitalist development and not merely some aberrant feature. By this we mean not that the actual form of uneven spatial development must remain fixed, but that the actual *process* of capitalist development is uneven and that this continually reproduces an uneven *pattern* of development, though not always in the same form. The last fifteen years, for example, saw a temporary relative convergence in unemployment rates for the standard regions, but this was an effect of increasing unevenness at other spatial scales, in the form of a massive decline of employment in metropolitan areas (especially inner-city areas) and the retreat of growth to smaller settlements in outer metropolitan areas (Keeble, 1976).

Given that the nature of capitalism is constantly changing, we should expect these spatial changes to be related to a new phase of development of the British economy. As has already been recognized in the regional development literature (e.g. Chisholm, 1978), the most obvious feature of this phase is that there is now little or no growth to redistribute in the hope of countering the regional problem by the traditional method of fostering and channelling industrial movement.

When considered in the context of Europe or the advanced (O.E.C.D.) countries in general, Britain as a whole appears as a laggard nation in economic terms. As we shall see later with reference to the example of the steel industry, the intra-national British regional problem is inextricably bound up with this larger context.

Britain's situation can be viewed in terms of three superimposed levels:

- a severe relative weakness of British domestic capital;
- a wider process of "jobless growth" in the advanced capitalist countries, especially in manufacturing;
- the general world economic recession.

Manufacturing capital in Britain has continued to become progressively more technologically backward, and as both cause and consequence of this, it has had unusually low levels of investment. At a time when it is more than ever necessary to innovate products and processes to improve its market position, British capital has been doing precisely the opposite by neglecting research and development as well as other parts of the "innovation process". Between 1967 and 1975, Britain was the only O.E.C.D. country in which the level of industry-financed research and development actually fell. Only in Britain was expenditure on research and development treated as an expendable activity, when profit margins were pressed, rather than as a necessary investment for long-term survival (Pavitt, 1980).

It must be stressed that the pressure to restructure and "modernize" has nothing to do with abstract ideals of progress, nor with simply satisfying a naturally insatiable consumer demand (cf. Manners *et al.*, 1972, p. 2), nor with replacing machinery that is simply worn out. It is a function of the necessity to remain profitable in the face of competition from other firms in product markets for sales, and investment markets for investment funds. Failure to respond to these pressures means failure to survive.

The pressures are transmitted throughout the world economy through market signals in terms of prices and costs and revenues of firms, but they originate from the development of newer, lower cost methods of production. It cannot be emphasized too strongly that the kind of economic theory which has traditionally informed economic geography and which uses *static* models, restricted to the sphere of market movements and ignoring the actual production process, inevitably fails to understand this dynamic of capitalist development and the upheavals in spatial development it causes. There is a spiralling process here in which the *response* to or effect of the pressures upon profitability (e.g. technological change) in one firm becomes the *stimulus* or cause of falling profits and subsequently restructuring or bankruptcy in other firms. The Conservative policy of "non-intervention" in the economy only serves to expedite the operation of this process and bring forward the fate of those firms which fail to invest.

Between 1962 and 1973, UK per capita investment was 30% of that in the US, 50% of that in France, and 60% of that in West Germany and Japan; and in 1978 total industrial investment in the UK was only 30% of the 1970 level. As a result, UK industry has low productivity and above-average import penetration in finished manufactures. An additional factor here which has disadvantaged UK capital has been the relative economic strength of the British working class in terms of shop-floor control of production. (The working class in many other European countries is often much better paid and is stronger in terms of participation in left political parties, but it lacks this shop floor, "economic" power.)

Sometimes, by depressing wages or finding cheaper fuel and raw materials, or finding locations with lower taxes and rates, or by pressing workers to speed up production, profitability may be maintained. But there are, of course, limits to the extent to which such savings can be made, and in the long run, as we have argued, survival depends upon introducing new products for which the market is not yet saturated and/or new production processes.

This, together with the British context of under-investment and low productivity has to be understood if we are to make sense of the apparent paradox where, on the one hand, labour costs are among the lowest in Europe while, on the other, wage increases (or resistance to wage cuts by means of failure to keep wages abreast of inflation) pose a real threat to British capital. While British wages have increased more slowly than the average for industrial countries, wage costs per unit of output have risen faster, because of chronic underinvestment.

In other ways, low wages are a problem rather than even a temporary solution for capital. A low paid population means a limited consumer market and hence limited scope for investment. Also, technological innovations which raise productivity are usually made first by multinational firms in the countries with the most affluent markets and which permit longer production runs and economies of scale, while older methods are retained in poorer countries (Pratten, 1976; Vernon, 1966). Another factor which could be seen as partly a response to these problems has been the perennial deflations which inhibited the long-term planning of investment in the 60s. (Rowthorn, 1971).

Yet despite this disturbing evidence regarding the depth of the crisis facing industry in Britain, it must be remembered that the effects are cushioned and disguised by the strength of the pound (due to North Sea oil and high interest rates) which has allowed the real wages of many of those fortunate enough to have a job to rise.

These problems are largely responsible for the profitability crisis which has developed in British capital, as in other O.E.C.D. countries. In Britain the profit margin in manufacturing (calculated in terms of gross profits as a proportion of net output) fell from 19·3% in 1966 to 3·4% in 1976, while in services it fell only from 29·8% to 27·2% (*Financial Times* 29.6.78). The problems of profitability and cash flow are being exacerbated by both high interest rates and the appreciation of the pound which, as a petrocurrency, rose by some 30% between 1976 and 1980. The resulting high exchange rate has already penalized engineering exports in particular. The February 1980 report of the Engineering Employers Federation illustrates the growing price disadvantage suffered by UK firms in foreign markets: 11% in relation to West Germany, 30% to the US and 50% to Japan.

The second element in the crisis is the development of "jobless growth". Since around 1966, Britain and most advanced capitalist countries have experienced declining employment in manufacturing industry coupled with stagnant or slow growth in output. (*Financial Times* 30.4.1981). Figures 1 and 2 show this graphically. In a sense, jobless growth is always present in some sectors of a capitalist economy, where the number of workers per unit of output is lowered more rapidly than the demand for their products increases. However, in times of boom such as that of the post-war period before 1966, such sectors were outweighed by others in which both output and employment expanded. Generalized jobless growth in manufacturing after 1966 was temporarily concealed by the expansion in private and public

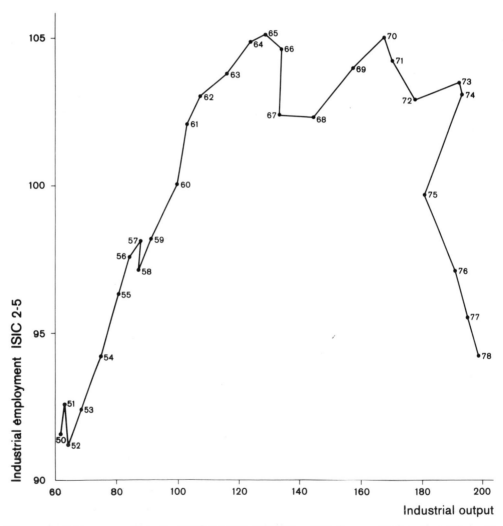

Figure 1. Jobless growth in the EEC-9 1950–78 1960 = 100. Source: Rothwell and Zegveld 1979, p. 20.

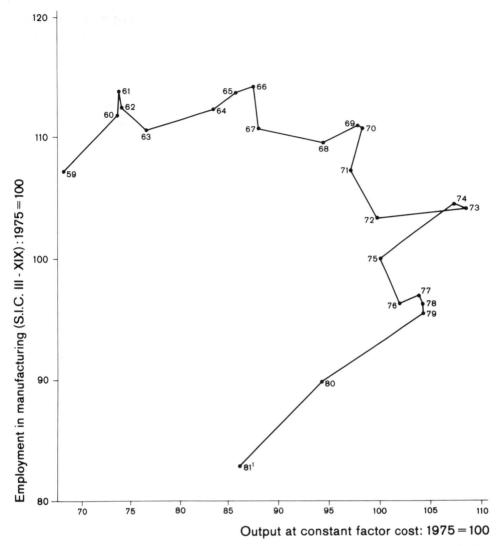

Figure 2. Jobless growth and decline in British manufacturing 1959–81 (numbers indicate years, superscript quarters). Source: Economic Trends.

service employment in the early 70s. Since then, the situation has been worsened by public expenditure cuts, by actual falls in *output* in manufacturing, and by the redundancies beginning to result from the introduction of microelectronic technology. Moreover, whereas it was possible in previous periods of jobless growth to point to several new industries which would increase their employment in future (e.g. the emergence of consumer durables in the late 20s and early 30s in Britain), there appear to be few significant contenders today.

This means that an increasing number of workers are now faced with the choice of losing their jobs to make way for new technology or losing them because their firms have *not* introduced it, and hence become uncompetitive. It also means that it is now, more than ever, utterly mistaken for geographers to assume that growth necessarily means employment growth or that declining employment necessarily means declining industry (Massey and Meegan, 1979; 1982).

The third element of the crisis as it is experienced in Britain, the world recession, is still more pervasive, but coincides in timing and severity with the development of jobless growth. It is most clearly indicated by falls in profitability and declines in rates of output increases beginning in about 1966, from the abnormally high rates (in long-run historical perspective) of the post-war boom. The so-called oil crisis of 1973 *deepened* the recession, but it certainly did not cause it (Mandel, 1975, 1980; Frank, 1980).

These kinds of change are rarely mentioned in the standard literature on the regional problem, which at worst, limits its interest in the economy to industrial location, ignoring *in situ* change and wider economic forces. Yet, together, these three elements of the crisis of British capitalism were for part of the autumn of 1980, producing a loss of 3000 jobs per day and unprecedented post-war unemployment rates in UK regions (see Table 1). The scale of recent manufacturing employment decline has been staggering even by post-1966 standards: between 1966 and 1976 some 1·32 m. jobs were lost, but between June 1979 and June 1981, manufacturing employment declined by 1·1 m. or 15·8% (Brown and Sheriff 1978; Department of Employment, August 1981). It should be noted that most of the resulting changes have and most probably will continue to occur *in situ* and not primarily in response to

TABLE 1. *Regional unemployment in Britain (July).*

	per cent	
	1980	1981
Northern Ireland	12·1	17·0
North	9·6	13·9
Wales	9·0	13·6
North West	8·4	13·0
Scotland	9·1	12·8
West Midlands	6·8	12·8
Yorkshire & Humberside	6·9	11·1
East Midlands	5·8	9·6
South West	6·1	9·4
East Anglia	5·2	8·6
South East	4·3	7·6

Source: Department of Employment Gazette (August 1981).

traditional "location factors" (cf. Dennis, 1978; Massey and Meegan, 1978).

At first sight the current strategy of "non-intervention" in domestic capital may seem counterintuitive and even self-destructive in this context, and many people have denounced it as such. An *over-simplistic* use of marxist theory might make it seem so. In a country in which economic power is concentrated in the hands of a minority by virtue of their ownership and control of the means of production, supporting the economy must mean supporting capital, on its own terms, strengthening it against overseas rivals. This argument is dubious on two counts. First, it cannot be assumed that the state always *recognizes* the general interests of capital; at least for limited periods it may be able to act in a way which is detrimental to capital before it is over-ruled and forced to capitulate (cf. Urry, 1981). It might be argued that this has in fact happened in so far as the government has frequently had to back down on its "non-interventionist" commitment, the most notable cases being British Steel and British Leyland.

The second criticism of the simplistic argument concerns the nature of the "interest" of British capital. From the point of view of Britain's stronger industrial and financial capital, the Conservative strategy has a certain logic. Although it is rarely recognized, while British *domestic* capital is weak, British-owned multi-national capital *overseas* is relatively strong. In 1976 the UK's overseas investment was second only to the USA and at £1735 m. was 37% more than West Germany, 69% more than France and 176% more than Japan (cf. Dicken, 1980).

Even the examples of "baling-out" British capital also seem to reflect this logic. Both Tory and Labour governments have repeatedly given assistance *on the condition that massive redundancies are made* and certainly not in order to save jobs. These were rescues of British capital, not British labour. It would not be too cynical to say that the firms welcomed the government doing their own "dirty work" for them. More particularly, in the case of British Leyland, it has been argued by Cowling that state intervention has been primarily a means of supporting the relatively profitable British *components* industry *which is now rapidly shifting its production to other countries* but which still needs British Leyland car assembly as a "captive buyer" (Cowling, 1981).

Also, it must be remembered that unemployment is primarily a problem for *labour*. It is not necessarily a problem at all for capital unless we include the indirect affects it has on driving up state payments to the unemployed at the very time when the government wants to reduce further taxation of companies. The CBI and some of the less guarded Tory ministers (e.g. Biffen) have repeatedly made the point that a substantial "shakeout" of labour is now a pre-condition for productivity and output growth in many industrial sectors. In this line, the *Financial Times* has argued that all is not unrelieved gloom (for capital!) because

UK business is reacting to the cost squeeze more by efficiency drives and attacks on overmanning rather than by resisting wage demands. The result is thus likely to be a shakeout and productivity improvement more reminiscent of the Wilson recession of 1966–67 . . . than that of the mid-1970's recession which was associated with stagnant productivity . . . Thus although UK output may hold up in line with the more optimistic forecasts, unemployment may rise with the most pessimistic (*Financial Times* 31.1.1980).

It is this "shakeout" plus closure of unprofitable branches that is now contributing to the changes in (regional) unemployment patterns noted above. The work of Massey and Meegan (1979) on the electrical engineering sector shows that it is usually (and understandably) the older more labour-intensive plants which are closed down first, and for historical reasons, these tend to be located in metropolitan areas, especially the inner cities.

In encouraging these effects of "free market forces", the government, despite its pro-small firms rhetoric, inevitably supports larger firms which are better able to respond to competition by large-scale investment. Nevertheless, as CBI criticism showed in the winter of 1980–81, even large firms have criticized the Conservative government for being insufficiently supportive in some ways, and this lends some credibility to the views that the government is not always aware of capital's interests, and that these interests are diverse.

Having looked at some of the main features of the crisis as it affects Britain, we are now in a position to interpret the regional impact of state intervention. It will be noted that we have not said simply "regional policy". For too long, regional analysis has overlooked the simple but crucially important point that the state affects regional development in far more ways than those which come under the ambit of "regional policy". For example a region having an over-dependence on nationalized industries will experience the effects of policies other than regional policy (e.g. National Coal Board and British Steel Corporation). What is more, as will be shown in the case of South Wales, there is only occasionally, and largely accidentally, any consistency among the various forms of state activity which affect regional development, whether they be sectoral industrial policies, employment policy, regional policy or nationalised industry policy.[2] As can be seen from Table 2, some forms of public expenditure (for example on central and miscellaneous services, the functioning of the labour market, support for nationalized industries and general support for industry) have been highest in the relatively "prosperous" South-East. Particularly interesting (in view of what we have said on the importance of innovative investment) is the distribution of expenditure on "industrial innovation".

Several other misconceptions about regional policy remain popular. It is still common to portray it as primarily a welfare instrument for generating employment where it is most needed, but its role in the post-war period has been neither continuous nor predominantly welfare-oriented. Regional policy

TABLE 2. *Regional distribution of regionally relevant expenditures on trade, industry and employment* (*average for the period 1969–70 to 1973–74*).

Type of expenditure	Region										Share of each programme in G.B. total
	North	Yorks. and Humberside	East Midlands	East Anglia	South East	South West	West Midlands	North West	Wales	Scotland	
Regional support and regeneration	29·0	2·2	0·2	0	0	2·1	0	16·5	16·0	34·0	16·5
Industrial innovation	2·0	0·5	20·9	1·0	22·3	28·5	4·3	7·4	0·1	13·0	16·1
General support for industry	15·0	6·1	4·2	2·7	23·3	5·1	6·7	14·2	8·1	14·6	37·9
Support for nationalized industries	10·1	11·1	9·2	3·6	27·8	3·9	7·9	14·7	7·2	10·2	12·9
Regulation of domestic trade and consumer protection	4·7	14·2	0	9·6	14·4	9·5	14·2	23·7	9·6	0	0·1
Functioning of the labour market	8·4	7·8	5·5	2·3	31·3	5·4	8·1	14·6	6·3	10·4	9·6
Central and miscellaneous services	6·3	3·2	1·0	0·4	58·8	2·2	2·3	6·6	11·0	8·4	6·1
Total	11·5	5·3	6·8	1·9	21·9	8·0	5·2	13·1	8·1	16·2	100·0
Region's share in GB population 1971 Census	6·1	8·9	6·3	3·1	31·9	7·0	9·5	12·5	5·0	9·7	
Ratio of share of expenditure to share of population	1·885	0·596	1·079	0·613	0·687	1·143	0·547	1·048	1·620	1·670	

Source: Northern Region Strategy Team (1976, Table 6.2) "Public Expenditure in the Northern Region and other British Regions 1969/70–1973/74, Technical Report, No. 12.

was effectively suspended for an entire decade between 1948 and 1958 (Pickvance, 1981). To be sure, there has been plenty of political pressure from the development areas for regional policy. Sometimes this has come not only from labour but from capital, when and where it saw investment opportunities in declining areas, and sought the bonuses and enabling measures of regional policy. We cannot always assume that regional policy is the "independent variable" and industrial (re)development the "dependent variable".[3]

Whatever the *source* of political pressure for regional aid, the predominant types of response of the state have been those which favoured capital, and necessarily so, given that economic development is primarily in the control of capital. This means that although working class political pressure for regional policy is clearly enough determined by need, it is only met if capital can satisfy its own different requirement of profitable operation. Prior to the present phase of jobless growth, increasing both output and employment simultaneously was possible within this criterion of profitability in most cases, though still not necessarily equally so in every region. It was therefore possible for the state to make its aid to firms conditional upon a certain level of employment creation.

Then, in 1966, investment grants were introduced *throughout Britain* with a 20% increased differential for development areas: these grants were paid to firms irrespective of any employment created and as such they constituted a major incentive to capital-intensive firms. From 1967 to 1976, a Regional Employment Premium was available to *all* firms in development areas according to the number employed, (though with a sexist form of weighting which gave higher subsidies to men than women and juveniles). Nevertheless, the overall balance of regional policy incentives was still geared to capital-intensive activities.

We would argue that the real significance of investment grants (as opposed to the previous system of tax allowance in the form of "free depreciation") was that they were an immediate cash injection during a period when firms were beset by profitability and liquidity problems. That is to say, regional policy, far from being a simple welfare measure to the *region*, became a means whereby financial aid was channelled to industrial *capital* which happened to be in the regions.

> In other words the "regional" element of the policy is completely subsidiary, and is an example of the way that thinking in terms of spatial units can conceal the real social processes involved. (Pickvance, 1981)

To avoid this kind of illusion, it is helpful to distinguish between development *of* a region, which implies benefits for all or most people and activities in the region, and development *in* a region which implies that the benefits are largely restricted to capital in terms of expanded output and/or profit. The term "regional development" may seem harmless enough, but it can conceal a great deal. Regions are not unitary objects but extremely complex aggregates of activities: some of which are highly interconnected, others virtually independent; some with compatible interests, others with contradictory interests. As we shall see, these differences and contradictions are particularly important in South Wales, but in *any* region there are inherent but complex contradictions between labour and capital and often also, a range of more limited conflicts between different kinds of capital.

Regional policy took a further shift away from any welfarist content in 1976 when the Regional Employment Premium (REP) was abolished as part of the most drastic single cut in regional expenditure ever. Regional policy was now geared still less to *direct* employment creation in the regions and had become primarily a support to the profitability and liquidity of firms. Many commentators criticized the bias towards capital-intensive industry,[4] but without realizing that the form of incentives is largely determined by the requirements of industrial capital; the abolition of REP signals a recognition of the material inability of the vast majority of manufacturing capital to sustain employment (see Table 3 for recent British experience). And even when it was at least arguable that regional policy had, in REP, an employment function, it was often criticized by friends and foes alike for merely slowing down the process of "shakeout" rather than increasing employment.

Another longer-established type of non-welfarist regional policy has cleared sites, and provided industrial estates and advance factories and public utilities. This is merely a regional guise for the role of the state in providing "general conditions of production" for capital (cf. Lojkine, 1976). Although we tend to take it for granted, one of the particular and problematic features of a capitalist economy is that the fragmentation of production into numerous separately-owned and controlled units all competing anarchicly

TABLE 3. *Investment and employment in Britain, for leading industrial sectors (1964–73).*

	% Increase in Plant and Machinery	% Decrease in Employment
(1) Coal and petroleum products, chemical and allied industries	67·7	8·5
(2) Other metals engineering and allied industries	33·5	11·9
(3) Bricks, pottery, glass and cement	68·1	14·2
(4) Construction	101·3	16·8
(5) Food, drink and tobacco	63·5	9·4

Source: Essential Facts on Unemployment (CIS Anti-Report No. 14).

discourages firms from undertaking investments which might be used without payment by competitors. The *general* interests of capital might be served by having certain kinds of training for labour or particular kinds of infrastructure such as docks and container ports, but individual capitals can rarely co-operate in their provision as each one will try to off-load the costs onto others so that a stalemate is reached where none are provided. The state bears these costs when it runs industrial training schemes, builds "Skill-centres" and sets up industrial estates and new towns. It also tends to overproduce them in comparison with capital's needs, especially in times of economic recession and in regions where political demands for jobs are particularly strong. Yet governments typically have to pretend firstly that providing some of these necessary material conditions for capital accumulation is virtually a sufficient condition for attracting investment, and secondly that if and when this comes it will mean significant job creation. In short, what is propagandized as a welfarist measure to encourge the development *of* a region, is not even sufficient to guarantee development *in* a region.

In a period of jobless growth, any employment expansion in one area is inevitably coupled with decline in another. The conventional response to redundancies and closures is to try to attract new industry to the affected area. Usually the numbers of jobs attracted fail to match those lost, but the problem is still largely seen in terms of "balancing the books" as if the processes involved in new investment (and sometimes, with it, job creation) were entirely independent of those involved in disinvestment and job loss. This view is shared as much by large sections of the labour movement as by the government. What is not noticed, because it rarely operates merely within the confines of a small area, is that there is a causal connection between investment and disinvestment. When jobless growth is generalized, even where new investments do create a limited number of jobs, they simultaneously threaten the jobs of larger numbers of workers in other competing higher cost, lower productivity plants, usually in quite different places. This also occurs by the normal mechanisms of the search for higher labour productivity and profit, but in a period of jobless growth it rarely has the effect of expanding employment in new sectors.

So it is not merely that the loudly trumpeted "catches" of new investments in areas of high unemployment create pitifully small or sometimes even negative changes in comparison with the numbers already lost: the problem is *worse, because the new investments will necessarily but indirectly, cause still further job loss.* Given the complexities of the structures of competition and location patterns of industries in the capitalist world market, it would be virtually impossible to trace the operation of this kind of causal mechanism systematically. However, individual examples are cited often enough in traditional regional economic geography books where the demise of a local industry is attributed to competition from Japan or wherever. In this respect the process is ordinary enough, but what is now *extra*ordinary is that, particularly in Britain, it is generalized and not compensated for by new employment-generating industries.[5]

Unfortunately, recognition of this process all too often becomes displaced and blamed upon regional policy, which is then accused of fostering development in the assisted areas *at the expense of* industry in the inner cities and metropolitan suburbs. This argument in turn gives rise to calls for "a regional policy for the London docklands" and suchlike. The state's response to this welfarist demand is, as usual, in terms favourable to the interests of capital accumulation, only this time in the form of "new enterprise zones" (see Anderson, this volume). This false train of argument is not purely and simply a matter of regional or local chauvinism; it has been actively reinforced by the selective vision of geographers which has grossly overemphasized the importance of industrial movement relative to *in situ* change. For instance, between 1966–74 it has been estimated that there was a decline of 310 100 jobs in manufacturing employment for greater London. Of this loss, only some 9% was a result of moves to the development areas, while 18% resulted from moves to locations *within* the South-East and East Anglia. The latter are obviously not attributable to regional policy as these do not have assisted area status, but even in the case of the development areas we might reasonably assume that at least a few of the moves would have occurred without the incentive of regional aid. By far the most significant feature of the job loss from London was that no less than 73% stemmed from closures and shrinkage at remaining plants (Dennis, 1978; see also Massey and Meegan, 1979b). The political implications of these findings, and of the recognition of the nature of jobless growth for countering regional chauvinism and beggar-thy-neighbour policies, are considerable.

These broad economic changes plus the alarming decline in growth rates and profitability discussed earlier led to a shift of emphasis in state policy in which regional considerations increasingly had to take second place to policies aimed at *national* economic recovery. The 1972 Industry Act of the Conservative government was designed to dispense state aid along sectoral as well as spatial/regional lines; while the "industrial strategy" of the succeeding Labour government had no spatial dimension. Nevertheless, it had a differential regional effect; it largely benefitted the South-East because this had large concentrations of employment in major favoured sectors such as industrial engines, construction equipment, office machinery, electronic components and domestic electrical appliances (see Table 2). Here, state non-regional policy worked in a contrary direction to state regional policy.

The role of regional policy as aid to capital was further elaborated with the creation of the Scottish and Welsh Development Agencies: an event which caused more than a little agitation in the English Development Areas. This signalled an attempt to make Scotland and Wales more reliant on *in situ* growth than on the previous method of inter-regional movement from England. These agencies cannot be said to represent any major commitment to employment creation through industrial investment. Although the WDA claimed that industrial investment would be its main priority, its annual report for 1977/78 showed that this item represented a meagre 5% of total expenditure in 1978. Instead, this agency concentrated its activities on providing "the general conditions of production" in the shape of land clearance and advance factories. With considerable justification, the Wales TUC view the investment functions of the WDA as nothing more than those of a traditional merchant bank. Once again, it is clear that the state is obliged to intervene in such a way that capital can respond in its own terms.

Over the last few years, and in the near future, capital has not and is unlikely to be able to create new employment on a socially required scale, and hence the once consensual and unexceptional demands for full employment have now taken on a semi-revolutionary character. Moreover, to isolate regional policy as evidence of the political resolve to solve the problems of uneven development is akin to saying that an army batallion is primarily dedicated to health and safety because it has a medical unit.

As unemployment and closures rise, there is greater scope for intended and unintended divisive effects among the working class as each locality attaches increased importance not only to the general volume of investment and disinvestment but to its location. As we show in the next section of the chapter, government and employers have been quick to exploit these possibilities of divide and rule strategies.

This new economic situation also marks and has warranted an abandonment of the policies of social-democratic consensus that has characterized post-war politics. A bi-partisan political consensus (known as "Butskellism") characterized much of the post-war period, sustained by the continuous, if slow growth of the British economy. And, since 1966, both Labour and Tory governments have resorted to broadly similar corporatist repertoires of political management, e.g. "tripartite" bargaining between TUC, CBI and government and a reluctant willingness to underwrite "deals" with increased public expenditure. However, in 1976 the Labour government effectively pronounced the end of the "Keynesian era" and inaugurated a regime of public expenditure cutbacks allied to monetarist cash limits. The Thatcher administration, therefore, did not pioneer "monetarism" but, rather, *extended* it: the novel features of the 1979 Tory government lay in its ideological celebration of the so-called "free-market"; its open endorsement of social inequality to restore "incentives"; its break with "tripartite" bargaining and its resolute attack on the organizations of the labour movement. Thus, when we speak of the break with consensus politics we refer to this post-1979 attempt to introduce a new political form of management which, above all else, tries to elicit a populist conservatism in the working class so that *they* will endorse the "work ethic" and market criteria.

Although the Tory strategy of imposing market criteria may be too draconian for some capitals, especially for small firms, and misguided even in terms of the general interest of capital in its neglect of investment, it is in other ways decisively and aggressively pro-capitalist. The economic signals to which capitalist firms respond are not those of *need*, but of ability to pay and scope for profitable production; capital in the form of money is the objective, not satisfaction of social needs. In this general sense, a reassertion of market criteria, of exchange-value over use-value, of profit over need, is pro-capitalist, as is the deliberate exacerbation of already-high unemployment levels through reducing wage demands and labour militancy. Despite the ideological rhetoric of "rolling back the frontiers of the state", such actions as the imposition of greater central government control over local government, the strengthening of the police force, the increased regulation of recipients of state benefits, all show that Thatcherism involves not a weak but a strong state, attempting to discipline the masses to accept the anarchic freedom of the market (cf. Hall, 1979).

In the field of regional policy, the Conservatives have extended the changes already started by the previous Labour government in terms of lowering the priority attached to regional, as against national needs. The Tories have cut regional aid by £233 million and whereas the assisted areas formerly covered 40% of the employed population, this figure has fallen to 25%. The CBI responded by reaffirming their need for regional aid, provided it was in the form of investment grants and did not involve any revival of employment considerations (CBI, 1980). Given that jobless growth characterizes so many sectors, aids to investment are very likely to promote job *loss*, though not necessarily in the places where the grants are received.[6]

Thus far we have confined ourselves to a general discussion; we now proceed to a more concrete analysis of the regional problem in a case-study of the recent steel crisis in South Wales.

3. The case of South Wales and the steel crisis

The aim of this section is to document some of the major components of the crisis in South Wales: a region which illustrates particularly clearly the uneven impact of the recession. South Wales has been called a "nationalized region" (Humphrys, 1972) owing to its heavy dependence upon the public sector. Of Welsh employees, 40·5% work in the public sector as compared with 29·6% for the UK, and this has made the region particularly vulnerable to public expenditure cuts. These include not only the effects of the £233 m. cut from regional policy expenditures in Britain as a whole, announced in July 1979, but also the severe contractions of the interrelated and still dominant steel and coal industries. Moreover, as we shall show, the private sector in Wales has also suffered heavily in the recession.

The steel industry is particularly significant in South Wales: between 1945 and 1963 it was one of the central determinants of output and employment growth in the region, and by the latter date it was the leading steel district, employing a total of 58 360 (Morgan, 1981). Despite having the largest output of crude steel in the mid-60s, South Wales had the lowest regional level of steel consumption. In other words there was a marked absence of the highly profitable metal-using industries, indicative of a general failure to realize the political commitment to diversify the employment structure. Moreover, contrary to the euphoric reports of a successfully reconstructed economic base in South Wales in the early 1960s, the British Iron and Steel Federation had already, in 1963, expressed deep concern about the future health of the Welsh steel industry in view of its low profits, under-utilization of capacity and the increasingly fierce international competition.

The full implications of the over-dependence of South Wales on the steel industry were revealed by the massive redundancies projected for Wales in BSC's 1973 Development Strategy. In this, the first major restructuring of the nationalized steel industry, Wales had its steel labour force depleted by 25%: nearly three times greater than the job loss in any other steel district.

Against this background and in response to the Tory edict that BSC should be profitable in 1981, the Corporation announced in December 1979 a capacity reduction from 20 m. to 15 m. liquid tonnes per annum with a consequent job loss of some 52 000. As Tables 4–6 and Figure 3 show, South Wales was once again the major victim.

BSC publicly decided upon what it termed its "soft option" for Wales, which entailed the joint run-down of both Llanwern and Port Talbot by 50% so that together they would produce 2·8 m. tons rather than their former total of 5 m. tons. It appears that this "soft option" emerged as the result of a struggle both within the BSC senior management and between BSC and the Department of Industry: the calculation seems to have been that a total closure of one plant would have provoked hostile union reaction. Fear of the latter is also evident in the further round of BSC redundancies (20 000), announced in December 1980, which affected these two plants less than might otherwise have been expected.

TABLE 4. *BSC employment and redundancies – 1973.*

	Total Male Employed	Total BSC Employed	Total BSC Redundancies	Redundancies % of Employed
Scotland	1 201 000	25 100	6 500	25·8
Northern	767 000	40 600	6 000	14·8
North West	1 665 000	10 200	3 500	33·4
Yorks./Humber.	1 193 000	44 600	4 000	9·0
E. Midlands	851 000	24 300	8 500	35·0
W. Midlands	1 374 000	12 600	4 000	31·5
Wales	592 000	66 700	17 500	25·2

Source: BSC: Ten Year Review Strategy (1973).

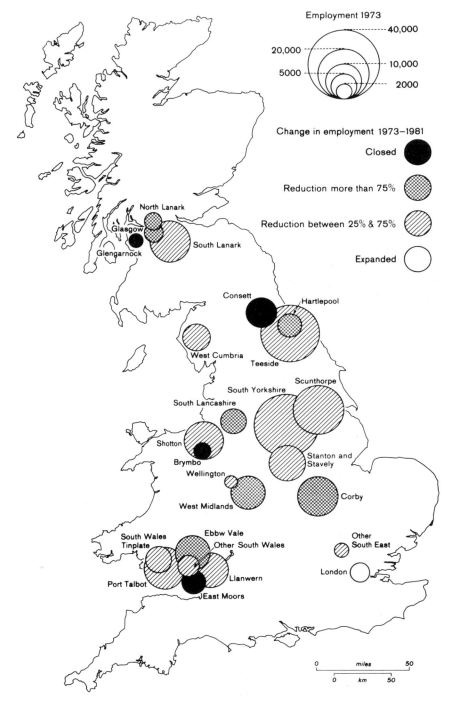

Figure 3. The regional impact of industrial policy: employment decline in the British Steel Corporation. Sources: BSC Manpower Statistics and Annual Reports.

TABLE 5. *BSC redundancies in Wales – 1973.*

Works	No. of Redundancies	% of Total Redundancies
Shotton	6 500	37·3
Ebbw Vale	4 500	25·6
East Moors	4 500	25·5
Others	2 000	11·6
Total	17 500	100·0

Source: BSC Ten Year Development Strategy (1973).

However, this compromise meant that both plants would effectively operate at some 50% of their design capacity, so that costs would still be prohibitive, and it was widely believed that this was but a stepping stone to the total closure of either Llanwern or Port Talbot. Whatever the ultimate solution, it is difficult to see how both can remain open given the financial targets of the Tory government imposed on BSC and the further contraction of the steel market in the UK and Europe. So much was admitted by Ian MacGregor, the new BSC chairman in evidence to the Committee on Welsh Affairs (Minutes of Evidence, BSC, question 1306).

It is now common to attribute the current steel crisis to BSC's excessively optimistic investment programme which it initiated in 1973 and which, in

TABLE 6. *BSC cuts: 1979.*

Present workforce in iron and steelmaking:	153 000
Proposed closures:	Job Losses
Consett	4 000
Hallside (Scotland)	600
Proposed partial closures:	
Scunthorpe	2 800
Llanwern and Port Talbot	11–15 000
Further cuts in rolling mills	2 500
Proposed reductions at surviving plants:	12 000
Announced closures of iron and steelmaking:	
Corby, Shotton and Cleveland	13 000
Already agreed at local level at a number of works:	8 000
Planned Remaining Workforce:	100 000

Source: Financial Times (12.12.79).

1976, accounted for a staggering 17% of total UK manufacturing investment. But it is essential to locate the failure of the 1973 BSC investment
strategy in the relative decline of metal-consuming industries in Britain, and
in the relative under-investment that has characterized British industry
generally. The overcapacity caused by BSC's planning is partly attributable
to the over-optimistic growth forecasts of private capital in the metal-using
sectors. As one BSC planner put it:

> Whenever we discussed the future prospects of a metal-using company or an
> entire industry we were shown V-shaped graphs. The customers' sales were
> always at the bottom of the V at that particular moment – but about to soar
> away upwards in future years. (*Financial Times* 12.2.79)

In fact, although demand for manufactured goods rose by 1–2% per year
from 1971–78 in Britain, imports of these goods rose by 6·5% per year. As a
result, metal using sectors have continued to decline. Mechanical engineering, which accounts for 15% of BSC's domestic sales was expected to grow
by 1–2% per year but is now expected to decline by 2% per year. In 1979 BSC
believed that production in the car, truck and tractor industries which
account for 20% of its sales would continue at the same level: now it
forecasts a 1·5% per year decline up to 1985. Similar downward revisions of
forecasts were made for the other two major steel-using sectors: miscellaneous metals and the construction industry.

On the face of it, it might seem that British domestic industry was over-
whelmed by an extraordinary wave of mass over-optimism, but to believe this
would be to miss the fundamental causes which lie much deeper in the
structure of a capitalist economy than mere managerial attitudes. It must
never be forgotten that capitalist economic development is not directed by a
social plan drawn up in advance: rather, development, and indeed recession,
are nothing but the outcomes of a multitude of unco-ordinated plans made
by separate units of capital, each trying to "hedge its bets" on what others
will do and trying to forecast the future economic context. Within each firm,
there is an extremely careful control of the "*technical division of labour*"
involved in producing any one product, whether it is carried out in one plant
or in several stages in different plants; the relative numbers of different kinds
of workers has to be planned in advance. However, between separate firms
(and even between separate products made within a firm), that is at the level
of the "*social division of labour*", there is not planning but anarchic competition (cf. Marx, 1976, Chapter 14; Massey, 1978). At this social level, the
unintended effects of a multitude of changes in technology, in the balance of
power between capital and labour in controlling production, and changes in
demand and prices throughout the world economy continually alter the
profitability of each sector.

The quantitative relation between the volume of goods and services ("use-
values") actually produced and the prices at which they exchange is con-

stantly being altered in unplanned ways through these processes. The primary signals upon which decisions are made regarding investment concern not the former "use-values" but "exchange-values".[7] At the level of the social division of labour, investment is planned in exchange-value terms according to expectations of profit, but this does not always guarantee that volumes and flows of use-values (goods and services) will be co-ordinated. Trying to plan production on this basis is therefore like trying to navigate with a faulty compass. There are therefore inevitable *disproportionalities* in the social division of labour: proportionality or equilibrium is the exception rather than the rule. Despite the highly interconnected nature of the economy, the relative growth of each part is only co-ordinated *a posteriori*.

One of the reasons for nationalizing the whole or major parts of key, "strategic" sectors such as steel is to enable short-term exchange-value considerations to be over-ridden where necessary so as to prevent shortages arising which might damage other sectors. This is expressed in the "cushioning" of nationalized industries from the need to make a profit, although governments vary in the extent to which they are prepared to relax this criterion. But "cushioned" or not, the criterion which really matters is not that it provides the necessary volume of goods and services that are needed elsewhere in the economy, but that its books are not too far out of balance. There may be thousands of socially-needed uses for the unsold products and unused capacity of private and nationalized capital, but unless these are reflected in appropriate "market signals", they will not be met.

Also, the "technical division of labour" is often planned on a long time-scale, as in the case of BSC's Ten Year Plan, and enormous commitments of capital are made. The firm only discovers whether it has estimated its market share correctly several years, sometimes more than a decade later, when conditions have changed radically.

However, while this can explain why disproportionalities between sectors of the economy should arise, it does not show why they take the form of overproduction and overcapacity on such a widespread scale. To account for this we need to consider the rising scale of production. In many sectors, the optimal scale of production grows more rapidly than does the market. Because increased scale of operation so often means lower costs per unit of output, no individual firm can afford to fail to invest up to the optimal level even though it is quite impossible for all firms to sell at this level simultaneously. So as the size of industry increases, the "stakes" get higher, and both gains and losses grow. It must also be appreciated that where the market for a commodity has become internationalized, state intervention can only affect the technical division of labour of its own domestic capital, not the social division of labour in the international market. This is a further reason why state support for firms in this situation, be they privately-owned or nationalized, does not overcome the anarchy of the capitalist market, but merely operates within it.

Figure 4. British Steel Corporation, Port Talbot, 1972 (courtesy BSC).

Nationalization has therefore only modified the nature of capital, and frequently the modifications have only served to create further problems. BSC, for example, was impeded in its accumulation of funds through successive state policies which subsidized private buyers of steel by denying BSC price increases. This meant that it was ill-equipped to meet cyclical reductions in demand with revenue reserves; in fact, delays and refusals of price increases were estimated to have cost BSC some £783 m. between 1967 and 1973.[8]

Other European steel producers have been adversely affected by the recession too, but none has cut capacity and labour as severely as BSC. The EEC has taken the view that community steel production ought to be reduced by 6 m. tons and yet BSC is *itself* cutting production by 40% of this European reduction. And even before this current cutback was effected, BSC was already ahead in the European league in terms of reduced production levels. Table 7 shows particularly well the uneven impact of the recession on the European steel industry.

TABLE 7. *Crude steel production (monthly averages in thousand tonnes).*

	1976	1977	1978	1979*	
Belgium	1012	938	1051	1118	(+9·5%)
Denmark	60	57	72	67	(+10·5%)
France	1935	1842	1903	1934	(−0·05%)
Germany	3535	3249	3438	3886	(+9·1%)
Italy	1955	1945	2024	1994	(+2·0%)
Luxembourg	380	361	399	416	(+17·4%)
Netherlands	432	410	466	484	(+10·8%)
UK	1856	1710	1693	1825	(−1·7%)

* 11 months.
Source: I.S.T.C., (*New Deal for Steel*, p. 20).

On the other hand, it has to be remembered that many of the countries which managed output growth in this period were serving considerably more bouyant metal-using industries than those in Britain. In this way, the uneven impact of the recession in the European steel industry is related to its uneven impact in the metal-using industries according to their relative efficiency and technological development: overcapacity is widely shared, but the scope for recovery is not, hence the desperate response in Britain.

The uneven pattern of government subsidies for steel production across Europe has been one of the major points of contention in the crisis. It also serves to show how inaccurate are the popular assumptions of a simple contrast between a self-financing private sector of capitals responding purely to market signals and a heavily-subsidized and internally co-ordinated public sector. While the Belgian steel industry receives a £15 per ton subsidy for coking coal, and the German and French industries £11 and £9 respectively, BSC receives £2 per ton. The German steel industry, which is *privately* owned, also receives subsidies for rail freight, labour (for short-time working), research and development and electricity (I.S.T.C., 1980, p. 53–5).

The inability of the capitalist state to regulate the social division of labour *within* the public sector is illustrated very strikingly by the relationship between the nationalized coal and steel industries in South Wales. Of the regions' coal output, 40% is in the form of coking coal for the local steel industry.[9] The threat to the coking pits, of which there are 18 out of the South Wales total of 37 collieries, arises from the reduced demand from BSC and government policy of switching to overseas sources of coking coal, such as Australia.

This will of course be a serious blow to the "regional development" of South Wales, but as we have argued, the interests of the working people of a region cannot be expected to be reflected in the interests of capital, whether private or public. In fact, reduction of capacity on peripheral coalfields such as that of South Wales has been seen as a way of weakening dependence on their more militant workforces.[10] Nor is this some simple conflict between the interests of the (often private) overseas coal producers and the publicly owned domestic coal industry, for the NCB itself is involved in a coal consortium in Australia! The Port Talbot steelworks is already supplied exclusively with imported coking coal, and the threat to Llanwern is already clear in view of the fact that imports from Ruhrkole are already being delivered under a contract which runs until 1982. (Interestingly, its price is some £2 per ton higher than South Wales coking coal.) These facts bring home the points that the determinants of regional development are increasingly non-local and international, even where nationalized industries are concerned, and that forms of state intervention other than regional policy have a profound effect upon regions. In this case, the Welsh TUC have estimated that the contraction of steel and coal and associated "ripple" effect on local industries will produce a loss of 51 000 jobs over three years.

These losses compound those that are occurring independently of the steel crisis in the private sector in Wales. In the first eight months of 1980 there were 44 000 *notified* redundancies in Wales, of which half were estimated to be related to the contraction of the steel industry. This compares with a figure of 16 000 for the first eight months of 1979.

As in other regions, these losses in the private sector are partly attributable to the Conservative economic strategy of using a high-valued exchange rate and unprecedentedly high interest rates, which has put enormous pressure on company liquidity. The consequent "de-industrialization" is, however, also superimposed on the effects of a general technological backwardness of much of British industry and a continuation of jobless growth in advanced-country manufacturing (Figure 1). It has often been considered that "branch plant economies" such as the private sector in South Wales are more vulnerable to closure in a recession by parent firms outside the region. This thesis has obvious attractions for advocates of nationalism, but little evidence or argument has been put forward to support it. The general pattern in South Wales seems to suggest that it is not the Japanese, American and German-owned branch plants which are closing and contracting, but the smaller UK-owned ones.[11]

The severity of the crisis in South Wales, and the daunting scale of even modest remedial action, is evidenced by the fact that, even with the help of regional policy, only some 30 000 jobs in *new* manufacturing industry were created between 1967 and 1977; that is, it has taken a decade to provide the number of jobs that are being destroyed in the current crisis alone. Another indicator of the severity of the problem is that South Wales was in a worse position in terms of redundancies than other Special Development Areas in the three years up to 1979, i.e. before the present steel crisis (see Table 8).

TABLE 8. *Number of redundancies – 1977/79.*

Region	Working population	Redundancies
S. Wales	1·7 m.	53 700
Strathclyde	2·5 m.	47 800
Merseyside	1·5 m.	42 700
Tyneside	1·5 m.	35 900

Source: Standing Conference on Regional Policy in South Wales *South Wales and the 1980 Steel Crisis* (p. 23).

The Standing Conference report calculates that £380 m. is needed (including regional aid) to provide 20 000 new manufacturing jobs in order to maintain the South Wales economy in its pre-steel crisis position (p. 13). So far, the Tory government has provided £48 m. for a cash programme of advance factories in the Port Talbot and Newport areas, and it is highly unlikely that more funds will be forthcoming. As the experience of previous ventures of this sort shows, if and when advance factories are occupied, it is often by firms which were currently quite viable anyway moving from other areas rather than new firms. Two of the more "successful" advance factory estates at Ebbw Vale have only managed to provide some 2000 jobs to replace the 5400 that have been lost in the steelworks since 1973.[12]

The scale of the crisis in South Wales and elsewhere in the UK raises important questions as to the role of the labour movement in partially acquiescing to such large scale redundancies and, of more long-term significance, the potential for intra-class conflict within the labour movement over the location of new employment and where closures will fall. Both elements were recognized in a BSC confidential document in which the BSC Chief Executive argued that:

> The scale and rapidity of the necessary manpower reductions in South Wales is of a magnitude never encountered before in a relatively small geographical area. Superimposed, as these manpower reductions are, on those associated with the recent closures of East Moors [Cardiff – authors] and Ebbw Vale, etc., a strong and growing reaction has been generated to what is seen by a wide cross-section of people . . . as a grossly unfair transfer of business and employment from South Wales to the North.[13]

This recognizes both the growing reaction plus the potential and actual divisiveness of closures in a multi-plant/multi-regional organization such as BSC.

The labour campaign against closures in South Wales fully revealed the problems which face the working class in organizing at a regional level. In the absence of a national alternative strategy and a national campaign, the unions in coal and steel in South Wales were clearly addressing mere effects. More than this, they were inhibited by the unresponsiveness of the "superstructure" of labour organization; the cancellation of the Welsh general strike, originally called by the Wales TUC for 21 January 1980, was largely the result of opposition from the "real" TUC which thought a Welsh initiative might precipitate a form of response which the traditional union hierarchy might not be able to control.

The problems of organizing at an inter-sectoral level within a "regional economy" are enormous precisely because the latter is increasingly just a local conjuncture of economic and political forces (some of them closely interrelated in their development, others functionally independent) which span far outside the region and indeed the nation.[14] The progressively decreasing unity of regional economies does not weaken the scope for divisive effects on the working class of a region but rather strengthens them. In this case, a formerly relatively simple coal and steel-based community is diversified across a range of new and unrelated industries. In fact, though it was once accurate to speak of "coal communities" in South Wales, and an organization (the South Wales Miners' Federation) which had some success in unifying often geographically isolated communities, the basis for this unity has been weakened by both economic and cultural changes (Francis and Smith, 1979). Nevertheless, as the political battles over the BSC closures across Britain show, "spatial" loyalties and *area*-based demands all too frequently supplant *class*-based action.

Here, there are many important but largely unresearched questions: how is it that traditional strongholds of "economic" militancy give rise to extensive support for Labourist policies, in particular those that assume that the answer to the problems generated by capitalist uneven developments is a drive to induce more capitalist accumulation into the region in the hope of making "it" more competitive, forgetting that if this were successful, other regions would become less competitive. Responses to "the regional problem" in Britain have traditionally been posed within this framework. The problems of uneven development will never be solved by attacking symptoms. An *anti*-capitalist, socialist national economic plan is at least a necessary condition for undermining the divisive origins of capitalist uneven development.

4. Conclusion

At a superficial level, the recent history of regional decline in areas such as South Wales is familiar enough, and indeed has become a part of our daily "media diet". There is a danger that those of us living in the more fortunate localities within the pattern of uneven development who have not been so directly affected by the recession may become complacent and unshocked by mass unemployment, de-industrialization and the loss of the economic basis of many communities. There is also a danger in any area of seeing such events as part of a sequence of calamities, each one separate but caused by an external nature-like force called "recession", which we all suffer and which must simply be "weathered" until existing forms of social organization recover.

Against such views, we have tried to show that these calamities are in fact rooted in the basic structures of capitalist society and are exacerbated by crisis. This crisis, in turn, is nothing more than an (unintended) outcome of multitudes of unco-ordinated decisions made by individual firms and governments. Firms experience crisis as an external conditioning force to which they are subject, but without realizing that they are part of the structures which produce crisis. But they experience it very differently from their work-forces.

Terrible though redundancies and closures are, they have assumed a "taken-for-granted" character in which their wider significance is lost. They signify in the starkest possible terms the nature of the relation between capital and labour: workers are "free" to work for whatever employer they can find, but there is no guarantee that sufficient numbers of owners of capital will find it profitable to employ them; lack of ownership and control of the means of production denies the unemployed the use of their skills even when those skills are most needed; money capital in the form of investment funds is highly mobile and can be switched around the world to wherever prospects for profit are best while its material effects (fixed capital) and its origins (labour) are left behind relatively immobile in abandoned industrial communities.

If we understand "class" merely in the sociological sense of a group of people sharing similar characteristics, the identification of particular classes always seems somewhat subjective and arbitrary. If we understand class as being defined in terms of a social relation between owners and non-owners of the means of production, the objective experience of redundancy and unemployment ("objective" because it happens *to* them, regardless of their wishes) could not make its existence more brutally clear.

Uneven development is not simply a geographical pattern but a process rooted in the capital–labour relation, in the division of society into classes, in the uneven relation between use-value and exchange-value, in the anarchy of the social division of labour, in the inequality of the relative mobilities of capital and labour, in the unequal gains and losses from competition, and in the increasing scale of production. And the process always takes place in a context which is itself the result of earlier uneven development.

The capitalist state is subject to this same process of uneven development. Although politically-organized labour has made the post-war British state very different from that of the inter-war period, nationalization has not become the keystone of a socialist strategy as many had hoped in 1945. Particularly with the further internationalization of capitalist markets and the coming of the recession, nationalized firms and industries such as the British Steel Corporation, the National Coal Board and, more recently, British Leyland, have become increasingly subject to the same pressures as private capital.

The British state has also been obliged to attempt to ameliorate the effects of uneven development through regional policy, but it can only do so by trying to orchestrate the same process in a different way; the "solution" is always another instance of the same process that was responsible for the problem. As we have seen in South Wales and as others have documented elsewhere (Austrin and Beynon, 1979), many of the factories which were closed or which have made redundancies and gone onto short-time working are the same ones which were welcomed in the sixties and early seventies. Here, as in other regions, the new industry was encouraged both by state agencies and by the official labour movement. Now jobless growth has made the material basis for such alliances even more flimsy; unless they belong to a sector not affected by jobless growth, and also are leading firms, any new plants will have the probably unseen effect of displacing jobs elsewhere.

It should also be clear that state policy with respect to the economy and regional development is crucially affected by the changing nature of capitalism: by the increasing size of firms, by the development of multi-national firms, by the crisis, by the power of organized labour, and in Britain by the respective weakness and strength of British domestic and British overseas capital. Likewise, the historical development of regional policy cannot be seen as a gradual learning process in which benign governments try out new combinations of welfare and economic measures against a political and economic background which is neutral except for slight variations caused by the alternation of Tory and Labour governments.

Our analysis also shows that the relationship between different types of state intervention is often contradictory, but this, like the "bad management" of BSC, should be seen in the context of their operation within the anarchy of the social division of labour, where concepts of "rational action" have limited meaning.

Finally, it should be clear by now that it is no longer possible for geographers and others to argue that the encouragement of new investment and the redistribution of existing employment are *solutions* to the "regional problem". Likewise, parochial solutions to regional problems, whether they come from industrial development officers trying to attract firms to Wrexham, Washington, East Kilbride or wherever (all of which of course, we will be told, have "large pools" of skilled and willing labour), or from the labour movement, are not solutions at all. This is not to say that nothing can be done at the local level, but that most of what can be done will have to be in alliance with other areas as part of a wider strategy to wrest economic power from the divisive control of capital.

Acknowledgement

We thank Martin Upham, of the Iron and Steel Trades Confederation for his help and encouragement.

References

Austrin, T. and Beynon, H. (1979). "Global outpost: the working class experience of big business in North East England", *University of Durham Working Paper.*
British Steel Corporation. (1973). "Ten year development strategy".
British Steel Corporation. (1979). "An accountability report".
Brown, C. J. F. and Sheriff, T. D. (1979). "Deindustrialisation in the UK: background statistics", NIESR Discussion Paper No. 23.
Chisholm, M. (1978). Regional policies in an era of slow population growth and higher unemployment, *Regional Studies*, **10**, 201–213.
Confederation of British Industry. (1979). "Memorandum on Regional Policy".
Cowling, K. (1981). Can the British car industry survive?, *Marxism Today*, **25**, 8, 7–13.
Dennis, R. D. (1978). The decline of manufacturing employment in London, *Urban Studies*, **15**, 63–73.
Department of Employment. (1981). Table 1·2, *Gazette*, August, HMSO, London.
Dicken, P. (1980). Foreign direct investment in European manufacturing industry: the changing position of the UK as a host country, *Geoforum*, **11**, 289–313.
Dunford, M. (1977). Regional policy and the restructuring of capital, University of Sussex Working Papers in Urban and Regional Studies, 4.
Dunford, M. (1979). Capital accumulation and regional development in France, *Geoforum*, **10**(1), 81–108.
Financial Times, (1981). The spectre of jobless prosperity, 30 April.

Fine, B. (1975). "Marx's Capital", Macmillan, London.

Francis, H. and Smith, D. (1980). "The Fed: a history of the South Wales miners in the twentieth century", Lowrence and Wishart, London.

Frank, A. G. (1980). "Crisis in the world economy", Heinemann, London.

Hall, S. (1979). The great moving-right show, *Marxism Today*, **24**, 2, 26–29.

House of Commons (1973). Second report from the Expenditure Committee, "Regional Development Incentives", HC327, HMSO, London.

House of Commons (1977/78). Select Committee on Nationalised Industries, "The British Steel Corporation", HC26, HMSO, London.

House of Commons (1979/80). Committee on Welsh Affairs, "The Role of the Welsh Office and Associated Bodies in Developing Employment Opportunities in Wales", HC731 HMSO, London.

Hudson, R. (1978). Spatial policy in Britain: regional or urban?, *Area*, **10**(2), 121–122.

Iron and Steel Trades Confederation, (1980). "New deal for steel".

Kay, G. (1975). "Development and Underdevelopment", Macmillan, London.

Keeble, D. (1976). "Industrial location and planning in the United Kingdom", Methuen, London.

Keeble, D. (1980). Industrial decline, regional policy and the urban-rural manufacturing shift in the UK, *Environment and Planning A*, **12**, 945–962.

Lojkine, (1976). Contribution to a Marxist theory of capitalist urbanisation, *in* C. G. Pickvance (ed.) "Urban Sociology: Critical Essays", Tavistock, London.

Mandel, E. (1975). "Late Capitalism", New Left Books, London.

Mandel, E. (1980). "The second slump", New Left Books, London.

Manners, G. *et al.* (1972). "Regional Development in Britain", Wiley, London.

Marx, K. (1976). "Capital", Penguin, London.

Massey, D. (1979). In what sense a regional problem, *Regional Studies*, **13**, 233–243.

Massey, D. and Meegan, R. (1978). Industrial restructuring versus the cities, *Urban Studies*, **15**, 3, 273–288.

Massey, D. and Meegan, R. (1979). "The geography of industrial reorganisation", *Progress in Planning*, **10**(3), 155–237.

Massey, D. and Meegan, R. (1982). "The anatomy of job loss: the how, where and when of employment decline", Methuen, London.

Moore, B. and Rhodes, J. (1973). Evaluating the effects of British regional economic policy, *Economic Journal*, **83**, 87–110.

Moore, B. and Rhodes, J. (1976). Regional economic policy and the movement of manufacturing firms to Development Areas, *Economica*, **43**, 17–31.

Morgan, K. (1981). "State policy and regional development in Britain: the case of Wales", unpublished D.Phil., University of Sussex.

New Statesman. (1980). 28 March.

Pavitt, K. (ed.) (1980). "Technical innovation and British economic performance", Macmillian, London.

Pickvance, C. (1981). Policies as chameleons, *in* M. Dear and A. Scott (eds), "Urbanisation and urban planning in capitalist society", Methuen, London.

Pratten, C. F. (1976). Labour productivity differentials within international companies, *University of Cambridge Department of Applied Economics, Occasional Papers*, **50**.

Rothwell, R. and Zegveld, W. (1979). "Technical change and employment", Frances Pinter, London.

Rowthorn, B. (1971). Imperialism in the 1970's – unity or rivalry? *New Left Review*, 69.

Standing Conference on Regional Policy in South Wales. (1980). "South Wales and the 1980 steel crisis" (Available from Mid-Glamorgan CC).

Sweezy, P. M. (1949). "The theory of capitalist development", Monthly Review Press, New York.

Urry, J. (1981). "The anatomy of capitalist societies", Macmillan, London.

Vernon, R. (1966). International investment and international trade in the product cycle, *Quarterly Journal of Economics*, **80**, 190–207.

Notes

1. House of Commons (1973). p. 7.

2. This was the case even before 1945, see Morgan, 1981.

3. This assumption is not questioned in such influential assessments of the effects of regional policy as that of Moore and Rhodes (1973; 1976). Dunford (1977; 1979) has shown how state regional policies in Italy and France have often followed rather than led regional (re)development.

4. Note that subsidizing capital-intensive industry does not *necessarily* mean subsidizing jobless growth, for it might be possible for employment still to increase slowly if capital-intensive industry is expanding in output terms. For a discussion of possible combinations of employment and output trends, see Massey and Meegan (1979b).

5. It was the threat to established UK producers in consumer electronics that led Thorn to oppose the planned Hitachi TV plant in the North in 1977. But Hitachi later entered a joint-venture with the UK's GEC in South Wales. Consider also, Ford and BL opposition to the proposed Datsun car plant in the UK in 1981.

6. Employment conditions have, since 1966, been gradually detached from regional policy, with the exception of "section 7 aid", under the 1972 Industry Act: this aid can result in *job-loss* if the project promotes a more viable level of employment, see Morgan, 1981, Chapter 3.

7. We have made some short cuts in our theoretical account here, by eliding the differences between value, exchange-value and price. Readers who would like to pursue the matter are advised to consult Fine (1975), Kay (1975), Sweezy (1949) and of course Marx's *Capital*. We do not believe that the "difference made by these differences" is great enough to warrant the enormous digression which would be required to communicate their meaning successfully to readers untutored in marxist economic theory.

8. House of Commons (1977/78). Vol. 1, para. 76.

9. The South Wales coal industry is being contracted for these, and other reasons, e.g. high costs because of appalling geological conditions and under-investment. See Morgan, 1981.

10. A recent Cabinet paper, leaked to the *New Statesman*, said that a nuclear programme would free energy production: ". . . from the dangers of disruption by industrial action by coal miners". (*New Statesman*, 28 March, 1980).

11. Private communication from the Development Corporation for Wales.

12. See BSC (1979).

13. House of Commons (1979/80). Vol. 1, p. (viii).

14. A "branch-plant" economy presents formidable problems for the labour movement, as local managements frequently have little autonomy, and multi-plant firms can threaten to transfer production to a less "troublesome" site. See Austrin and Beynon (1979).

THREE

Social relations at work and the generation of inner city decay

A. FRIEDMAN

(October 1981)

1. Introduction

The existence of a substantial number of people in Britain, many concentrated in inner city areas, living in substandard housing, overcrowded and with poor amenities, is clearly related to their low incomes and high frequency of unemployment. This rather obvious fact seems finally to have been established in the urban deprivation literature (see for example, Gans, 1973a, 1973b; Rutter and Mage, 1976; and Thrift, 1978). Associating urban deprivation with the poor economic performance of "disadvantaged" groups in labour markets implies that local authorities, in their role as providers of housing and other amenities, cannot be viewed as responsible for the generation of urban deprivation (though they may exacerbate or alleviate the problem). Many of the Community Development Projects came to this conclusion in the 1970s (Coventry Community Development Project, 1975, Community Development Projects, 1977).

But once urban deprivation is associated with relative economic performance in labour markets, obvious policy prescriptions do *not* immediately emerge. Instead a further question emerges: Are wide disparities on the market primarily supply- or demand-generated? Is relatively poor performance on the market due to physical or personality "defects" in the individuals concerned, which they "bring to" or "supply to" the labour market? Or do firms on the market offer a set of jobs with poor and uncertain rewards, independent from the characteristics of individual workers? Do firms demand, or require, or prefer, groups of people who will do relatively badly on the market? Of course this will be a difficult question to answer unambiguously one way or another. In many cases both factors will be

REDUNDANT SPACES?
0-12-058480-8

important. Nevertheless, the difference in policy prescriptions which follow from these very different explanations is enormous. If the answer comes primarily from the labour supply side, either one may try to encourage these individuals to change their attitudes and acquire more desirable characteristics, or one may believe the best policy is to do nothing.

Doing nothing would follow from assuming these characteristics to be unalterable (perhaps because they are inherited), or that they represent the choices of people with as much choice as anyone else. In this latter case, poverty and poor housing are assumed to be the "fault" of the poor. The state should not aim to make these choices any easier by alleviating the plight of the poor. This seems to be the attitude of the Thatcher government (1979 – ?).

If one believes these supply factors to be environmentally determined, the right policy would be to alter those environments which generate "deviant" characteristics. Moving council tenants out of inner city areas, breaking up large agglomerations of disadvantaged groups and making it easier for children to escape these environments through better education facilities would then "solve" the problems. Such policies have been pursued primarily by Labour governments and certain local authorities since the war.

But what if the source of relatively low incomes and high frequency of unemployment is to be found primarily on the demand side of labour markets? What if the normal operation of firms in market economies requires separate groups of workers who are paid less than the rest and who are easily laid off? Little clear policy has been formulated on the basis of this being the primary source of urban deprivation. I would suggest that one reason is the lack of analysis putting forward the demand side position clearly and in some detail. In the following sections such a framework is outlined and then used to examine the sources of urban deprivation in Hillfields, an inner city area of Coventry.

In the past few decades Coventry has been transformed from the major growth city of Britain to an area of high unemployment, even by the standards of Britain's current state of acute depression. Coventry was a showpiece of British capitalism from the late 1880s until the 1960s. During that time Coventry grew faster than any other major city in Britain (Friedman, 1977, p. 247). Average wages in Coventry's engineering industry had been consistently between 35 and 40% higher than wages for comparable engineering labour in the rest of the country from 1946 to 1969 (Friedman, 1977, p. 209). In 1966, 58% of households were owner-occupiers in Coventry compared with 47% for Great Britain as a whole. Unemployment rates in Coventry in the first post-war decades were generally less than one half those for the country as a whole.

Yet near the centre of this boom city of Britain certain areas have been nearly as depressed and deprived as any inner city area of deprivation in the country. Why had this apparent anomaly persisted throughout nearly a century of generally good times for Coventry? Why, when Coventry persistently had unemployment rates well below the national average, did an area like Hillfields in Coventry's centre have unemployment rates well over the national average and generally twice Coventry's rate? (For example, in 1971 unemployment in Coventry was 3·8%, but in Hillsfields 7·4% were unemployed, – Coventry Community Development Project, 1975.)

It may be argued that Hillfields has contained a massively high proportion of people with physical or personality defects, but this supply-oriented answer does little to explain the fact that Hillfields was the showpiece of Coventry area in the early nineteenth century. Wages were once highest, unemployment levels lowest in Hillfields compared with the rest of Coventry. Did the majority of people living in Hillfields suddenly acquire serious physical or personality defects? Were the sons and daughters of those early hardy and acceptable specimens available on the labour market, born with terrible disabilities? Did all the "good" ones leave and a lot of "bad" ones take over the majority of Hillfields area? In Section III, I will show that what happened to Hillfields was generated primarily from the demand side of the labour market. It was not primarily a reflection of the supply side. In the section which follows, a framework is presented which will allow analyses of the structure of the labour market, and changes in that structure, from the demand side.

2. Framework for analysis

If the source of low incomes and high frequency of unemployment among significant minorities is to be found on the demand side of labour markets, it seems obvious that the next step should be to look closely at how the demanders of labour, generally the top managers of private business firms, manage their workers.

The essential departure of the following model from most neo-classical and Marxian models is to assume that there is no "One Best Way" to operate a firm. The top managers who run firms make strategic decisions, (especially with regard to their organisation of workers), which have clear consequences on the fortunes of different groups of workers.

Of course top managers cannot make strategic choices without any constraints. Market forces do force some actions in response to changes in competition in both products and labour markets, but the way top managers respond to these pressures will depend on the existing strategies pursued, as well as the degree of flexibility allowed by profit rates of the recent past. Also there are internal pressures requiring strategic decisions by top managers. Within firms top managers perform two sorts of roles. They co-ordinate complex processes, and they implement systems for maintaining authority over workers. Each of these activities involve uncertainties. Machines can unexpectedly break down, managers' lines of communication may get disrupted, and, most important for the following discussion, worker resistance to managerial authority is a continual, and sometimes unpredictable factor.

In the following four sections, types of *managerial strategies* for maintaining authority over workers will be outlined and related to pressures from markets and from worker resistance. Finally the consequences of these strategies will be related to the physical environment.

2·1 Managerial strategies

When managers buy workers' capacity to work on labour markets, they buy a particular sort of commodity. Labour capacity is peculiar for two reasons: First workers are particularly malleable, you can get somebody to do something once he is employed beyond what may have been specified in the original employment contract. Second, workers are ultimately controlled by an independent and often hostile will. These two peculiarities of labour capacity occasion two types of strategies which top managers pursue for maintaining authority over workers. In the first type of strategy, what I call the Responsible Autonomy type, managers try to accentuate the positive peculiar aspect of labour capacity, its malleability. Workers are given responsibility, status, and light supervision. Their loyalty towards the firm is solicited by encouraging venom against competitors, by fancy sports facilities, by co-opting trade union leaders, etc. In the second type of strategy, what I call the Direct Control type of strategy, top managers try to reduce the amount of responsibility of each individual worker by close supervision, and by setting out in advance and in great detail the specific task workers are to do.[1]

Both types of managerial strategies have serious limitations. These limitations stem from their common aim, to maintain and extend managerial authority over people who are essentially free and independant, but who have alienated their labour capacity. Ultimately, the direct control type of strategy treats workers as though they were machines, assuming they can be forced by financial circumstances or close supervision to give up direct control over what they do for most of their waking hours. Ultimately, the responsible autonomy type strategy treats workers as though they were not alienated from their labour capacity by trying to convince them that the aims of top managers are their own. Both types of strategy involve a contradiction. People *do* have independant and often hostile wills which cannot be destroyed, and the aim of top managers ultimately is to make steady and high profits, rather than to tend to their workers' needs.

Management is an active process. To maintain stable and high profits requires continual reorganization of systems of co-ordination and lines of authority in response to changes required by fresh worker resistance, new technologies, and other types of competitive challenges. But once any type of managerial strategy is implemented, it cannot be changed radically within a short period of time. Direct control strategies require well-defined lines of authority and a high proportion of white-collar staff. Responsible autonomy strategies require an elaborate ideological apparatus for co-opting workers' leaders and the rank and file themselves, as well as relative employment security. To switch suddenly from a strong responsible autonomy strategy to a direct control strategy, or the other way round, would cause severe disruptions.

Besides the difficulty of changing strategies quickly, each type of managerial strategy appears to generate its own peculiar form of inflexibility. With a high degree of direct control, managers will find it relatively difficult to move workers around factories or to change their methods in response to machine faults, mistakes in co-ordination, changing techniques or changing product demand. Each change will require complex and time-consuming planning, communication and implementation of new detailed work tasks. With a high degree of responsible autonomy, top managers will find it difficult to fire workers or to replace workers' skills and direct control with new machinery, without undermining the ideological structure upon which responsible autonomy is founded.

Many of these propositions have been clearly demonstrated during the history of the UK car industry (Friedman, 1977, Chapter 14). For example, while people in Britain these days consider the car industry to be inherently strike-prone, in fact the high proportion of strikes in the industry is a relatively recent feature. From 1949 to 1958, the average annual number of working days lost per 1000 employees for the UK vehicles industry was 344. Comparable figures for 1959–68 and 1969–75 were 650 and 1250. As a percentage of total working days lost per 1000 employees, the vehicles industry represented 12·8% in 1949–58, but 19·7% in 1959–68 and 20·5% in 1968–75 (Department of Employment, various years). Similarily Coventry's record of strike-proneness rose tremendously from the mid 1950s. In Coventry almost all the strikes recorded were in the car industry or at engineering firms supplying the car firms. The number of strikes recorded in the Labour Gazette and the Department of Employment Gazette for the Coventry area rose from 11 in the 1935–44 and 1945–54 periods to 23 in 1955–64 and then to 69 for 1965–1972.

The usual sociological explanations of strike-proneness can not explain this *change* in degree of strike-proneness. If strikes are primarily stimulated by mass production techniques, large plant size, large firm size or piece-work payment systems, why was the British car industry relatively strike-free during the 1930s, 1940s and early 1950s, when all the above factors characterized the industry? What happened in the mid 1950s was not the introduction of mass production techniques, not tremendous growth in size of plant or firm compared with the 1940s, nor a change in payment systems. Rather, in 1956 widespread redundancies heralded the collapse of the employment security which was fundamental for the responsible autonomy strategy which top managers in the car firms were pursuing, (particularly in Coventry where labour market supply was scarce).

Top managers can reduce the inflexibility inherent in their strategies by splitting workers into various groups and applying different types of strategies towards different groups. Encouraging divisions among workers often weakens overall worker resistance, but dividing workers according to managerial strategies applied also helps to counteract the inflexibility peculiar to each type of strategy. The employment security of one group of workers can be more easily assured if cost reduction is achieved by laying off members of other groups first. Also if workers in the second group are more easily laid-off and if the division between the groups is widespread throughout society, then the reserve army for the second group will be larger, and it will be easier to impose greater direct control over the second group within the enterprise.

Dividing workers into groups will also make it easier for top managers to reverse directions with either group. The privileges of the group to which top managers apply responsible autonomy strategies may be more easily undermined if a mass of unprivileged workers are readily available. Also disruption arising from disputes with groups experiencing direct control management may be bypassed if the work they do could be done by others.

Top managers can only effectively split their labour force if workers of one group do not act in solidarity with those of the other groups. This usually means that it is easier for top managers to divide their labour force along lines in general division in the society as a whole. Groups of workers who are subjected to the responsible autonomy type of strategy (what I call central workers) are usually male, white, adult, native people. Groups of workers who are subjected to a direct control type of strategy (what I call peripheral workers) are usually females or non-whites or adolescents or immigrants. (Combinations of these characteristics make peripheral status even more likely.)

There is considerable evidence equating peripheral status with general social discrimination. Rates of unemployment are generally much higher for black workers compared with whites. For example, Davidson (1964) found black unemployment four or five times higher than white worker levels in Great Britain between 1961 and 1963. Also, during recessions, unemployment among black workers rises more quickly than for whites (Wright, 1968, see also Doherty, this volume).

Breugel (1979) finds a similar pattern dividing men and women, while Castles and Kosack (1973) cite a great deal of evidence showing this peripheral pattern for immigrant workers. Interestingly, Castles and Kosack also find that unemployment rates and fluctuations have been greater for female black immigrants compared with male black immigrants, (p. 91).

2·2 Interface; managerial strategies/market conditions

When competitive conditions are severe, top managers will move towards direct control type strategies and they will try to reduce the proportion of central compared with peripheral workers. In severe product market conditions, top managers will try to reduce costs quickly. This will involve laying-off workers. This will be difficult when managers are using responsible autonomy type strategies. Similarly, when firms enjoy a high degree of monopoly power they will be able to enjoy a luxury of a higher proportion of central workers and the pursuit of responsible autonomy type strategies. The former prediction is most likely when severe competitive conditions in product markets are accompanied by oversupply in labour capacity markets, the latter when loose competitive conditions are accompanied by undersupply in labour capacity markets.

These predictions seem to have been bourne out for changes in strategies by top managers in the UK car industry, and especially for those sections of it located in Coventry (cf. also Rogers, this volume, for Birmingham in the Great Victorian Depression). Top managers moved toward Responsible Autonomy strategies during the two world wars when they were able to sell anything they could produce at a high profit to the government. Soon after the First World War they reverted to direct control strategies when the economy went into recession in 1921/22. These strategies prevailed until the Second World War. After the war, responsible autonomy strategies were maintained reflecting the extremely strong demand for British cars abroad and the high home demand (which was protected by a 33⅓% tariff). While the employment security which was required for responsible autonomy strategies was rocked by stop–go politics requiring redundancies in 1956, 1961, and 1965, it was not until the late 1960s that strategies clearly reverted back to direct control. This move was marked by the introduction of Measured Daywork schemes. For evidence on the timing of these shifts see Friedman, 1977, Chapter 14.

Evidence for centre-periphery patterns along social divisions was cited in the previous section. Perhaps the major division between central and peripheral workers within firms follows lines of skill and the division between white collar and manual workers (though the latter distinction has been breaking down with the de-skilling of certain clerical and secretaries jobs, Braverman, 1974). Changes in the proportion of central and peripheral groups have followed market conditions and changes in managerial strategies in the UK car industry. The ratio of white collar to manual workers generally rose in recessions during the 1950s and 1960s (Friedman, 1977, pp. 241–243). As Rhys said in reference to the car industry at that time,

> as demand falls it is easier to lay-off production workers quickly but more difficult to cut down on the 'fixed' labour content such as managerial and technical staff (1972, p. 442)

While this pattern is common for short-term fluctuations in demand, the major long-term deterioration of the UK car industry from the late 1960s has meant that the 1970s have been marked by attempts by the car firms to reduce the proportion of white collar central workers permanently. It was significant that the only union to oppose Chrysler's major redundancy plan in Coventry during the 1975/1976 crisis was the Association of Scientific, Technical and Managerial Staffs.

Top managers of firms are able to react to severe product market conditions either by increasing the proportion of peripheral workers within their own firm, or by developing links with smaller suppliers and distributors which place these smaller firms in a peripheral position relative to the first firm. Centre–periphery relations can exist between firms as well as between workers within a single firm. Top managers of firms can cut costs quickly by reducing orders from smaller firms and by refusing to pay bills to these smaller firms, as well as by laying-off workers.

Centre-periphery patterns between firms within engineering industries have been particularly significant. Wages in the smaller firms supplying parts and components to the major car firms are generally lower than for the car firms. One reason for this is the higher proportion of peripheral workers within these peripheral firms. These firms generally employ a higher proportion of women than the major car firms (Friedman, 1977, pp. 244–246). Data for Coventry shows that during recessions the supplier firms shed labour *before* the major car firms indicating that the major car firms cut their contracts with suppliers as a first reaction to product market deterioration (Friedman, 1977, pp. 126–126).

2·3 Interface; enterprise/workers

Central workers are those who are considered by top managers to be essential for securing high profits in the long-run. Some workers may be so considered as individuals because of their skills or their contribution to managerial authority. Some workers may force top managers to consider them central workers as a group because of the strength of their resistance. During recessions the employment positions of central workers will be protected, while peripheral workers will be readily laid off.

Peripheral workers are those who can be easily replaced by others within the enterprise or by others from outside the enterprise. What they offer top managers is the ability to make their operations more flexible. With a large ring of peripheral workers top managers will find it relatively easy to reduce their labour force in step with falling output without suffering severe disruptions.

Generally, the groups of workers top managers consider to be peripheral will be unskilled and semi-skilled manual workers (skilleu manual workers to a lesser extent), and lower level administrative staff such as clerical workers and secretaries. (Although clerical workers and secretarial staff may be treated as central workers if top managers believe them to be necessary for maintaining managerial loyalty or efficiency.) Along with lower employment security, peripheral workers will generally be paid less and suffer worse working conditions than central workers.

Ultimately, in an unplanned capitalist system, no worker's employment position can be permanently secured. Long-run changes in technology, in market conditions and in political climates all reduce the permanence of any group of workers' central position. The stability of large firms will depend, in the short-run, on their ability to find peripheral means to absorb fluctuations, but in the long-run, in order to survive, those firms will have to be able to *shift their centres*. (cf. Murgatroyd and Urry this volume, looking at the example of Lancaster).

The consequences of such a shift will be very great on any group of workers because involuntary unemployment generally results in a de-skilling process. Unemployment will mean more than loss of earnings, loss of prestige, and loss of self-confidence. If the next job is taken with a different firm, status and earnings increments acquired within the worker's old firm will generally be forfeited. If the next job taken is also in a different industry, the workers' skills will often be inappropriate and therefore unremunerated. Strong evidence for this de-skilling via employment has been found by Hill (1973) and Daniel (1974). Thus the decline of an industry, for whatever reason, is likely to send many people into a vicious circle of decline and deprivation as they tumble from central to a peripheral status (cf. Byrne and Parson, this volume).

2·4 Interface; workers/physical environment

Labour is not highly mobile. It is difficult for people to move home. This means that once industry has declined in an area, the area itself will become even more depressed than would be indicated by short-run of unemployment. Those workers who are best able to maintain their central status will also generally be most mobile, and so those workers representing the highest earning capacity will generally leave the area. Those who remain will be those least able to secure central positions and therefore the area will gradually develop higher and higher proportions of peripheral workers. Peripheral workers will be less able to maintain the areas's housing stock and local authorities have generally been prejudiced against spending a lot of money on such areas. Privileged workers are prejudiced against moving into neighbourhoods where peripheral workers live (particularly if the distinction is clearly racial), and against having peripheral workers move into their own neighbourhood.

Thus peripheral workers remain in areas of deprivation in spite of especially high rates of unemployment during trade recessions. There, they form a pool of cheap labour, easily available to top managers when trade revives.

3. Hillfields and Coventry

In the section which follows, the framework for analysis just presented will be applied to help understand what happened to Hillfields. It is important to remember that the plight of Hillfields is merely an example of what can happen to an area quite apart from the characteristics which the people living in that area bring to the labour market. A further example of the relative importance of demand side-factors at the labour market for understanding relative prosperity or deprivation of any area is the drastic change or fortune which the whole of Coventry (and the West Midlands) has suffered during the past few years.

3·1 Hillfields prosperity: central area

Hillfields, Coventry's first suburb, was built just outside the city wall in the 1820s and 1830s. Its establishment reflected strong demand for silk ribbons, Coventry's major trade. Houses were purpose-built for weavers, with large windows lighting workshops on the top floor. Only first-hand journeymen (skilled weavers who owned their own looms), could afford to move to Hillfields. This left less well-off journeymen's journeymen and the growing number of factory hands in workshops (then called factories, though at first not steam-powered), in the increasingly cramped city centre.

3·2 Hillfields decline: centre shift

In Hillfields, most merchant manufacturers pursued Responsible Autonomy strategies. First hand weavers were given silk and returned ribbons on Saturdays. During the week, weavers' time was their own and they often took "Saint Monday" and "Saint Tuesday" holidays as well as Sundays. Increasingly weavers were pressed into the growing number of steam factories in Coventry's city centre during the 1840s and 1850s.

Here weavers' time was supervized and weavers were gradually forced to work at a more even (and often quicker) pace. As steam increased the comparative advantage of the factory, Hillfields' domestic weavers were pressed to abandon the list of prices and to turn their own homes into cottage factories. The first they resisted while the second they pursued with vigour. But while Hillfields weavers fought their merchant manufacturers over the factory and lower earnings with some measure of success, the whole area was losing out to French and Swiss manufacturers who were already paying lower wages and who had moved to factory production earlier.

In 1860, with the Cobden Treaty, French ribbons entered England free of duty and Coventry's silk ribbon trade collapsed. The manufacturers over-threw the list of prices after a six-month strike. In the city it was the Hillfields weavers who suffered the most. Cottage factories and home work-ing were the least efficient methods of weaving because they did not allow as deep a division of labour. Though the centre of the Coventry area shifted away from Hillfields and back to the city centre, the entire region remained in a wretched state during the 1860s and 1870s. A national fund was set up to relieve Coventry in 1860 and 1861.

As the years of depression wore on, weavers began the long process of adjustment to declining industry. Cottage factories reverted to hand power or were converted into proper factories. Many were closed altogether. Many Hillfields weavers had to journey into town to work in the dreaded factories. Many apprenticed their sons to watchmakers. Others left Coventry altogether.

In both Coventry and Hillfields, partly because the demand for ribbons was strong, partly because the supply of labour power was physically limited by the land available for housing in Coventry and its suburb (Coventry was surrounded by commons which could not be developed), weavers were well organized. Male weavers were strong enough to protect their supply of labour from women by effectively insisting women only be allowed to work the simplest hand looms. Weaver strength meant that the list of prices, ensuring "just" earnings, remained in force until 1860, forty years after it had disappeared in nearby areas. Strong weaver resistance also meant steam power was late in coming to Coventry.

The central position of Hillfields and Coventry weavers was based on a periphery of weavers in the surrounding villages. During the boom period of trade cycles, the extent of weaving in villages grew. During recessions it declined, thereby cushioning the effects of short-term cycles in the central area. Because 75% of them were women and children, most village weavers used only the simple, less efficient looms. Because village weavers had no list of prices, they were paid less than what central area weavers received, even when working with the same looms, and working for the same merchant manufacturer.[2]

This centre–periphery pattern was based on more than a geographic division. It was based ultimately on the insecure employment consequences of an unplanned system of production whose aim is profit, combined with a work force who could be *socially* divided. It was the lack of solidarity between Hillfields and Coventry workers on the one hand, and village weavers on the other hand, which manufacturers used to achieve rapid cost reductions with little disruption.

While Hillfields weavers suffered more than other city weavers, those in the villages suffered most. They had no nearby factories to walk to, nor were there other trades to turn to. Population fell even more drastically in these villages than in Coventry after 1860.

From the late 1880s, with the development of first the bicycle industry and then the car industry, Coventry's fortunes revived. People began moving back into the area. But now those who came to live in Hillfields were not the most skilled. The housing stock in Hillfields was old with relatively small units compared with new suburbs built on the former common lands. Those already living in Hillfields had inappropriate skills for the new industries. The only major new firm to move to Coventry to take advantage of Hillfields labour was Courtaulds (1905). But Courtaulds came to employ the plentiful supply of cheap *female* labour in Hillfields and the surrounding villages (especially Foleshill). It was the low wages which Courtaulds could get away with paying these workers, rather than their skills, which attracted Courtaulds to the area.

3·3 Hillfields deprivation: the peripheral area

From the late 1880s Coventry had been (until recently), this country's fastest growing and richest major city. Nevertheless Hillfields did not revive. In the past when Coventry's major firms had been growing quickly, many people who came initially to Hillfields managed to move after a short time to Coventry's better housing areas. Particularly after the 1920s and 1930s, when new housing estates were built in suburbs close to the car factories, those workers who could afford to, either left Hillfields or entered those new housing estates when first coming to Coventry. Much as the movement of first-hand journeymen to Hillfields in the 1820s and 1830s left those in the city centre with the worst housing conditions, so the movement of more privileged workers to newer areas of the city left those in Hillfields with the worst housing conditions.

During the Second World War, Hillfields suffered considerable bomb damage. In the Development Plan, Hillfields was designated as one of the three comprehensive development areas. While Hillfields did receive aid, top priority was given to reconstruct the city centre and new housing estates. This resulted in twenty years of delay in implementing the redevelopment plans for Hillfields, twenty years of planning blight.

In 1951 only 2·5% of Hillfields property was judged unfit, but by 1961, more than 25% was unfit. In 1971, 52·2% of private households in Hillfields were without the exclusive use of hot water, bath and W.C. (compared with 20·2% for Great Britain and 19·9% for Coventry as a whole). Those who could afford no better than the miserable housing available in Hillfields were generally the aged, the unskilled and the disabled. In 1971, 21% of Hillfields' male workers were classified as unskilled compared with 6% for Coventry as a whole. Car ownership and owner occupation were also much lower in Hillfields compared with the rest of Coventry.

Not only were those living in Hillfields working in peripheral jobs, but also Hillfield's people tended to work for peripheral firms. In 1971, 7·2% of Coventry's workers were employed by firms in the metal-working industries other than the fifteen largest firms in Coventry. But 12·1% of those living in Hillfields were so employed. Also a high proportion of Hillfields workers were employed by Coventry Corporation (10·2% compared with 2·3% for Coventry as a whole). Most of these were not working as administrators, clerks or school teachers. In fact 92·5% were manual workers. Finally, Hillfields people were more likely to be unemployed than those in the rest of Coventry. In 1971, 7·4% of Hillfields people were unemployed and actively seeking employment compared with 3·8% for Great Britain and 3·7% for Coventry.

While no more up-to-date figures for Hillfields are readily available, a survey of Foleshill, the area of Coventry adjacent to Hillfields (to the north), was carried out in mid-1976. This showed Foleshill unemployment rates at 13·9% compared with Coventry's rate of 6·9% (City of Coventry, 1979). In 1981, a member of the Department of Architecture and Planning estimated that unemployment rates in Hillfields and Foleshill were likely to have continued to be about double the Coventry rates (private conversation). This would mean a staggering rate of unemployment in September 1981 of 33%!

4. Conclusions

The really noteable feature of Coventry at present is not the wide difference in relative prosperity between different neighbourhoods. While a centre–periphery pattern still exists in the Coventry area, it is now obscured by the general depression of the area. British car manufacturing as a whole has fallen to a peripheral position within world car manufacturing. The consequences of this shift on Coventry have been enormous. While unemployment has risen in Britain throughout the past few decades, the concentration of Coventry jobs in car manufacturing and car component supply has meant that Coventry's unemployment rates have risen much faster than for the rest of the country. By 1974, Coventry's umemployment rates had caught up with the average rate in Britain, but since then, and especially during this past year, the rate of job loss in Coventry has been immense. In September 1980, 10·9% of Coventry's labour force were on the unemployed register compared with 9·5% for all of Great Britain. By September 1981, 16·7% of workers in Coventry were unemployed compared with 12·2% for Great Britain as a whole (City of Coventry, 1980 and 1981). By 1980, average weekly pre-tax earnings of male manual employees in the vehicles industry in Britain had fallen below average earnings for manufacturing industry in general (City of Coventry, 1980).

The signs of depression and of coming deprivation grow steadily in Coventry. Pubs and restaurants are half empty. Shops in the city-centre are not repainted. The lists of unsold houses at the estate agents are enormous. Incidents of racial violence, especially of stabbings, are reported in the

Coventry Evening Telegraph with alarming frequency. Reports of concern about prostitution also appear regularly.

In this paper I have argued that the source of urban deprivation is not to be found merely in "defective' attitudes or characteristics of certain groups of workers. Those people currently unemployed in Coventry did not suddenly acquire undesirable labour market characteristics during 1981 or even over the past decade, just as the people of Hillfields did not change their attitudes and physical characteristics during the nineteenth century. Rather the inter-action of unstable markets with the counterplay of managerial strategies and worker resistance must be considered as a fundamental source of relative deprivation in market economies. If this is so, then government policies to counter-act urban deprivation which do not attempt to alter these funda-mental factors, both *within* private firms and between firms and markets can, at best, only *temporarily* alleviate some of the worst consequences of centre–periphery relations.

References[3]

Braverman, H. (1974). "Labour and monopoly capital: the degradation of work in the twentieth century", Monthly Review Press, New York.

Bruegel, I. (1979). Women as a reserve army of labour: a note on recent British experience, *Feminist Review*, **3**, 12–23.

Castles, S. and Kosack, O. (1973). "Immigrant workers and class structures in Western Europe", Oxford University Press, London.

City of Coventry. (1979). "Foleshill social survey report".

City of Coventry. (1980). "Quarterly monitors of the local economy".

City of Coventry. (1981). "Monthly reports on employment".

Community Development Project. (1977). "The costs of industrial change", CDP, London.

Coventry Community Development Project. (1975). "CDP Final Report", CDP Information and Intelligence Units, London.

Daniel, W. W. (1974). "A national survey of the unemployed", Political and Economic Planning, London.

Davidson, R. B. (1964). "Commonwealth immigrants", Oxford University Press, London.

Department of Employment (various years). *Gazette*, HMSO, London.

Friedman, A. L. (1977). "Industry and labour", Macmillan, London.

Gans, H. J. (1973a). "People and plans", Penguin, London.

Gans, H. J. (1976b). Poverty and culture: some basic questions about studying lifestyles of the poor, *in* P. Townsend (ed.), "The concept of poverty", Allen and Unwin, London.

Hill, M., Harrison, R. M., Sargeant, A. V. and Talbot, V. (1973). "Men out of work", Cambridge University Press, Cambridge.

Mansfield, E. (1968). "The economics of technological change", Norton, New York.

Marx, K. (1970). "Das Kapital, Vol. 1", Lawrence and Wishart, London.

Prest, J. (1960). "The industrial revolution in Coventry", Oxford University Press, London.

Rhys, D. G. (1973). "The motor industry: an economic survey", Butterworth, London.

Rutter, M. and Madge, N. (1976). "Cycles of disadvantage: a review of research", Heinemann, London.

Thrift, N. (1979). Unemployment in the Inner City: urban problem or structural imperative? A review of the British experience, *in* D. T. Herbert and R. J. Johnston (eds), "Geography and the urban environment", John Wiley, Chichester.

Wright, P. (1968). "The coloured worker in British industry", Oxford University Press, London.

Notes

1. These strategies are explained in more detail in *Industry and Labour*, (Friedman, 1977, Chapters 5 and 6).

2. Much of the information about Hillfields in the nineteenth century comes from Prest (1960).

3. Community Development Project (CDP) reports are now available from 85–87 Adelaide Terrace, Benwell, Newcastle upon Tyne.

FOUR

The restructuring of a local economy: the case of Lancaster

L. MURGATROYD and J. URRY
(September 1981)

1. Introduction

In this chapter we will consider how one particular local economy within Britain has been reorganized over the past twenty or thirty years. We will suggest that this reorganization, reflected in the apparently simple changes in the relative size of manufacturing and service employment, is in fact the product of complex relationships between the underlying "restructuring" of the various industrial sectors pertinent to the locality. Thus, industrial location and employment changes are not simply the consequence of certain general processes which are merely developed to a lesser or greater extent in any particular local economy. Any such economy must rather be seen as a specific conjuncture, in both time and space, of the particular forms of capitalist and state restructuring within manufacturing and service industries. As Massey argues:

> the social and economic structure of any given local area will be of complex result of the combination of that area's succession of roles within the series of wider, national and international, spatial divisions of labour. (Massey, 1978, p. 116)

There are three important implications of this "structural" approach for the analysis of industrial location and employment change. (See Storper, 1981, for a brief overview of the "structural" analysis developed within the Conference of Socialist Economists Regionalism Group.) First, the changing forms of the spatial division of labour, especially the shift away from a high degree of regional specialization, derive from new patterns of capital accumulation. In particular, they reflect the internationalization of capitalist accumulation and the development of "neo-Fordist" methods by which the labour process is controlled (see, amongst many sources, Aglietta, 1979; Massey, 1979; Perrons, 1981.)

Second, changes in the location of industry are not to be explained simply in terms of "economic" or "political" factors; location is rather to be understood in relation to those forms of economic restructuring within and between industrial sectors which are necessitated by the requirements of capital accumulation (see Massey, 1977, on a critique of the conventional literature on industrial location). However, relations between classes, and other social forces, also significantly affect patterns of economic restructuring, and the latter themselves, influence social relations within particular localities to a substantial extent. (This has been well shown in the case of Wales, by Cooke, 1981).

Third, problems of uneven development cannot be analysed simply in terms of "regions" and of regional growth or decline. With the growth of national and international branch circuits there has been a decrease in the degree to which productive systems are centred upon a particular region (see Lipietz, 1980b, and Massey, 1978, 1979). This is related to the dispersal of new manufacturing employment on a periphery-centre pattern and to some consequential decline in regional variations in unemployment and economic activity rates between the mid-1960s and the late 1970s (see Keeble, 1976, pp. 71–85, and Dunford *et al.*, 1980, pp. 12–13). This homogenization among the peripheral regions has also been partly reinforced by the growing concentration of the functions of conception and control within the South East region of the UK (see Crum and Gudgin 1977; Buck, 1979, among many sources). Similarly, in terms of industrial change, Fothergill and Gudgin conclude that "there are much greater contrasts within any region than between the regions themselves" (1979, p. 157; more generally see Urry, 1981b).

One example of such contrasts may be seen in the North West, in which Lancaster is situated. In 1966, this was one of only two regions said to possess a "regional" industrial structure (see Fothergill and Gudgin, 1979, pp. 170–2, 174–6). Yet even in this case we find considerable intraregional variations in the recent period:

(i) in the percentage change in male employment 1960–77, between $-27 \cdot 7\%$ (Liverpool) and $+15 \cdot 6\%$ (Crewe) (ignoring the new towns in the region);

(ii) in the percentage change in female employment 1960–77, between $-33 \cdot 5\%$ (Rossendale) and $+58 \cdot 7\%$ (Northwich);

(iii) in the 1980 ratio of female:male employees, between $0 \cdot 534$ (Warrington) and $1 \cdot 165$ (Southport);

(iv) in the unemployment rate, between 5% and $13 \cdot 7\%$ (Crewe and Liverpool; June 1980) (Department of Employment, ERII).

In this chapter we shall consider these three points in some detail, in particular in relation to the de-industrialization of the Lancaster sub-region (which we will refer to simply as "Lancaster"). This local economy is situated in the north of the North-West Planning Region (north of Preston and Blackburn), and consists of the former urban districts of Lancaster, and Morecambe and Heysham, as well as extensive surrounding rural areas from the Fylde to the Lake District, and from Morecambe Bay in the west to the Peninnes in the east. It constitutes a relatively self-contained labour market, with only 7·6% of residents in the district travelling elsewhere to work and 8·7% of these working in it living outside (Census of Population, 1971; in general, see Murgatroyd, 1981, for background details).

Lancaster has, like much of the rest of the UK, been "de-industrialized" in recent years. However, we would suggest that this change in the pattern of employment, consisting of a shift out of manufacturing into either service employment or unemployment, results from a number of underlying processes whose impact in different regions and localities varies greatly. In other words, there is no simple "de-industrializing" process by which national and subnational economies develop, with one kind of economic activity automatically replacing another as dominant. The Fisher-Clark thesis of a natural history of industrialization, with extractive, manufacturing, and service sectors each dominating the economy in their turn, seems at best specific to Western Europe (see Sabolo, 1975, Singelmann, 1978, and Urry, 1981, pp. 7–13, for general discussion). And even here, the rates and patterns of industrial change vary widely. In France, for example, there has been some shift directly from primary to tertiary industry, while West Germany, supposedly the most advanced European economy, is one of only two in which manufacturing employment is *still* larger than service employment (see Marquand, 1980, p. 27).

To say that a local, regional, or national economy has been 'de-industrialized" is, then, merely a way of *describing* certain shifts in the structure of employment; it does not provide any kind of explanation (see Blackaby, 1978; Singh, 1978; Showler and Sinfield, 1981; Barratt Brown, 1981, for further discussion of de-industrialization). Britain as a whole has experienced "de-industrialization", in recent years, in the sense that manufacturing output has fallen (from a peak in 1973), and manufacturing employment has shrunk (by nearly two and a half million between 1966 and 1981). However, this term in fact *conceals* highly diverse processes, affecting different localities in different ways, depending upon their location within pre-existing and new forms of the spatial division of labour. Hence, part of our project is to demonstrate the inadequacy of notions of both "de-industrialization" and the "region" in characterizing the diverse and complex processes of economic and class restructuring.

In the following we shall show how the "de-industrialization" of Lancaster has resulted from a combination of such processes. Although during the 1950s and early 1960s this subregion was an important site for private manufacturing investment, the national and international reorganization of capital produced a rapid decline in Lancaster's manufacturing base from the

1960s onwards. We shall focus on three manufacturing industries in greater detail, to show how their particular forms of restructuring had the effect that most of the new employment generated was located outside Lancaster, whether abroad or elsewhere in the UK. We shall also briefly consider the restructuring of the service industries in the locality. We then turn to some of the implications of the process of capitalist restructuring in Lancaster, for local politics and for the state. There is a brief conclusion.

2. The restructuring of Lancaster's economy

2·1 Employment in Lancaster

Tables 1 and 2 indicate the main changes in the structure of employment in Lancaster, the North-West Planning Region and the UK between 1951 and 1977. Overall, there was a major reduction in manufacturing employment in Lancaster, from around 17 000 to 9000 jobs, and considerable employment loss was recorded in all those industries with a substantial labour force. At the same time, there have been major increases in many of the service industries, such that employment increased by 5000 over the period, 1951–77. Female employment and unemployment both grew, and while the total population had expanded by 13%, there was an 11% fall in the employed population.

These overall changes did not occur smoothly over the thirty-year period, as Figure 1 shows. During the 1950s and early 1960s, manufacturing and service employment both grew considerably, by 9·5% and by 13·2% respectively between 1952 and 1964 (Fulcher *et al.*, 1966; unless otherwise stated all data between 1952 and 1964 comes from this source). Employment in a number of manufacturing industries grew considerably: textiles by 32·3% (1349 employees), engineering by 56·5% (360), clothing and footwear by 17% (124) and floor-coverings and coated fabrics by 25% (1002). Although the long-established local furniture industry was run down (the main factory closed in 1962), an oil refinery and chemical plant were developed and became major local employers. Certain categories of service employment also showed very substantial rates of employment growth; notably distribution 38%, insurance, banking 35%, professional services 42%, and public administration 19%.

During this period, there was a strong demand for labour, and unemployment was minimal. The labour force increased by over 4000, at a rate about equivalent to the national rate but faster than the average for the North-West region. Much of this increase was accounted for by in-migration, and female employment also increased slowly, but even with these expansions in the labour force, local employers found increasing difficulty in recruiting labour in the early 1960s.

Over the next fifteen years, the situation altered dramatically. Manufacturing employment fell from 16 700 in 1961 to 11 200 in 1971 dropping to 9000 in 1977 (Department of Employment). By contrast, employment in the service sector expanded steadily through the 1960s from 23 000 in 1961 to 26 800 in 1971, and rose more sharply during the early 1970s to reach 29 400 by 1977, that is, from just over one-half to two-thirds of total employment between 1961 and 1977 (Table 2).

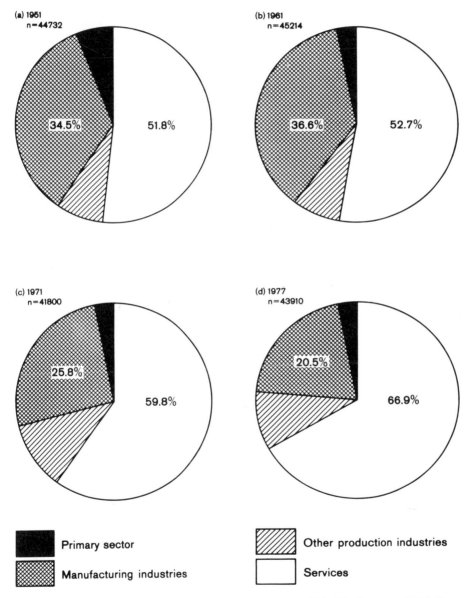

Figure 1. Employment in Lancaster by industrial sector, 1951–77. Sources: 1951 Census of Population; 1961–77 Department of Employment.

TABLE 1. *Sectoral shifts in employment, in selected years 1951–1977 Lancaster, the North-West region and Great Britain.*

	Sector	1951*	1960	1966	1971	1977
Lancaster	Production industries[a]	42·8	45·2	44·8	34·2	31·1
	(of which) manufacturing[b] industries	34·5	36·3	33·7	25·8	20·5
	Service[c] industries	51·8	52·5	53·7	59·8	66·9
	Total	49 732	43 178	43 335	42 604	43 910
North-West Region	Production industries	51·1	57·2	54·8	51·8	45·3
	Manufacturing industries	46·2	48·2	45·9	44·6	38·4
	Service industries	42·8	42·0	44·5	47·7	54·1
	Total	3 029 100	2 976 700	2 995 500	2 773 900	2 636 000
Great Britain	Production industries	45·6	50·9	49·5	47·4	41·0
	Manufacturing industries	32·9	39·2	37·9	38·3	32·5
	Service industries	46·9	42·3	48·4	51·0	57·2
	Total	22 134 689	22 817 000	24 065 000	22 509 000	22 172 000

* There are some discrepancies with data presented elsewhere, due to unclassified employment. Sources: 1951 Census of Population (April); other years from Department of Employment (June).
[a] Industries II–XXI in 1968 Standard Industrial Classification.
[b] Industries III–XIX in 1968 SIC.
[c] Industries XXII–XXVIII in 1968 SIC.

TABLE 2. Changes in employment in Lancaster travel-to-work-area, 1951–1977.

Industry Groups	1951	1977	Change 1951–77	% Change 1951–77	1951 % of total	1977 % of total
Agriculture	2601	636	−1765	−67·9	5·2	1·9
All production industries	21 018	13 694	−7324	−34·8	42·3	31·1
includes:						
Manufacturing	16 949	9075	−7934	−53·2	34·1	20·5
includes:						
petrol and chemicals	2324	1076	−1248	−53·7	4·7	2·5
metal and engineering	1893	1198	−695	−36·5	3·8	2·7
textiles, leather and fur	5205	1754	−3451	−66·3	10·5	4·0
timber and furniture	1184	162	−1022	−86·3	2·4	0·4
plastics, rubber, linoleum and others	4126	2761	−1358	−53·2	34·1	20·5
All service industries	24 271	29 374	+5143	+21·2	48·8	66·9
includes:						
transport and communications	4934	3073	−1861	−37·7	9·9	7·0
distribution	5836	5322	−508	−10·1	11·7	12·1
professional and scientific services	3 726	10 459	+6733	+180·7	7·5	23·8
miscellaneous services	6725	6815	+90	+1·3	13·5	15·5
Total Employment	49 732	43 910	−5822	−11·7	100·0	100·0
includes:						
females in employment	14 203[a]	19 103	+4900	+34·5	28·5[a]	43·5
registered unemployed	241[a]	3030	2789	+1160%	1·7%[ab]	6·9%[b]

⋆ Sources: 1951 Census of Population. 1952 and 1977, Department of Employment.
[a] 1952.
[b] Unemployment rate.

This structural shift has also had significant effects upon the differential employment of men and women locally. Between 1951 and 1971, male employment fell by 1200, while female employment rose by 4900. The economic activity rates for men fell from 81·4% to 72% (with 67·4% in employment), while the female rate rose from 31·8% to 36·8% (Census of Population, 1951, 1971). As a result there was an increase in the ratio of female to male workers in the subregion; by 1977 it had risen to 0·74, slightly higher than the mean for the North-West which had always shown high female activity rates (Department of Employment). The general shift towards the service industries is related to the increased feminization of the Lancaster labour force since the proportion of women employed in these industries is high. However, there has also been a shift *within* the service sector towards increased feminization (from 49·1% to 54% between 1971 and 1976; Department of Employment, ERII).

Two further labour force characteristics should be noted here. First, there has been a considerable growth in declared part-time employment especially during the 1970s. The proportion of the labour force which was part-time rose from 18·1% to 22% between 1971 and 1977 (Department of Employment); in 1951, only 5% of employees in Lancaster M.B. worked part-time. Second, like elsewhere, there has been a long-term increase in the numbers of registered unemployed.

Up to the mid-1960s, Lancaster was a significant centre for capital accumulation, and this led to a considerable labour shortage. However, from 1965 this became less the case, and the local unemployment rate rose above the national average. The male rate in particular has increased steeply, and a growing gap between the national and local rates has developed.

We will now consider what explanation we can provide for this shift in the pattern of employment over the post-war period. We will begin with the decline in manufacturing employment. One obvious explanation of this is simply that the industries present in Lancaster 1956/60 were those which were about to decline in employment nationally (such as cotton textiles and related industries which were already declining in the rest of Lancashire). However, Fothergill and Gudgin (1979) show that the industrial structure in Lancaster's manufacturing sector in the late fifties was in fact exceedingly favourable in comparison with other areas. They say:

> Expressed as a percentage of 1959 employment the worst subregional employment structure for *manufacturing* was North-East Lancashire (−20·0%), reflecting its heavy dependence on the declining cotton industry, and the best was Lancaster ... dominated by a handful of firms in growing industries (1979, p. 169)

They also show that the industrial structure remained favourable throughout the sixties, when those manufacturing sectors represented in Lancaster expanded in the UK as a whole.

The explanation of the decline in manufacturing employment (3300 between 1959–75) cannot, therefore, be the existing industrial structure. The alternative is that established firms failed to grow, or at least to expand employment, and closed or shrunk instead, while the locality failed to attract mobile employment which was being generated elsewhere in the sixties and early seventies. Conversely, the relatively large expansion of Lancaster's service sector could not have been predicted from the structure of service industries in 1959, but was due rather to the movement of services (such as the University) into the subregion, and the disproportionate growth (or lesser decline) of those already present, such as health services and tourist-related trades. This pattern in Lancaster was directly the converse of that in neighbouring subregions (see Fothergill and Gudgin, 1979, pp. 170–1). In South Lancashire, Mid-Lancashire, North-East Lancashire, and West Yorkshire, there was a highly unfavourable industrial structure for manufacturing, while that for services was favourable. In Lancaster, as we have seen, there was a very favourable industrial structure for manufacturing, while that for service employment was unfavourable.

Their analysis suggests then that the decline of Lancaster's manufacturing base rests with the "poor performance" of existing capital combined with the inability to attract substantial new plants into the subregion during the 1960s. Hence at a time of very considerable industrial restructuring, with considerable new plant mobility, Lancaster failed to attract such investments and its existing capital became progressively unable to compete with the new plants being established (see also Massey and Meegan, 1978, as well as Morgan and Sayer, in this volume).

Fothergill and Gudgin have attempted to explain the overall pattern of employment change in terms of the division between urban conurbations and semi-rural areas. It was in the former, and especially in the large conurbations, that manufacturing employment decline has been most marked. This has resulted from the *in situ* contraction of employment and plant closures (1979, p. 169). And it was in the less industrialized, semi-rural areas that the most substantial relative increases in both manufacturing employment and total employment have been recorded (1979, p. 189). The Lancaster subregion, in terms of its rural/urban characteristics, fits into a category showing very considerable growth of manufacturing employment in this period (between 16·3 and 17·9%). However, by singular contrast, manufacturing employment in Lancaster actually *fell* by 22% over the same period.

Two points follow from this discussion. First, Lancaster *should* have experienced considerable increases in manufacturing employment, given both its industrial structure in 1959 and the "performance" of similar less heavily industrialized subregions. But second, identifying a locality in terms of its urban/rural characteristics glosses over a number of highly diverse determinants of employment change. Overall it is more important to identify the place that a particular locality occupies in relationship to the changing spatial division of labour, and hence why in *certain* cases *in situ* expansion or new plants will be developed within smaller less urbanized centres. We will now consider the forms of restructuring of the manufacturing and service sectors in the Lancaster economy.

2·2 Restructuring in the manufacturing sector

We will begin by summarizing the main developments in the structure and ownership of the local manufacturing sector as a whole. First, there has been a significant increase in the numbers of establishments and of enterprises. In 1964 there were 58 manufacturing firms in the Lancaster subregion while by 1979 there were at least 135 separate manufacturing establishments employing over ten people. Table 3 gives a rough indication of the changing size distribution of manufacturing firms in Lancaster.

TABLE 3. *Size distribution of manufacturing firms in the Lancaster TTWA, 1964 and 1979.*

1964		1979		
Size of "firm"	No. of firms	Size of "establishment"	No. of establishments	Percent employees
Up to 100	35	10 to 100	109	23%
101 to 250	15	100 to 1000	24	57%
251 to 500	3	1000 and over	2	20%
500 and over				
Total	58	Total	135	100%

Sources: Fulcher *et al.*, 1966, p. 14; Industrial Strategy for Lancaster (1977) updated with figures from City Planning Department and from *Who Owns Whom*.

The number of small manufacturing firms in 1964 was particularly low. This may be connected with the tightness of the local labour market at the time; small firms found it hard to attract labour (Fulcher *et al.*, 1966), and the abundance of jobs may have lessened the attractiveness of self-employment. Between 1961 and 1971, however, there was a 10·7% increase in self-employed males (excluding professionals and farmers), and a 24% increase in the number of employers and managers in small establishments. Altogether, one tenth of economically active males in Lancaster were self-employed by 1971, which was twice the national level, and there are indications that there were some further increases during the seventies (see Murgatroyd 1981).

So while there has been a substantial increase in the number of manufacturing firms in Lancaster, at the very same time, the subregion has been de-industrialized and manufacturing employment has dropped to about one-fifth of total employment. The increase in number of firms is largely accounted for by a substantial increase in the number of small enterprises. By 1979 there were 109 firms employing between ten and a hundred employees compared with 35 employing below 100 in 1964. Indeed it is interesting to note how successful the subregion has been in establishing and attracting small manufacturing firms. Partly this may have resulted from the efforts of the City Council to encourage the establishment and growth of such firms, not simply because this is the only alternative, but also because of the perceived problems caused by dependence on "externally controlled" capital. This problem was graphically highlighted when the Lansil works owned by British Celanese (part of Courtaulds) closed in 1980. This episode also shows very well the limitations of the popular "small firm solution" to industrial decline. This one closure caused more jobs to be lost than had been created by small firms during the *whole* of the 1970s (see also Brimson, 1979, on the weakness of the small firms strategy).

Since the late 1950s, a high proportion of manufacturing employment has been in firms which were controlled from outside the immediate area; and there has been a slight increase in this proportion as shown in Table 4.

TABLE 4. *Ownership of manufacturing industry in Lancaster TTWA.*

Nature of Company	1964	1968	1977
(1) Subsidiary/Branch is externally controlled			
Percentage of total firms	43%	40%	30%
Percentage of employment in manufacturing	73%	68%	77%
(2) Independent			
Percentage of total firms	57%	60%	70%
Percentage of employment in manufacturing	27%	32%	23%

Source: Lancaster City Council (1977).

Subsidiaries or branches of large companies tend to be the larger establishments. A considerable number of locally based firms were taken over by, or merged with, other companies over this period. These include the takeover of Waring and Gillows by Great Universal Stores in 1962; the merger of J. Williamsons (founded by Jimmy Williamson, the "Lino King") with Nairns of Kirkcaldy in 1967 and its later take-over by Unilever in 1975; the affiliation of Storey Bros to the Turner and Newall Group in 1977; and the take-over of Lansil Ltd first by Monsanto and then by Courtaulds in 1973. This dependence of the local economy upon a small number of large externally controlled firms has been noted by the local planning department, who say that:

> . . . it is significant that a very high proportion of closures and redundancies declared during recent periods of recession have been in firms who are under external control, i.e. 'pruning the branches to encourage growth'. (Lancaster City Council: 1977, Appendix IIIc)

The "branches" are located in Lancaster.

It is also important to note here that *all* the large manufacturing firms in Lancaster are now externally controlled, while independent ownership is much more characteristic of the very small firms. Moreover, hardly any of the large plants were established by major multinationals; rather they were locally-owned firms which were *acquired* by (or merged with) large companies based elsewhere. In other words, external takeovers have been far more important for the employment structure of Lancaster than have patterns of branch-plant migration (except in the 1940s and 1950s with the establishment of a fertilizer and ammonia plant by ICI and of a refinery by Shell). Lancaster has not therefore developed as a branch-plant economy in the sense of branch-plants moving in (a few exceptions include Hornsea Pottery, and Angus Fire Armour); rather, existing plants have become branches.

An interesting comparison can be made here with the neighbouring Northern Region; Smith shows that in the region the external branch-plant sector was responsible for 80% of the new establishments and over 90% of the new employment that was created in establishments with over 100 workers between 1963 and 1973 (1979, p. 433). By contrast the indigenous sector was responsible for a mere 5·4% of new employment in the same period, rather similar to the situation in Lancaster. And again, as in Lancaster, firms acquired externally tended to have a fairly high closure rate, a relatively low rate of new establishment formation, and a strong tendency to reduce employment levels. Employment loss in the Northern Region was concentrated among the indigenous sector and the externally acquired sector, and there are the main forms of manufacturing ownership in Lancaster. Within these employment losers, it is the externally acquired sector which shows greater redundancy rates, as can be seen from Table 5.

We will now consider three forms of restructuring of industrial sectors which will generate different spatial patterns of employment decline (see Massey and Meegan, 1982). They are "intensification", "investment and technical change", and "rationalization". *Intensification* is the process of increasing the productivity of labour with little, if any, loss of capacity and no investment in new forms of production. Such a reorganization of production will generally entail less change in the distribution of employment than

TABLE 5. *Redundancies and closures in Lancaster 1962–77.*

	Independent Firms		"Externally Controlled"	
	Number made redundant	Average number Employed	Number made redundant	Average number Employed
1962–70	176 (4·8%)	3654	2574 (26·1%)	9863
1971–77	419 (18·0%)	2330	1630 (20·1%)	7798

Sources: Fulcher *et al.*, 1966, p. 14 and Lancaster City Council (1977).

any of the other forms of reorganization. In the second type, *investment and technical change*, there is heavy capital investment in new forms of production and as a result considerable job-loss, often highly unequally distributed among job-types and skills. The third form, *rationalization*, produces closure of capacity without new investment or change in technique. Massey and Meegan attempt to show how in each of 32 separate industry Minimum List Headings (M.L.H.), which accounted for a job-loss of 312 100 between 1968 and 1973, one or other of these three forms can be seen as the dominant cause of employment decline.

The restructuring of the British economy in this way has had important spatial implications, and Lancaster seems to have been one of the casualties. Lancaster's manufacturing employment was concentrated in industries in which "investment and technical change", or "rationalization" were to occur, rather than "intensification". To demonstrate this in detail is beyond the scope of this chapter; instead, we will discuss the broad trends in the three principal manufacturing industries. In June, 1971, linoleum, plastics and floor-coverings (M.L.H. 492), man-made fibres (M.L.H. 411) and fertilizers (M.L.H. 278) employed 2502, 2015, and 911 people respectively, and between them accounted for 46% of all manufacturing employment in Lancaster. By 1977, employment in these industries had fallen by 41%, 66% and 32% compared with their 1971 levels. What, then, were the forms in which production in these industries was reorganized, to produce such a fall in their employment in Lancaster?

(1) Floorcoverings, linoleum, plastics, etc.

Table 6 indicates the employment trends in this census industry grouping (M.L.H. 492). (It is difficult to compare the statistics over the whole period, because of changes in industrial classifications; neither is it possible to disaggregate beyond this level since these industries are grouped together in a single M.L.H. and more detailed statistics are not available.)

During the 1950s this was a relatively buoyant industrial sector with a
25% increase in the local employed labour force. However, during the 1960s
there was a sharp decline in employment within this sector. The local results
were that:

> ... the major company since the 1860s, the Mills [Williamsons], were forced
> into a defensive merger with a major rival; the merger led to considerable
> rationalisation, the disposal of surplus asset and the consolidation of both
> administration and production at the headquarters of the former rival [Nairns],
> in a government development area [Kirkcaldy]. (Martin and Fryer, 1973, p.
> 168: names in brackets added)

In fact, all floor-covering production was transferred to Kirkcaldy and the
Lancaster plant mainly concentrated on PVC wall-coverings instead.

TABLE 6. *Local and national employment in linoleum, plastic
floor-coverings, leather cloth, etc. industries.**

	1952	1964	1971	1973	1977
Lancaster TTWA	4019	5021	2502	1888	1483
United Kingdom	13 800	13 800	13 500	16 000	14 300

* MLH 492 in the 1968 Standard Industrial Classification.
Sources: Fulcher *et al.*, (1966) and Department of Employment (various years
and unpublished data).

Linoleum manufacture had long been established in Lancaster, having
developed from sail-cloth and oil-cloth production in the nineteenth
century, and much of the equipment was therefore outdated. The market for
these products deteriorated sharply with the development of plastics, and
later of cheap carpets based on man-made fibres. Local firms did diversify
into PVC sheeting and various kinds of coated fabrics and wall-coverings,
but much of this was achieved by the adaptation of old machinery rather than
by substantial new capital investments and the use of new forms of production technology. The main production change within this industry has been
the decline in linoleum and the development of plastic floor coverings. This
resulted from a combination of two processes: rationalization and the almost
complete disappearance of manufacturing capacity in linoleum, and technical change and investment within plastic floor and wall-coverings. This
has had dramatic employment effects.

Overall, the rate of decline in this sector has been far faster in Lancaster
than in the UK as a whole. The changes in the M.L.H. nationally are shown
in Table 7. Nationally, restructuring (including closures) has been accompanied by some expansion in the newer sectors of this M.L.H. grouping.
This has not occurred in Lancaster.

Figure 2. The old Williamson Linoleum factory, named after the "Lino King" Jimmy Williamson. Now partly used by Unilever to produce vinyl wallpapers.

(2) Fertilizers

In contrast to the floor-coverings industry, there have been enormous increases in output, capital expenditure and productivity in this industry (M.L.H. 278), as Table 8 shows.

Both output and productivity increased ten times over the period 1963–78, while capital investment increased nine times between 1968 and 1978 (all in money terms). The increases in productivity in fertilizers were greater than for any other branch of the chemicals industry between 1970 and 1975 (see COI, 1978, p. 17). The capital investment was concentrated in the development of new, very large, low cost manufacturing plant; by the late 1960s there were six major plants in the UK (ICI at Avonmouth, Billingham, Immingham; Fissons at Avonmouth, Immingham; and Shell at Ince Marshes, see Warren, 1971, especially pp. 194–200). As a consequence there was a 20% reduction in the numbers of both establishments and

TABLE 7. *Developments in the linoleum,*
leather cloth and plastic floor-coverings industries,
in the UK 1963–1977★

	Number of Enterprises	Number of Establishments	Number Employed
1963	38	53	20 000
1968	41	56	17 300
1970	41	51	18 800
1973	44	55	16 500
1977	49	56	14 4000

★See note to Table 6.
Source: Census of Production.

TABLE 8. *Output, productivity and capital investment in floor-coverings* and fertilizers* 1963–78.*

	Net output £m.		Net output per head £		Total capital investment	
1963	36·7	33·0	2041	1644	10·1	3·5
1968	70·9	38·4	3674	2224	8·3	3·7
1970	81·6	47·4	3708	2530	16·1	4·4
1974	214·6	77·7	10 875	4653	26·1	8·2
1978	366·2	117·0	19 312	8963	71·2	n.a.

* Industries in MLH 492 and MLH 279 of the 1968 Standard Industrial Classification. Note changes in classification in 1969, 1973 and 1979. All figures are in monetary terms.
Source: Census of Production.

enterprises between 1963 and 1978. Moreover, these enormous increases in output were achieved with little or no increase in total employment in the fertilizer industry (see Table 9). The fertilizer industry is a very good example of "jobless growth" where the process of restructuring took the form of "investment and technical change". What then were the consequences for the Lancaster economy?

Table 9 shows the decline in employment from the early 1950s. The workforce fell in the main local plant (ICI at Heysham) for two main reasons. First, ammonia production was abandoned in 1977, and concentrated in the larger plants, especially in the North East. And second, the fertilizer made at Heysham (Nitrogel) could not compete with the new fertilizer (Nitran) which had been developed by ICI in the mid-1960s. The Heysham plant is disadvantaged in that its capacity is too small (500 tons per day compared to 1500/2000 tons at more modern plants) and because none of its main production capacity dates from later than 1962 (source: interview with management). Again we see how capital accumulation in manufacturing industry has not led to reinvestment in Lancaster, and that this decline results from the development *elsewhere* of newer, cheaper manufacturing capacity. Even moderate-sized plants producing for a specific regional market (for example, the ESSO plant at Warboys, Essex) are unable to compete with the major plants listed above (see Warren, 1971, pp. 197–8).

TABLE 9. *Employment in fertilizer production in Lancaster and the UK 1952–1977.*

	1952	1964	1971	1974	1977
Lancaster	2285	1869	911	768	624
UK	n.a.	n.a.	11 400	11 800	11 600

Sources: Fulcher *et al.*, 1966; Department of Employment.

(3) Man-made fibres

Production of man-made fibres (MLH 411) began in Lancaster in 1928 with the establishment of Cellulose Acetate Silk Co. Ltd (later known as Lansils), in an era of considerable national expansion in the production of cellulosic textile yarns (i.e. rayons). By 1929 there were 32 national competitors; yet in the next 30 years one firm, Courtaulds, came to dominate the production of rayons. In 1962, for example, Lansils was the only other producer of cellulose acetate (see Monopolies Commission, 1968, Cowling, 1980, and Coleman, 1980, Chapter 8). However by the early 1950s the market for rayon was being eroded by the development of synthetic fibres (especially nylon and later polyesters) and of improved cotton. Courtaulds itself diversified and came to dominate production in all sections of the textile industry, except weaving which remained rather fragmented.

In 1978 there were 303 enterprises and 368 establishments in M.L.H. 413: weaving of cotton, linen, and man-made fibres. Courtaulds partly overcame this fragmentation by establishing their own weaving plants, for example, at Skelmersdale (see Knight, 1974, Cowling, 1980.). Lansils itself was finally taken over by Courtaulds in 1973/4.

Two conclusions are important here. First, as Table 10 suggests, man-made fibres constitute a sector in which investment and technical change has been particularly marked, especially in the period up to 1970 (see Ewing, 1972, Chapters 4 and 5 on some of the main technical changes). These figures conceal the shift from cellulose-based fibres to synthetic fibres. Courtaulds itself has been able to enlarge its monopoly position by moving into synthetics, and by vertical integration (see Counter-information Services Report, 1974). Second, the effect of this in Lancaster has been the closure of Lansils in 1980, after a long period of decline. Courtaulds justify closure with reference to annual losses of £91 000, but more fundamentally this resulted from failure to update or replace machinery since first installation in 1952. It is true that the reorganization of the textile industry as a whole: mergers, acquisitions, technical changes, and new plants in development areas and abroad (see Counter-information Services, 1974, and Newbould, 1970), produced new accumulation away from the traditional

Figure 3. The Lansil works, taken over by British Celanese (part of Courtaulds) in 1973 and closed in 1980. Its main product was cellulose acetate yarn for the textile industry.

TABLE 10. *Main developments in the UK man-made fibres industry 1958–78.*

	Enterprises	Establishments	£m. Net output	£ Per person	Total Employment (1000)	Total Expenditure (£m.)
1958	10	30	49·5	1360	36·4	10·7
1963	7	26	108·8	2918	37·3	11·7
1968	5	26	163·0	4043	40·3	24·4
1970	9	26	172·8	4014	43·1	41·4
1974	27	43	293·9	6917	42·5	37·3
1978	24	36	297·3	8538	34·8	27·3

Source: Census of Production (figures are in monetary terms).

Lancashire textile towns. But we might have expected Lancaster to have been protected from some of the worst consequences of this process because of its involvement in the production of man-made fibres rather than cotton. However, this did not occur, showing how accumulation in the 1950s was followed by disinvestment in Lancaster in the 1960s and 1970s. The total number of textile workers in the travel-to-work-area has declined from 5500 in 1964 to 1800 in 1977 (source: Fulcher *et al.*, 1966, and Department of Employment).

To summarize, Lancaster benefitted from accumulation in manufacturing industry in the 1950s, and by the end of the decade had high representation in a number of growing industrial sectors. However, these were sectors that were to experience "investment and technical change", and "rationalization", particularly because of the increased centralization of ownership. New plants were established elsewhere, while existing plants based on earlier technologies shed labour. Local branches of multi-plant companies were run down, as these companies restructured their production away from Lancaster. While the number of small manufacturing enterprises swelled during the later period, these did not provide sufficient employment to offset the decline in the larger establishments. It is interesting to note that of those industries in which there was much less job-loss in Lancaster, two appear as "intensifiers" between 1968 and 1973, according to Massey and Meegan (1982, Chapter 3). These are textile finishing (M.L.H. 423), whose employment in Lancaster fell from 432 to 278 between 1971–7 and footwear (M.L.H. 450) whose employment fell from 549 to 414 (source: Department of Employment).

2·3 The reorganization of services

We will now consider how restructuring in service sector industries has affected Lancaster. First of all, however, it is necessary to distinguish between service *industries* and service *occupations*. The former are those industries with a product which is classified as a service rather than a tangible good, and include transport and communications, distributions, professional services, and so on (see Gershuny, 1978, for a helpful discussion). The latter, service occupations, are like service industries in that they are normally defined in contrast with the *physical* production of commodities, and include managers, professionals, clerical and sales workers, health and educational workers and so on. The most important implication of this distinction is that there are many workers within manufacturing industry who are located within the service occupations. Grum and Gudgin (1978, 5) estimate that by 1971, 34·6% of manufacturing workers were what they term "non-productive" in this sense.

So another way of expressing the de-industrialization thesis is to point out that the absolute number of "direct production workers" had fallen from 6·5 m.

in the late 1950s to 5·2 m. in 1975 (Crum and Gudgin, 1978, p. 5). Partly this reflects the changing industrial structure, so that roughly speaking the later an industry develops, the higher the proportion of non-productive workers employed within it (66·1% in periodical publishing compared to 10·8% in miscellaneous wood and cork manufacture; see Crum and Gudgin, 1978, p. 6). It also reflects the socialization of non-productive labour within firms, and the differentiation of the functions of management between a large number of agents as conception is increasingly separated from execution.

We can also identify some distinctive factors which affect the labour process within service work. First, it is generally not easy, and in certain cases impossible, to accumulate the service-commodity. Hence, labour-power has to be expended more closely to where the consumer demands it, and this has implications for the spatial structuring of such industry. It is also more difficult to standardize the product and hence to fragment the labour process as in manufacturing industry. There is also some degree of control maintained by many service workers over the nature of their work. This is true even within distribution, clerical and secretarial work, and is particularly marked in the case of so-called "people-work" (see Stacey, 1980).

In the service sector, capital (and the state) tend to economize on labour costs, not principally through direct increases in productivity (though this of course happens) but rather through the employment of sectors of the labour force which can be employed at less than the average wage for white males. In most of the major capitalist economies, there have been much larger increases in the employment of women than of men in the growing service sector. (A significant exception to this is West Germany, where large numbers of "guestworkers" have been employed). In the UK, women are now five times more likely to be employed in service than manufacturing industry (see Marquand, 1980, pp. 30–1). This development is connected to some de-skilling of service employment (see Lipietz, 1980a). We should note that such variations in women's participation rates will have significant implications for the cost of reproducing labour power, the size of local labour reserves, and the levels of organization and politicization of the labour force; all of which may in turn affect patterns of industrial restructuring.

What then has happened to the service industries in Lancaster? Between 1951 and 1977, the numbers employed in them increased by 21%, as compared with a 23% increase nationally. As Table 2 above shows, this constituted an increase of over 5000, at the same time that total employment had fallen by nearly 6000. However, this overall expansion conceals a number of divergent trends.

Figure 4 shows that between 1960 and 1979 employment in transport and communication declined by over one third, while that in professional and scientific services almost trebled (up 180%). Other service industries maintained fairly steady levels of employment. In the relatively large size of the

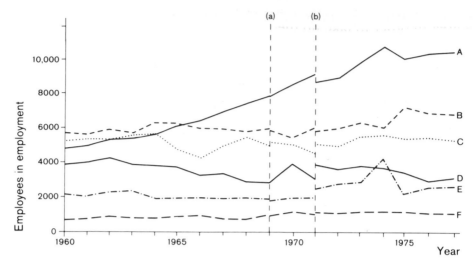

Figure 4. Employment in service industries, Lancaster travel-to-work area, 1960–77.
Key: (a) change in classification   C   distribution
     (b) change in base   D   transport and communication
     A   professional and scientific services   E   public administration
     B   miscellaneous services   F   insurance, banking and finance.
Source: Department of Employment.

transport sector, and the small numbers employed in financial services and government administration, Lancaster was fairly typical of the North-West as a whole. During the 1950s Lancaster had a lower proportion of people employed in professional and scientific services than was the national average (7·5% compared with 7·9% nationally), and in this also it resembled the average for the North-West Region (see Marquand, 1980). However, during the 1960s and 1970s, the expansion of the sector resulted in strong local concentration of employment in these services. Of the employed labour force in Lancaster, 20% were in this Industry Order (25) in 1977, compared with 16% nationally.

Many of these shifts result not from changes in local markets or other indigenous factors, but from decisions taken at a national level, mainly concerning changes in the railway, education and health system. As in the case of manufacturing industry, the domination of the transport and the professional and scientific services (Industry Order 25) by organizations which extended beyond the boundaries of Lancaster resulted in reorganization which affected the locality to a disproportionate extent. While the "market" for many of these services is local, in the sense that health and education authorities cater for those living within their boundaries, there has also been a concentration in Lancaster of specialized areas of health care (e.g. mental hospitals, geriatrics), and of higher education which serve a population far wider than that permanently living in the travel-to-work-area.

Both employees and clients in these services are geographically mobile into the area in order to take up the jobs or services available in Lancaster (see Murgatroyd, 1981).

The tourist industry is the other major employer in the area. Here again, there is a net invisible export from Lancaster via the geographic mobility of the clientele, a large proportion of whom travel from other parts of the North-West (Riley, 1972). "Miscellaneous Services" (Industry Order 26) and "Distribution" (Order 23) are the two industries most closely connected with tourism.

In 1951 "miscellaneous services" (which includes cinemas and theatre, sport and recreation, betting and gambling, hotels, restaurants, public houses, clubs, etc. . . .) was by far the largest service industry in the area, accounting for 13·5% of all local employment; double the proportion nationally. As Fig 4 shows, there were fluctuations in the level of employment in this sector, but by 1977 the net increase since 1951 was minimal, despite their increased *share* of employment locally.

Similarly, distributive trades maintained a steady level of employment over the period, apart from a drop in the mid-1960s attributable to selective employment tax. The steady level of employment in this sector resulted from to opposing forces; nationally, retailing employment declined due to a shift towards large-scale outlets, but the population serviced by retailers in the Lancaster district increased, due to a high rate of in-migration of professional and retired families (Lancaster City Council, 1980). The local multiplier effects of the expanded health and education services, more than made up for the slight decline in tourist-related employment over the period (Lancaster City Council, 1977).

Although little detailed information is available concerning changing ownership patterns in the local service sector, it is clear that there is a trend towards external ownership of the large enterprises in this sector, just like in manufacturing. There is also an increasing local dependence on public sector employment in educational and health services. Not only has an increasing proportion of the local population come to depend directly on the state sector for employment, but also a great deal of employment in other services depends on the incomes generated by these sectors. As manufacturing employment declines, the economy of Lancaster has become increasingly dependent on the level and direction of state expenditure.

2·4 Summary

In conclusion to this section we should note how there has been a substantial shift in the character of this locality over the past thirty years. In 1950 the local economy was dominated by a small number of private manufacturing employers, who were involved in numerous commodity and inter-personal linkages with the locality and with the surrounding textile-based region. In 1980, the state is the dominant employer, and the fortunes of the small private employers depend upon the expansion or contraction of state expenditure, principally within the service sector. Relatively few large manufacturing establishments remain, and they have limited linkages with other locally based firms.

It is worth briefly considering how general this kind of shift is. Perhaps the most helpful attempt to systematize such developments is that the Lipietz (1980b). He suggests that regions have become increasingly specialized in terms of the distribution of economic activities among them, and that each region has developed one of four types of "vocations", as follows:

> *Type One regions*, poles of financial and technological management;
> *Type Two regions*, skilled manufacturing; (which presupposes an "industrial past");
> *Type Three regions*, offering reserves of labour that can be regarded as unskilled, since they are produced by the obsolescence of previous industries, and in which activities such as assembly (using unskilled workers) are developed;
> *Type Four regions* in which rural depopulation has taken place, and for which tourism and military camps are the "vocation".

Bearing in mind that Lancaster is not a region in Lipietz's sense (and spatial polarization does not seem as strong as Lipietz suggests, at least in Britain), we can ask whether its restructuring can nevertheless be analysed in terms of Lipietz's categories. Despite the historical position of Lancaster as a local commercial and manufacturing centre, and the growth of the university (which, it was hoped, would provide local spin-offs in high technology manufacturing), the district has not developed as a strong centre for "financial and technical services". The headquarters and Research and Development sectors of large manufacturing plants have tended to move out of the area, and employment in financial services is fairly small.

Lancaster also has not developed as a type two region, partly because of the precipitous decline in the existing manufacturing industries which rendered obsolescent many of the existing skills. In some ways it has developed as a type three region, precisely because of this shift away from established "skilled" manufacturing employment. And in relationship to mobile private manufacturing capital, it has nothing to offer which is different from the vast number of type three localities found throughout both the advanced and backward capitalist countries (see Fröbel, Heinrichs, Rowolt, 1980; Perrons, 1980, on the new international division of labour).

However, Lancaster has become an important centre for service employment, especially by the state, but also privately through the tourist industry. In that sense it displays elements of Lipietz's type four region, where university/health care replaces military camps! This suggests that Lipietz's categorization needs refining, both in relation to more precise localities (rather than general regions), but also with regard to the particular *combinations* of capitalist and state manufacturing and service activities found within them and which give rise to the peculiar characteristics of any locality. In the next section we will briefly discuss how some of these characteristics bear upon the forms of economic and political struggle within Lancaster.

Figure 5. The Gillow furniture factory which produced high quality furniture from the nineteenth century to 1962. Symbolically, this was the first site of the University of Lancaster.

3. State policies, politics and struggle

There are three significant issues to deal with here. First, why was Lancaster unable to attract the mobile new employment that was generated in those industries undergoing technical change and making new investments? Second, what have been the characteristic features of the economic and social relations in Lancaster that have influenced this failure? How far can these relations be described as those of paternalist capitalism? And third, what have been the consequences of the changes in the ownership and the structure of employment upon local struggles; has a state paternalism replaced private corporate paternalism?

3·1 Regional and local industrial policies

On the first question we may begin by noting that Lancaster is part of the North-West Region, and this region has performed very badly in employment terms over the recent period. Stillwell maintains that the North-West was among "the least attractive regions in which to locate industry" (1968, p. 10 and see Fothergill and Gudgin, 1981) This meant that other regions attracted the mobile plants which made a major difference in employment terms. This produced cumulative disadvantages for those less-favoured areas, as the age of the region's capital stock got progressively older and less competitive with the new plant being established elsewhere.

Lancaster should have been partly protected from this effect, given its relative expansion in the 1940s and 1950s. However, this was not sustained, partly because the North-West Region has not constituted an important force politically (in comparison with Scotland or Wales, for example), and partly because Lancaster has had little chance of making effective representation on its own (although it has maintained Intermediate Area Status). The labour movement never developed a strong regional base here, by contrast, for example, South Wales or North-East England (see Cooke, 1981; and Morgan and Sayer, this volume). One crude indicator of this is given by the fact that the proportion of people voting labour in Lancashire has generally been lower than in corresponding regions. (In 1974, 50·1% in Lancashire voted Labour, compared with 59·4% in the North-East.) Lancaster itself comprises two constituencies, yet the first Labour M.P. was not elected until 1966, although the proportion of manual workers in the labour force was over 50% until the 1960s.

The local state has concentrated upon two policies: first, to attract new service employment within the public sector, hence the university and expanded hospital services; and second, to develop small manufacturing firms. The latter policy was introduced in the early 1960s (after the closure of the Gillow furniture workshops following the take-over by Great Universal Stores), and it was consolidated in the late 1960s and 1970s. This has not been substantially changed, even when unemployment began to rise. Land and technical and financial assistance were made available and a "seed-bed" experiment was set up to help very small firms to become established. Preference for these facilities were actively given to those small firms, with "high quality" products, in technologically-based industries (Lancaster City Council, 1977). A substantial number of such firms were successfully brought to (or started in) Lancaster, using the facilities provided by the council and the university through *Enterprise Lancaster*, and also helped by the *Small Firms Club* initiated by the city council. Large-scale manufacturing investments were less strongly encouraged by the local council throughout the sixties and early seventies, and Lancaster's designation as an Intermediate Area during the era of Regional Policy after 1972 did not facilitate the attraction of large-scale capital during a period of massive industrial restructuring. In general, regional policy has benefited those areas which experienced full special Development Area status during the central period of regional policy (*c.* 1965–1975) at the expense of other regions (see Cambridge Economic Policy Review, 1980). However, the impact of regional policy should not be over-estimated, since the period in which it was particularly developed was also that in which the most substantial restructuring of capitalist industry took place (see Moore and Rhodes, 1977, and the critique in Massey, 1978a).

3·2 Restructuring class relations and local politics

We have already noted that the Lancaster subregion has not been an area with a strong labour movement, but contrary to right-wing commentators, this did not result in the attraction of large flows of capital to the subregion, so that they might profit from the quiescent (or "realistic") labour force. It has been argued that the quiescence of the Lancaster labour force has resulted from the paternalist character of social relations both within workplaces and between the local firms and the city (see Martin and Fryer, 1973, on the firm of Williamsons; and see Urry, 1980, for some sceptical comments). Norris defines paternalism (of the sort once found in Lancaster) as existing where inequalities of economic and political power are "stabilized through the legitimating ideology of traditionalism" (Norris, 1978, p. 471–2). He suggests that there are four components to such an ideology: "gentlemanly ethic", "personal dependence", "localism", and a "gift relationship".

While traditional forms of paternalism clearly no longer existed by the 1960s and 1970s, vestiges of these practices are indicated by the responses of the local labour movement to the mass redundancies and plant closures which have characterized 1980 and 1981. These events elicited fatalistic responses from the labour force, and the only negotiations that took place were about the terms of redundancies, their necessity being accepted from the start. Despite an understanding that the closure of Lansil plant (1980) by Courtaulds was caused, not simply by low company profits, but by the company's worldwide restructuring plans, the workers from Lansil's eventually appeared grateful to accept the minimal redundancy payments made by Courtaulds's (source: interview with shop steward). This kind of response was in sharp contrast to the occupation simultaneously taking place at Gardners in Eccles, only 40 miles away, and to similar protests elsewhere. Such action was not seriously considered in Lancaster by any of the workforces affected by redundancies, rather notions of the "gentlemanly ethic" and the "gift-relationship" prevailed.

The main active response was also characterized by attitudes associated with paternalism, namely localism and personal dependence. *The Save Lancaster Campaign* was established by the Trades Council late in 1980, in the wake of several redundancy announcements, and the emphasis of the campaign was firmly on the locality rather than on class politics. This campaign did not gain much active support even at this time, and it withered away after a few weeks. Most of those affected preferred either to depend on the provisions of the state and the efforts of the city council, or to find individualistic solutions to unemployment. It may well be that the blossoming of small businesses during the 1970s was an accommodating local response to the decline in employment in older manufacturing firms, and in addition, the existence of a large (traditional) petit bourgeoisie (the self-employed) probably undermined collectivist protests.

We have already mentioned two of the strongly localist responses to the industrial restructuring which has affected the Lancaster area, namely the *Save Lancaster Campaign*, and the City Council's initiatives to encourage the establishment of new small businesses whose local inter-linkages (and hence presumed local control) would be more marked than in the case of externally owned and controlled plants. Although there was considerable controversy within the labour movement about its involvement in such local initiatives, it would seem that the forms of capitalist restructuring made it difficult for employers and city officials to resist the claims of labour to have some say in future developments. Indeed, to some extent, it appears that the labour movement had more involvement in trying to "save" the city's industry than have most other groupings; certainly more than the major transnational companies who happen to have one of their plants in the locality (except Unilever). Part of the efforts of the city council have been directed to getting such companies to take some responsibility for the effects of their decisions. Yet, at the same time, the efforts of the labour movement to preserve capitalist manufacturing activity in the locality clearly deflected labourist struggles away from the traditional issues of the wage-relation or the forms of capitalist control, concentrating them instead on presenting the city as a suitable site for capitalist accumulation. To some extent the labour movement has also put its weight behind the "small firms strategy", being apparently unaware of the deficiencies of such strategy (see Brimson, 1979).

To the extent that social relations in Lancaster were once characterized by "corporate paternalism", this may have been replaced by a kind of state paternalism. Clearly the local labour force (and indeed the local economy) is dependent to a crucial degree upon the state, and it has responded gratefully when announced cutbacks are less than they might have been. A good recent example has been the attitudes of gratitude and deference exhibited locally when the Manpower Services Commission created considerable temporary employment in the area. However, it may be more appropriate to regard the responses to heightened "external control" of the local economy as characterized more *by fatalism* than by paternalism. A number of other developments in local politics took place over this period, which cannot be discussed here. In particular, various "oppositional fragments" have emerged, which have been concerned with struggles in the area of consumption as well as than production. Such issues as ecology, sexual politics, transport, leisure and the arts have grown in importance locally, as the service sector has come to dominate the area's industry; many of those active in such "fragments" being either employed in the service sector, or unemployed. The restructuring of the local economy has therefore involved not only the undermining of traditional forms of class conflict, but also the development of new struggles, and a restructuring of local politics (see Urry, 1981a for further comments on these.)

4. Conclusion

We have thus tried to show how the Lancaster economy has been transformed as a consequence of its location within the changing forms of the spatial division of labour. During the period of post-war reconstruction, based on the expansion of national capital, Lancaster benefitted and developed in a number of growing industrial sectors. But with the industrial restructuring of the 1960s and early seventies, a new, in part international, spatial division of labour developed from which Lancaster failed to benefit. Indeed since its fixed capital was of a previous vintage, the effect of the new round of accumulation was to undermine those industries established within the previous round. The main expansion was in state service employment, and partly in private service employment. There was an increasing gap between the relatively skilled employment available in the service sector (especially that of the state) and that de-skilled employment available in the private manufacturing sector. The political composition of Lancaster interestingly reflects this particular combination of forms under which the local economy has been restructured.

Acknowledgements

We are very grateful for the assistance, advice and encouragement of other members of the Lancaster Regionalism Group. We are also indebted to the Department of Employment, to Mr R. H. Kelsall of Enterprise Lancaster, and others, for providing us with information, and to Mr M. Lee for assistance in processing it. This work has been financed by the Human Geography Committee of the S.S.R.C., 1980–1. Photographs were taken by Amy Urry.

References

Aglietta, M. (1979). "A theory of capitalist regulation", New Left Books, London.
Barratt Brown, M. (1981). "Britain in crisis", Spokesman, Nottingham.
Blackaby, F. (ed.) (1978). De-industrialisation, *NIESR Economic Policy Papers*, **2**, Heinemann, London.
Brimson, P. (1979). "Islington's multinationals and small firms: magic or myth", Islingtons Political Economy Group, London.
Buck, T. (1979). Regional class differences, *International Journal of Urban and Regional Research*, **3**, 516–26.
Cambridge Economic Policy Review 1980. Urban and regional policy with provisional regional accounts 1966–78, *CEPR*, **6**, 2, Department of Applied Economics, University of Cambridge.
Central Office of Information (COI) (1978). "Chemicals", HMSO, London.

Coleman, D. C. (1980). "Courtaulds: an economic and social history", Clarendon Press, Oxford.

Cooke, P. (1981). Class relations and uneven development in Wales, Paper presented for British Sociological Association Annual Conference, Aberystwyth, 1981.

Counter Information Services. (1974). Courtaulds, inside and out, *CIS Report* **10**, CIS, London.

Cowling, K. (1980). "Mergers and economic performances", Cambridge University Press, Cambridge.

Crum, R. E. and Gudgin, G. (1977). Non-production activities in the UK manufacturing industry, *Brussels Commission of the European Community Regional Policy Series*, **3**.

Department of Employment. (1971). "British labour statistics 1886–1968. Historical abstract", HMSO, London.

Department of Employment. (various years). "British labour statistics yearbook", (various years) HMSO, London.

Dunford, M., Geddes, M. and Perrons, D. (1980). Regional policy and the crisis in the UK: a long-run perspective, *International Journal Urban and Regional Research*, **5**, 2, 377–411.

Ewing, A. F. (1972). "Planning and policies in the textile finishing industry", Bradford UP with Crosby, Lockwood and Son, London.

Fothergill, S. and Gudgin, G. (1979). Regional employment change: a subregional explanation, *Progress and Planning*, **12**, 155–220.

Fothergill, S. and Gudgin, G. (1981). "Unequal growth: employment change in British cities and regions", Heinemann, London.

Fröbel, F., Heinrichs, J. and Rowolt, D. (1980). "The new international division of labour", Cambridge University Press, Cambridge.

Fulcher, M. N., Rhodes, J. and Taylor, J. (1966). The economy of the Lancaster sub-region, *University of Lancaster Economics Department, Occasional Paper 10*.

Gershuny, J. (1978). "After industrial society? The emerging self-service economy", Macmillan, London.

Keeble, D. (1976). "Industrial location and planning in the UK", Methuen, London.

Knight, A. (1974). "Private enterprise and public intervention: the Courtaulds experience", George Allen and Unwin, London.

Lancaster City Council. (1977). "Industrial strategy for Lancaster", Lancaster Town Hall, unpublished.

Lancaster City Council, (1980). Population change in Lancaster district, "Lancaster City Council, Monitor Report No 1".

Lipietz, A. (1980a). Inter-regional polarisation and the tertiarisation of society, "Papers of the Regional Science Association 44".

Lipietz, A. (1980b). The structuration of space, the problem of land and spatial policy, *in* J. Carney *et al.*, (eds), "Regions in crisis", 60–92, Croom Helm, London.

Mackay, R. and Thomson, L. (1979). Important trends in regional policy and regional employment – a modified interpretation, *Scottish Journal of Political Economy*, **2**, 3, 233–260.

Marquand, J. (1980). The role of the tertiary sector in regional policy, Commission of the European Communities, *Regional Policy Series No 19*, Brussels.

Massey, D. (1977). Towards a critique of industrial location theory, *in* R. Peet (ed.), "Radical Geography", Methuen, London.

Massey, D. (1978). Regionalism: some current issues, *Capital and Class*, **6**, 106–125.

Massey, D. (1979). In what sense a regional problem?, *Regional Studies*, **13**, 233–243.

Massey, D. and Meegan, R. (1978). Industrial restructuring versus the cities, *Urban Studies*, **15**, 3, 278–288.

Monopolies Commission. (1968). "Man-made cellulosic fibres: a report on the supply of man-made cellulosic fibres", HMSO, London.

Monopolies and Restrictive Practices Commission. (1956). "Report on the supply of linoleum", HMSO, London.

Moore, B. and Rhodes, J. (1977). The relative decline of the UK manufacturing sector, *Cambridge Economic Policy Review*, **8**, 2. Department of Applied Economics, University of Cambridge.

Murgatroyd, I. (1981). De-industrialisation in Lancaster: a review of the changing structure of employment in the Lancaster district, *Lancaster Regionalism Group Working Paper*, **1**, University of Lancaster.

Newbould, C. D. (1970). "Management and merger activity", Guthstead, Liverpool.

Norris, G. (1978). Industrial paternalism, capitalism and local labour markets, *Sociology*, **12**, 469–89.

Perrons, D. C. (1981). The role of Ireland in the new international division of labour: a proposed framework for regional analysis, *Regional Studies*, **15**, 81–100.

Riley, S. (1974). "Tourism, its impact on retail trade", Tourism Research Unit, Department of Marketing, University of Lancaster.

Sabolo, Y. (1975). "The service industries", ILO, Geneva.

Showler, B. and Sinfield, A. (eds) (1981). "The workless state", Martin Robertson, Oxford.

Singelmann, J. (1978). "From agriculture to services", Sage, London.

Singh, A. (1977). UK industry and the world economy: a case of de-industrialisation, *Cambridge Journal of Economics*, **1**, 113–136.

Smith, I. J. (1979). The effect of external takeovers on manufacturing employment change in the Northern Region between 1963 and 1973, *Regional Studies*, **13**, 421–437.

Stillwell, F. (1968). Location of industry and business efficiency, *Business Ratios*, **2**, 5–15.

Storper, M. (1981). Towards a structural theory of industrial location, *in* J. Rees, G. Hewings and H. Stafford (eds), "Industrial location and regional systems", Croom Helm, London.

Townroe, P. M. and Roberts, N. J. (1980). "Local-external economies for British manufacturing industry", Gower, Farnborough.

Urry, J. (1980). Paternalism, management and localities, *Lancaster Regionalism Group Working Paper*, **2**, University of Lancaster.

Urry, J. (1981). De-industrialisation, households and forms of social conflict and struggle, *Lancaster Regionalism Group Working Paper*, **3**, University of Lancaster.

Warren, K. (1971). Growth, technical change and planning problems in heavy industry with reference to the chemical industry, *in* M. Chisholm and G. Manners (eds), "Spatial policy problems of the UK economy", Cambridge University Press, Cambridge.

FIVE

Industrial decline, restructuring and relocation: Aston and the Great Victorian Depression

N. ROGERS

(January 1982)

1. Introduction

During the 1970s and 1980s we have become accustomed to a state of economic depression in Britain. Industrial closures, lower living standards, the movements of industry to cheap-labour countries, the abandonment of the inner city areas, the decline of previously prosperous regions, the constant talk of "the new technology" and the demands for new working practices; all are commonplace both in the media and in daily life. In short, we are now used to living in the midst of a restructuring of industry and society in general. The irony is that the same thing happened 100 years ago, the same solutions were proposed, and yet in many cases the areas that are now worst affected were the "solutions" of the late nineteenth century.

The "regional", or more recently "the inner city", problem is generally associated with the decline of "traditional industries", and, less frequently, with the growth of new ones. In Britain, the late nineteenth century is a key period in which much subsequent decline and growth had its origins. Hobsbawm (1968) argues that the significant period was the Great Victorian Depression 1873–96. During this depression, British capital, for the first time, faced effective international competition in many industries as a result of rival indigenous development and the improvement in international communications during the mid-nineteenth century. From this time on, international contexts increasingly set the parameters of both the problems and the solutions for Britain's economy. An analysis of change must therefore have a global as well as an historical dimension.

This chapter uses the example of changes in the Birmingham area at the end of the last century to illustrate the similarities between economic crises and their effects in capitalist societies. The Birmingham area is particularly interesting as it consisted of a diverse manufacturing base, unlike areas such as the North East of Britain which were dominated by a few main industries. Furthermore, the restructuring process made necessary by international competition perpetuated this diversity, replacing declining trades with new growth industries, so that the area continued to develop. A major feature of the changes made during the Depression was the rapid transformation of the production technology. Prior to 1870, Birmingham was dominated by many small workshops, with a differentiated work force with varied skills organized in a finely graded hierarchy. After 1890, the major industries had largely gone over to factory based, mechanized production, with a greater use of unskilled hands. The character of Birmingham industries had therefore undergone a fundamental, but not a total, shift. The new pattern of industrial and social life was mirrored in the development of the urban built form.

The chapter starts by discussing the international nature of the Great Victorian Depression and its general national manifestations. The next two sections outline the general picture of the changes that occurred within the Birmingham region, as these had a direct impact on Aston. There is then a detailed study of Aston itself which considers its early development, the non-industrial changes at the social level, the process of economic and industrial restructuring, and the political and social consequences.

2. The Great Victorian Depression 1873–1896

The Great Depression has a voluminous literature in which little is agreed (Aldcroft and Richardson, 1969). While it started as an apparently conventional crisis and slump, it continued as something rather more protracted and alarming. The main points of agreement are that Britain, for so long the leader and exporter of the new capital goods, e.g. railways, shipping, etc. was finally confronted by effective competition. In part this is due to the integrative effect of improved transport, in part due to the spread of protectionist trade measures particularly during the Depression. There is also evidence to show that the competition was based on cheap labour or mechanized production. Finally there was an integration of world food markets and a great drop in prices: for example wheat prices declined by 77% in Britain between 1860–90.

A royal commission set up to examine this worrying development reported that a depression in trade and industry had existed since about 1875. This

> meant a diminution, and in some cases an absence of profit . . . neither the volume of trade nor the amount of capital invested therein has materially fallen off, though the latter has in many cases depreciated in value.

Agricultural prices were falling and there was an increased production of all commodities such that supply was much in excess of demand. Furthermore

> . . . the accumulation of capital . . . and the greater severity of the competition which results from this accumulation tend to lower the rate of profit. This tendency is of course checked by any expansion of trade . . . there has been in recent years a marked absence of such expansion . . . We have no doubt that the chief agency in perpetuating this state of things is the protectionist policy of so many foreign countries . . . which has become more marked during the last 10 years than in any previous period of similar length. (R.C. 1885, Vol. IV, 16)

Birmingham businessmen (R.C. 1885, Qu.1515ff.) agreed with these conclusions. Overproduction was common due to the amount of plant laid down in the period 1870–73, and much of it was closed in the ensuing crisis, particularly in small establishments. The main problem was seen as foreign competition.

> It is possible to the present day to put manufacturers in four or five different countries in competition. Twenty years ago that was not possible . . .

Consequently,

> Many trades that formerly had their centre in Birmingham solely for the world's supply are now distributed for competition between four or five different countries.

These foreign countries had, it was argued, a trading advantage for;

> . . . protective duties secured to the manufacturers in those countries the absolute command of their home markets at a very high price, and that consequently getting a very large profit under that protective duty . . . it enabled them to sell in England at a very low price and at a very low profit.

However, it is clear that tariff differences, *per se*, were only part of the problem. Disparities also existed at the point of production, and here the two most significant factors were relative wages and productivity.

In 1886 the US consul for Birmingham reported to Washington his reasons for the local depression in trade and industry. For guns, cutlery, edge-tools and scissors he blamed German, French and Belgian wage rates which were half those in Birmingham, while American production was more mechanized as well as protected by tariffs. Brass, pens, buttons and jewellery all suffered competition from cheap labour in Europe. The Board of Trade, also interested in this question, compared working class income and expenditure in a number of countries, a summary of which is given in Table 1.

Wages in Great Britain were higher than in France and Belgium and lower than those of the USA (German figures were only available for incomes below £1/15/0 a week. But here they were on average £1/0/6 a week, while in GB they were £1/19/0.) The US consul for Birmingham even claimed, in

TABLE 1. *Comparative statistics on working class incomes and expenditure 1890–91 (£.s.d.).*

	Germany*	Belgium	USA	France	GB
Average income per week	19/4	1/2/7	2/6/5	1/5/6	1/3/11
Total food expenditure	9/5	10/11	17/8	11/6	15/8
Rent expenditure	1/8	2/3	6/6	2/6	3/9
Total expenditure	19/4	1/3/4	2/3/2	1/3/6	1/12/3

* For incomes below £1/15/0 per week only
Source: Board of Trade 1903, 235.

December 1883, that "necessaries" in America were cheaper although the wages in New York and Chicago were twice the English rates.

Such evidence is clearly suggestive rather than indicative. Overall, however, the contention regarding cheap labour is fairly well supported. The question of relative productivity is far less clear-cut.

Some comparative figures on productivity have been provided by Aldcroft and Richardson (1969). As can be seen in Figure 1 there was a stagnation in average output per person in the UK, from 1890 to 1913, that is not apparent elsewhere. While making the caveat that this average hides individual differences, Aldcroft and Richardson argue that this reflects a lack of technological advance in productive methods; reinvestment in Britain tended to be in old technology.

> The worst symptom of Britain's industrial ills . . . was the extent to which her entrepreneurship and technology was defensive. She was no longer in the van of technical change; instead, even the best of her enterprises were usually being dragged in the wake of foreign precursors, like children being jerked along by important adults (Richardson, 1969).

Current parallels are rather striking.

Figure 1 also shows that in Britain output per worker increased *more* rapidly than other countries between 1880 and 1890, even on overall average figures. Further, Aldcroft and Richardson refer explicitly to the way in which the old capital goods industries, like iron and coal, dominate the statistics. These industries were marked by active disinvestment (see Carney *et al.*, 1975) and so depress the rise in productivity even more. Consequently this earlier rise in productivity must have reflected substantial growth and investment in other industries and other areas. The evidence given later will show that Birmingham was one such place. Nevertheless, the general comparative point is still valid. Rates of productivity increase were on average greater in Germany and the USA than in Britain.

The overall picture was therefore one of higher wages, lower productivity increase, overproduction and, ultimately, a loss of profits. The problem was largely interpreted as protectionism by other nation states but protectionism was only part of the story as British firms were competing against the lower wage rates or the greater mechanization and higher productivity of foreign rivals. In the most general sense, therefore, British capitalists were under pressure to "restructure" their businesses. In some cases this led to a total disinvestment and a shift to a new product altogether; in other instances it meant a reinvestment in new productive methods and sometimes a relocation of production. Finally, if possible, wage rates were also cut as a short-term expedient, particularly where the trade unions were weak.

In the Birmingham area all three strategies were adopted, but it was the second – reinvestment in new methods and location – that had the greatest impact. This was because Birmingham industries of the time were in the main still organised along pre-factory system lines. The restructuring of

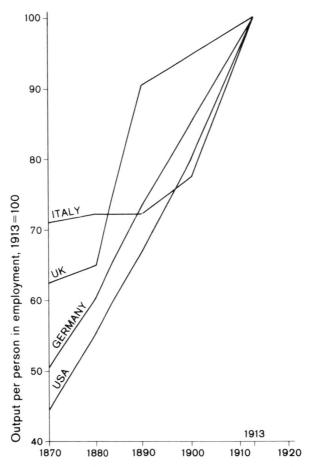

Figure 1. Relative productivity of British manufacturing 1870–1913. Source: Aldcroft and Richards on p. 126.

these industries, as a result of the economic recession, gave rise to other changes in the social, political and urban structures of the Birmingham area. Taken together these changes marked a transformation into a new stage of accumulation and development.

3. Industry and labour in Birmingham before the Great Depression

Productive relations in this period were dominated by the "Factor" system. This was in many ways an early form of capitalist relationship. Essentially the "factor", or merchant, organized and co-ordinated production by a series of small-masters in small workshops. Alternatively, outworkers were directly employed, the factor being responsible for materials and marketing. There was also the practice of "stand renting" to individuals within a workshop with a common source of machine power. There was no necessary productive connection between the workshop owner and such a tenant. The average size of workshop appears to have been about twenty persons (Eversley, 1968) and Fox (1955) claims that most were between five or ten persons. The main activities of Birmingham's economy at the time, focused on metal working, made the continuation of this system possible. They were characterized by higher levels of manual skills, a wide and varied range of commodities with little standardization, and very little mechanized production.

The development of production was restricted by the "factor system" in two ways. First, the factor was the main (and limited) source of finance; and secondly, he enabled his subcontractors to specialize, thereby developing a very fine social division of labour. Within the workshop the division of labour was also detailed. This derived from the practice of paying piece rates to the subcontractor, while he paid day rates to his labourers. There was also a substantial use of boys, not only to depress wages but to curb the demands of the underhands.

There was therefore a fine gradation of employers and workers, and this led to a blurring of wider class distinctions. Fox concludes:

> The organizational division into two levels of labour thus had profound effects upon industrial relationships. In the first place it split the ranks opposed to the employers and factors by setting up a conflict of interests between the small master and his underhands. And, in the second place, it greatly mitigated the bitterness of struggles waged by the master craftsman alone against the factor, by giving him the status of employer . . . The difficulties were heightened by the fact that nowhere in this pattern of status was there any impassable gulf . . .

Another commentator observed:

> . . . This classless 'reasonable' approach to union affairs inevitably pegged wages to the trade cycle; it was the inescapable outcome of the political and industrial alliance with the employers. (Corbett, 1966, p. 43)

Organized labour (if not all the working class) was also politically and ideologically well integrated into the dominant Liberal hegemony. For example, Wright (1977) documents the incorporation of working-class leaders into the local Liberal party machines, albeit in lowly positions. Fox emphasizes the links between religious non-conformity, Liberal politics and the predominant view of industrial grievances being seen in individualistic, not class terms. The generally accepted picture of class relations in Birmingham is therefore one of low levels of organization and conflict, unless on non-class lines, and high levels of political and ideological integration.

By 1873 Birmingham had developed as the trading and financial centre for the West Midlands, as well as a major productive centre. Its industries were based on metal-finishing trades using raw materials or semi-finished products, often made in the Black Country. The main industries in this period were guns, jewellery, buttons and brass-working, all of which were diverse in production methods, use of labour and products. Other industries included edge tools, fire irons, saddlery, harness, nails, screws, pens, hollow-ware, etc., which were often closely associated with the main trades. This early Victorian development had been associated with colonial develop-ments and the steady increase of domestic consumption. Spatially it had created a band of industry around the central commercial and financial district, with certain offshoots, for example to the north into and around Aston. The climax of this old industrialism came in the boom of 1869–73. The trade cycle was on an up following the 1866 financial crisis; colonial trade was expanding, while the Franco-Prussian war created extra demands for military equipment and other goods no longer supplied by the pro-tagonists. The result was a working of old capacity to record levels, and the laying out of new plant. Consequently 1871–73 saw a general rise in output and prices. 1872 had been "rarely equalled and never surpassed for its great and general prosperity." (Allen, 1929, p. 199). The short-term effect of this boom was to improve the competitive position of foreign producers through its inflationary effect on prices and wages within Britain.

4. Birmingham during the Depression, 1873–96

The position of industry in Birmingham was greatly affected by foreign competition during the Depression, and, once established, the resulting situation continued up to 1914 (Allen, 1929). Two trades, guns and buttons, are particularly interesting. These had been staples in Birmingham's economy, and they also represent well the more general picture.

The gun trade had boomed during the American civil war (1861–64). However, in concentrating on this "easy" market, it lost the "bread and butter" cheap gun market. Belgian firms, concentrated in Liège, where labour was cheaper, took over. In addition, the American producers of military rifles introduced mechanized production and this dramatically cut

Figure 2. The mixture of workshops and housing that made up Birmingham's industrial core before the Victorian recession, photographed in the 1940s (courtesy Bournville Village Trust).

costs. Consequently this market was also lost, at least in America. Consular figures show a drop in Birmingham sales to America from \$379 000 to \$212 000 in the period 1882 to 1891, and this was when the main change had already occurred. This was despite the introduction of machinery by one Birmingham firm in 1883, halving the costs of production. The result was a retreat into the specialized hand-built sporting gun trade. This trade remains in Birmingham but cannot, of course, support mass industry or employment. The button trade has a similar history. Of thirteen leading firms in 1853, four were left in 1860 and only one by 1910, with no substantial replacements.

Not all established industries completely disappeared as a result of the Depression. However, those that survived were substantially restructured in terms of corporate structures, sources of finance, labour processes and often location. Many firms in Aston came into this category and are discussed later. Alternatively, new industries were started which capitalized on the skills of the existing work force at the same time as they introduced new labour processes and working methods. Some of the new industries were set up during the Depression, for example bicycles, while others started a few years later at the beginning of the new century, such as electrical goods and vehicles. The trade of these new industries boomed as the figures for the bicycle trade with America indicate. Between 1890 and 1891 bicycle exports rose from \$325 000 to \$622 000, and steel tubes from \$275 000 to \$352 000, despite the American attempt to impose protective tariffs.

The new and the restructured, older industries that emerged from the Depression had a number of characteristics that marked them out as different. First, they were based on new technology and the use of steel. There was a demand for improved capital goods and machines, rather than cast components. Cycle parts are a good example. The result was a shift in old industries to new products, the development of the machine tool trade, the development of electrical engineering and a new chemical industry. In addition there was a major development in consumer goods, including electroplate ware, food and drink (Cadbury's is perhaps the most famous name emerging during this period).

The second feature of new industries was their scale of operation, which Smith (1968) sees as deriving from corporate strategies during the depression. These strategies were basically those of integration, which meant a centralization of the control over capital and often the process of production, as well as the elimination of competitors. Vertical integration involved the extension of a company's activities to cover those of its erstwhile suppliers and customers. An example of vertical integration with world-wide effects was Cadbury's, with Cadbury's-owned plantations in the colonies ultimately leading to Cadbury-owned cocoa houses in Birmingham streets. Horizontal integration was a question of amalgamation and elimination of competitors, e.g. Tube Investments who look over Birmingham Climax tubes in Aston.

In general the main period for such amalgamations was post 1895, and this was associated with the rise of the public company.

Before 1880, the predominant form of finance was through partnerships and the reinvestment of profits. Although limited liability had been legally possible since the early 1860s, it was not introduced to any great extent until "the commercial difficulties of the eighties" (Eversley, 1968). The problems of surviving the Depression led to a replacement of personally owned and partnership firms by limited liability companies.

The new industries, and the surviving older industries, thus tended to develop in the same direction. They were bigger in plant size, limited if not public companies, often the result of mergers. As the evidence of the Birmingham Chamber of Commerce to the 1885 Royal Commission points out, such firms had greater access to capital, greater productive capacity, the ability to stock-pile in the then common situation of overproduction, and they were able to take greater investment risks. These developments were paralleled by other changes in the labour process.

Most important was the disappearance of the "factor", and with him went the "overhand". Both these groups were replaced by the new structure of managers being adopted as firms increased in size. An additional pressure on factors was the development of retailing and wholesale marketing, which cut into their middleman function. Finally, the "factors" role as a source of credit was no longer possible, for this had been taken over by larger and more effective financial institutions such as banks and holding companies. (These last two changes also had an important spatial manifestation which I will not deal with here; central area redevelopment became dominated by chain stores, department stores and banks.)

Within the labour process a number of trends can be discerned. The Factory Acts of the 1840s and 1860s, and the 1870 Education Act set limits to the employment of women and children. Similarly the 9-hour day, introduced in 1872, shortened the working day. These events reinforced the trends towards more organized, standardized and mechanized production. The result was a decline in the need for skilled men, except as toolsetters and engineers, and an increased use of cheaper female machine operatives. This was further facilitated by the use of gas and electric engines in the smaller workshops.

Allen concludes:

> Yet if in the actual production of finished articles the necessity for a great deal of skilled labour had passed away in many industries, the new methods of manufacture called into existence bodies of skilled workers for such inter-mediate processes as tool-making and tool-setting . . . These developments involved a new grouping according to sex . . . For example, in several very different industries, the skilled men who had made up the labour force during the old era began to be superceded by semi-skilled female machine operatives . . . the advance of the power-press carried them into trades where they had

previously had no part . . . Where no important mechanical changes occurred, the proportion of women then remained the same . . .

After 1890 women also began

> to appear as warehouse hands, as typists and as clerks – developments which were also associated with the new methods of management and of office routine. (Allen 1929, p. 340–41)

The increased size of plant made city-centre development for manufacturing prohibitively expensive, even if sites had been available; consequently sites were developed on peripheral, greenfield areas. Aston was one such area, where in addition cheaper land in the river valley, the canal, and later the railway, made the area even more attractive. Other examples of this trend toward greenfield development were Bournville (Cadbury), Witton (Kynoch's and GEC), Saltley (Metro-Cammell) and Small Heath (BSA). The overall trend was for new firms to be further out.

5. Industrial change and the locality; Aston 1850–70

The previous section outlines the two major responses to the changing international economy, and the British recession: industrial collapse or industrial restructuring. Both of these had important locational implications. In this section, I shall concentrate on the trend towards industrial relocation, using the example of Aston.

Aston Manor, as it was known up to 1911, was an area that bordered most of the northern edge of Birmingham. It remained largely undeveloped during the industrial revolution, although several small pockets of housing were built to house workers from north Birmingham. By 1851, the Manor's population was only 6426 living in 1437 dwellings. Up to 1851 approximately half of the Manor remained unavailable for building as it was part of the private estate comprising the Manor Hall and its Park. However, after 1851 the owners, Greenaway, Greaves and Whitehead, bankers in Warwick, started to auction off small plots. By 1865 a substantial area of the Park had been sold for private building and the rest, including the Hall, had finally been sold to Birmingham Town Council. In effect these sales triggered off a series of changes in the land ownership patterns in Aston that were later reflected in new buildings during the 1870s and 1880s.

Before the 1880s industrial buildings in Aston were confined to a few firms located on the boundary with Birmingham, e.g. Yates (edge tools), Philips (brass-forging) and Ansells (Brewing). Apart from these large premises, there were many of the small workshops that characterized Birmingham industry at that time. By their very nature these workshops tended to be scattered throughout the residential areas. It was not until after the sale of the park land, the construction of cheap housing and the exodus of industry to suburban greenfield sites during the 1880s that a distinct industrial area developed in Aston. It was this combination of factors that in effect produced Aston as a factory suburb for the first time. Instead of small workshops on the edge of the countryside, Aston became dominated by industrial factory premises with the latest technology.

Aston was not a "new" industrial area in the sense of reflecting new industrial development different from Birmingham as a whole. Rather it reflected the transformation of the existing industrial structure. A comparison of the occupational distributions for Birmingham and Aston shows that Aston was typical of the economic structure of the Birmingham area. The main concentrations and trends within the occupational structures are the same throughout the period. Similar concentrations also emerge from an analysis of firms found in a street sample of Aston.[1] When grouped into census categories, machines/implements (15 premises in 1881) and dress (36 premises) emerge as most numerous, with metal-working (8 premises) and animal substances: e.g. chemicals, glue, varnish; (5 premises) as the next largest distinct group. (The number of premises under the heading "dress" is a little misleading as there were a large number of small shop-size premises, particularly in boot-making, as well as the larger button manufacturers.) It is perhaps the variety of trades that is impressive, however, and in the 44 streets examined, there were 31 different trades represented. These are shown in Table 2.

Table 3 shows most of these streets in order of distance from central Birmingham, and gives the number of commodity-producing properties and their average Gross Estimated Rental (GER) value for rating pruposes (GER is taken as an index of property size).[2] In 1871 the table shows a concentration of such property in the south eastern, inner area of Aston nearest to existing development. Compared with later years, the average value of industrial properties in 1871 was low, only £91 GER; and all properties were assessed at below £500 GER. (The waterworks, assessed at £2500 GER has been excluded from the analysis; this is not properly manufacturing plant.) Only three sampled streets had more than £1000 GER in total, and fully 80% of industrial properties were below £40 GER – where a corner shop would normally be assessed at around £20.

In 1871, then, Aston was already an "industrial" but essentially prefactory area. Its industries were based on a large range of products in several sectors, overwhelmingly in small premises and workshops. In this respect Aston was typical of Birmingham as a whole before the Great Depression.

6. Aston during the Great Depression

In terms of the restructuring of production and economic activity as a whole, Aston was very similar to Birmingham. Production of new commodities started; skilled labour was replaced by machines and unskilled, sometimes female, workers; and the new technology was housed in new factories.

Detailed examples of these changes in Aston are given later but first it is important to consider why Aston was an attractive place to relocate or expand companies during the depression. In this respect the answer lies in factors outside the workplace.

The main period of expansion for industrial premises was 1876–86. Very little of this was situated on the old Manor Park land auctioned off in the 1850s and 1860s, but that sudden release of land had the effect of bringing other lesser holdings onto the land market. Consequently, land with good

TABLE 2. *Productive properties in all streets sampled, Aston 1871–1891.*

Trade	1871	1881	1891	Trade	1871	1881	1891
Coachbuilder	1	3	2	Rolling Mills	1		
Glass	2	1	3	Wood bird-cage		1	1
Dressmaker (?)	1	1	8	Mineral water		1	1
Hosier	1		1	Photo frame		1	1
Watch and clock	1	3	2	Shovel manufacture		1	1
Bootmaker	8	23	23	Soap		1	1
Sheet iron	1			Call bell		1	
Brick and tile	1	1		Brass forger		1	1
Varnish	3	2	1	Brush		1	2
Grease	1	1		Tram workshop		1	1
Manure	2			Bicycle		1	4
Revolver and rifle	1	1	1	Electro-plate		1	
Boatbuilder	2	1	2	Draw plate-maker		1	1
Metal-rollers	1	2	3	Cooper		1	
Baker (?)	2	3		Carriage axles		1	1
Rivets	1	1	1	Eyelet		1	1
Gun-work forger	2	1	1	Whip			1
Lamps	1	2	1	Printer			2
Hats	2			Steel tubes			2
Oilcloth	1			Iron foundry			1
Boxes	1			Spindle and screw			1
Chain and sash	1			Umbrella			1
Brewer	1	6	4	Rope			1
Brass founder	2	2	1	Chemical			1
Paint	1		1	Enamel signs			1
Edgetools	3	3	1	Electric light			1
Timber	1	1	1	Glue			1
Cabinet case	1			Gas fittings			1
Pearl button	1		2	Hurdle manufacture			1
Uranium refining	1	1	1	Tin plate			1

Source: Kelly's Street Directories.

TABLE 3. *Streets arranged in order of distance from central Birmingham showing number and average GER for production properties 1871–91.*

Street	1871		1876		1881		1886		1891	
	No.	Av.	No.	Av.	No.	Av.	No.	Av.	No.	Av.
Nursery Terrace	1	133	2	141	2	141	2	161	3	99
Aston Road North	5	69	9	74	13	95	10	165	10	147
Avenue Road	1	15	1	15	1	10	1	9	1	9
Chester Street							2	147	2	148
Holland Road									1	40
Park Lane	3	36	2	24	1	30				
Rocky Lane	4	120	4	301	5	303	6	268	4	289
Catherine Street	4	51	4	44	3	130	5	114	5	134
Portland Street					1	68	2	133	2	250
Wharf Street	4	136	6	137	6	142	5	162	5	159
Wainwright Street	4	88	1	140	5	113	5	117	6	107
Lichfield Road	17	268	7	553	30	210	16	247	14	91
Park Road			1	205	2	198	4	158	4	216
Thimble Mill Lane	1	173	2	97	2	97	2	5	2	05
Church Lane	1	4	1	260	1	140	1	140	2	73
Vicarage Road									2	24
Queens Road					3	147	3	163	3	141
Grosvenor Road					1	13				
Sutherland Street									1	20
Plume Street							17	117	13	129
Aston Lane			3	63	4	51	5	113	6	92
Totals	59	91	54	165	91	148	103	146	107	119

Streets with one small premises omitted.
Sources: Ratebooks and Kelly's Street Directories.

access to communications and the commercial and financial centre of Birmingham (and hence the region) was actually available for purchase. The sale of the Park land was significant in a different way, for it was here that the cheapest housing was built, adjacent to what was to become the new industrial area. Most of the housing was put up in the period 1875–77, and it was a major factor in the reduction in the cost of living for the working class inhabitants in Aston.

While Aston is unlikely to have been unique, the Depression's impact on living standards was particularly concentrated as the area was predominantly a working-class suburb. By 1881 there was 14% unemployment among the employable male population with a compensatory increase in working mothers. The medical officer of health argued that this gave rise to a lower standard of infant care and a consequent rise in infant mortality. Further deaths came from children sharing the parental bed and being smothered, while the smallest babies were undernourished as the mothers' diets were inadequate for breast feeding. Dr May also recorded a sharp rise in the number of lodgers during the depth of the Depression as a means of sharing the rent. He summed up the working class experience as follows:

> The working classes have now become quite accustomed to very low wages, and the continued cheapness of the necessaries of life has made this less difficult for them.

This cheapness is borne out by the 34% drop in a national retail price index, in this period 1873–87. Nevertheless, and in spite of substantial reductions in the incidence of food adulteration in Aston (amounting to 50% since the 1878 Act according to the M.O.H.), it is clear that costs and standards of living for the working class of Aston were very low. While the national trend in house rents for large towns, including Birmingham, was upwards (BOT, Vol. 2, 31) Aston seems to have been an exception in this respect.

The development of cheap housing in Aston in the mid-1870s had a marked effect on the area's character, and was probably one of the main reasons that firms set up or relocated within the Manor. If housing was cheaper, the supply of cheap labour would be more assured and pressure for wage increases would be lessened. The period 1875–77 was characterized by a boom in house-building at national level (Mitchell and Deane, 1962), so Aston was typical of the norm in that respect. However, particular types of house were built in Aston, very much determined by the pattern of land ownership and the nature of local building industry. With land released in small plots sold in the parkland auctions, and developed by small builders, back-to-back housing gave the best possibilities of commercial return to be made, especially as other more salubrious areas had already captured the middle and upper class market in speculative housing.

Houses in Aston were built for cheapness, to low standards and with inferior workmanship. By 1883 Dr May records that most were already deteriorating, often to the point of being unfit for human habitation; a sufficient indictment of the speculative builders of the period. But, at the same time, rents fell, by as much as 30%–50% between 1870 and 1883.

One consequence of the building boom in cheap houses was to attract young families, which partly accounted for the higher than average birthrate in Aston. (In 1876 Aston reached 43·8 births per 1000 inhabitants, compared with an average of 37·6 per 1000 for British towns as a whole.) Aston's housing also attracted people displaced by the Birmingham Improvement Scheme, then getting under way during the Chamberlain mayoralty of "municipal improvement". The overall increase in population, coupled with changes in the demographic structure were to have political consequences in the early 1880s.

The cheapest, back-to-back, type of house was not the only type to be built in Aston, for instance in the Lozells area a whole set of streets was laid out for artisan houses with gardens. The Lozells development was, however, an exception, and by 1891 Aston was very definitely a poor working-class suburb. In 1891 Aston had 9% more housing rated under £10 than the twenty major provincial towns. Furthermore, the housing stock was increasingly spatially segregated according to its rateable value. A typology of Aston's housing is given in Table 4. Given the development of both new factories (employing new production methods), and cheap housing, what were the resulting changes in population and occupational structure? Every occupational group (except agricultural workers) increased absolutely, but relative shifts are very marked. The most dramatic change was the large increase in the "unnoccupied class' between 1871 and 1881, particularly evident for industrial workers.

The second main feature was the increased industrial employment of women, especially between 1881 and 1891. This was most noticeable in the machines and implements sector, in chemicals (including explosives) in mineral substances, and in the general and unspecified residual sector. In this latter category were 488 "undefined factory workers", a 200% increase on 1881. Two other areas of increased women's employment were as clerks and teachers. In both increasing unemployment and the increse in women workers, Aston reflected the trend for Birmingham as a whole.

The study of industrial properties of 1891 in Aston reveals concentrations in the same trades as in 1871, that is in machinery/implements and dress. However, there is also evidence of new developments, especially of changes of commodities produced. There is a growth in the carriage and harness business, including the new bicycle business which was to boom in the 1890s. Similarly the development of trams in the early 1880s (in Aston) is seen in the tramway workshop in Lozells Road. Another trade allied to bicycles, though with far wider applications, was the steel tube trade which expanded in the 1880s and 1890s, two large examples of which were established in Aston by 1891. Other new industries that set up in Aston in the

Figure 3. Birmingham's new industrial suburbs. Better quality tunnel-back housing, photographed in July 1941 (courtesy Bournville Village Trust).

TABLE 4. *Housing types in Aston 1891.*

Total (%)	GER (£)	Description	Densities (Net Acre)	Class of Occupant
1	£24	Large wing terrace	8·6 houses, 46·5 persons	Middle class
11	£20	Small wing Terrace		Artisan
24	£12–£15	Tunnel back	10–31 houses; 44–163 persons	
		Small tunnel		Labourer
		and		
64	£0–£11	back-back in courts	Open/infill	Casual working poor
			42–57 houses; 225–281 persons	
			Closed	
			59–110 houses; 267–510 persons	

Sources: Aston Manor Rate books; Anderson, R. 1969.

1880s were electric lights and gas fittings. Of the already established industries, brewing expanded as did metal rolling and the food industry.

In the period 1871–1891 there were two distinct trends involving the location and size of industrial buildings, as shown in Table 3. First, the size of plant increases, either by addition or by investment in new buildings; and second the new plant is located further out from the centre. An example of the former is Rocky Lane, and of the latter Plume Street. Frequency curves of plant size distribution (by GER) provide further detail (Figure 4). In 1876, it can be seen that the smaller properties, up to £40 GER, had already succumbed to the recession while medium-size plants were still in business. However the curve also shows the increased proportion of larger plants in the sample. This is even more significant in the 1881 curve, which shows the reduction in the numbers of both small and medium premises in business as one would expect in a slump. The 1891 position, during the new boom, was one of basically larger plant with a return of smaller units. In fact the period 1876–86 sees the most additions to the stock of productive buildings in the Rate Books, the average value of each building added being £124 prior to 1881 and £131 after. Reinvestment was taking place during the depression, when interest rates were low as well as profits. The scale of investment in buildings had increased substantially since 1871, when the average GER for industrial buildings was only £91. In addition, the number of sample streets with some form of industrial production had increased by over 50%.

The Depression therefore had a number of effects in Aston. First, it led to an increased employment of women, particularly in industry and as clerks. This was a direct means of reducing labour costs; another was the lack of employment generally, leading to wage-cutting. The glut of bad-quality houses reduced rents in Aston, against a wider trend, and reduced pressure on wages. Secondly, there was a change in some of the activities in the area, with new commodities being produced. Thirdly, small capitals dropped out of production during the recession. Fourthly, the general trend was for investment in enlarged properties, and this had a certain spatial element in the extension of the built area north-eastwards. The trend to locating the new large-scale production units in the suburban areas was not exclusive to Aston. However, in conjunction with neighbouring Saltley, it was one of the main areas of development in this period.

This general picture of the restructuring of economic activity within Aston can be further illustrated by three grouped-case studies of particular trades; brewing, clothing and edge-tools.[3]

The first group is the brewing industry. Aston was important in brewing as it was above large supplies of unpolluted artesian water. The biggest brewery was the Ansell's brewery in Park Road which survived until 1981. The original building was started in 1858 on a site bought in the early 1850s sales of Park land, when Joseph Ansell senior moved out from Gosta Green.

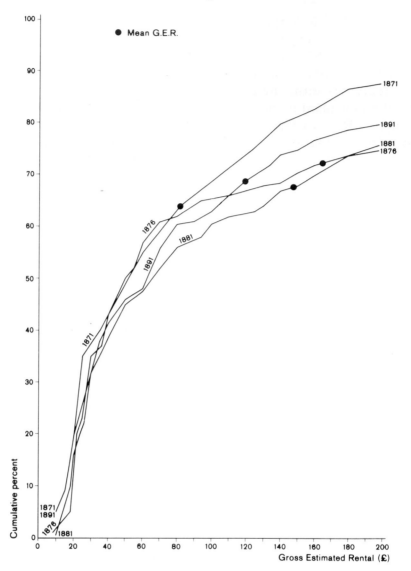

Figure 4. Size distribution for industrial buildings, Aston 1871–1891. Source: rate books.

In 1881 the first of five plans was submitted for consecutive extensions to the plant during the 1880s, resulting in a GER of £572 in 1891. Not only were the Ansells major employers, but they were also prominent in local Liberal and Conservative politics.

A similar history can be found in some of the other breweries, e.g. William Rushton's Lion Brewery in Aston Road. The brewery was part of a development on Josiah Robins's land to the south of the Park land. In the 1880s he added four buildings to the existing plant. Alfred Homer's Vulcan

Brewery also had four separate extensions in the 1880s. Both these companies went public in 1898.

Apart from the breweries, the growth of the food processing industries is seen in the establishment of Barrett and Co. at Aston Cross, and the location of the Midland Vinegar Co. a little to the north. These developments are part of the more general development of the food industry mentioned earlier in connection with Cadbury. Midland Vinegar was established in Aston in 1875, and was a factory with modern equipment. Not only did it have automatic bottling machinery, but was able to operate day and night shifts, indicating a successful business and reliable plant. It is still in existence as part of the Smedley group, its site being marked by the 'H.P. Sauce' tower in north Birmingham.

The second grouping is also consumer oriented, and comes under the heading of "dress", and is a very significant indicator of the wider international trends mentioned earlier. Buttons had been a major staple in the Birmingham economy which went into sharp decline during the Depression due to foreign competition based on cheap labour or mechanization. The only long-term survivor was located in Aston, namely Thomas Carlyle. As opposed to its earlier widespread location in Birmingham, in this way the industry became highly concentrated in space. Smith (1965) calculates a location quotient of 4·0 in 1881 increasing to 30·0 by 1911.

In the 1870s Thomas Carlyle was a button manufacturer in Alma Street (Aston New Town), as were Harrison and Smith. In the 1880s he submitted ten separate plans for buildings on a new site, and by 1884 he moved his business. In the meantime Harrison and Smith had been bought by Walter Evans in 1880, a prominent Tory, who then added five new buildings. Carlyle's premises were as large as Ansells brewery and in the 1890s his business continued to grow. In 1897 it became a public company and in 1899 he took over Player Bros. In 1904 the firm was described as a "virtual monopoly of the button trade" (Ironmonger 30·7·04). In 1907 a new company was formed to take over Plant, Harrison and Smith and Carlyle Ltd. This was Buttons Ltd., and it still existed in 1967. In the circumstances it is clear that the survival of both Harrison and Smith, and Carlyle, particularly the latter, was associated with a major reconstruction of production, indicated by the investment in new buildings in the 1880s. It must also have been associated with new production technology to survive the foreign competition.

Another established industry of a more general nature than buttons was the edge-tool trade represented in Aston by J. Yates and Co., a firm established in 1793 and located in Aston by 1848. Yates and Co. made edge-tools and became leaders of the trade. The progress of the trade and of Yates illustrates many points concerning international competition, the Depression and the restructuring of production.

The general trade position during the period is given by Smith's (1965) references to the journal *Ironmonger*. The trade was based on exports, and to maintain production, wages of necessary skilled craftsmen could not easily be cut (*Ironmonger*, 8·3·1879). However, by 5·7·79 the journal noted that the Depression had reached the trade in Birmingham. Continued production in Birmingham may well have been due to the movement of the trade from Sheffield, because of strong unions there, as reported by the *Ironmonger* (22·6·78). The Depression, however, meant a drop in prices, not in demand. On 15·1·81 it was reported that machinery was producing higher quality goods than the traditional hand processes. In response to this, as much as to lower costs, the larger firms in the industry were introducing "considerable mechanization".

In 1881 the "factor" system, so important to the export trade, was severely critized in the edge-tool industry. Throughout the year a controversy raged over the relative merits of American and British axes sold in Australia. It was argued that the factors had given producers inferior specifications, or bought the cheapest goods, in order to undercut American prices. The result was a bad reputation, less orders and a decline in trade. Faced with this example of mercantilist perfidy, many firms started direct trading, thereby contributing to the absorption of marketing functions into firms' management.

In November 1885 a slow return of demand for "better tools", i.e. British trade marks, was noted. However in January 1886, agents for German trowels had set up in Birmingham itself, an indication of the strength of the competition. A surplus of production that same year led to the development of the Chinese market, at that time dominated by various Imperial interests. On 12·2·87, a review article noted that the increased competition had revolutionized production methods, through an increase in mechanization and youth employment since 1880, and a loss of smaller firms. There were currently 4000 people employed in the Birmingham area. In February 1893, the journal noted that the trade was concentrated in a few hands. One of these was Yates and Co.

In 1864, Yates employed 3–4000 people and was the largest firm in the trade in Birmingham. It had at least two works: one in Pritchett Street the other at Rocky Lane, Aston. In 1871 the GER of the Rocky Lane plant was £349; this had doubled by 1881. The firm at this stage was an exporter to both colonial and foreign markets, hence its normal stocks were valued at between £20–30 000 because of its relatively long turnover-period (*Ironmonger*, 9·6·83). In the wake of the 1881 controversy, the Ironmonger reported (13·1·83) that the firm had put in new machinery to compete with the axe production of their American rivals Collins. In September 1886 the hoe mill was reopened, possibly because of the new Chinese market, though there was also a general increase in business. In February 1891 the Company went public with a capital of £50 000 and a workforce of 400. The new company took over the edge-tools works and the adjacent sawmills, though the family's pewtering, electroplate and bedsteads businesses seem to have been kept separate. In 1893 Pritchett Street was closed and moved to Rocky Lane. A centenary article in the *Ironmonger* that year noted that the firm's export trade was now supplemented by domestic trade. Yates' involvement in direct trading was shown in R. P. Yates convalescent tour of India and Australia in 1888–9 when he visited their agents.

The history of Yates in this period illustrates some of the different components that go towards restructuring a firm during a crisis period. First, there was the introduction of new machinery. Secondly, there were the five new buildings erected during the 1880s. Thirdly, there was the development of new trading areas and methods. Fourthly, there was the eventual concentration of production on one site, as well as the partial centralization of control and capital in a new limited company. It is also one of the few available examples of an increased capitalization. Taking the partial index of building value and the labour force, the former increases from £349 to £1115 (including sawmills) while the workforce remains virtually stable. The value of machinery has not been recorded, but we can expect this to also have substantially increased.

The new buildings mentioned in these examples are only 21% of all buildings put up for production purposes between 1880 and 1891. Clearly then many other businesses were either expanding or locating in Aston, although the examples given were probably the most significant contributions to the area's economic development. From 1885 to 1891, buildings were going up at over seven per year with a peak in 1888 of 14. As noted earlier, these tended to be larger on average than the buildings of the 1870s.

The particular examples discussed above give support to the more general picture of Aston and Birmingham presented earlier. In particular the emergence of large and in some cases almost monopolistic firms can be seen in certain trades. Associated with this was the increased mechanization of production and the growing employment of women and youths. The case of Yates and Co., particularizes the general picture of an increased capitalization in trades restructuring to meet new levels of competition. The changes in company financing discussed by Smith are amply illustrated with the larger companies becoming public before the smaller ones.

The expansion and changes in the Aston economic base are thus clearly seen as the result of changes brought to the Birmingham economy by the Depression. The response of the area's capitalists can be seen in the buildings put up with the new investment. The restoration of competitiveness resulted in generally larger buildings often further from the centre of Birmingham. The special attraction of Aston for brewing has been mentioned. More generally, however, there were a number of factors in Aston's favour. First, it was relatively undeveloped, for historical reasons, and consequently had cheaper land available. Secondly, there was the Birmingham and Fazeley canal, though its importance was diminished since the development of the nearby Curzon Street marshalling yards.

Thirdly, the rates in Aston were less than in Birmingham at least from the mid-1870s onwards. Finally, and probably most attractive, a cheap labour force in cheap housing was available.

7. Political and social consequences

The many and varied changes in the economy resulting from the national recession promoted new political problems and issues at all levels. Nationally, there was a debate between Free and Fair Traders over the question of introducing import controls in the form of tariffs. There was also the rise of the New Trade Unionism associated with the spread of the factory system and the growth in the numbers of semi- and unskilled workers. At the local level the continued expansion of towns, the redevelopment of city centres and the displacement of the urban poor, continued to focus attention on sanitation, housing and education. The parameters for the resolution of such issues were laid down by the economic situation and made even more difficult by the effective culmination of the trend towards central control of local government in the Local Government Act of 1871.

Throughout the nineteenth century local politics were dominated by practical questions such as highways, drainage, housing standards and school provision. These problems were treated in a non-party political manner (where large portions of the working class were disenfranchized), rather they were defined in apolitical, almost technocratic, terms. The main polarity tended to be between the "spending" and "saving" factions in the local political institutions. However, increasingly, as the century progressed, local political institutions became politicized as part of the nation-wide conflict between the Tory and Liberal parties.

By the 1880s the combination of economic recession, increasing demands for social infrastructure, the institutional centralization of government, the widening gulf between the major political parties, and the final straw of the Irish Home Rule Bill, led to a major schism in the dominant Liberal party. Disaffected Liberal-Unionists started the move that would later take them into the reformed Tory party. As a result of the demands for local-based expenditure, the allegiance of the lower middle-class also shifted from the Liberals to the Tories. Finally, the remaining radical Liberals found themselves supplanted or allied to the nascent Labour party (Crossick, 1977; Fraser, 1976). As a major Liberal area, Birmingham, and to a lesser extent Aston, experienced many of these trends.

Corbett (1966) gives the evidence for the rise of the New Unions in Birmingham during the 1880s. In 1885 there were 25 societies, with as many branches, affiliated to the Trades Council. By 1893 there were 56 societies with 66 branches. He also described the emergence of a more militant attitude within organized labour. Wright (1977) has shown how the divisions within the Liberal party at national level led to a local situation in which organized labour as well as general working class demands for reform were being neglected. Consequently, on 14th September 1893 the Trades Council resolved to support independent labour representation in Parliament. As Kynaston (1976) shows, this shift in the political orientation of organized labour was a general phenomenon. Fox concludes that the effect of the Depression in the Birmingham area was to introduce new, often mechanized work processes, and to change the social relations of production from a graded hierarchy to a polarized employer/wage labourer dichotomy. As a consequence there was greater solidarity and a tendency to a more structural and class definition of issues.

The political developments in Aston were mainly associated with local affairs rather than the broader issues of class relations. As the area's economic and physical development was compressed into a relatively short period, the political changes were both rapid and complex.

Early development, up to 1877, gave rise to problems connected with unmade highways and sewerage. While Aston residents soon elected a Highway Surveyor, it took a court action, brought by the water company, to establish a Local Board of Health in 1868 and a basic system of main drainage. At this stage the Board was drawn from the Liberal concensus that embraced capital (the Ansells), reformers (Dr May) and lower middle-class representatives. The Liberals also dominated the School Board.

The rapid development of Aston following the sales of the Park land, in particular the construction of the cheap housing in the mid-1870s that attracted young families, meant a rapid rise in the need for expenditure on social infrastructure. Roads required "making" and "adopting". The high proportion of children in the population required the statutory educational facilities, and this time Westminster was obliged to resort to legal pressure. Pressure to introduce by-laws to prevent back–back housing was resisted until all the relevant sites had been completed, by a local board containing many of the leading "developers" of Aston. Underlying these debates was the fundamental question of whether Aston should be merged with Birmingham, or incorporated as a separate Municipal Borough. This question remained unresolved until 1911, but the legal debates and the "expansionist" plans of local Liberals had direct financial implications.

With the rapid growth of Aston and its population in the 1870s, the level of Local Board expenditure rose sharply, and so, therefore did the rates. In 1879 a Ratepayers Union was formed, and this was supported mainly by the lower middle-class of shopkeepers and small businessmen. Shortly afterwards the Tory and Liberal Party Associations were formed for local political purposes. Debates over expenditure on highways, schools, the new Local Board offices and the desirability of becoming a municipal borough were henceforth highly political. The position of the Tory interests was considerably strengthened as many of the new industrial investors in Aston followed R.P. Yates and supported that party. This setback for the Liberals was further compounded after the 1884 Reform Act gave working-class males the vote, for, by the General Election of 1892 it was considered worthwhile to put up a Labour candidate in Aston. In this respect, therefore, Aston would appear to have been typical of the radical developments in the Birmingham area at the time.

Overall, the development of Aston had caused the break-up of the local Liberal consensus. Capital interests were increasingly represented by the Tories, while the lower middle-class were moving in that direction via the Ratepayers Union. The reforming element of the Liberals remained with the party after the split with the Liberal-Unionists; but their erstwhile support among the organized working class was progressively adopting a more independent position with respect to parliamentary representation. Aston was therefore representative of wider social trends.

8. Conclusions

This case study has illustrated a number of general themes that are typical of economic crises in capitalist societies. While the geographic scale at which the manufacture of the economic changes are found is different in the 1980s, the underlying similarities with the 1880s are distinct and discernible. Furthermore, trends started in the last century are still to be seen evolving in the present day.

The Victorian Depression was a result of the advent of international relativities, such as in wage rates and productivity, becoming the defining parameters for domestic, British capital. It involved major and often protracted periods of restructuring that either successfully re-established the accumulation process (as in Birmingham), or resulted in a prolonged period of decline (as in North-East England). At company and plant level, restructuring took the form of new productive technology and corporate structures. At the industry level there was a loss of firms, amalgamations and sometimes the total disappearance of the industry from a particular area, supplanted by international rivals.

The transformation of the productive process moved the local social formation from one stage, or level of development, to another. The skilled artisan in the small workshops of a semi-capitalist economy became semi- or unskilled workers in the new factory-based economy producing a different range of commodities, often in an entirely new location. This transformation was matched in the social and political sphere outside work. The old Liberal party institutions and individualistic hegemony were broken up and gradually replaced by a realignment that was more overtly class-oriented in nature.

At the local level, the central importance of land ownership as an important determinant of how the social changes became physically apparent in the built form is also clear. Apart from the relative cheapness of the land, the existence of a working-class suburb in Aston with a very low standard of living proved an incentive to industrial investment. Existing premises grew, and new premises were on a generally larger scale to house the new technology. Not only was there a segregation of land uses, consequent upon the beginnings of the "flight to the suburbs", but within the housing stock there was a development of distinct spatial patterns in the value of houses. The emergence of exchange professionals (such as estate agents) and speculative builders in Aston suggests that this was a conscious policy. Following the passing of the Public Health Acts, this policy became the cornerstone of town planning.

In common with the present day, the political debates at local level during the Victorian Depression were primarily focussed on the question of public expenditure. It was the conflict between the demand for rate income to finance the manifest needs for social infrastructure, and the lack of economic success from which to supply that demand, that finally shifted the crucial lower middle-class support from the Liberal to the Tory party. The economic recession fragmented the earlier political alignments, and it was several more decades before the resulting factions coalesced into new political institutions. It remains to be seen whether the 1980s is witnessing a similar political phenomenon, but it is certain that the underlying economic issues remain the same.

A major conclusion is therefore that local changes in economic, political and urban structures are reflections of far wider processes. The factors that promoted the development of Aston were predominantly located outside the area itself. An understanding of any particular part of Aston's development is dependent upon an understanding of its relationship to the whole process and the other structures involved. The terms of reference for any explanation cannot be bounded spatially; nor, we can add, should they be isolated within the bounds of traditional social science disciplines that also emerged during the Great Victorian Depression.

References

Aldcroft, D. and Richardson, H. (1969). "The British economy 1870–1939", Macmillan, London.

Allen, G. C. (1929). "The industrial development of Birmingham and the Black Country, 1860–1927", Allen & Unwin, London.

Anderson, R. A. (1969). An anatomy of Aston, unpublished dissertation, Birmingham Polytechnic.

Aston Medical Officer of Health. Annual Report, 1874–1911.

Board of Trade (1903, 1905, 1909). "Memorandum, statistical tables and charts on British and foreign trade and industrial conditions", (three volumes).

Carney, J. Hudson, R. and Lewis, J. (1975). Coal combines and inter-regional uneven development in the UK, *in* D. Massey and P. Batey (eds), *London Papers in Regional Science*, 7, Pion, London.

Corbett, S. C. (1966). "The Birmingham Trades Council 1866–1966", Lawrence & Wishart, London.

Crossick, G. (1977). "The lower middle classes in Britain 1870–1914", Croom Helm, London.

Eversley, D. (1968). Birmingham industry, *Victoria County History: Warwickshire*, Vol. 7.

Feinstein, C. H. (1973). "National income expenditure and output of the United Kingdom 1855–1965", Cambridge University Press, Cambridge.

Fox, A. (1955). Industrial relations in nineteenth century Birmingham, *Oxford Economic Papers*, **7**, 1, New Series, 57–70.

Hobsbawn, E. (1968). "Industry and Empire", Pelican, London.

Kynaston, D. (1976). "King Labour", Allen & Unwin, London.

Wright, G. H. (1913). *Chronicles of the Birmingham Chamber of Commerce*, Birmingham Chamber of Commerce.

Wright, R. A. (1977). Liberal Party organization and politics in Birmingham, Coventry and Wolverhampton 1886–1914, with particular reference to the development of independent labour representation, unpublished, Ph.D. thesis, Birmingham University.

Notes

1. In order to be able to analyse the development of the built form in Aston, a sample of 44 streets was drawn from a total of 138 streets in the area. These were then traced through the Ratebooks for 1871, 1876, 1881, 1886, 1891 and all the properties' gross estimated rentals were recorded. The sample aimed to cover all areas of the manor.

2. The Gross Estimated Rental (GER) of a property is the rental valuation of that property for one year. It is mainly a calculation based upon the space standards and quality of the property, rather than its market price. The Rateable value of the property is a percentage of the GER. The percentage varies, but from 1871–1891 it remained at 80%.

In itself building size is an unsatisfactory measure of growth and change in production process: the same building can have different uses. However, expansion does indicate investment, and corroborative information of the time suggests that new building was usually part of the introduction of new production processes.

3. These examples and many of the more obscure references are drawn from a typescript copy of Smith, B.M.D. (1965). *A Directory of Midland Industry*, which is kept in the Local Studies section of Birmingham Central Reference Library. It lists and abstracts references to Birmingham's industries, 1870–1914, alphabetically, by industry, in date order. It is an essential starting point. The references to the building put up come from the Building Plan records for 1880–91.

SIX

The state and the reserve army: the management of class relations in space

D. BYRNE and D. PARSON

(January 1982)

1. Introduction

This chapter is about the state, "its" spatial policies and the restructuring of the working class. It is concerned with the changes in the form of the working class which are being forced on that class by the contemporary character of capitalist production, and in particular it is concerned with the way in which spatial policy contributes to the forcing of those changes and to attempts to "manage" the consequences of them. The chapter is informed by our version of an "autonomist" account of these developments. This is not a perspective which has been much employed in understanding this area, at least in relation specifically to spatial policy, and it will be necessary to outline the essential elements of such an approach. We will then go on to look at spatial policy in general in relation to the restructuring of the working class and in particular in terms of the consequences for that part of the working class which we can describe as the "stagnant reserve army" or, and this has slightly different implications, as the "surplus population". Here we will be concerned with what we want to call "reserve space", and we will attempt to illustrate what is happening by a specific focus on the processes of housing administration which are concerned with spatially segregated "reserve" or "surplus" areas and with the management of that part of the working class forced to live in these areas.

There is one thing we want to emphasize right at the beginning of this piece. What we are describing is a working class in struggle, and in many ways in defeat. The processes are ones which *now* seem to have very unpleasant implications for the conditions under which working-class people live and for their capacity to change those conditions. *Nonetheless*, if there is one thing which is central to our understanding of what is going on, it is that the working class is not the passive object of developments where the subject, the actor, is simply "Capital" or the capitalist state. We are dealing here with struggle, and struggles require fighters in the plural. If we are attempting to outline the spatial form and consequences of the present crisis, then we are doing it in the framework asserted recently by James O'Connor:

> ... crisis theory must be formulated in terms of what has been *made* to happen in history and what can be *made* to happen in the future, rather than in terms of what has happened and what will probably happen. Crisis theory thus meaningfully explains social action when and only when it has become a weapon in the hands of the working class movement (1981, 327).

That the structure of the working class is changing is something which ought to be apparent from simple observation. In the United Kingdom we now have 3 million unemployed. This becomes 4½ million if we define unemployment as the *Irish* Poor Law Commissioners did in 1837, i.e. as "those who have not work and want it", and include those on "Youth Opportunity Programmes", "Training Opportunity Programmes", and "Community Employment Projects", the early retired and unregistered women. The proportion of those in work engaged in manufacturing industry has declined from 45% in 1951 to 27·5% in 1981, and the total number of manufacturing workers has declined from 8·8 million in 1951 to 5·8 million in 1981. These changes are examples of what Braverman, following Marx, has called changes in the "social division of labour": "the way in which labour has been shifted between different branches of the economy". We also have to consider "the way in which the nature of work has been altered within different branches", that is: "the changing detailed (or technical) division of labour" (see Friend and Metcalf, 1981, 47). In other words there have been important changes in where people work, how they work and if they work. Far from representing the dawn of the post-industrial era based on slave robots and offering the life of the Athenian elite to humankind, it is perfectly clear that these changes have been for the worse. In general they have been emmiserating. As Sweezy pointed out in his introduction to Harry Braverman's seminal *Labor and Monopoly Capital*:

> Marx's General Law of Capital Accumulation, according to which the advance of capitalism is characterized by the amassing of wealth at one pole and of deprivation and misery at the other ... far from being the egregious fallacy which bourgeois social science has long held it to be, has in fact turned out to be one of the best founded of all Marx's insights into the capitalist system (1974: xii).

However, these developments have not affected all the working class in the same way, although it is clear that they have the same very general implications for all working-class people. Rather to a very considerable degree they have taken the form of the reinforcement of *divisions* within the working class with the associated transfer of an even larger proportion of the class to the emmiserated side of the divide. This is the consequence of that restructuring which is occurring through the processes most generally and simply described as "de-industrialization" (changes in the social division of labour) and "de-skilling" (changes in the detailed division of labour). What we are getting is a massive increase in "the stagnant reserve army of labour", or as Friend and Metcalf prefer to describe it "the surplus population". Both these terms come from Marx but, as we have already suggested, they differ slightly but quite importantly in terms of implication. As we hope to demonstrate an autonomist account suggests that "stagnant reserve army" (SRA) may be a more useful formulation, but it is worth giving both definitions here as a starting point for our considerations:

> The third category of the relative-surplus population, the stagnant, forms a part of the active labour army, but with extremely irregular employment. Hence it furnishes to capital an inexhaustible reservoir of disposable labour-power. Its conditions of life sink below the average normal level of the working class; this makes it at once the broad basis of special branches of capitalist exploitation. It is characterized by a maximum of working time, and minimum of wages. We have learnt to know its chief form under the rubric of "domestic industry" . . . Its extent grows, as with the extent and energy of accumulation, the creation of a surplus population advances. But it forms at the same time a self-reproducing and self-perpetuating element of the working class, taking a proportionally greater part in the general increase of that class than the other elements (Marx, 1976, 602).

Marx's definition emphasized three inter-related aspects of the SRA that we will address in this chapter: its consequences for the organization of production, the emmiserated conditions of its reproduction, and the fact that the SRA is "self-reproducing and self-perpetuating".

Friend and Metcalf very specifically distinguish what they call the "surplus population" from "the reserve army of labour". They say:

> The term "reserve army of labour" has an economistic flavour, omitting class consciousness and class organization from its terms of reference; moreover the surplus population embraces a wider section of the working class than those who are just unemployed and as such is more useful in analysing life in the older working class areas than the concept of the reserve army of labour (1981, 25).

We think they are wrong here for reasons which will emerge in our discussion of the autonomist perspective, but their description of the surplus population both has great value *as a description*, and provides us with a way into considering a different analysis of the situation they are describing:

> . . . these groups include all those who are long-term unemployed; most of those for whom periods of unemployment alternate with dependence on temporary or casual part-time work; those participating in the bottom reaches of the "black economy" outside the tax system; all those who are totally

dependent on state benefits or forms of charity (including the mass of pensioners, the chronically sick and disabled, and single parent families on social security); and those people who, although in regular employment in labour-intensive sweated occupations or the state service sector, earn wages signficantly below the national average and who live in households where the standard of living only exceeds the minimum poverty line because of the receipt of means tested benefits. This broad definition embraces the majority of those living in urban areas who are unemployed because they are marginal to the requirements of capital in terms of the direct production of surplus value during the current long wave of stagnation, but does not draw a hard and fast distinction between them and the low paid who are in work or those who are excluded from the workforce because of age and childcare responsibilities – because in practice the line is often crossed by individual people (1981, 119).

It is very important to realize, as ought to be apparent from the very considerable and intentional similiarity between Friend and Metcalf's description of the contemporary character of the surplus population and Marx's definition of the SRA that there is nothing new about this group. There are all sorts of different terms for describing them and for differentiating them from the rest of the working class. In the late Victorian and Edwardian periods, the distinction between the "respectable working-class" and the "residuum" was perfectly well understood, and was the basis, as we shall see, for the central elements of coercive social policy. In the specific context of work, the difference has been described by radical versions of bourgeois social-theory in terms of dual labour-market conditions. One recent way of conceptualizing the division which we have found particularly useful is Andy Friedman's distinction between "central" and "peripheral" workers (see Chapter 3 in this volume), albeit that we would want to extend this distinction beyond the realm of work, of "direct" production as it is usually understood and develop an account of centrality/peripherality in the sphere of reproduction as well as production.

Friedman defines central workers thus:

> Central workers are those whom top managers consider to be essential to secure high long-run profits, particularly when product demand or general business conditions are depressed. Workers may be considered central as *individuals* because of their skills, their knowledge of their contribution to the exercise of managerial authority; or they may those who, by the strength of their collective resistance make themselves essential to top managers *as a group* (1977, 109).

It is the second half of this definition which is most important for us because it illustrates the autonomous power origins of "central status". Of course this central status is not a stable one. An important theme in the autonomist account of the development of the capitalist relations of production is the way in which new technology and organization of production through "scientific management" have been used together precisely to destroy the central status achieved collectively by workers in struggle. A very straightforward example of this is provided by the history of the establishment of dockers' unions, the first general unions of the residuum, the long battle for de-casualization of dock work finally achieved during the last war, and the consequent introduction of container cargo handling and roll-on/roll-off vessels as a way of destroying this hard-won central status and peripheraliz-ing the workers who stuff and strip the containers off the dock.

An important background theme in this chapter is the general "periph-eralization" of production which is occuring in the UK and US economies at the present time. If we go back to Marx's definition of the SRA, we will see that he referred to it as "the basis of special branches of capitalist exploita-tion". When we talk about the peripheralization of production we mean the way in which the relations characteristic of these "special branches" are becoming generalized in capitalist production as a whole. Peripheralization is a strategy developed by capital in response to working-class iniative: the intensification of mechanization in order to increase the extraction of rela-tive (as opposed to absolute) surplus-value due to working-class agitation for the ten-hour day as described by Marx in *Capital*[1]; the development of Taylorism and Fordism in response to the unionization drives and militant working-class activity in the early twentieth century; the flight of capital to "peripheral" regions and countries from the 1930s onwards (e.g. the loca-tion of the car industry in the UK outside traditional industrial areas in the 1930s and the contemporary location of electronic assembly in SE Asia) which has always been directed at avoiding the demands on capital by the organized working class; the increase of the SRA through the current "neo-Fordist" use of information technology (see Braverman, 1974; Palloix in CSE, 1976; Duncan, 1981; Perrons, 1981). Class struggle in this context is not a monolithic uni-dimensional process, rather it proceeds as a set of fragmented hierarchies of centres and peripheries. In speaking of centres and peripheries, we are not trying to employ an obscure form of geometric marxology, but instead are attempting to conceptualize the way in which the social and spatial forms of class relations are manifest as a result of the development of the class struggle.

We are now almost ready to attempt an explicit delineation of our version of the autonomist perspective as opposed to our implicit use of it thus far. Before doing this we want to look, very briefly, at recent history and the position of the SRA in relation to it. Gough in his description of the characterization of this golden age of the Keynesian political economy in the 1950s and 1960s, makes the point that the mobilization of latent reserve armies of labour from agriculture, non-industrial regions and housewifes, even taken together with the rapid growth of labour productivity:

> . . . failed to prevent the major supplies of labour being absorbed and therefore 'over full employment' from developing. This in turn strengthened the bar-gaining power of labour in all post-war countries, though at different tempos

Figure 1. Early Sunday morning, Upper Parliament Street, Toxteth, Liverpool 6 July 1981. Police prepare to fire CS gas, with night vision image intensifier (left); shotgun for firing CS gas (right) and CS gas gun (behind). (Photograph: John Sturrock, Network).

in each. Thus, whether or not there was an initial committment to pursue full-employment policies, the very dynamism of the capitalist economies brought it about by the end of the 1950s at the latest. This in turn increased the economic and political leverage of the organized working class to obtain improvements not only in money wages but also in the social wage (1979, 72).

This is an account of the virtual disappearance of the SRA in metropolitan capitalism, and one which suggests that the SRA was re-created in some way during the present crisis. O'Connor provides us with a summary of the rationale which:

> suggests that the crisis-induced recreation of the reserve army of labour is a lever of accumulation *to the degree that it is a lever of 'capital restructuring'*. This means that the layoffs during the early stage of economic crises permit capital to re-establish its domination over the working class which is in turn a social and political pre-condition for restructuring the means of production and relocating industry. Concentration and centralization of capital, increases in production efficiency, and industrial relocation in turn generate more unemployment. This means that in subsequent short or long-term economic expansions an ever larger reserve army is available to throw into production (1981, 315–316).

As O'Connor makes absolutely clear this is only the "capital-logic" part of the story; the "economistic" side which leaves out class relations and actions. We need to add in class autonomy and the role of the state in reproduction, but let us here note that the metropolitan SRA-surplus population has been re-created in the present crisis out of next to nothing at the time of the long boom. In this particular sense, the 1980s, look more like the 1890s than the 1960s. The role of state spatial policy in all this is a key theme in this paper.

2. The Autonomist perspective

As we understand it, the autonomist perspective involves two central and related propositions. The first is one which has been implicit in our account of developments in the position and form of the working class: it is the assertion of the active autonomous character of the working class in refusing work, where work is the fundamental form of social control imposed on it through the commodity form. This, then, is the source of crisis in capitalism. As Harry Cleaver puts it:

> with the working class understood as being within capital yet capable of autonomous power to disrupt the accumulation process and thus break out of capital, crisis can no longer be thought of as a blind 'breakdown' generated by the mysteriously invisible laws of competition. Beginning with Antonio Negri's work on Marx's crisis theory, crisis has been reinterpreted in terms of the power relations between the classes and competition has been located as only one organization of this relation. Marx's understanding of crisis as a

means to restore the conditions of growth is seen in terms of restoring adequate control over the working class. Thus 'the modern crisis' emerges as a phenomenon of two moments: a first, in which the working class struggle imposes crisis on capital, and a second, in which capital tries to turn the crisis against the working class to restore command (1979, 62).

This "class struggle" account gives us a very different method for understanding the processes involved in the peripheralization of production and of the working class. What we are dealing with when we consider the massive expansion of the SRA is a process of under-development, if we understand this term in the autonomist sense. We quote again from Cleaver:

> (D)evelopment and underdevelopment are understood here neither as the outcome of historical processes (as bourgeois economists recount) nor as the processes themselves (as many Marxists use the terms). They are rather two different *strategies* by which capital seeks to control the working class . . . they are always co-existent because hierarchy is the key to capital's control and development is always accompanied by relative or absolute underdevelopment for others in order to maintain that hierarchy . . . By development I mean a strategy in which working class income is raised in exchange for more work . . . The alternative strategy, in which income is reduced in order to impose the availability for work, I call a strategy for underdevelopment (1977, 94).

We think that this makes very obvious sense if we are thinking about the position of the workers in "the special branches of capitalist accumulation", and about the general role of a reserve army in affecting the capacity of workers to struggle at the point of production. In this context, the development of the "new sweatshops" (see Green *et al.*, 1979), and the union-busting and real-wage cutting of the likes of Michael Edwards at British Leyland, can be interpreted as dependent on the expansion of the Reserve Army of Labour in general, both as a mechanism of attacking the "centrality" of employed workers and as the basis for the expansion of "peripheral" production. We should note here that in this sense "peripheral" does *not* mean unimportant. On the contrary, capitalism cannot function without the peripheral production at any time, and it is essential in crisis as one part of the basis of capital's attack on the working class. One of the reasons why we prefer the term "Stagnant Reserve Army" to "Surplus Population" is that we think Marx's formulation of the notion of SRA emphasized the importance of "peripheral production" in a way in which "Surplus Population" does not, although we would note that it is abundantly clear that Friend and Metcalf's definition of the contemporary character of the surplus population corresponds exactly to our description and includes workers in "peripheral production".

Our major difference with Friend and Metcalf stems from the second central proposition of the autonomist perspective, that is the notion of the "social factory". The crucial point in the idea of "social factory" is the importance of the arena of the reproduction of labour power for capitalism.

The demarcating character of capitalism as a system is that labour-power is a commodity, that wage labour is the dominant form of labour relation. Labour-power has to be "reproduced", in the immediate sense of workers having to be housed, clothed and fed, in the future sense of the need to raise new generations of workers and in the ideological sense of providing workers ready and willing to work in a capitalist context. It is very well worth noting that in the early years of industrial capitalism neither the physical nor ideological reproduction of the working class was unproblematic. Factory and Public Health legislation had to be introduced so that urban industrial workers could continue to survive and produce. In other words, wages alone were not enough to reproduce labour-power. Long political and moral struggles took place before capitalism was generally accepted as natural, or at least assented to. The state became involved in the process, acting as the collective capitalist, the guardian of the integrity of the system and doing that which was necessary but not done by individual capitalists[2] (see Doyal, 1980 for an excellent discussion of all this). Reproduction means more than just physical reproduction. It involves a whole complex of ideology, acceptance, involvement in the system. It is a process in which the role of women as wives and mothers is crucial and the major recent development of reproduction theory has been socialist-feminist in character (cf. Mackenzie and Rose in this volume). Let us use Cleaver again to put this formally:

> (Mario Tronti) focuses on how the analysis of circulation and reproduction in Volume II of *Capital* also involved the reproduction of classes. This insight meant that the equation of capital with the 'factory', characteristic of marxist political economy, was clearly inadequate. The reproduction of the working class involves not only work in the factory but also work in the home and in the community of homes. This realization brought into sharp focus the importance of Marx's long discussion of the reserve army in Volume I's chapters on accumulation. Accumulation means accumulation of the reserve army as well as the active army, of those who work at reproducing the class as well as those who produced other commodities (besides labour-power). The 'factory' where the working class worked was the society as a whole, a social factory. The working class had to be redefined to include non-factory workers (1979, 57).[3]

The notion of social factory clearly indicates that the autonomous activity of the working class is not confined to the traditional workplace, production narrowly conceived, but also occurs in the social factory, the sphere of reproduction. We therefore have to consider reproduction as an arena of class struggle and class strategy. Essentially what we want to suggest is that an autonomist account of the current crisis must involve consideration of crisis as produced by the action of the working class in reproduction as well as production. In other words, reproduction is also being peripheralized. Hilary Partridge is getting at this when she says in her interview with Negri:

> Reading 'Capitalist Domination and Working Class Sabotage', I was struck particularly by your discussion of public spending and the wage, parts of

which I quote: "Public spending and the wage are themes to which analysis, the theory and practice of revolutionaries will continually have to return, because in a situation of discontinuity in the cyclicity of the class struggle, the problem of public spending will, in the coming years assume the same import- ance as the wage, narrowly defined, has had in years past", and later: "The privileged place of the wage in the continuity of proletarian struggles must, today, be extended to the struggle over public spending cuts. Only this struggle can enable the full self-recognition of the proletariat; can attack directly the theory and practice of income-as-revenue". This seems to me a very important concept for the strategy and tactics of working class struggle today. The mass vanguard of the proletariat movement is no longer to be found at the point of production, on the board and largely masculine shoulders of the factory worker guaranteed by powerful trade unions, but amongst the traditionally weaker sectors of the proletariat – women, the unemployed, immigrants and so on – the major consumers and providers of welfare services. The nurses in struggle for improved wages and conditions and thus improved nursing facilities in the hospitals, women demanding the provision of refuges and nursery facilities, youths demanding more cultural and social facilities, now move from the back pages of the annals of socialist historiography to take on capital as major protagonists of the class struggle (1981, 137; see Negri, 1979, 109–110).[4]

As we shall see, and as Negri if not Partridge clearly realizes, this is no new struggle. Indeed we want to give autonomist action in reproduction a crucial status and examplify in relation to spatial policy and the role of the state. First let us return to our criticism of Friend and Metcalf. If we look at their definition of "surplus population", we can immediately see that they are aware of the importance of reproduction. Our point is this – we must think of reproduction as class struggle; that means we need an active definition of those involved and Reserve Armies, even if stagnant, sound more active than surplus populations. We really need a new term.[5] What we are on about here is people in production and reproduction who have been "decentralized" and "emmiserated" as part of the "under-development" of the working class which is a central strategy of capital in a crisis caused by the offensive action of the working class in production and reproduction. We now turn to a consideration of the interrelated activities of the state in both these spheres as expressed in spatial terms.

3. Spatial Policy and the production/reproduction of the SRA

In understanding the working-out of the processes described in the first half of this paper, it is important that we recognize the actual mechanisms by which "capital" maintains its hegemony and creates a hierarchical fragmen- tation of the working class. To do this we need to pay attention to the role of the state. We have to be careful here. Both of us are very keen to avoid the kind of abstracted structuralism which derives from analysis in which "capital" and "the state" are treated as categories separate from their human components. Our work is explicitly *not* deductive and abstracted in intention. Nonetheless if we tread carefully, work on the basis that the essential character of the state is succinctly indicated by its identification as: ". . . a committee for the management of the collective affairs of the whole bourgeoisie", and also remember that any attempt at understanding the role of the state in mass democratic capitalist societies has to recognize the reality of mass democracy, the important complex nature of reformism, and the role of the *capitalist* state as a venue for class conflict while it remains capitalist, then we can at least make a start. That elaborate set of qualifications is necessary and deliberate.

The development of spatial segregation as a component of social policy in the UK illustrates the relevant point particularly well. In the UK, the very formation of a mass reformist social-democratic party was intimately associated with the relationship between the state, especially the local state, and the response of socialists to the segmentation of the working class in relation to the capitalist organization of production and reproduction (see Byrne, 1980, 1981). In the late nineteenth and early twentieth centuries, that is to say after that crucial differentiation of the UK working class into the respectable working-class on the one hand and the "residuum" or "dangerous poor" on the other, the social policy of the state was very largely concerned with the management of the latter group. If we are to understand what was going on then we must immediately realize that the "respectable working class" was not the creation of the bourgeoisie. We reiterate that it created itself in the struggles over the length of the working day and the very transformation of metropolitan capital's central rationale from the expropriation of absolute surplus value to that of the expropriation of relative surplus value was contingent on the auto-genesis of this central group. The contradictory status of this central working class is an area of concern for many marxists historians.[6] The relationship of the state to the residuum located in transport and industrial production in the East End of London, which group was the product of the decomposition of production in London alongside the development of production in the UK as a whole, is described by Stedman Jones in *Outcast London* (1971). It is important for our analysis that we recognize the forms of resistance exemplified by the new unionism and the Poplarist[7] model in relation to the local state, as specific class resistance to the process of underdevelopment represented by the vertical decomposition of production in London and the associated state activities, particularly in relation to the East London Poor Law Unions.

The history of reformism and the social policy of the state in the UK during the twentieth century is one in which capital undertook an offensive on the central working-class of the regions. Before 1910 these groups were, with the important exception of their relationship with the state educational system, scarcely at all the object of social policy. This offensive operated in a context in which the central working-class had achieved control of many local states through the democratic process, and had initiated pre-figurative if contradictory housing reforms. In many mining areas, the central working-class employed their electorally achieved control over the administration of poor relief to finance quasi-insurrectionary, if defensive, strikes (see Ryan, 1976). This period represented a second phase in the under-development of the working class in the UK, using under-development again in the sense defined in the first half of this paper. It was very precisely out of the reaction of the working class against this offensive that the complex of welfare and regional policies of the 1945–51 Labour Government developed. In many senses the urban component of the New Deal in the United States had the same status, although the consolidation of reformist labourism as the dominant class ideology of the working class in the UK has had profound implications for the character of the state's relationship with that class.

A very important point about the long boom of the 1950s and 1960s was the virtual collapse of segregation within the working class, at least as far as processes of reproduction were concerned. We want to illustrate this point by reference to something which provides a framework for the management of the contemporary SRA, differences in housing quality. Swennarton has recently described in detail the extent to which the quantum jump in the design quality of working class housing provision immediately after the first world war in Britain was a consequence of working class struggle (1981), and the history of class struggle about housing quality in Britain is well documented (see for example Melling, 1980). The point is that after 1919, as a consequence of autonomist working-class action in the politics of reproduction (see Byrne and Damer, 1977) that part of the reproduction of the working class in Britain which involved shelter, always involved the state, although only between 1945 and 1951 did the state have a monopoly over the direct provision of even new stock.[8] After 1919 it was very clear that the housing of the residuum or SRA was going to be a state responsibility. In the 1930s, with the development of massive area slum-clearance schemes necessitated by the need to ensure physical reproduction, the SRA became to an ever increasing degree tenants of the state, and in a period of working-class defeat, they were the worse housed (se Byrne, 1980). In the long boom, when the SRA "disappeared" and the working class in Britain was on the reproductive offensive, state provision of housing was of high standard. It was not until the 1960s that the building of the differentiatedly worse rubbish began again. Council Housing in Britain is the concrete embodiment of class struggle about reproduction: superb in the 1920s, bad in the 1930s; good in the 40s and early 50s, and bad in the "flats" boom of the 60s. Of course there are local variations, which are the product of local struggles (see for example North Tyneside CDP, 1977 Vol. 1). The state has had to manage these shifts, and has played a major role in the whole process of crisis management in relation to struggle in reproduction. Housing is not only history in bricks and mortar; the variation in its quality is the key to spatial management of the SRA, to the use of space as a mechanism for differentiating and dividing the working class in British urban areas today. We want to return to this in a moment, but first we want to go back to theory by looking at the relationships among the state, capital and the working class in contemporary circumstances.

Since the 1920s in Britain conflict over reproductive issues has overwhelmingly been conflict in which the working class have been engaged with the state, and capital has been off the stage. This is true even for housing where capitalist production and provision retain massive importance. However, the fact that the appearance is one of conflict between class and state most certainly does not mean that capital has been subsumed into the state. Rather as we implied earlier, we regard the state as in the first instance concerned with ensuring the continued accumulation of capital (see Miliband, 1978). The period which began with the creation of the long boom is one in which the distinction between economy and politics in capitalist societies has increasingly collapsed as the state has been drawn into the business of facilitating the restructuring of capitalist production. This is a complex and contradictory process. Regional policy and planning which have served as key mechanisms in this restructuring had in origin important reformist content (see Morgan and Sayer in this volume). Nonetheless it is essential to note that they were from the beginning separated from democratic local state control and placed under corporatist administration (see Byrne, 1982). It seems as if capital could, for a time, cede the local administration of reproduction to the working class. Control of production has never been so ceded, and the direct instrumental involvement of class representatives of capital in the administration of these activities is of great continuing importance (see Benwell CDP, 1978).

We would like to focus on one aspect of state spatial policy in which reproduction and the production requirements of capital were compounded; that is the second phase of new town development in the UK which began in the 1960s at the end of the long boom and was directly associated with the restructuring of capital. At this time, the state was being forced to accommodate its policies to the new organization of capitalist production dominated by multi-national corporations. A very clear example of how all this operated is provided by the history of planning policy in the Belfast region. Here the working class was divided by sectarianism, and had never achieved local labourist hegemony. Until the 1950s the politics of the local state, Stormont, were dominated by local "Orange" capital, particularly the medium-sized local capitalists involved in the linen industry. In the 1950s, the collapse of the employment base and the threat to the Orange political system posed by mass unemployment among protestant workers forced the "protestant state" to develop planning policies which facilitated multi-national penetration. The Mathew Plan for the Belfast Region was sectarian reformist in intent and restructuring in practice. In terms of production, it facilitated the de-skilling process contingent on the movement of production to green field sites (see Massey and Meegan, 1977).

These production-centred activities had reproductive implications. The Belfast Transport Plan necessary for the infrastructure of green-field branch plants, required the physical destruction of Belfast "communities". The people who would in consequence require rehousing were chanelled to the "growth centres" to provide the labour force for the multi-nationals' plants (see Wiener, 1976). Hudson has described the development of Washington New Town in the North East in similar terms (1979). What happened at this point was that housing, a reproductive activity involving the state,[9] became subordinated to production's requirements. This could only happen because of the political condition of the working class and in particular because of the weakness contingent on the incorporation of the class' formal political leadership into corporatist administration. In the special case of Northern Ireland sectarianism and some incorporation of trade union officials were the equivalent factors. The effect of New Town-centred housing policy was to socially peripheralize, *at least in potential terms*. The immediate conditions of workers and residents in new towns were often "central" in character, but in manufacturing the change in "the technical division of labour", the de-skilling involved in the re-organization of the production, facilitated the ability of multi-national capital in subsequently locating the production away from the metropolitan working-class in order to take advantage of cheap labour-power in "newly industrializing countries".

Historically the SRA has always *tended* to be spatially segregated. Friedman has described the general residential conditions of peripheral workers:

> Peripheral workers will generally live in less pleasant areas. They cannot afford to keep up their neighbourhood. They cannot afford to move to a "better" neighbourhood. Local authorities are prejudiced against spending a lot of money on such areas (except to make way for commercial development). Privileged workers are prejudiced against moving into neighbourhoods where peripheral workers live (particularly if the distinction is racial), and against peripheral workers moving into their own neighbourhood . . . Thus peripheral workers remain in areas of deprivation . . . There they form a pool of cheap labour, readily available to top managers when trade revives (1977, 137–138).

It is important to realize that differentiation in state housing policy facilitates this segregation and that the net effect of housing policy's subordination at the beginning of the present crisis to the requirements of multi-national capital has extended the effects massively into the working class. Friend and Metcalf in their analysis of London concentrate on the inner city as the locale in space of the surplus population. We would add many new towns and overspill estates peripheralized by de-industrialization in the very recent past. In these areas we find the contemporary SRA concentrated in "reserve space".

There is an obvious connection between this reserve space and the concentration of labour reserves in the third world. In a temporal manner Castells (1975) speaks of the SRA in the advanced countries as providing a nineteenth century proletariat for a twentieth century capital. The spatial equivalent to this observation is Montano's (1975) characterization of capital's strategy as not only taking the factory to the third world, but also taking the third world to the factory.

The question arises as to why the SRA is concentrated in reserve space and not scattered throughout the urban labour market. The answer lies in the complex and contradictory character of the process of the reproduction of labour as a class relation. On the one hand, capital through the state establishes the framework for the material maintenance of the SRA (through the social wage) and shapes the spatial character of the class relation through housing policy. On the other hand and at the same time those subjected to this process develop political consciousness through their own reproductive role, albeit that the character of that consciousness reflects the general complexity of state–class relations in democratic societies. Harris (1980, 14) observes that the significance is felt through its effects:

> . . . on the conditions under which labour power is being produced as a class relation.

The communities that result from all this are not merely reactive to the power of capital, but rather and simultaneously exist in spite of capital. On the one hand, these communities serve the interests of capital in that they reproduce their labour for the service of capital. On the other, they can reproduce themselves in a manner frequently antagonistic and autonomous to the interests of capital. Capital thus seeks both to maintain and to destroy these communities at the same time. Capital maintains its hegemony and suppresses this contradiction by the hierarchical fragmentation of the working class, spatially as well as through the intra-class divisions of other sorts (waged–unwaged, central–peripheral etc. . . . .). In such a manner, large working-class areas of the city exist as little more than a multiplicity of private households with little or no contact with one another, alongside the "communities" which have solidaristic relationships. Development coexists with underdevelopment as a strategy of enforcing this spatial fragmentation. At this level we see the emergence of a hierarchy of communities, differentiated by autonomous political and reproductive power that is posed against capital's means of social control. Thus reserve space is utilized by capital in the sense that a particular segment of the labour market is concentrated and in fact immobilized in space by various social controls and constraints. It is in this way that Montano (1975) speaks of "ghettoization" as an advanced capitalist tool.

It is worth contrasting this approach to spatial segregation with that traditional in urban analysis, where spatial segmentation has been a key theme for urban geographers and sociologists. Thus Timms in a book with the suggestive title of *The Urban Mosaic* states that:

> In the modern Western city, at least, much of the detailed differentiation between neighbourhood populations is accountable for in terms of no more than three or four underlying axes of differentiation; social rank, family status, ethnicity and urban mobility. The sociological structure of the city is formed in the interaction of these properties as this is acted out in the locational decisions of the urban population and in the physical constructions of the city builders (1971, 250).

In this statement the core of the traditional sociological perspective is apparent. That is to say the significant phenomena with which urban analysts are concerned describe the attributes of populations, not the relationships existing among those populations and among populations, capital and the state. The notion of the urban system as being in any relationship with production and reproduction was absent from this literature. A case study of Killingworth Township in North Tyneside provides an illustration of the way in which capital restructuring and spatial policy have had a compounding effect in terms of the recreation of the SRA and its spatial segmentation through the operation of the state housing system.

The first proposals for the development of some sort of New Town in the Killingworth area can be dated back to the production of the Northumberland County Council Development Plan in the 1950s. Newcastle City had already started to use the area as an "overspill zone" for population relocation, and it was clear that this part of South-East Northumberland was to have great significance in relation to the rehousing of slum cleared populations from urban Tyneside. At the time of the fourth amendment to the Northumberland Development Plan (1957), it was thought that the East End of Newcastle and Wallsend Municipal Borough were likely to generate an overspill population of about 18 000. The period of these discussions was also that of the development of regional policy as a solution to structural problems in providing employment. Thus in 1963, following on the (in)famous visit to the region by Lord Hailsham waring a flat-cap, the White Paper; *The North-East − a programme for regional development and growth* was published and the emphasis on industrial attraction as a key planning strategy was firmly established. The Killingworth plans were formulated in the early phase of "regionalism", but were always coloured by the emphases of that perspective.

Killingworth was not a New Town under the New Towns Act of 1948. Rather it was established under the Town Development Act of 1952 and as a Comprehensive Development Area under the 1962 Town and Country Planning Act. The Killingworth Project was approved by Northumberland

County Council in August 1958, although there were continuing difficulties with Newcastle City Council, the quite independent local authority area which was to provide the bulk of projected population by relocation of its inner city inhabitants. Indeed it was not until the late 1960s that Newcastle County Borough Housing Committee finally committed itself to housing development as part of the Killingworth scheme.

In the middle 1960s the development process actually began with the appointment of R. Gazzard as co-ordinating Architect-Planner, a position he had previously held at Peterlee New Town in County Durham. Around this time a variety of population estimates were produced. Thus *Killingworth Information Digest* of October 1968 suggested a population of 20 000 in the Citadel with a further 30 000 in surrounding areas of Longbenton looking to Killingworth for shopping and administrative activities. By this time the physical and industrial character of Killingworth had been decided upon. The specifications are to be found in the *Killingworth Township Handbook* of 1966 and in the 1968 *Information Digest*:

> Killingworth is conceived as a hard-edged 'castle town' set in a landscape of parkland and is approached by a causeway access across a sheet of water as a drawbridge crosses a moat (*Information Digest*, **3**).

> The Township will consist mainly of family houses in the medium density range i.e. 50/90 persons per acre. The housing density will be increased towards the town centre where it will be covered with a blanket of high density housing in stepped penthouses or multi-storey flat blocks based on the town centre itself (*Town Handbook*, **17**).

> The Township has been designed as a compact urban growth point for the accommodation of intensively developed small and medium sized industries with a limited potential for expansion employing 60–80 persons per acre . . . selection has therefore been concentrated on the precision engineering and electrical industrial together with service and maintenance industries able to contribute to the general development of the township (*Information Digest*, **6**).

Thus Killingworth was planned as a housing locale for about 20 000 people rehoused from inner urban Tyneside, as an industrial location for small and medium science and engineering-based industries, and as a shopping and administrative centre for about 30 000 people in the general Longbenton area. At the time the optimism was very great. Witness:

> Killingworth is therefore not just another housing estate but a Township of exceptional amenity designed for the needs of tomorrow as well as today. (Councillor Danny Hogg, Chairman Longbeaton Housing Committee, 1966) Now let us look into the future – is it conceivable that any responsible authority would allow so notable and imaginative a piece of urban construction to languish (R. Gazzard: Killingworth Architect/Planner, 1967).

Languish is perhaps too mild a word for what has actually happened. The industrial development has not materialized because the Township was finished just as the crisis took effect. The industrial estate was intended to provide an employment base of 6000–7000 jobs. There are now, even counting the promised employment in the Findus food-processing plant, less than half that number. The British Gas Research Station, which represents the science input offers few jobs to council tenants in the area except as cleaners etc. Councillor Hogg was right. Killingworth was built for the future, but it was not the future that he looked forward to. The Township makes a splendid ghetto: it even looks just like a gaol. In other words, the effect of the construction of Killingworth has been to immediately peripheralize its residents, both spatially and economically. Produced by the state at the end of the beginning of the crisis, it relocated a population precisely at the time when "meso-economic"[10] multi-national capital had no *direct* use for that population in that place. Killingworth's residents were forced into the SRA almost straightaway.

And what is the reproductive position of the inhabitants of this reserve space. Killingworth Towers were system-built rubbish. The effect has been that this development which was only completed in the mid 1970s is already "Difficult to let, difficult to live in and difficult to get out of" (Taylor, 1979). Taylor's two papers with this title show clearly that Killingworth far from being the "Science City" of tomorrow has become the ghetto of today. Of the three elements in Killingworth's public sector stock one, the "Towers", is disasterous with 55% of the residents having applied for transfers out of it. Another, the flat roofed "Old Garths" are merely poor housing. Only the conventionally built "New Garths" are acceptable and they are rapidly becoming a "medical ghetto". A housing career in Killingworth runs on the lines of if the Towers make you ill enough, then you might get into the New Garths before the Towers kill you. Taylor's study of allocations to Killingworth shows the way in which the Towers have taken over from the South Meadowell as the sump of North Tyneside, and the location of the worst

Figure 2. Killingworth Towers, North Tyneside.

treated of the SRA. In particular they are where the living in and the homeless get housed (Taylor, 1979, Table 1). Taylor concludes:

> From this interpretation it is clear that public intervention in housing will not radically alter the structural inequalities although it might change the spatial manifestations of the inequalities by dispersing the zone of transition (1979, 1307).

In reality North Tyneside (the conglomerate authority made up of the industrial towns of Wallsend and North Shields, Newcastle City's overspill area in Longbenton, the coastal suburb of Whitley Bay, and Pit Villages like Backworth and Burradon) has not had any "zones of transition" since immigration into the area ceased in 1920, following the collapse of the war industries responsible for Tyneside's massive growth between 1890 and 1920. Rather there have been locations for the SRA, when one existed. In inner North Shields in the multi-occupied riverside tenements until 1930, on the inter-war Meadowell Estate, made up of flats in blocks of four until the tenants forced the improvement of the area and now, among other places, in Killingworth.

It is very important to realize that the effects of these spatial policies are not confined to location. How is the SRA dealt with when you've got it where you want it, nicely tucked away in the ghetto. Housing Management is one answer, and indeed this particular strategy yet again proves the Geordie adage that "there's nowt new under the sun". The operation of coercive social work practice as a method of controlling the SRA was developed in East London in the 1880s by the Charity Organization Society. The particular innovation was the development of casework orientated towards the supposed inadequacy of individuals which was seen as the explanation of their condition. This remains the central basis of social work to this day. The collective equivalent which was explicitly informed by COS perspectives was detailed supervisory housing management as practised by Octavia Hill. This sort of activity was not accepted passively by its recipients. It played no small part in provoking that great socialist uprising of the East London residuum which was described by Engels:

> The revival of the East End of London remains one of the greatest and most fruitful facts of this *fin de siècle*, and glad and proud I am to have lived to see it (1892).

Like bad winters, coercive housing management seems to come round in the 80s of a century. Let us look at its contemporary form. Its object is "difficult to let" estates, but as the authors of a recent Department of Environment report indicate:

> The term (difficult to let) is misleading . . . in that such estates may be easy to let, but only to households in need of immediate rehousing who cannot afford to wait for an offer which really suits them . . . 'Difficult to Let' is a description

in most cases of the process whereby certain estates progressively accumulate a concentration of families who are on low incomes, who are unemployed or who have other related social problems. This tendency for families who are less able to cope to end up in housing which is in least demand we have called 'social polarization' (DOE, 1980, 1).

It's all so unfortunate. To be fair to the DOE authors, they do recognize that there is some system in this, at least to the extent that "social polarization" is only possible because some public sector housing stock is a lot worse than the rest. However, having "failed to cope" with capitalist underdevelopment and achieved the status of being unemployed, single-parent, low income (either as a wage or as a benefit) etc., and having been consigned to the dump, are the SRA then left to get on with it? No they are not, because one of their ways of getting on with it involves *inter alia* not paying their rent. We are not starry eyed "radical deviance theorists" about all this. Some of the individualistic vandalism, low-level criminality etc. which occurs in these locales is totally unproductive in any socialist sense. It causes some bother for the state's reproductive mechanisms and a lot more for the neighbours. Being unwilling to pay rent for rubbish is another matter, and even more of another matter is collective organization around the issue of the conditions of reproduction, autonomous action by SRA tenants as tenants.[11]

The DOE study was not merely intended to describe. It was very much an attempt at producing a strategy for coping with the problems represented by these ghettoes. Gateshead MBC on Tyneside provided some examples used by the DOE. According to a report produced by Gateshead CCP (Comprehensive Community Project: the managerial controlled successor to the CDPs, see Mayo, 1979), of Gateshead's 38 000 public sector dwellings (45% of housing stock and housing 57% of the population), some 3500 were "difficult to let" (CCP, 1978). The Labour-controlled local state's response is represented by the Springwell Project. Springwell is an estate of 850 conventional dwellings (albeit large and difficult to heat), built in the early 1960s for families slum-cleared from central Gateshead. Over their period of analysis, the CCP found that 66% of single-parent families and 75% of large families rehoused in the Wrekenton housing management area were allocated to Springwell, which contained about 10% of the available stock. The estate had a long history of rent arrear problems. The solution adopted was the establishment of the Springwell Area Management team, a joint project with housing and social services involvement. It consists of eight community workers who, among other things, are concerned with breaking down the tenants mistrust of the local authority. The Team's role is generally defined thus:

> The Team will make an important departure from traditional practice by adopting the casework system which will enable them to identify problems at an early stage and take appropriate action, as well as monitoring and reviewing problems (Springwell Project, 1980, 3).

This is of course precisely the coercive casework management style devised by Octavia Hill for the residuum in the East End in the 1880s, and here it is being applied to their equivalents in the 1980s. The procedure is currently being extended, using "Inner Area Partnership" funding to another estate, St. Cuthbert's Village, with a history of organized tenant militancy. Of course these schemes are contradictory. For example they do improve repairs

Figure 3. St. Cuthbert's Village, Gateshead.

procedures and local authority committment to the general environment of these estates, but they also collect rents and co-opt protest. That is what the DOE sees as the function of community development in such locales (DOE, 1980, 9). These ghettoes are one locale in space of the SRA today. Their extent is growing. In Liverpool, according to a *Guardian* article of 8 Jan. 1982, 25% of all Local Authority housing is "difficult to let". Housing, far more than Income Maintenance which is the other major area of state activity involved in the reproduction of the SRA, can and does serve as the basis for collective resistance. The North East Tenants Organization is by far the most important "reproductive" specific organization on Tyneside, and to a considerable degree it is based in the "difficult to let" estates. The SRA has been recreated and emmiserated as a mechanism for coping with the crisis but it is fighting back. We turn in conclusion to the implications of that struggle.

4. Conclusion

This paper has attempted to employ the autonomist perspective in understanding the character of spatial policy in Britain in the context of the current crisis. We have emphasized "ghettoization" in the framework of the city as a strategy of capital in this "war of position"[12] because we think this is of crucial importance in relation to the ability of the emmiserated part of the working class to act on its own behalf. As we shall see, we regard spatial location as of crucial importance in providing a potential for such action. We have also drawn attention to the "under-developing" character of regional policy, and the implication of our account is that the process of peripheralization and the creation of "reserve space" are central and related aspects of the development of the contemporary crisis. There is a lot more to reserve space than just the existence of council-house ghettoes. Policies like the development of enterprise zones (see Anderson, this volume), and at a slightly earlier time the Category D settlement policy for the mining villages of County Durham need to be interpreted in this way just as much as does the ghettoization with which they are so often associated.[13]

Nonetheless ghettoization is a useful area to consider both because it is important in itself and because it reveals some of the strengths and weaknesses of the autonomist account. Historically Tyneside, the locale of our case material, has a history of centrality in production and in related class action. Tyneside's unions date back to the organization of Pitmen, Keelmen and Seamen in the "Trinity" in the sixteenth century. In 1871 the 9-hour day strike won by the Tyneside engineers, with the support of the First International which helped prevent the recruitment of Belgian and German blacklegs, was one of the key working-class victories in establishing centrality and shifting capital's focus to relative surplus value. Although the Tyneside working-class is the product of massive immigration, it is not divided on ethnic or sectarian lines.[14] In the late nineteenth and early twentieth century, Tyneside's importance in coal production, arms manufacturing and shipbuilding made it a central place with a predominantly central working-class.

And yet there was division. The Board of Trade Report of 1908 on Wages, Prices and Rents in the principle working-class towns identifies "occupationally" based wage differential and rent-based residential segregation (see North Tyneside CDP, 1977). What seems to us to be of the greatest importance is the recognition of the way in which the working class challenged these divisions, always in a contradictory way, but challenging them nevertheless. The long-term demand for "full employment" (which is by no means the same thing as a demand for work) was one part of this challenge and so successful was class action that under-employment disappeared for all practical purposes (i.e. with the exception of casual work in construction and outwork as domestic production). At the same time the class was on the offensive against the quality base in housing segregation, and indeed differentiation in reproduction in general. The outcome was a massive increase in the social wage. This was the action of a working class which has been described as unique in Europe in that until the present crisis, its last major defeat was in the period after 1926. It is this twin offensive in production and reproduction that has provoked the crisis of today.

This relatively homogenous working class with its well co-ordinated offensive in both production and reproduction has been extra-ordinarily difficult to contend with. Ghettoization has been one strategy for dividing and setting against, putting the respectable to control to the residuum. A history of Labour-Council management of ghetto areas, which areas have nevertheless been bastions of support for the Labour Party, well illustrates the effectiveness of such an approach. A history of Labour-Party control of urban Tyneside since the 1960s is a history of crisis management by the political organization of the working class. St. Cuthbert's Village, the "difficult to let" estate, was used as the set for the siege estate in the recent TV film *United Kingdom* (which dealt with the taking over of an "overspending" Labour-controlled local authority by a central government Commissioner, filmed December 1981). It is very important to realize that the relations between Gateshead's Labour Councillors, overwhelmingly drawn from the respectable, older and central working-class (and this matters because it determines job history), and the overwhelmingly "residual" residents of St. Cuthbert's Village are a great deal more complex than being a matter of identity and support, as was suggested in the film. And this is in a place with no ethnic or sectarian basis for division!

On the face of things, these developments can support that version of the autonomist account which assigns revolutionary potential to the marginalized "social proletariat" alone, acting *against* the "traditional" or central working-class whose unions and political parties are incorporated in the state system. This mirror image of Poulantzian distortion, which defined the working class as only those who directly produced surplus value, seems to us to be absurd. However a rejection of this absurdity does not involve a rejection of the importance of struggle in reproduction *and* peripheral production. As Negri says:

> Now at this point I should answer those jackal voices that I already hear howling: I am not saying that the Mirafiori (Fiat's major plant) worker is not an exploited worker (this is the extent to which you have to go in order to polemicize with jackals!). I am saying that the 'Party of Mirafiori' must today live with the politics of the proletarian majority and that any struggle which is restricted purely to the necessary struggle in the factory, and which is not linked to the wider majority of the proletariat is a position that is bound to lose. *The factory struggle must live with the wider majority of the proletariat.* (Negri's emphasis, 1979, 110)

In Gateshead as we write (January 1982), the overall registered unemployment rate is 20%. In the working-class ghettoes the *real* unemployment rate clearly exceeds 50%. The marginalized are now the majority, and in Gateshead and places like it that is a new thing. It is in this context that ghettoization matters.

In the past one of us who is active in local politics on Tyneside has had reservations about "autonomous" tenants' action. On reflection he is now persuaded otherwise. Even in this homogeneous place we need to realize that the autonomous struggles of the various sectors of the working class are successful only in the complimentary interaction of struggle. To seek immediate alliances on ideological grounds against the common enemy will only subsume one struggle to another and perpetuate the hierarchical fragmentations that have been imposed on the class by capital. To break down these hierarchical divisions of the class (which are in fact the key to capitalist power) is the aim of the working class, but the nature of this division must be realized; capital controls the working class by mediating power through one sector of the class to dominate another. That is what Labour councillors are doing to ghetto residents.

The problem that autonomist analysis leaves unresolved here is the problem of the party. The Labour Party on Tyneside is even more hegemonic than the Communist Party in Italy. What is the relationship of autonomous struggles by the marginalized to the Party? Clearly they must not be surbordinated. Equally it seems to us that mere confrontation with the party as party is wrong. We can do no more here than identify what seems to us to be a crucial absence in autonomist analysis, one of which many "autonomist" writers in Italy are perfectly well aware.

We want to return for a moment to thinking about struggle in the ghettoes. Let us say explicitly what we see as happening here. For those without work, common spatial location in reproduction is serving as the basis for collective action. That is why the ghetto, a mechanism for division, is contradictorily a source of class action. But crucially important as reproduction is, it is not the whole of life for all ghetto residents. Many remain involved in production and especially peripheralized production. They have the status of "massified workers", part of that growing segment of workers who are unskilled interchangeable components in the production process: a group corresponding in many respects to what Marx called the "floating" form of the reserve army. Underemployment is back with a vengeance. We have reservations about a notion of "social proletariat" in that it seems to ignore this production experience which, as Friend and Metcalf have suggested, belongs on the emmiserated side of any divide in the working class. The character of production experience in this sort of work is clearly one which poses major difficulties for collective action. It is part-time, isolated, weak. The traditional answer has been general unions, but with the rare and now it seems temporary, exceptions of those male workers for whom general unions have achieved central status, such unions organized on bureaucratic formats are perhaps the best example of why "Poor Peoples' " movements fail (see Piven and Cloward, 1977). Here again location in reproduction is crucial, because historically it has served as the basis for the production organization of the residuum and may well do so again. It is the *potential* for collective action about reproduction and production which is the basis of the contradictory character of spatial segregation. This is what we are getting at when we talk about the collective power of "the reserve community".

Let us conclude on a hopeful note. Our account as we said at the beginning has been one of defeats and emmiseration, and nevertheless we assert the capacity of the working class for transforming this situation. We have both been involved for a long time in community action. What we have got from the autonomist perspective in relation to the situations with which we have been dealing is a coherent *if incomplete* account of the logic of that action. Certainly on Tyneside the working class is beginning to stagger back onto the offensive, considerably after the marginalized inner-city and black working-class of Liverpool and Brixton. The main movement at the moment is among the ever-growing residuum in the ghettoes. As O'Connor says, it's a matter of what is made to happen.

Acknowledgements

The authors are grateful for discussion of an earlier draft at the Urban and Regional Seminar, LSE. Photographs for figures 2 and 3 by David Byrne.

References[15]

Ball, M. (1978). British housing policy and the housebuilding industry, *Capital and Class*, **4**, 78–99.

Benwell Community Development Project (1978). "The making of a ruling class", Newcastle.

Boggs, C. (1976). "Gramsci's Marxism", Pluto, London.

Branson, N. (1980). "Poplarism", Lawrence & Wishart, London.

Braverman, M. (1974). Labour and monopoly capital: the degradation of work in the twentieth-century, *Monthly Review Press*, New York.

Byrne, D. S. (1980). The decline in the quality of council housing in inter-war North Shields, *in* J. Melling (ed.), "Housing, social policy and the state", Croom Helm, London.

Byrne, D. S. (1982). Class and the local state, *International Journal of Urban and Regional Research*, **6**, 1, 61–82.

Byrne, D. S. and Damer, S. (1980). The state, the balance of class forces and early housing legislation, *in* M. Paddon (ed.), "Housing, construction and the state", Political Economy of Housing Workshop, CSE, London.

Castells, M. (1975). Immigrant workers and class struggles in advanced capitalism, *Politics and Society*, **5**, 1, 33–66.

Comprehensive Community Project (1978). "Review of housing allocation system", Gateshead Metropolitan Borough Council.

Cleaver, H. (1977). Malaria, the politics of public health and the international crisis, *Review of Radical Political Economics*, **9**, 1, 81–103.

Cleaver, H. (1979). "Reading Capital politically", Harvester Press, Brighton.

Duncan, M. (1981). Microelectronics: five areas of subordination, *in* L. Levidow and B. Young (eds), *Science, Technology and the Labour Process*, CSE, London.

Conference of Socialist Economists (1976). "The labour process and class strategies", CSE, London.

Department of Employment. (1980). "An investigation of difficult to let houses", HMSO, London.

Engels, F. (1952). "Preface" to the English Edition of "The Condition of the Working Class in England in 1844", Allen & Unwin, London.

Foster, J. (1977). "Class struggle and industrial revolution", Weidenfeld and Nicholson, London.

Friedman, A. (1977). "Industry and Labour: class struggle at work and monopoly capitalism", Macmillan, London.

Friend, A. and Metcalf, A. (1981). "Slump city: the politics of mass unemployment", Pluto Press, London.

Gough, I. (1979). "The political economy of the welfare state", Macmillan, London.

Harris, R. (1980). Community action and class struggle in Kingston, *Union of Socialist Geographers – Newsletter*, **5**, 4–6.

Hudson, R. (1979). New Towns and spatial policy – the case of Washington New Town, *in* G. Ives and T. Lobstein (eds), "Proceedings of the Bartlett Summer School", University College, London.

Holland, S. (1975). "The socialist challenge", Quartet, London.

"Information Digest 1978". (Killingsworth Township), Killingsworth.

Marx, K. (1977). "Capital" (Vol. 1). Progress Publishers, Moscow.

Massey, D. B. and Meegan, R. A. (1978). Industrial restructuring versus the cities, *Urban Studies*, **15**, 3, 273–288.

Mayo, M. (1979). Beyond CDP: reaction and community action, *in* M. Brake and R. Bailey (eds), "Radical social work practice", Edward Arnold, London.

Melling, J. (ed.) (1980). "Housing, social policy and the state", Croom Helm, London.

Miliband, R. (1977). "Marxism and politics", Oxford University Press, London.

Montano, M. (1975). Notes on the international crisis, *Zerowork*.

Negri, T. (1979). Capitalist domination and working class sabotage, *in* "Red Notes Working class autonomy and the crisis", CSE, London.

North Tyneside CDP. (1977). North Shields: working for change in a working class area – the action groups, Final Report, Vol. 4.

North Tyneside CDP (1977). North Shields: working class politics and housing 1900–1977", Final Report, Vol. 4.

Partridge, H. (1981). Interview with Toni Negri, *Capital and Class*, **13**, 129–138.

Piven, F. and Cloward, R. (1977). "Poor peoples' movements – why they succeed and how they fail", Vintage Books, New York.

O'Connor, J. (1981). The meaning of crisis, *International Journal of Urban and Regional Research*, **5**, 3, 301–329.

Perrons, D. (1981). The role of Ireland in the new international division of labour: a proposed framework for regional analysis, *Regional Studies*, **15**, 81–100.

Ryan, P. (1976). The poor law in 1926, *in* M. Morris (ed.), "The General Strike", Penguin, London.

Springwell Project (1980). "Initial Statement", Gateshead, Metropolitan Borough Council.

Stedman Jones, G. (1971). "Outcast London: a study in the relationship between classes in Victorian society". Oxford University Press, London.

Taylor, P. J. (1979). Difficult to let, difficult to live in and sometimes difficult to get out of, *Environment and Planning A*, **11**, 1305–20.

Timms, D. W. G. (1971). "The urban mosaic", Cambridge University Press, Cambridge.

"Township Handbook", (1966). (Killingsworth Township), Killingsworth.

Wiener, R. (1976). "The rape and plunder of the Shankill", Notaems, Belfast.

Notes

1. Absolute Surplus Value is the SV expropriated from a given product by paying the worker less for the same work or the same for more work. Thus it was the form of expropriation which lay behind disputes about the length of the working day. Relative Surplus Value comes into the picture when the productivity of labour is increased by the use of machinery and/or the cost of reproducing labour power is reduced by a cheapening of food, housing etc. With this form of exploitation, the workers may be better off in a material sense, but their rate of exploitation is increased because they retain a smaller proportion of a larger product.

2. This formulation does not merely replace capital by the state. Rather it is a way of thinking about the relations among capital, the state and the working class without adopting the get-out procedure of talking about the state as "relatively autonomous" from the capitalist relations of production. Baldly put, our argument looks functionalist, but the intention is quite the reverse, because the autonomist activity of the working class extends into the realm of the state. This brings in the problem of reformism, and we should note that we find the autonomist account seriously inadequate in contending with the relationship between reformism and the working class.

3. All this amounts to is a rejection of "workerism". There is a tendency in Italy within Autonomia which does regard the "social proletariat" i.e. the reproductive workers, as the only force against capital. As we show in the conclusion, this is not Negri's position, and is completely at variance with the significance that the autonomists and their predecessors, notably C. L. R. James, have attached to the labour process in production.

4. Partridge is over-reacting. A careful reading of the history of the working class in capitalism shows us that since the 1870s, reproductive struggle has been a major part of class struggle for the metropolitan working-class, particularly in Britain. Negri is clearly aware for example of the importance of the inter-war National Unemployed Workers Movement in this context.

5. As we indicate in the conclusion, we have reservations about the term "social proletariat" because its emphasis on reproduction does not allow for a consideration of the position of those in peripheralized production.

6. For example Foster, 1977.

7. That is the radical reformist activities of the Poplar Guardians and Borough Councillors, and their imitators in many labour local authorities, during the 1920s (see Branson, 1980).

8. This actually extended for practical purposes until 1954, but the Macmillan programme of 1951–1954 was clearly a lead into the reviving of private sector provision and the reassertion of owner-occupation. The point is that in principle, since 1890, and in practical terms since 1919, the state in Britain has been directly engaged in housing provision because the private market was not adequate for the physical or social reproduction of the whole of the working class.

9. Of course the *production* of housing is production like any other. While we regard Ball's (1978) account as the epitome of capital logic, his assertion of the importance of production of houses, in considering the development of housing policy, is pertinent.

10. The term is Holland's (1975). It describes a situation in which multi-national enterprises operate beyond the micro-economic level of a multiplicity of firms. We think the "meso", which means middle, is an erroneous description. Holland puts this level between the "micro"-firm and the "macro"-national economy, but the central relevant part of his thesis is that meso-economic firms are so large and multi-national as to be beyond the control of states operating at the level of national economies.

11. For a series of examples see North Tyneside CDP, 1977, Vol. 4.

12. The term is Gramsci's (see Boggs, 1976).

13. Category D refers to a policy in County Durham planning whereby "redundant" pit villages were to be eliminated through planning and housing policies and their populations concentrated in new growth centres. Category A was a growth centre; Category B was slow growth; Category C was slow decline and villages were put into this category, so it is said, if they had stone-fronted buildings in the front street; Category D stood for destroy.

14. For example there has been no anti-Irish action on Tyneside since the 1860s, although Tyneside's population contains as large an Irish Catholic element as Glasgow, and very nearly as large an element as Belfast.

15. Community Development Project (CDP) Publications are now available from 85–87, Adelaide Terrace, Benwell, Newcastle upon Tyne.

SEVEN

Industrial change, the domestic economy and home life

SUZANNE MACKENZIE and DAMARIS ROSE

(April 1982)

1. Introduction: "separate spheres" and the reproduction of labour-power in the city: the need for a synthesis

For the last fifteen years or so, conference papers, seminar discussions and "comment" sections of geographical journals have been forecasting and identifying a transition (or, less kindly, a crisis) in geographic theory and method. This is hardly surprising. As geographers, we are concerned to understand changing relationships between people and the environment, and the nature of these relationships appeared increasingly more fluid and less certain. By the late 1960s and early 1970s, geographers found themselves living in the midst of a bewildering variety of protests and problems. These coalesced in community-action movements, youth and student movements, ethnic movements, anti-war movements, workers movements, nationalist movements, ecological movements and so on. All of these were expressions of hitherto invisible conflicts (at least as far as geographers were concerned) in the fabric of social life. And, all of these movements appeared to make unprecedented and apparently interconnected demands upon space and resources. In other words, they seemed deeply geographical.

A growing number of urban geographers became concerned and involved with these movements and the problems they expressed: as observers, as community advocates and as urban dwellers. In the process, they "discovered" a great deal about urban process and the lives of city residents; they "discovered" ghettoes, inner-city decline, noise pollution, social injustice. They also found that geographic data and the categories within which it had been confined had escaped from the computer and had become objects of urban struggle, while the "subjects" of social analysis had become activists in urban struggle. Sayer (1979) provides a useful commentary on the dichotomy between "understanding models" and "understanding the city".

One of the most hallowed analytical separations in human geography was that between "economic" and "social" geography: between the analysis of the location of industries and commerce and analysis of the spatial patterns of residential environments and "communities". This division of intellectual labour was predicated upon the assumption that there was a natural separation in society between the production of goods and services on the one hand, and the neighbourhood, home and family life, on the other; in other words between the "sphere of production" and the "sphere of reproduction of labour". Geographers viewed the real spatial fragmentation of the various dimensions of human life in the typical modern western city (places for work, places for living in, places for shopping, places for education, places for amusement, and so on), and concluded that these various dimensions warranted analytically-separate sub-disciplines or "special interest fields". Even the nascent radical and Marxist urban theory was distracted by these spatial and functional separations of home and wage workplace, and so neglected those processes linking the "non-capitalist" sphere of home, family and community to the "capitalist" sphere of industrial production and circulation. It too divided its analysis into "consumption" issues and "production" issues.[1]

This paper attempts to bridge this analytic separation by outlining the relationships between the major activities that go on in the home and those that go on in the workplace. We ask precisely how the domestic economy, and home life, have been related to the development of specifically capitalist ways of organizing production. And, through examining this relationship historically, we seek to move closer to an analytical synthesis of the "separate spheres". Our analysis will situate these historical processes within the developing geography of the city, which they also help to shape. In doing this, it will discuss the emergence of "common sense" understandings of home life, and it will draw out the specific importance of changes in women's activities, within and outside of the labour-force, in directing the shifting interrelationships of "home" and "workplace". First of all, however, we shall try to show *why* it is important to bridge this analytical gap.

If geographers assumed that there was naturally a separation between home life and working life, between the residential suburb and the factory or office, it seemed to them equally natural that this separate sphere of home life would be maintained as a "domestic economy" by the suburban wife and her nuclear family. While the "ideal home-maker" was rarely an explicit presence in geographic theory, in the application of this theory to policies for housing and suburban development, she was an essential, if shadowy, part of the scenario of the "ideal home".[2] The words of a spokesman at a recent international symposium on housing policy explain why:

The home must be more than just shelter. It should be a place where the family unit . . . can live in comfort, with peace of mind, and in a climate which will enable the repair and regeneration of mind and spirit so necessary in today's society. This ideal state is difficult to achieve. (Millward, 1977, 70)

In other words, while the home was a "separate sphere" from that of working life, it played a crucial part in maintaining "today's society" both on a day-to-day and generational basis, precisely *because* it was such a separate sphere in terms of space and social relations. For the home was the haven, the refuge, the place where the physical and emotional maintenance of the worker was carried on, readying him to go back to work in the morning, clothed, fed, satisfied, and relatively willing to put in an efficient day's work on the production line or in the office. The home was also the place where children were created and raised in an environment that would encourage them, too, to grow up to be relatively willing and efficient workers in modern capitalist society. Central to this process was the domestic labour of the housewife.

This day-to-day and generational renewal of people-as-workers, carried on in the home, is an important part of what marxists refer to as the "reproduction of labour-power", which, in its simplest sense, means the renewal of the capacity to work.[3] Since home life plays such an important part in this reproduction process, it clearly should not be separate in analytical terms from industrial life, from the "sphere of production". Indeed, if labour-power were not continually reproduced in the commodity-form (that is, workers having to sell their labour as a commodity for a wage, because they have no access to independent ways of making a living), and at a particular socially defined standard, the capitalist economy would not continue to function. William Beveridge put this very well in his 1942 report which effectively set the guidelines for the post-war British welfare state:

The great majority of married women must be regarded as occupied on work which is vital enough though unpaid, without which their husbands could not do their paid work and without which the nation could not continue.

Yet, until recently, geographers were able to ignore these connections, largely through ignoring the women who actively *made* the connections in their everyday work as keepers of the ideal home. Geographers ignored the fact that women were workers who reproduced labour-power through domestic production.

However, by the 1970s, the daily lives of women were clearly revealing not only the existence of "functional" connections between the two spheres, but were also forcing a recognition of some major problems that were emerging as a result of this separation. For women's roles were multiplying, while the geographical separations of the different spheres remained writ large in the relatively fixed spatial structure of the city and suburban milieux. Women's increased participation in the waged and salaried labour-force, added onto their domestic and community roles, started to pose significant practical challenges. Those concerned with the restructuring and relocation of industry and commerce were confronted with the "feminization" of the labour force: the increasing proportions of women engaging in wage labour (see Table 1 for the British case). As we shall see, it is impossible to understand either the nature of the changes in female labour-force participation or the tendencies for women to be concentrated in certain types of employment without considering their links to changes in women's domestic and community work.

TABLE 1. *Women's participation in wage-labour force, Britain 1921–1971.*

Year	Percentage of women over 15 and over in wage-labour force*	Percentage of married women in wage-labour force	Percentage of married women aged 45–54 in wage-labour force
1921	32·3	8·7	8·4
1931	34·2	10·0	8·5
1951	34·7	21·7	23·7
1961	37·4	29·7	36·1
1966	42·2	38·1	49·8
1971	42·7	42·2	56·3

* except 1921 when figures relate to those aged 12 and over, and 1931 when figures relate to those aged 14 and over.
Source: Census of Population.

Many other urban issues are also affected by the shifting relationships between women's waged work and their work as reproducers of labour-power. These include community movements, patterns of income distribution in cities and regions, journeys to work, shopping and residential patterns, demographic trends and needs for particular social services in specific locations. But only in recent years has serious attention been paid to the impacts of women's dual roles on these aspects of urban and regional development, and the impact on women of a legacy of urban spatial structure and social infrastructure that was not designed for women's dual roles in the contemporary city.

At first, geographers defined the "problem" solely in terms of the constraints imposed on women's activity patterns by the existing spatial and social context, and how women could, and "should", adapt to this "given" context. For instance, they documented the special peculiarities of women's journey-to-work patterns, and investigated the time–space constraints imposed upon their lives by the geographical separation of the places where their waged, domestic and community-based work had to be carried out. None of this research questioned the nature of the "dual role" itself, or the reasons for its enshrinement in a city of "separate spheres".[4]

However, the challenge posed to geographical analysis, and to the future of the city, was and is more fundamental. It could not be met by research using standard geographical assumptions and frameworks. The daily lives of a growing number of women, combined with the emergence of feminism as a powerful social force, are actively denying and attacking the "commonsense" view of a separate sphere of home life, serviced by women, as a "deep and natural desire" to which all aspire. Through collective action in housing struggles and community movements, through more private struggles within the home and family themselves and through theoretical work, many women have challenged the "naturalization" of the domestic sphere as the place where they should reproduce labour-power in a form suitable for the continuance of capitalist production. Feminists have demonstrated that, for women in their domestic role, the ideal single-family home has always been primarily a *workplace* for their reproductive work, and often a very oppressive and isolating one, rather than a haven.[5] This remains true even when they are also wage- or salary-earners outside the home (the classic "dual role").

To understand the import of these changes and challenges for urban life and urban analysis, we need a perspective on the city which focusses on the relationship between the social production and circulation of commodities and the reproduction of labour-power. These relationships are complex and constantly changing.

We have suggested that the home is a key site of the day-to-day and generational reproduction of labour-power, and that this is oriented towards fulfilling the needs of capitalist production. However, this "need" for an "appropriate" mode of reproduction of labour-power does not explain the historical *origins* of, and specific development of, the separate "domestic sphere" of home life itself. This sphere is viewed today as natural and inevitable. We shall argue, however, that the history of the "separate sphere" has to be investigated in the context of working-people's struggles around control over the means of production and subsistence: struggles that were integral to the development of industrial capitalism.

We shall also argue, as suggested in this introduction, that the maintenance of a separate sphere of the domestic economy and home life in the present-day city is generating a number of conflicts, which geographers need to address. These conflicts have been mobilized by feminist practice and theory to challenge not only the spatial organization of geographic theory and the city, but also the rationale for the maintenance of the separate sphere itself in its present form. They must be analysed, we hold, in terms of the relationship between the "sphere of production" and the "sphere of reproduction".

The remainder of this chapter will attempt to use these preliminary analytical insights to guide an historical analysis of the interactive processes shaping the direction of industrial change, the specific development of the domestic economy of the household, the generation of "commonsense" social definitions of home life and the experience and meaning of these definitions for working men and women. Empirically, we root our analysis in British and North American urban and industrial development from the beginnings of industrial capitalism to the present day.

2. The transition to capitalism and the redirection of household production

2.1 Work and home life in feudal society

We refer here to European society from about 900 to the early stages of capitalist development in the 1500s. Within this period, society changed a great deal, but was generally characterized by a unity of production and reproduction of labour. The household was a producer of goods that were primarily for its own use. The rhythms of production were regulated by the need for the items produced. In rural areas, households produced most of what they consumed. The work involved in the production of goods, and the work involved in the reproduction of labour-power, were unified both spatially and functionally in the pre-capitalist household. The household itself controlled its own means of production. There was, none the less, a division of labour by age and sex within the household, and its organization was in general patriarchal (Tilley and Scott, 1978, 21).

In towns, households also produced some goods as commodities for sale and purchased many necessities in the market-place. Yet the household was still largely in control of the resources it needed for production and subsistence.

Feudal society was no utopia. Class and gender relations were frequently oppressive. Levels of subsistence for peasants and for poorer urban dwellers were generally low, and, from necessity, hours of work were often long, while work itself was often arduous.

On the other hand, however, working hours and the organization of work-processes were self-regulated, while work cultures were closely knit with the cultures of the community. Often, unrelated workers lived with the family (Mumford, 1961). Work cultures were convivial, and despite their arduousness, embodied elements of "play" (Clayre, 1974). These features, combined with the spatial proximity or identity of workplace and home, minimized both the necessity and the possibility of separate blocks of space and time whose role was *defined* in terms of escape and recovery from working life. Indeed, there is considerable evidence that the position of women, especially those who owned property or were guild members, was far less restrictive than in early industrial capitalist society (Beard, 1962; Clark, 1968).

2.2 The transition to capitalism

The transition to industrial capitalism eventually destroyed this self-regulating unity of production and domestic life, and fundamentally transformed the nature of the domestic economy as well as the nature and purpose of household production. Nonetheless, this process took several hundred years to become fully effective in all branches of industry in Britain and Continental Europe.[6] The small-scale production of commodities by the household and workshop came increasingly under the sway of merchants and middlemen with links to an increasingly national and international economy. Production became less and less oriented toward immediate need, and more and more oriented toward making profits to reinvest in expanded production in order to create more profits. The household economy became more tied to the world of the market. It became dependent for its subsistence on selling first goods and then its own labour for cash. The viability of independent producers was being undermined. In urban areas, they had lost access to their means of production through intractable indebtedness to merchants who increasingly controlled trade, and through the process of competition itself. In rural areas, agricultural people were dispossessed of their means of subsistence in the process of the consolidation of vast amounts of capital and land in relatively few pockets. The creation of these two "poles" allowed capitalists to put the new labour-force to work in the new factories and thus to set in motion the dynamic of surplus-valve production and self-expansion of capital: the production of value and surplus value, the continual separation of workers from what they produce, accumulation and reinvestment for further profit; in other words: the motor of industrial capitalism (Dobb, 1963; Thompson, 1966; give detailed historical examples for particular industries and areas).

Initially, however, the location of production remained entirely in the household and small workshop, under the "putting out" system. The day-to-day, hour-to-hour carrying out of the labour process remained under control of the household. But the urban merchant or "factor" gathered an increasingly large share of the surplus product, while the processes of trade concentrated wealth in the hands of the nascent urban capitalists (Marx, 1959, 332–334 and 1976, 1022–1023). "Productive" and "reproductive" work were still largely spatially unified in the household, but they were diverging in terms of their purpose. The motive of profit for its own sake came to regulate the household's production to an ever-increasing degree. The "unity" of the household was preserved but its independence was being eroded (Zaretsky, 1976, 46).

As the factory system spread to more and more branches of industry, the old small workshops increasingly lost their independence as productive units. While some of these workshops survived in "subordinated" forms (in effect parts of the factory, but located outside it), small producers increasingly lost control over their means of production and were thrown into the groundswell of the factory labour-force. This happened on a massive scale in England in the early nineteenth century when the leading domestic industry (cotton textiles) was transformed into the leading factory industry (and see Rogers, this volume, for a later case and its spatial effects). The combination of capital and technological innovations helped to revolutionize the production process, vastly increased the productivity of labour, and made possible production for profit on a scale hitherto unthought of (Marx, 1976, 560– 562). Machinery was used to "work up" global resources on a mass scale. Goods were produced for an expanding world market. The potential for capital's expansion now appeared limitless (Anderson, 1977; Engels, 1952; Mumford, 1961).

At the same time, the possibilities for change in human social relationships also appeared infinite, and frighteningly so. This expansion of capitalist production initially took place through a lengthening of people's working hours, including those of women and children: to such an extent that it threatened to destroy the family. While workshop production under the sway of profit-seeking merchants had led to a deterioration in the conditions of work and life in the household, the *form* of the household had been preserved. But now the pre-capitalist household was all but destroyed. Its economic base had been completely eroded. Its human base was now being shattered as people's working hours were lengthened to the biological maximum, and even beyond. They were paid the barest subsistence, or even sub-subsistence wages. There was no time for a "domestic sphere" in which the goods and services necessary for the reproduction of workers could be produced through household production, because women and children were also at work in the factories (Rowbotham, 1977, 57–59). Moreover, there was no physical space for such production in the appalling housing conditions that resulted from impoverishment in the overcrowded factory towns (Gauldie, 1974, 145–148).

The pre-capitalist household, with its unity of production and reproductive work, had been destroyed, but there was as yet nothing to replace it. Meanwhile epidemics such as cholera swept industrial cities and extremely high rates of infant mortality (Gauldie, 1974, 101–112) demonstrated forcefully that labour-power was not being reproduced adequately, neither from the consideration of the continued expansion of capitalist production nor from the point of view of working-class people themselves (Anderson, 1977; Engels, 1952). This resulted in the emergence of struggles *for* a separate "domestic sphere", safe from the heedless ravages of the factory. These were struggles which embraced some peculiar political alliances. Their outcome (like the Factory Acts in Britain which regulated working hours and conditions by age and sex) had crucial effects upon the development of the working-class household, which became an institution with a new and very specific type of domestic economy. As we shall now see, out of these struggles, new definitions of "home life" emerged. Crucially, at the same time, industrial capitalism was consolidated as a social system.

2.3 The struggle for a "separate sphere" and the creation of the new working-class family

This near-demise of family life in the industrial cities gave rise to widespread concern in mid-Victorian society (Thompson, 1963, 339–349). After lengthy and concerted campaigns by workers in the Industrial North, the Ten Hours Act was passed in 1847. This Act reduced the permitted hours of female and child labour. It provided the impetus for larger industrialists to shift toward reorganizing production processes so that profits would be extracted through fewer, more productive workers working shorter hours (Marx, 1976, 429–38).[7] At the same time, the Ten Hours Act marked the first in a whole succession of concerted measures by the state to promote and support a stable working-class family. The home was to be maintained as a "separate sphere" in which a reasonably healthy workforce could be reproduced with "appropriate" values and attitudes (Wilson, 1977, 11–15, 27–30).

Through a combination of changes in the form of exploitation of labour, the beginnings of a Welfare State and (as we shall see) a variety of struggles by working people, a new working class family began to evolve in the second half of the nineteenth century. This was far removed from the pre-capitalist household. Domestic labour, carried out mainly by the wife with help from older children, was still directed toward producing some goods for use within the household. Putting purchased goods to use in household consumption and carrying out services for household members became more central to domestic workers. A fundamental change, however, was that domestic labour now had to reproduce workers whose surplus labour would be appropriated and turned into profits for capitalists. Unless some household members sold their labour-power in exchange for a wage, the family could not obtain the basic needs of food and shelter.

Thus, the "domestic sphere" was now a primary site of the reproduction of labour power for the purposes of capitalist production. Working-class women's work within the home thus became subordinated to the imperatives of the capital accumulation process, even though the forms in which many household tasks were carried on remained unchanged from the precapitalist period. Moreover, domestic workers now had to provide physical and emotional maintenance for wage-earning husbands, who, unlike those in precapitalist society, had little or no control over their day-by-day, hour-by-hour working lives. The alienated workers would return home from work tired and very much in need of a haven (Luxton, 1981, 43–41; Rose, 1980, 73–75).

Home and workplace thus became increasingly entrenched as separate spheres (Rose, 1980, 72–3; Zaretsky, 1977, 29–35). For working-class men, the home had become a necessary haven. For their wives, however, no such separation existed. The home was primarily their workplace, and in some ways it had become a more oppressive one.

Yet the working-class household was not created and passively moulded in the "long-term interests" of capital. As capitalist processes spread into more and more branches of production, working people, both men and women, struggled to establish a separation of their daily lives from the domination of capitalist processes. The struggles for a shorter working day were struggles for time to live out and reproduce their labour outside the arena of market forces (Curtis, 1980, 125–127; Humphries, 1977, 29–33). Households also tried to maintain economic independence from the processes of capitalist production and accumulation in whatever ways were possible.

For example, many working-class families tried to produce part of their subsistence from the land, especially in the more peripheral rural areas where hard-rock mining and quarrying were predominant, but where people were not fully separated from access to the means of subsistence. A major motivation behind efforts to obtain freehold cottages with one or two acres of land (in West Cornwall and North Wales for example) was to reduce household dependence on the mining wage. Such garden plots and smallholdings typically involved the labour of all family members, and made a real difference to people's daily lives, especially in times of bad trade and recession (although by "subsidizing" the costs of reproduction, they also often enabled employers to keep wages down; Rose, 1981b, 17–22). Campaigns for allotment gardens in urban areas had similar motivations (see *Select Committee on Smallholdings*, 1889).

The separation of urban households from access to the means of production was not achieved at an even rate in all branches of industry, and the transition to a "real" subordination of labour to capitalist production proceeded irregularly (Marx, 1976, 590–592 and 595–610).[8] This uneven pace of capitalist penetration was both reflected in and affected by household struggles to retain control over production. For example, in Northampton, which was dominated by the relatively "backward" shoe-making industry, small workshop production in or adjacent to people's houses persisted even as factory-based production was expanding in the town (Fox, 1958, 137; Rose, 1981, 22–24). New workshops were set up, using a combination of unwaged family labour and one or two hired hands, while production involved often elaborate forms of subcontracting. Over time, the general tendency was for these workshops to become less and less independent. The masters of these workshops (usually the male heads of households) struggled, however, to retain some independence. They tried to maintain forms of petty commodity production in which they would control both the labour process and the *purpose* of production. Yet, increasingly, they were forced to direct their production toward the demands of large employers and middlemen. While many of the small masters still owned their means of production, sometimes including their own houses which were also their workshops, they were losing control over work schedules and hours of work. In particular, the labour of wives, children and hired "boys", now often had to be super-exploited in order for the production unit to survive. Fox (1958, 137) provides a good example for the Northampton shoe industry.

By the late nineteenth century, state agencies were coming under increasing pressure from large employers to stamp out these remaining "domestic workshops". They wanted the exploitation of labour through relative surplus value to be fully established among all employees. This was necessary in order to equalize the rate of profit within the clothing and shoe industries and also to establish the conditions for greater mechanization and speed-ups of production lines so that productivity would be increased. The central government was, however, reluctant to act. Internal Home Office documents indicate a strong concern to maintain the ideology of the home as the place where the working-man was in control of his life without interference from the state. Nothing was to be done that would "violate the principle of the Englishman's home is his castle".[9] Evidence to the 1892 *Royal Commission on Labour* similarly indicates a reluctance to antagonize the respectable working-man engaged in domestic workshop production.

However, worker struggles to maintain the home as an independent site of non-capitalist *production* were ultimately unsuccessful for the majority of working people, who became fully proletarianized. Yet state agencies were anxious to maintain the home as the separate sphere of *reproduction*: the private "castle" wherein the worker would be reproduced.[10] Ideologically, this was of great importance in the battle to force male wage-earners to acquiesce to a working life of alienated labour and to the capitalist "work ethic". This working life would seem to them worthwhile, or at least tolerable, if the wages it paid could obtain another, separable life: a private haven for rest and recreation (Rose, 1980, 72–75).

Crucial in this ideological struggle in late nineteenth century capitalist society were the twin concepts of "respectability" and "thrift" as applied to home life (Gray, 1976; Tholfsen, 1976: Rose, 1980). From the late-Victorian bourgeois viewpoint, if the regularly employed working class and their wives were imbued with the virtue of respectability and thrift, workers would be motivated to develop a material stake in the expansion of capitalist production. They would want to improve their home and family life by the purchase of consumer goods. Ideally, they would in time become homeowners, thus acquiring a "material stake in the country" (Dickens, 1978; Ehrenreich and

English, 1975; Hayden, 1981). Higher wages and shorter working hours were seen as encouraging these values; workers could concede further losses of control over their labour processes in return for more time and money for the domestic sphere (Stearns, 1975, 310ff).[11]

At the same time, thrift and respectability were strongly upheld by the regularly-employed working-class and emerging "lower-middle-class" (Gaskell, 1977; Gray, 1976). But (and it is important to stress this), their values and aspirations were not fashioned mechanically through an inculcation of "bourgeois ideology". It was true that those who had shown evidence of thrift were classed by administrators of the Poor Law and by Victorian charities as members of the "deserving poor" if and when they fell upon hard times, and that as such they were accorded better treatment (Rose, 1981b). House purchase, for example, was one very visible way of demonstrating thrift. But home-ownership and other forms of saving could also provide real security for a family against unemployment, bad trade or old age (Rose, 1980, 73). The practice of thrift then, was an integral part of struggles by many working-class people for some modicum of security, rather than a demonstration of an existing and fixed "status" that marked them off as being aligned ideologically with the bourgeoisie (Reid, 1979, 5).

In general, the more separated the domestic labour-process became from the processes of social production, the more workers' struggles were aimed at building up another life *outside* their work in, and for, capitalist production and accumulation. These struggles were sometimes directed at setting up in small business. Sometimes they were aimed at obtaining land for a small holding. Yet, where there was no possibility of using life-beyond-work in this way, workers' resistance to capitalist domination was expressed through whatever channels remained open. Male wage-earners tended to struggle for a home life that would ameliorate the physical and emotional wear and tear of their working lives as much as possible, that would provide a sphere of "compensation" and alternative non-capitalist environment (Rose, 1980, 72–75). They consciously aimed to build up the home-as-haven and to have a woman to service it and take care of them and their children (Nichols and Beynon, 1977, 193–194).

Crucially, however, such a home was far more of a haven for men than for women for whom it was a domestic workplace. In this way a new polarization between men and women was set up; the needs and desires of alienated male workers contributed to the oppression of domestic workers and enabled the household to function as the "ideal" mode of reproduction of labour (Luxton, 1981, 45–46; Mackenzie, 1980, 20–21; Rose, 1980, 73–75; Rowbotham, 1977, 32–3; Zaretsky, 1977, 62–66). Domestic labour had become "more than a labour of love".[12]

Of course male wage-earners still engaged in wage-workplace based struggles that entailed active resistance to oppressive and exhausting working conditions, and challenged capitalists' "right" to surplus-value. However, the range of issues across which labour unions and male socialists organized was very much restricted by their experiences of the domestic sphere as "non-working life" and increasingly ignored the needs of domestic workers (Rowbotham, 1977, 91–107). Home and work, the "economic" and the "social" were becoming increasingly separated in the actions and experiences of men and women.

A separate sphere of home life had thus been created. It evolved in specific ways, in the context of the historical dynamic of industrial capitalism and workers' struggles against the subordination of all aspects of their lives to the imperatives of capitalist production. This separate sphere, with its peculiar domestic economy and functions, appeared, by the early twentieth century, to be a "natural" centre of reproduction of working-class labour power. But, as we have indicated, the process of creating this separate sphere also created new divisions between the location and type of work carried out by men and women. And these divisions, in turn, created a new problem: the "woman question", which threatened not only the "ideal family", but the whole system of reproducing labour power.

3. The threat to the "separate sphere": the emergence of the "woman question"

By the late nineteenth and early twentieth century, charities and, later, state agencies took on an increasing responsibility for aspects of the reproduction of labour-power, helping to support the working-class family (Mackenzie, 1980, 48–55; Wilson, 1977, 3–58; 98–115). But these also contributed to increases in the range of available employment opportunities for women. Education, health care and social services all primarily employed women. These new jobs had emerged partly as a result of the development, by middle-class women, of the "helping professions". Middle class women were able to become teachers, social workers and nurses while working-class women worked in the more "menial" supporting services (Kessler-Harris, 1981, 119–125). At the same time, the increasing complexity of the economy led to a massive growth in office employment and the emergence of a burgeoning "new middle-class" of white-collar workers in commerce, corporate organizations and bureaucracies (Braverman, 1977, 293–304). The many secretarial and clerical posts which were created were filled mainly by women, including many of working-class background (see Table 2; also Braverman, 1974, 353–4; Kessler-Harris, 1981, 95–101).

The combined effect of all these developments was to provide the possibility of greater economic independence for many women. This added force to the demands of middle class women (frustrated by their constricted sphere) for the vote, for access to higher education, for unrestricted professional careers and so on. But these opportunities for women's economic emancipation were very widely seen as a threat to the respectable "ideal family", the

TABLE 2. *Women and men in the labour force, Britain 1951–1981.*

Year	Total labour force	Men in labour force (in millions)	Women in labour force	Women as % of total labour force
1951	22·6	15·6	7·0	31
1961	23·8	16·1	7·7	32
1971	25·1	15·9	9·2	37
1976	25·6	15·8	9·3	38
1982 (estimate)	26·0	15·6	10·4	42

Source: Social Trends, 1980; *Employment Gazette*; Labour Research **71**, 3, 1982.

relations of domination and subordination it embodied, and the ethos of the bread-winner committed to work diligently to keep his family.

And as the public sector took over more and more aspects of what had been family production and services, and as the norm of the bourgeois ideal woman became more entrenched, women's waged role came to assume first an unnatural and then a dangerous appearance. This became known as the "woman question".

Meanwhile, in some industries productivity had increased sufficiently to enable the payment of higher real wages to male workers in response to worker demands (Stearns, 1975, 310ff). Some sections of organized labour agitated for a "family wage". The motives for this were mixed and complex, but included concerns to keep women at home to take care of the male bread-winner. This was one element in the respectable household discussed above. While there was no unanimity on the family-wage issue, trade unionists' widespread acceptance of the concept "a woman's place is in the home" militated against the implementation of the principle of equal pay for work of equal value (Barrett and McIntosh, 1980).[13] In any case, most working-class women had to contribute financially to the household income: the "family wage" was a myth for the day-to-day lives of their families (Bowley and Burnett-Hurst, 1915; Tilley and Scott, 1978). Moreover, home-ownership, the epitome of "respectability", could rarely be achieved by those in urban-industrial areas without at least two incomes in the family.

However, the ideology of the family wage and of "woman's proper sphere" became an important force in limiting women's opportunities and reshaping the relationships between domestic life, home and wage workplace, especially in the inter-war period. In the first place, the widespread accept-ance that women's paid work was of secondary importance to their domestic labour reinforced the tendency for them to be segregated occupationally into jobs defined as "low status" and paying little (Taylor, 1977). Secondly, the spatial isolation of these women in the new suburbs of this period further restricted their employment opportunities. Many women who still needed to earn cash coped with this isolation by doing "outworking", taking in boarders, doing light cleaning or child-minding (Davidoff, 1979; Luxton, 1980, 173–5).

In fact, the development of separate suburban environments in the maturing industrial/commercial city was itself of crucial importance in the establishment of the home as separate sphere and in the enforcement of the social definition of a woman's place as being in the home. It is to a discussion of the relationships between historical processes of suburbanization and the form of reproduction of labour-power that we now turn.

4. The "suburban solution" and the new domestic economy

4.1. The "separated sphere" in the new suburbs

Among bourgeois families the process of suburbanization had been going on for some time (Mumford, 1961). During the early nineteenth century they had begun to move into distinct residential districts. Whole sections of the city became devoted to the activities of reproduction. In these areas, specialized services grew up, such as churches, schools and surgeries, which complemented the reproductive work of the family.

By the late nineteenth and early twentieth centuries, this process was extending to "respectable" working-class families and to the emergent lower middle-class. In cities like London, the new suburbs were socially as well as functionally segregated (Gaskell, 1977; Stedman Jones, 1976, 207; Olsen, 1979, 232–244). The desires of these groups to move out to an "exclusive" suburb were influenced not only by the prospects of much better living conditions than in the increasingly congested inner city, but also by a fear of "sinking back down into the mire of the city and the working-class" (Walker, 1978). This fear was made all the more real by the continued threats of unemployment faced by many skilled workers (Stedman Jones, 1976, 287–8). Their concerns to make themselves distinct from the "underclass" of casual workers was expressed not only through an emphasis on keeping an overtly "respectable" household (as discussed above), but also by locating this home in a neighbourhood where privacy could be maintained and children raised free of "bad influences", away from the stigmatized slums (Gray, 1976, 98; Meacham, 1977, 86–87).

The desires of these various groups of suburban and would-be suburban residents interacted with, and were taken full advantage of, by the operations of speculative housebuilders who promoted "healthful" suburbs (Dyos, 1961, 122–137; Mackenzie, 1980, 74–77). The urban landscape, rather than comprising a mosaic of homes and factories, began to resemble a patchwork of neighbourhoods and districts. Of these, some were devoted to social production, some to the circulation of goods and capital, while others were devoted primarily to the activities of the reproduction of labour-power: residential suburbs made up of single-family dwellings complemented by shops, schools and services for the family.

By the early twentieth century, in "mature" industrial commercial cities, wage workplaces and homes were often many miles apart, linked by rail and street-car or tramlines designed for commuters.[14] By the 1920s, urban planning and zoning regulations had become explicitly oriented towards reinforcing the "city of separate spheres", spatially segregating residential, industrial and commercial land uses (Perin, 1977).

At the same time, urban planning and neighbourhood design *implicitly* embraced the principle of "a woman's place is in the home" (Hayden, 1980, 170). Homes and neighbourhoods were designed for the nuclear family with a full-time housewife primarily engaged in rearing young children, preparing them for an adult life from which they were carefully cut off (Jackson, 1973, 167–8). Family life was isolated spatially from the world of wage-work and the "moral" temptations of the city (Markusen, 1980, 30–31; Olsen, 1978, 207–219). A popular magazine published by the Hearst Corporation characterized the suburban home as "the third parent". Not only was this suburban environment predicated on the labour of a full-time suburban housewife, it also made it very difficult to organize the domestic economy and home life in any other way (Social Planning Council of Metro Toronto, 1979, 55; Wekerle, 1979, 1980).

The history of suburbanization clearly should not be viewed only in terms of deliberate attempts to establish an "ideal family" in a separate sphere. But up to World War II, suburban environments were most effective in helping to entrench women's role as primarily a "private" domestic one. In this sense, the suburbs were a partial solution to the "woman question" of the early twentieth century, as the legitimate sphere of women's activities was confined to the home and neighbourhood (see Mackenzie, 1980, for an extended discussion of this in Toronto).

4.2. *Home economics: the new science of the separate sphere*

The suburban environment also enabled the actual *role* of the housewife to be extended and elaborated. The single family home in its suburban neighbourhood provided a material space where women could practice the newly-conceived science of "home economics". This had far reaching implications.

As we have seen, by the early twentieth century, the home and the feminine role had taken on a new meaning. Although the home was a separate sphere and women's domestic role a separate role, they were functionally integrated into the processes of social production and the reproduction of capitalist social relations.

Women carried out the activities of reproduction in the family in a milieu that was distinct from but subordinated to the pressures and demands of an advanced capitalist society with an increasingly complex division of labour. The home was portrayed as a microcosm of society: and the cornerstone of the "new society". As such, it had to be imbued with the principles of business and of scientific method. In the words of one domestic science writer, the home was "part of a great factory for the production of citizens" (quoted in Ehrenreich and English, 1979, 151).

For bourgeois women and the wives of those workers who could earn a "family wage", the home economics movement of the early twentieth century reinforced the ideal of the nuclear family. It elevated the status of women's domestic role while giving them a "science" to absorb their potentially threatening energies in an appropriately "feminine way". Home economics was also extended to the poor through the education of girls in the school system and through the "missions" of private philanthropists to women in low-income neighbourhoods, as part of their training in reproducing the new industrial labour force (Mackenzie, 1980, 86). Similarly, the germ theory of disease introduced a scientific standard of household cleanliness, and cleaning became an issue of public health and morals (Wright, 1975, 41). Finally, a growing range of "household commodities" were now coming onto the market. These were deemed essential to the proper running of the home. Consumer goods and innovative marketing techniques proliferated (Ehrenreich and English, 1979, 162–4; Wright, 1975, 43).

The elevation of the status of women's domestic labour was an important aspect of the home economics movement. Women's roles as housewife and mother were to be respected, to be deemed of equal importance to society as the "public" work of men. The continued restriction of women to the home was legitimated by a "separate but equal" pedestal which, in fact, bound women more tightly to the home than before.

Thus the extension of the possibility of the ideal home and the ideal family for large sections of the working-class fundamentally changed both the ideological and economic roles of the family and entrenched the new social definition of the home. The home was not only a place of retreat from economic life for wage earning-men, it was also the cornerstone of a new type of social life, based on women's unwaged domestic work.

At the same time, the definition of "a woman" became something separate from "the norm". Women became associated with the "human qualities" of love, sexuality and irrationality which were excluded from the supposedly "masculine" logic of the marketplace. As the home became the negative image of the world of work, so women became "the other" (Ehrenreich and English, 1979, 17).

The "woman problem" then, was apparently resolved by placing women's

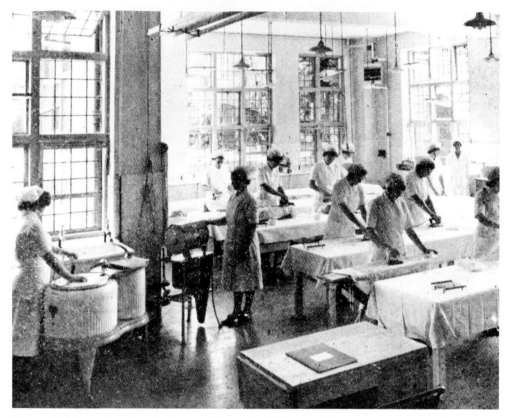

Figure 1. Laundry class, Leicester Domestic Science College, around 1946. From "The Housing Digest", prepared for the Electrical Association of Women by the Association for Planning and Regional Reconstruction. Art and Educational Publishers 1946.

activities and concerns in the home and neighbourhood. Yet, as we shall see, the extension of the concept of the ideal family into the reality of working-class life, while alleviating the symptoms of one set of historically-created problems, laid the basis for the emergence of new conflicts.

5. The problems of production and reproduction in the first half of the twentieth century

We have seen how the new definition of the home, and of women's place in it, bound the household more firmly to market relations, while simultaneously reinforcing an unprecedented gender-typed separation between the "home" and the "economy". Women and children became more dependent on a single wage-earner while becoming less able to affect the course of developments in the wage–labour sphere.

However, despite the hegemony of the dependent housewife role over all aspects of women's life, women were neither passive nor silent in the "ideal"

Plan of work for four-bedroomed house with a family of three schoolchildren:

6.45 a.m.	Make early morning tea. Wake children.
7.0	Open up house. Draw back curtains, etc. Start preparing breakfast. Husband does solid fuel fire.
7.15	Dress self and supervise children.
7.40	Finish preparing breakfast and serve.
8.0	Get family off to school.
8.15	Clear and wash breakfast.
8.40	Make beds and do daily work upstairs.
9.40	Do daily work downstairs.
10.15	Cooking. Make preparations for evening meal.
11.0	Break for tea.
11.15	Special work (see below).
12.30 p.m.	Prepare and eat snack lunch.
1.15	Tidy kitchen. Finish off special work.
Afternoon:	Shopping, mending, ironing, gardening, etc.
4	Get tea for self and milk and cake for children on their return from school.
5	Put on evening meal.
6	Serve hot meal for whole family.
6.45	Supervise younger children's bedtime.
7.15	Wash up supper dishes. Pack husband's lunch for next day.

Special Work:

Monday	Washing.
Tuesday	Turn out three main bedrooms in rotation. Fourth bedroom when necessary.
Wednesday	Turn out sitting-room and dining-room in alternate weeks.
Thursday	Bathroom, lavatory, hall and stairs.
Friday	Weekend shopping in morning. Extra cleaning of kitchen in afternoon.
Saturday	Extra baking.

till a major clearing up session is needed. Encourage your family to take their share and not to leave everything for Mother to clear up. Good cupboards, shelves and plenty of pegs for clothes will immeasurably help in the tidying-up process.

Bathroom and Lavatory Cleaning: Bath and basin should be cleaned immediately after use, so keep a cloth and paste cleanser handy for the purpose. Clean the lavatory pan each morning.

Kitchen Cleaning: See chapter on Easier Housework.

Once-a-Week

Turning out Rooms: Though this is one of the more difficult jobs to fit into the routine, a regular turning out of each room does pay, and immensely simplifies spring cleaning. The ideal is a once-a-week for each room, but this is probably not possible for the single-handed housewife. Decide how much time your plan of work allows for house-cleaning and then turn out each room in rotation; you will probably find it possible to do them all about once a fortnight.

Follow a methodical routine in turning out your rooms, and you will save yourself time and energy. Here is a suggested order of work for the living-room:

1. Open the windows.
2. Remove flowers; empty ashtrays, waste paper basket, etc.
3. Clean out grate and re-lay fire.
4. Vacuum-clean curtains, upholstery and carpets. If no vacuum cleaner is available, cover upholstered furniture with dust sheets, shake the curtains gently and clean the carpet with a stiff brush.
5. Mop and polish the surrounds.
6. Clean the windows, and the paintwork where necessary.
7. Dust window ledges, wainscotting and all polished furniture. Polish where necessary.
8. Shake the rugs before replacing them. Rearrange room.

Arrange for chimney sweep. (This last task is not necessary if smokeless fuel is used.)

MARCH
Interior decoration. Spring-cleaning. Cleaning of soft furnishings and carpets. Spray wardrobes, etc., with moth repellent.

APRIL
Finish off spring-cleaning. Preparations for Easter. Preserving eggs.

MAY
Cleaning and storing of winter clothing and furs.

JUNE
Fruit preserving, drying herbs.

JULY
Jam making, fruit and vegetable bottling. Order winter fuel. Have gas fires cleaned.

AUGUST
More preserving. Family holidays.

SEPTEMBER
Pickle and chutney making. Arrange for exterior decorations. Check up on necessary repairs to guttering, windows, etc. Spray wardrobes, etc., with moth repellent. Pot indoor bulbs for Christmas blooming.

OCTOBER
Wash and store summer clothes. Check up on heating apparatus. Examine the lagging of tanks and pipes.

NOVEMBER
Preparation for Christmas; make cakes, puddings, mincemeat. Christmas shopping. Send overseas parcels and letters by surface mail to arrive in time for Christmas.

DECEMBER
Christmas shopping and decorations. Further Christmas cooking and preparations.

Spring Cleaning
Modern labour-saving methods and equipment, together with a better understanding of household routine, have done a lot to simplify spring-cleaning, but however carefully you have followed your daily and weekly cleaning schedule, there is always a certain amount of special cleaning to be done early in the year.

Figure 2. Excerpts from the "Good Steward's" duties – daily, weekly, monthly. From "The Happy Home", the Good Housekeeping Institute and The Gas Council. Waverley Book Co, undated (but probably produced in the late 1940s).

homes and communities of inter-war suburbia. They struggled to overcome the isolation and powerlessness of their position, to compensate for their simultaneous dependency on and separation from the wage labour sphere.

For housewives, the home and the community were (and remain today) first and foremost workplaces of domestic labour. Their activities in this period were aimed primarily at improving and gaining more control over their conditions of work-at-home and life. These activities took the forms of both individual struggles within the household for less arduous and time-consuming housework, and more space to plan and do it in, and also of more collective struggles against the social definition of the home as the purely private and isolated sphere of their labour.

Many of these struggles were mediated through the male wage-packet and the internal distribution of family resources. So Young and Willmott (1962, 189) refer to the extended family as "women's trade union . . . organised in the main by women and for women". Other struggles were organized through informal networks of neighbours, exchanging information and material resources as well as "swapping" services such as shopping and child-care, and also through more formal organizations such as Women's Institutes, Townswomen's Guilds, voluntary service organizations and women's sections of political parties. These networks acted directly to change housewives' working conditions, as well as providing information and education and pressing for the extension of state services.[15] For example,

> (t)he Women's Co-operative Guild (founded in 1883) organised housewives into consumer co-operative societies. By 1930, the guild had some 67,000 members. . . . Women in the guild became advocates on issues of education, health and maternity care. (Tilley and Scott, 1978, 207)

With no market mechanism to match individual male wages with the size and special needs of particular families, there were growing pressures for state services to "make-up the difference" for large families, and those without a regularly employed wage-earner. The struggle for various forms of "social insurance", especially widows' pensions and support for orphans and family allowances were led by women, both in parliament and in the community (Wilson, 1977, 98–125; Barrett and McIntosh, 1980).

Campaigns for birth control and the limitation of family size were also a significant part of women's attempts to control both their physical health and their conditions of work. Bourgeois and middle-class women had been limiting their families since the 1870s at least, and the first birth-control clinics in England were set up in the 1920s, largely by women for women. "The birth controllers" actively campaigned for extension of women's control over their own fertility.[16] By the 1930s, the use of some kind of birth control had become widespread (Leathard, 1980).

However, this increased control by some women over their biological destiny raised fears about the decline of the "British race", about economic and cultural stagnation attendant on a static, and in future perhaps even dwindling population size.[17] Social researchers Titmuss and Titmuss declared that "capitalism is a biological failure" (1942, 116). Pressure was exerted to produce more and healthier children, through the extension of social services to improve the conditions of family life, and to compensate households for the costs of parenthood (Ferguson and Fitzgerald, 1954; Political and Economic Planning, 1948).

Demands were also made for the expansion of services for the increasing proportion of elderly people who were dependent on a dwindling proportion of younger productive workers (Moroney, 1976; Titmuss, 1958). At the same time, slum clearance and relocation policies:

> promoted the isolation of the suburban household worker by ending the extended family and community network that previously helped informally to collectivise household work in urban areas. (Markusen, 1980, s31)

This led to some new problems arising out of the old "solutions":

> The isolation of the housewife implies a diminution of social resources available to her to cope with crises associated with child-bearing and rearing, thus rendering child-bearing less attractive. Hence falling family size, increasing alienation among housewives/mothers, and increasing demands on the social services by "normal" families, are all different sides of the same coin. (Harris, 1976, 59)

The campaigns for better housing, social insurance, medical services and education contributed to a new shift in the relations between production and reproduction. Just as the reproduction of the nineteenth century labour-force called forth rudimentary state interventions, so the increasingly complex social division of labour and the increasing separation of home and workplace in the mid-twentieth century raised demands for a universal "welfare state".

Yet the institution of the welfare state raised its own set of problems. As Elizabeth Wilson points out:

> the welfare state is not just a set of services, it is also a set of ideas about society, about the family and about women, who have a centrally important role within the family, as its lynchpin. (Wilson, 1977, 8)

Welfare services were developed to support the "separate" family and to support women in their roles as mothers and housewives. They therefore relied on a particular definition of "femininity" which "is central to the purposes of welfarism" (ibid.). But at the same time, they led to demands which necessitated changes in this social definition of femininity. The simultaneous expansion of welfare services and of the consumer goods sector in post-war British society raised the demand for wage-labour once again. This expansion, coupled with the low "natural" increase in population in the 1930s (due to family limitation), led to a labour shortage. Labour shortage, combined with the continuous need for a family centred around the work of the housewife, led to another adjustment in the female labour-process: the development and expansion of "dual roles" for women after the Second World War and up to the present time.

6. Dual roles for women: intersection of the "separate spheres"

The possibility of women's dual role was based on the same conditions as its necessity: the active changes in demography, the labour process, of family and community life which were effected by women and men in the inter-war period.

First of all, the limitation of family size through birth control has led to a new life-cycle for women. Although more women than ever become mothers at some time in their lives, they have fewer children in a shorter space of time. Combined with the decline in three-generation families and the tendency for children to leave home sooner, these factors have contributed to an increase in the number and proportion of one and two-person households. In 1979, only 43% of households in Britain contained children; this figure is dropping, and in turn about 10% of those with children were "lone parent" households. This "stripping down" of the family has been reinforced both by changes in employment opportunities and housing policies. The former have led to increased geographical mobility of labour while the latter have provided mortgages and council housing primarily for nuclear families. At the same time, life expectancy has increased, and at a rate faster for women, since the general decline of the birth rate in the 1930s. Writing in 1968, Myrdal and Klein point out:

> Whereas fifty years ago, a woman spent on the average fifteen years of a considerably shorter life-span in actual child-bearing and nursing of babies, the corresponding average is three and a half years today, assuming she marries at the age of 22, this represents only 6–7% of the remaining years of her life. The family functions of women, for which . . . women were set aside, have diminished radically. (Myrdal and Klein, 1968, 20)

While women and men have been defining and living out these new household sructures, the growth of state services to the family and community, and the expansion of capital into the mass production of consumer commodities have been altering the content and conditions of domestic labour and women's work within the community. Women's altered life-cycles and these new goods and services, combined with alternative employment opportunities, have demonstrated that maternity and housework need no longer be full-time, life-time jobs. In addition, the escalating cost of commodities now needed to maintain the domestic labour process (most especially housing) increasingly necessitate that the average family have two full-time wage or salary earners.

6.1 Women, wage labour and regional change: the British experience since 1945[18]

In the context of all these interlocking developments, women were actively encouraged to enter the wage labour force from the end of the Second World War. Restrictions on married women in the civil service and in teaching were removed in the 1940s. In the words of the *Economic Survey*, 1947:

> the need to increase the working population is not temporary, it is a permanent feature of our national life . . . women now form the only large reserve of labour left and to them the government are accordingly making a special appeal. (quoted in Wilson, 1977, 156)

Women, especially married women, entered the labour force in growing numbers. In Britain, between 1951 and 1971, the wage-earning population increased by 2·5 million. Of these, 2·2 million were women. By the end of the

1970s, women formed 40% of the British labour force, of whom a large proportion were older married women (see Tables 1 and 2). In 1979, 52% of all mothers with dependent children were in waged work, including 28% of those with children under 5 years.

Women not only sell their labour-power for a wage, while continuing to carry out domestic duties; they also provide a particular form of wage labour. Because of their dual role, women's wage labour has particular advantages and disadvantages for employers. The disadvantages stem from the fact that women's wage work has to "fit in" with their domestic responsibilities. New shift schedules, part-time work, new forms of sharing and dividing tasks, and the relocation of "routine" office jobs to the suburbs, all acknowledge the need to adjust the labour process to the entry of large numbers of women who have, or are assumed to have, major domestic responsibilities (Freeman, 1980). This adjustment goes on not only in traditional sectors (manufacturing, nursing, teaching), but is also built into the newly expanded service and clerical sectors. Nevertheless, although part-time employment for women is common in Britain (although most wage-working women in Europe are employed full-time), many work full-time and often for long hours. Often, the poorer women or those with least resources work outside the home the longest. A 1979 survey of a poor working-class district in Huddersfield found that the average daily duration of employment, for working mothers (including part-time workers) was 5·2 hours. But for black mothers, working full-time this rose to 8·0 hours and for Asians to 8·5 hours (Jackson and Jackson, 1980).

The advantages to employers of women's wage labour stem from the same source. First and foremost, women's earnings are, on average, lower than those of men. In 1980 in Britain, women's earnings averaged 72% of men's.

> While the average male manual workers earned £111 a week gross, the corresponding figure for full-time manual women workers was only £68. For non-manual workers, the figures were £151 and £83 respectively. (Counter Information Services (CIS), 1981, 9; see also Brueghel, 1977)

Despite increasing unionization among women workers (see Table 3) and examples of militancy (perhaps the majority of recent factory occupations in Britain have been sustained by women), it is generally assumed that women workers are less well-organised and less likely to protest over pay, conditions or closure.

Lower average pay for women partly reflects the type of jobs held by them (for example, women teachers are concentrated in the less well-paid primary school sector). It also reflects lower grading for similar or even identical work (thereby circumnavigating the provisions of the Equal Pay Act), and concentration of women workers in structurally weak sectors, offering lower wages all round. Segregation by type and level of job has actually *increased* during the twentieth century to the disadvantage of women. So while women

TABLE 3. *Women as percentage of total union membership: Great Britain 1961–1978.*

Year	Women as Percentage of total union members
1961	20
1964	21
1970	25
1974	27
1978	29

Source: Department of Employment Gazette.

accounted for 24% of skilled manual workers in 1911, this had decreased to 13·5% in 1971. For unskilled manual workers, usually with lower paid and less secure jobs, the opposite trend occurred: from 15·5% in 1911, women made up 37·2% of the 1971 total. By 1971, 91% of all foremen [*sic*] and supervisory jobs were defined as male jobs, whereas 82% of all personal service jobs (including office workers) were defined as female jobs. Only the relatively small managerial and administrative group seems a partial exception to this trend (see Table 4). There was a slight decline in job segregation during the late 1970s (Hakim, 1982). But, as Hakim points out, the relatively small effects of Equal Opportunities and the Sex Discrimination Act (both passed in 1975) were quickly reversed by the recession. Job segregation is exacerbated by the fact that women often interrupt their waged work to become mothers, usually in their early twenties. It is assumed that it is the mother, not the father, who is expected to give up paid employment for unpaid, but full-time, child care. This is in turn perpetuated by the low pay of "women's work", and the low status of child care.

Women are also concentrated in "female" sectors of the economy, either without a tradition of union organization, or with an emerging tradition of "feminine" sacrifice and caring. These sectors often offer low pay as a whole, so women become doubly penalized. Over 70% of all women wage workers are in service industries, often doing work similar to what they do at home. In 1980, "over half of all female manual workers were in catering, cleaning, hairdressing and other personal services, and more than half of the non-manual women are in clerical and related occupations" (CIS, 1981, 8). Wage rates for women full-time workers in occupations like cleaning and catering are only around 50–60% of the average full-time male worker (rates of pay for part-timers are even less, see below). Even relatively high-wage "female" jobs receive relatively low pay. Nurses and secretaries/typists earn only 70–80% of the average male rate of pay. Clerical work has always been

TABLE 4. *The percentage of female workers in some major occupational groups, Britain 1911–1961.**

Occupational groups	1911	1921	1931	1951	1961	1971
Non-manual workers						
Managers and administrators	19·8	17·0	13·0	15·2	15·5	21·6
Higher professionals	6·0	5·1	7·5	8·3	9·7	9·9
Lower professionals and technicians	62·9	59·4	58·8	53·5	50·8	52·1
Foremen and inspectors	4·2	6·5	8·7	13·4	10·3	13·1
Clerks	21·4	44·6	46·0	60·2	65·2	73·2
Shop assistants and sales	35·2	43·6	37·2	51·6	54·9	59·8
Manual workers						
Skilled	24·0	21·0	21·3	15·7	13·8	13·5
Semi-skilled	40·4	40·3	42·9	38·1	39·3	46·5
Unskilled	15·5	16·8	15·0	20·3	22·4	37·2

* Note that 1941 figures are not available; ironically so, for these would presumably have shown massive increases in the percentage of female workers.
Source: Hakim (1982).

seen as a relatively superior and accessible occupation for women, but the Equal Opportunities Commission anticipate that with the introduction of new office technology, as many as 17% of these jobs will disappear by 1990. Of the women employed in manufacturing industry, nearly 40% are employed in three sectors: clothing and footwear; textiles; and food, drink and tobacco where (women account for 76%, 46% and 40% of total sector employment respectively). Over and above all the specific disadvantages suffered by women, these sectors are structurally weak, offering low rates of pay as a whole (for this section see Labour Research, 1982).

Finally, women are also far more likely to work part-time. Currently 84% of Britain's 4 million part-time workers are women, amounting to 40% of all women employed. Not only do part-time workers usually have lower wage rates than full-timers (see Table 5), but women part-timers often have lower rates than men part-timers. Even the legal applicability of the Equal Pay Act is in doubt for part-time work. Labour costs for the employer are further reduced because national insurance and employment overheads (e.g. sick pay, holiday rights etc.) can be minimized or avoided for part-time workers. Overall, 17% of all employees are now part-time women workers (Labour Research, 1982).

As well as economic compulsion, many women also take jobs to escape the boredom and isolation of the "ideal housewife" role. Nonetheless, this is

TABLE 5. *Average hourly earnings of female workers*,*
UK 1975 and 1980

	1975	1980
Part-time female rate as percentage of:		
full-time male	58·3	58·3
full-time female	70·5	71·7
Full-time female rate as percentage of:		
full-time male	82·7	81·2

* Excluding overtime
Source: Labour Research, 1982.

often a Faustian bargain. The dual role of housewife/mother and worker leads to heavy demands on women, especially as few men provide much significant help with domestic tasks or child care. This is compounded by the guilt women sometimes feel in deserting their prescribed ideal role. To quote from one recent study of women assembly-workers in three British food factories, they experienced:

> cumulative and additive effects of physically, mentally and emotionally debilitating demands and circumstances, from which a woman can see no escape . . . These women are caught in a constant and unremitting round of activity throughout their waking hours. (Shipman, McNally and Hill, 1981, 345)

Most of these particular women worked, in either role, from 5 to 6 a.m. up to 9–10 p.m., with little or no time for rest. Not surprisingly, up to one third of the sample showed symptoms of poor mental health and stress. This is not an uncommon situation, the Jacksons' (1980) surveys in Huddersfield and Manchester draw similar conclusions. While women *may* have equal opportunities in law, in practice this is not the case when jobs have to be fitted in with domestic responsibilities, and where work in the home also often precludes the time and energy necessary for organization of collective action.

These "advantages" of women's labour, coupled with concomitant restrictions of women's spatial mobility (Madden, 1977) are often exploited in the programmes of rationalization and restructuring being carried out in many industrial sectors. The relocation of factories from central cities to post-war suburban or small-town industrial estates was often a means of replacing a skilled, unionized male labour force with an unskilled, non-unionized and essentially geographically "captive" female labour-force. Sometimes these women had themselves been "relocated" to the post-war suburban housing estates and new towns or, with industrial change, "male jobs" were now scarce (see Morgan and Sayer, Byrne and Parson, Robinson, this volume). The organization of labour processes in the new female-dominated sectors is predicated on the assumption that, by definition, female labour is cheap and flexible, and that women work only for "pin money". Those processes of industrial restructuring which lead to greater unemployment and the de-skilling of jobs can also, paradoxically, lead to a relative increase in the employment of women in low-paid, unskilled work (see the figures for 1961 and 1971 in Table 4). Ironically enough, this trend is sometimes known as "feminization". As we will discuss below, this has been quite important to the changing location of industry and employment in Britain (Brueghel, 1977; Massey and Meegan, 1982).

This growth in female employment is highly differentiated within regions. The most dramatic rates of increase have been in peripheral regions of North East England, Wales, the South West, and (to a lesser extent) Scotland. In South Wales, for example, female activity rates increased from 40% in 1961 to 52% in 1977; in the Northern Region from 31% to 42%. These same regions have also witnessed large declines in male activity rates and male-oriented primary (coal mining) and secondary industries. Not only has male unemployment increased massively, but there has been a large growth in long-term, structural male unemployment. As Massey says "Not only are women increasingly absorbed into capitalist wage relations but with the continued decline of basic industries men are increasingly excluded from them" (1983; see also Massey and Meegan, 1982). These two trends are not unconnected.

In conventional regional analysis patterns of regional inequality and differentiation have usually been examined in terms of aggregate, or even just male, employment rates and/or income levels. This not only reflects intuitive discounting of women, both in the statistical sources employed and in the analysis, it also distorts our understanding of industrial and regional change. For instance, using such aggregate and male-oriented indices, Keeble claims that the period 1965–75 witnessed a striking convergence of nearly all these different indices of regional economic performance towards the national average (1976). However, not only was the national average performing badly (i.e. regional rates were getting equally *bad*), but this disguises substantial changes in the sexual, occupational and wage-rate composition of employment. For instance, looking at control of manufacturing industry in central Scotland, Firn (1975) noted the substitution of female semi-skilled and unskilled jobs for male skilled jobs, not only between sectors but also within them. Provision of new jobs thus often entailed a net wage reduction as well as de-skilling. Generalizing from research like this, Massey (1983) concludes that "convergence" implies not the end of spatial differentiation, but its existence in a new form. Changes in waged work will also be reflected, by necessity, in changes in domestic work.

The sexual division of labour is a vital dynamic in contemporary industrial and regional development.

Thus, industrial restructuring is not gender-neutral. Major trends have been de-skilling and the increase in assembly work, replacement of traditional primary and heavy industries by light manufacturing and service work, replacement of local industry by multi-national-owned branch plants, and a search for cheap, more docile labour. This changing division of labour as a whole implies both a changing spatial and sexual division. Even if regional analysts have sometimes been unaware of this, employers certainly have not been. To quote from firms newly located in North-East England:

> this opened as a cheap labour factory . . . we set up here because female labour was cheap

and (from a firm recently moved from Aberdeen):

> Aberdeen is a booming town, with high wages and only 2% unemployment . . . here there is cheap labour and a very large pool of female labour.

An employer in North-East England can conclude this section for us:

> . . . we are predominantly female labour orientated . . . the work is more suited to women, it's very boring, I suppose we're old-fashioned and still consider it as women's work . . . the men aren't interested . . . we changed from full-time to part-time women . . . especially on the packing . . . because two part-timers are cheaper than one full-timer . . . we don't have to pay national insurance if they earn less than £27·00 a week, and the women don't have to pay the stamp . . . the hours we offer suit their social lives . . .[19]

7. Dual roles and reproduction in the contemporary city: fragmentation and beyond

7.1 Dual roles and the mismatch of resources

At the same time as they are altering the nature of the wage-labour process, women are creating significant changes in the family and community. On the one hand, the wages women earn are rarely sufficient to ensure their economic independence. Rather, they are seen as a "supplement" to the family income, providing the "luxury" of a better domestic working environment through the purchase of "labour-saving" devices and convenience foods (Jephcott et al., 1962). But as women have less time for household services and the production of items for use in the home, these commodities become increasingly central and necessary to the domestic labour process. In turn, this reinforces the family's expectations. Furthermore, taxation and many essential costs (especially housing and transport) have tended to increase more than disposable incomes. The "supplementary" wage becomes essential. According to a report on women in the 1980s:

In 1979, 1·3 million men and 4·4 million women grossed less than £60·00 a week, below the supplementary benefits level for a 'standard family'. But however badly women's work is paid the loss of this so-called pin money pulls many families below the poverty line. If all employed married women were to lose their jobs, the number of families living below the poverty line would treble (Counter Information Services, 1981, 3–4).

The growth of women's wage work has also placed greater demands on community services: day care, school meals, home helps for elderly or infirm household members, old age homes and so on, while demands for wage workers to do these largely "female" jobs have pulled still more women into the wage sector.

Because of women's dual roles, all the changes in their lives become interdependent and mutually reinforcing: the content and context of women's wage and domestic work comes to be defined by the dual role. And this dual role calls for further changes not only in the wage labour but also in the domestic and community spheres. For both the family/community and the wage-labour sector, women's dual role has become a self-reinforcing necessity. The relation between production and reproduction has taken a new form.

Yet once again women have not been passive in the face of this restructuring of their lives. With the extension of the dual role, all aspects of women's lives have become social and political issues. And increasingly, this has placed women's daily activities in opposition to the space and process of the city of separate spheres. The re-emergence, in the 1960s, of the "women question" as a "social problem" expresses the fact that these changing social conditions were creating conflicts in women's daily lives which the prevailing ideology of "woman's place" could not mask.

In carrying out their dual roles, women are not "just" doing two separate jobs. As we've seen above, they are effecting a balance between home and wage workplace. Doing this in a city of separate spheres means bridging numerous separations. It means negotiating and synchronizing, in one life, a variety of conflicting roles.

Women's activities and the environments where they perform these activities are today more fragmented and differentiated than ever before. In one day, as part of her daily work, a woman can be a housewife, a companion, a mother, a wage-worker, a union member, a patient, a customer, a committee member, a client, a claimant, a demonstrator or community activist. Many of these activities are not only spatially and temporally separated, they also exact different types of behaviour and often make conflicting demands on women's lives.

To perform and reconcile all these roles, women need access to a wide variety of resources: flexible child care, shops and services with late opening hours, schools which provide lunch-time meals and supervision after school and vacation care for school-age children, and networks which care for elderly and disabled household members and provide help in emergencies. Women with all these roles also need flexible and frequent public transport, and flexible working hours in both the domestic sphere and wage workplace.

In practice, the city provides few of these resources. The home is often far from the places where a woman performs other aspects of her reproductive work: shopping, being a client of state services, or the mother of a child who is ill or having problems in school. The domestic sphere is also often widely

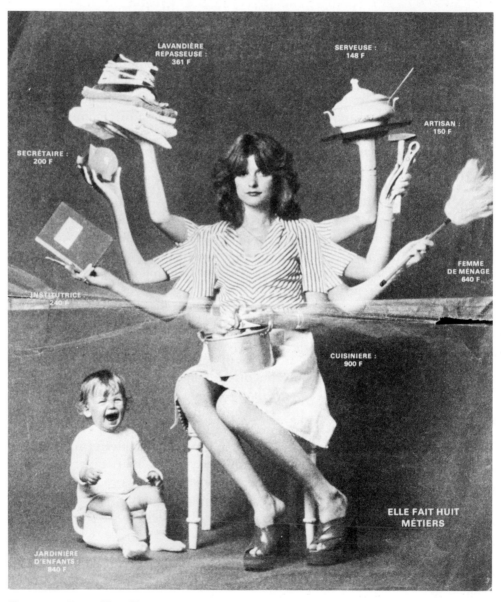

Figure 3. From *Vous* Françoise Kostolany, Photo Stern.

separated from the wage workplace. Hours tend to be rigid in all of these places. Inadequate transport and environments hostile to prams, push-chairs and toddlers often make it difficult to carry out all these activities. Child-care facilities in Britain are usually scarce and rudimentary, often positively harmful to the physical and emotional development of children (cf. Jackson and Jackson, 1980). Whereas, in the inter-war period, many of women's struggles were directed at compensating for the mismatch between women's domestic working conditions and an "outside economy", women are now at the centre of this mismatch. And this has called forth new forms of organization, increasingly influenced by feminist theory and politics. By the 1960s, women's disadvantages as wage-workers, community members and state clients, had become, in their interrelation, "women's issues". The environmental needs arising from women's changing and multiplying social roles were becoming collective political demands, both in the domestic community sphere and the wage workplace.

7.2 Domestic community based struggles: the British experience

Despite their dual roles, women still do most of the work in the home and community, and for many, this is the primary, or only, workplace. Of all family members, they are the most likely to be in contact with educational, medical and welfare services. They are the people most directly affected by inadequate or inaccessible services, by badly maintained homes or neigh-bourhoods (Conference of Socialist Economists, 1979; Leeds Political Economy Class, 1977).

The growing socialization of community life, the importance of state services and purchased commodities in domestic labour, have politicized virtually all aspects of women's domestic work. So although many struggles in the domestic sphere continue to be mediated by the family wage-packet, attempts to improve conditions increasingly mean "taking on" the state, or providing individual or collective alternatives to the gaps in state services.

Women are especially provoked to campaign in their communities for better and more equitably located services, for better home and estate maintenance, for housing construction and neighbourhood design that meet their needs, (Cockburn, 1977; Conference of Socialist Economists, 1979; Segal, 1979). And they are, as the persons primarily responsible for the demanding task of parenting, particularly concerned to struggle for increased control over the conditions of fertility, maternity, childbirth and childcare. It is in these areas especially that the extension of the welfare state has been a mixed blessing.

Women's control over their fertility has become an increasingly "public" and political issue. Facilities for female contraception have expanded greatly in the last four decades, largely under the auspices of the Family Planning Association. In 1967, this and other groups succeeded in liberaliz-

ing family planning law, while mammoth extra-parliamentary pressure
resulted in a liberalized abortion law in the same year (Leathard, 1980,
127–137). In 1976, contraception was recognized as a state responsibility
when "free" family planning services became available under the National
Health Service.

But the continued inadequacies of these services and constant challenges
to their existence has forced a growing range of pressure groups to defend
their existing provisions, while voluntary agencies attempt to fill the gaps.[20]
By the early 1970s, women's right to control their fertility had become a
central issue in the growing feminist movement. The National Abortion
Campaign, formed in 1976 to defend the Abortion Act and to pressure for its
full implementation, says in its statement of principles

> Women will only be able to take an equal part in society when we can decide
> for ourselves whether and when to have children. We believe that no one
> should have the right to compel us to have children we don't want or stop us
> from having the children we do want. This is an important and fundamental
> fight for women. The question of who controls our bodies and our lives is
> central to our campaign. (National Abortion Campaign, 1980)

Conditions of maternity and childbirth have also become social issues. In
contrast to the pre-war period, most children are born in hospital, and a
growing range of medical hardware and drugs is used in childbirth (Brighton
Women and Science Group, 1980). While the post-war expansion of maternal and infant welfare services has greatly reduced maternal and infant
mortality, it has also reduced women's control over the conditions of childbirth. Therefore, while women's organizations have pressed for improved
and extended medical, financial, social and legal support in maternity and
childbirth, part of this pressure has been directed at extending (or reassert-
ing) women's control over, and active participation in, the birth of their
children. This has been carried out both by pressuring within the Health
Services,[21] and by providing training and support to allow women to participate more fully in childbirth.[22]

The growth of social concern for the fitness, education and "requisite
numbers" of children by the Welfare State, and the concomitant growth of
women's wage-labour have made child care more and more of a public
concern. But as in other fields, women had had to organize to defend and
extend state provision for children under five, and to provide alternative
venues for collective child care and contact between parents. With the
growth of women's direct participation in child care organization, and with
the influence of feminism, the pre-war concern with the infant has
broadened to include concern for the mother's conditions of work and life.

For example, the National Campaign for Nursery Education was formed
in the mid-1960s to press for more and better nursery ~ducation and to
oppose cutbacks. The more militant and explicitly feminist National Child-

care Campaign, formed in 1980, claims that "childcare facilities are absolutely necessary and central to women's equality" and are a "major political issue" (National Childcare Campaign, 1981, 10). Local affiliates have organized pressure campaigns and occupations of day-care centres threatened with closure.

There are also a wide variety of groups which co-ordinate parent-run services. One of the largest of these is the Pre-school Playgroups Association. Formed in 1961, by 1981 it had an estimated 13 500 affiliated playgroups, running an average of 2–3 hours several times a week. These are generally parent-initiated and co-ordinated by a play-group supervisor with a rota of parent helpers. There has also been a tremendous growth of Mother and Toddler groups, informal meetings by mothers with their "under threes" for a few hours a week. These too are often parent-initiated and run. Women in many communities have initiated self-help groups, who exchange skills, ranging from household repairs to babysitting as well as running social events and holiday play schemes. Many of these services and groups are especially important to the growing number of single-parent families. Single-parent families have also organized their own groups to press for better services and to provide mutual aid.[23]

Wages in many reproductive jobs are relatively low, especially for those in the non-statutory sector. In 1981, the average earnings of playgroup supervisors was calculated at below £1·00 per hour by the Pre-school Playgroups Association. The PPA goes on to stress that there is in fact no proper wage for playgroup supervisors or helpers, for families could not afford to pay if there was. Rather, they receive "a token of appreciation" (PPA, 1978, 35). This is borne out by the Jacksons' work on child-minding in Huddersfield in the mid-1970s. Providing a low-cost service for poor parents, the average rate was no more than 7½ pence per hour for each child. Yearly running costs were around £4·00 per year for each child, as opposed to £700 for state day nurseries. Even so, weekly costs amounted to 10–15% of the working mothers' wages. Not surprisingly, standards of child care were usually positively harmful to emotional and intellectual development (Jackson and Jackson, 1980). Fortunately standards have improved since the mid-1970s, following pressure and action by the National Childminders Association (founded in 1977), although they are often still far from ideal.

The growth of female waged service-workers in the reproductive sphere: child care workers, school and medical staff, social workers, and so on, has thus been paralleled by an increasing number of unwaged workers in this sector. Therefore, in addition to a growing range of pressure groups within established professions like midwifery and nursing, there is an increase in communal organization among these newly recognized groups. The Pre-school Playgroups Association, the National Childcare campaign and the National Childbirth Trust are prime examples.

7.3 Wage workplace-based struggle

These changes in the nature and organization of reproductive work resulting from community-based struggles, combined with the growth of female wage-labour, are having profound effects on the trade union movement and other wage-workplace based struggles. However, there is still considerable resistance, in Britain and elsewhere, to making "women's issues" a priority or even (in some cases) organizing women workers (Coote and Kellner, 1980).

In taking on wage jobs, more women come to share the economic and political concerns of all wage-workers, especially the concerns of workers in badly paid, insecure jobs. As they are doing two jobs, these are concerns which women necessarily integrate with their domestic concerns and organizations. Despite their relatively low rates of unionization (Table 4), women's participation in the labour-force does increase actual and potential union membership, as well as accelerating the shift toward the numerical dominance of service workers within the trade-union movement (Coote and Kellner, 1980, 28).

Women's participation has also forced an extension of the arena of trade union concerns, making "women's issues" (equal pay and opportunities, sexual harassment, reproductive conditions, part-time and homework) into union issues. The 1975 Trade Union and Congress policy supporting "the right of all women to adequate services for contraception and abortion on request available free of charge on the National Health Service", and the 1978 support for outpatient abortion clinic in each Area Health Authority were the outcome of pressure by women in unions (National Abortion Campaign, 1980). Since 1976, the Labour Abortion Rights Campaign, affiliated to National Abortion Campaign, has organized two Trade Union conferences on abortion and positive legislation as well as mobilizing support to defeat restrictive legislation. Following pressure from the Women's Advisory Committee, the Trade Union Congress has given support to a national perinatal mortality campaign and has:

> devoted particular attention to measures which will assist pregnant women to a safe and healthy pregnancy and childbirth. The impetus for this initiative by the TUC has come from the strongly expressed views of women trade unionists as articulated through the affiliated unions and the annual TUC Women's Conference. (Trades Union Congress, 1980, 73)

The TUC has further recommended that unions extend workplace health education and negotiate time off for antenatal classes, and better maternity and paternity benefits (TUC, 1980, 75–80), and has prepared a "TUC Charter for the Under Fives".

This extension of trade-union concerns has come about partially through the presence of "dual role" women in unions. Additionally, women's labour-force participation and involvement in community actions are forcing changes in the division of domestic labour between men and women (Luxton, 1980). Thus some barriers to links between community and wage workplace action are being broken down. Further, an increasing number of associations of non-unionized workers, waged and unwaged, in the reproductive sphere, have direct links with the trade unions. The National Childcare Campaign has a Trade Union Liaison Committee; the Pre-school Playgroups Association, the National Campaign for Nursery Education, the Association for Improvement in the Maternity Services, and the Maternity Alliance all actively encourage trade-union contracts. The Labour Movement Fightback for Women's Rights, set up to co-ordinate protection and extension groups brings together a large number of diverse groups. In addition to many of those mentioned above, affiliates to Fightback include Women's Aid (refuges for battered women), the Claimant's Union (for those on social security), the National Council for Civil Liberties and the Child Poverty Action Group.

Many of these groups, union and non-union alike, are explicitly trying to change the relation between home and wage workplace. For example, they are campaigning for recognition that wage-workers are also parents, and that parenting is work that must be socially and economically valued and accommodated through, for example, altering parents' working hours to fit the school day, providing more flexible part-time work, and through extending community controlled alternative employment in reproductive areas.

7.4 *"Beyond the Fragments"*

The new forms of organization necessitated by women's dual roles often appear to be fragmented and internally divided. Yet they are also breaking down the fragmentation of daily life. In their attempts to extend control over and improve the conditions of work and life, women's demands extend the terrain of the political from the shop floor to the kitchen to the bedroom. Women's daily activities and feminist-influenced struggles thus embody a new element, both in their organizational structure and in their concrete priorities: an element which disputes and actively alters the dichotomy of home and workplace.

The conflicts in women's lives and their individual and co-operative struggles have been intensified as already inadequate support services have been cut back in the growing recession of the late 1970s and 1980s. Cuts in social services are causing the family to take on more jobs formerly done by state services. For example, the family becomes more responsible for the care of the elderly and handicapped as institutions for their care are closed or cut back. The deterioration in hospital and health services places a greater nursing burden on the family. Cut-backs in nursery care, the raising of school entering age, the discontinuing of school meals and shorter school hours all shift more responsibility for child care back onto domestic workers. Cut-backs in council housing construction and renovation and the selling of council houses are leading to deteriorating conditions of household labour and community life for those in council housing, and for those waiting, probably in vain, to be housed.

At the same time that the family is taking on more and more jobs, it has fewer and fewer resources with which to carry them out, especially in working-class households. Declining real wages exacerbate the difficulties of the housewife's job. She must work harder and buy fewer "convenience" commodities and services. Her growing domestic responsibilities make it more difficult for her to take on wage-work at the same time as increasing responsibilities demands increasing family resources. At the same time again, state cut-backs also decrease employment opportunities for women, while the decreasing level of household consumption of commodities leads to layoffs in light manufacturing sectors.

It is difficult to measure real unemployment among women, as many don't register at Job Centres, since many married women are not entitled to unemployment benefits, nor do most part-timers or homeworkers register. A Department of Environment survey estimated that in 1978, 45% of all women unemployed and seeking work didn't register (compared with 24% of unemployed men). Despite this however, the proportion of women registered rose from 27% of the registered unemployed in 1972 to 45% in 1978 (CIS, 1981, 19–20; Labour Research, 1982).

Women then suffer particularly acutely from the cut-backs, due to the specific nature of their dual role. It is women who, by and large, are responsible for the increased family workload, and for stretching out or compensating for declining family resources by increased production of goods in the home for domestic use in the reproduction of labour-power. And in taking on these new tasks in response to cut-backs, women are decreasing their prospects of getting employment outside the home.

Yet at the same time, the "separate sphere" of the home is becoming a wage workplace for many women. Many corporations are taking advantage of the renewed immobility of many women within the home. We are witnessing today a resurgence of "home-working", usually by piece rates, and mainly involving women who would otherwise have no source of employment. In 1980, there were an "estimated 200 000 to 400 000 homeworkers in Britain", but "by the nature of their work, homeworkers stay off government statistics", so this figure is likely to be underestimated (CIS, 1981, 14). Such work has little in common with the old-style domestic industries (discussed earlier in this paper), since it does not bring the workers concerned any control over the product, although it often involves working conditions and wages reminiscent of the horrors of the nineteenth century. A Low Pay Unit Survey found that " . . . in April, 1979, only 15% of homeworkers earned above £1·06 an hour" (CIS, 1981, 14). In times of recession, even major corporations may prefer to use such cheap female labour in homeworking.

The difficulties experienced by families whose activities have come to rely on a balance of state services, supplementary wages, domestic work and paid work in the home are expressed in a variety of urban protests and problems. These range from politically conscious community movements and new types of union activism, as discussed above, to less visible struggles within the home and family and vandalism in the streets (Friend and Metcalf, 1981, 121–145 and 161–170).

The conflicts which began to emerge in the 1960s and are being exacerbated by the deepening recession of the 1980s, suggest that the solution of separate spheres is fracturing under diverse attacks; these are converging and becoming visible as conflicts in women's lives.

8. Conclusion

We have argued in this paper against the analytic separation of social and economic processes in the city by geographers (and others), and suggested instead a perspective which sees urban development and change as a history of changing relations between the activities of production and reproduction of labour. Such a perspective is essential if we wish to understand women's activities and women's struggles to change their position. An understanding of women's activities and struggles is essential to many of the concerns of geographers, including problems and processes discussed elsewhere in this book.

We have suggested that changes in the relation between production and reproduction of labour, as it operated in the city, was a process of constant struggle. As these changes involved complex restructuring of women's work, women's struggles were especially central.

The gradual separation of productive and reproductive activities in the transition to industrial capitalism resulted in a new working-class family, partly through the struggle of working-class people to maintain some elements of control over their daily lives. The nineteenth and early twentieth century reshaping of the city into specialized "productive" areas in the central city and "reproductive" areas in the suburbs provided the conditions for a new relationship between production and reproduction. They allowed the extension of social services to the labour force in such a way as to support and mould the family, and provided a basis for the extension of a separate "housewife" role to more and more women. Throughout the early twentieth century, women struggled to overcome the conflicts of their isolated "separate position", struggles which contributed to the development of the Welfare State and women's post-war dual role.

The numerical and structural extension of the dual role was incubated in the landscape of "separate spheres". The birth of this role in the 1940s and

1950s, and its extension in the following decades, demarcated another shift in the relations between social production and the reproduction of labour power. Once again this shift was centred on the restructuring of the female labour process. But this time it was shaking the very foundations of "home" and "work" as separate spheres that supported the cycle of accumulation through their connections in function and their fragmentation in consciousness and political practice.

The shifting of activities and of social definitions of home life and women's roles, which bemused, disrupted and angered urban dwellers of the last century, appear to us now as aspects of a transition toward a new set of relations between production and reproduction, a different city with new activity patterns and new types of struggle.

However, it is far from easy to "collect" and explain these varied and apparently disconnected activities in our own period. This paper has tried to build some analytical bridges between the city's "separate spheres". We hope that it will go a little way toward clarifying the motivations and purposes of current struggles around the domestic economy and home life, which have bewildered geographers and other "urban experts", using different analytic frameworks. We hope this paper will stimulate debate about the possible future directions of these struggles, and their implications for our future life in the city.

The authors of this paper accept equal and full responsibility for its content. We wish to exonerate, and at the same time extend our warm thanks to the editors of this volume, and also to the following for their specific comments, criticisms and additions: Bob Beauregard, Robin Flowerdew, Gord Garland, Briavel Holcomb, Jane Lewis, Katy Oliver, Hilary Renwick and Sue Ruddick. We also thank the many others who have made essential contributions to our thinking, and provided much moral support, but whom we cannot name individually.

References

Anderson, J. (1977). "Engels' Manchester: industrialisation, workers' housing and urban ideologies", A political economy of cities and regions No. 1, Architectural Association, London.

Barrett, M. and McIntosh, M. (1980). The Family Wage: some problems for socialists and feminists, Capital and Class, 11 (Summer), 51–72.

Beard, M. (1962). "Women as a force in history: a study in traditions and realities", Collier, New York.

Bowlby, S. Foord, J. and Mackenzie, S. (1981). Feminism and Geography, Area, 13 (4).

Bowley, A. L. and Burnett-Hurst, A. R. (1915). "Livelihood and poverty", G. Bell & Sons, London.

Braverman, H. (1974). Labour and monopoly capital: the degradation of work in the twentieth century, Monthly Review Press, New York.

Brighton Women and Science Group. (1980). Technology in the Lying in Room in Brighton Women and Science Group "Alice through the microscope: the power of science over women's lives", Virago, London.

Brueghel, I. (1977). Women as an industrial reserve army: a note on recent British experience, *Feminist Review*, **3**.

Burnett, P. (1973). Social change, the status of women and models of city form and development, *Antipode*, **5**, 3, 57–62.

Clark, A. (1968). "Working life of women in the seventeenth century", Frank Cass, London.

Clayre, A. (1974). "Work and play", Weidenfeld & Nicholson, London.

Cockburn, C. (1977). "When women get involved in community action", *in* M. Mayo (ed.), "Women in the community", 61–70, Routledge and Kegan Paul, London.

Community Development Project Political Economy Collective (CDP-PEC). (1979). "The state and the local economy", Brookside, Seaton Burn, Newcastle-upon-Tyne.

Conference of Socialist Economists. (1977). "On the political economy of women", Stage 1, London.

Conference of Socialist Economists. (1979). "In and against the state. Discussion notes for socialists", CSE, London.

Coote, A. and Kellner, P. (1981). Hear this, Brother: women workers and union power, New Statesman Report 1, New Statesman, London.

Counter Information Services. (1981). "Women in the 1980's", CIS, London.

Curtis, B. (1980). Capital, the state and the origins of the working-class household, *in* B. Fox (ed.), "Hidden in the household: women's domestic labour under capitalism", Women's Press, Toronto.

Davidoff, L. (1979). The separation of home and work? Landladies and lodgers in nineteenth and twentieth century England, *in* S. Burman (ed.), "Fit work for women", Croom Helm, London.

Davidoff, L., L'Esperance, J. and Newby, H. (1976). Landscape with figures: home and community in English society, *in* J. Mitchell and A. Oakley (eds), "The rights and wrongs of women", Penguin, London.

Davis, W. J. (1910). "The British Trade Union Congress, History and Recollections", Vol. 1, TUC Parliamentary Committee.

Dickens, P. (1978). Social change, housing and the state: some aspects of class fragmentation and incorporation, 1915–46, *in* M. Harloe (ed.), "Urban Change and Conflict", Proceedings of a conference at York, 1977, CES, London.

Dobb, M. (1963). "Studies in the development of capitalism", International Publishers, New York.

Dyos, H. J. (1961). "Victorian suburb", University Press, Leicester.

Ehrenreich, B. and English, D. (1975). "The manufacture of housework", *Socialist Revolution*, **26**, 5 5–40.

Ehrenreich, B. and English, D. (1979). "For her own good: 150 years of the experts' advice to women", Pluto, London.

Engels, F. (1952). "The condition of the working class in England in 1844", Allen & Unwin, London.

Ferguson, S. and Fitzgerald, H. (1954). "Social service: UK history of the Second World War", HMSO, London.

Firn, J. R. (1975). External control and regional development: the case of Scotland. *Environment and Planning, A*, 7, 393–414.

Fox, A. (1958). "A history of the National Union of Boot and Shoe Operatives", Blackwell, Oxford.

Freeman, J. (1980). Women and urban policy, *Signs*, 5, 3. Supplement (Spring) S4–S21. (Entire supplement republished as G. R. Stimpson (ed.) (1981). "Women and the American City", University Press, Chicago).

Friend, A. and Metcalf, A. (1981). "Slump city: the politics of mass unemployment", Pluto, London.

Gaskell, S. M. (1977). Housing and the lower middle class, *in* G. Croissick (ed.), "The lower middle class in Britain, 1870–1914", 159–183, Croom Helm, London.

Gauldie, E. (1974). "Cruel habitations: a history of working-class housing, 1780–1918", Allen & Unwin, London.

Gray, R. (1976). "The labour aristocracy in Victorian Edinburgh", Clarendon, Oxford.

Gregory, D. (1982). "Regional transformation and industrial revolution", Macmillan, London.

Hakim, C. (1982). Job segregation: trends in the 1970's, *Employment Gazette*, **89**, 12, 521–529.

Harris, C. (1976). Comment on Willmott, *in* M. Buxton and E. Craven (eds), "The uncertain future: demographic change and social policy", Centre for Studies in Social Policy, London.

Hayden, D. (1980). "What would a non-sexist city be like?", Speculations on housing, urban design and human work, *Signs*, 5, 3, Supplement (Spring) S170–S187. (Entire supplement republished as C. R. Stimpson (ed.) (1981). "Women and the American city", University Press, Chicago).

Hayden, D. (1981). "The grand domestic revolution", MIT Press, Cambridge Mass.

Humphries, J. (1977). The working-class family, women's liberation and class struggle: the case of nineteenth century British history, *Review of Radical Political Economics*, **9**, 3, 25–41.

Jackson, A. (1973). "Semi-detached London", Allen & Unwin, London.

Jackson, B. and Jackson, S. (1980). "Childminders", Penguin, Harmondsworth.

Jephcott, P., Seer, N. and Smith, J. H. (1962). "Married women working", Allen & Unwin, London.

Keeble, D. (1976). "Industrial location and planning in the United Kingdom", Methuen, London.

Kessler-Harris, A. (1981). "Women have always worked: a historical overview", McGraw Hill/Feminist Press, New York.

Leathard, A. (1980). "The fight for Family Planning: the development of Family Planning Services in Britain, 1921–1974", Macmillan, London.

Labour Research. (1982). Working women in the 1980's, *Labour Research*, **71**, 3.

Leeds Political Economy Class (1977). "The need to change the way we live, the social base of Leeds", Worker Educational Association, Leeds Branch.

Loyd, B. (1980). Women, home and status, *in* J. Duncan (ed.) "Housing and identity", Croom Helm, London.

Luxton, M. (1980). "More than a labour of love: three generations of women's work in the home", Women's Press, Toronto.

Mackenzie, S. (1981). "Women and the reproduction of labour power in the industrial city: a case study", University of Sussex Working Papers in Urban and Regional Studies, No. 23.

MacMurchy, M. (1976). The Canadian girl at work, *in* R. Cook and M. Mitchinson (eds), "The proper sphere: women's place in Canadian society", 195–197 (originally published in 1919) Oxford University Press, Toronto.

Madden, J. (1977). A spatial theory of sex discrimination, *Journal of Regional Sciences*, **17**, 3, 369–380.

Mandel, E. (1978). "Late Capitalism", Verso, London.

Markusen, A. R. (1980). City spatial structure, women's household work and national urban policy, *Signs*, **5**, 3, Supplement (Spring) S23–S44. (Entire supplement republished as C. R. Stimpson, (ed.), (1981). "Women and the American City", University Press, Chicago).

Marx, K. (1959). "Capital Vol. III", Progress Publishers, Moscow.

Marx, K. (1976). "Capital, Vol. 1", Penguin, London.

Massey, D. (1983). "Industrial restructuring as class restructuring: production decentralisation and local uniqueness", *Regional Studies*, **17**, 2, 73–89.

Massey, D. and Meegan, R. (1978). Industrial restructuring versus the cities, *Urban Studies*, **15**, 3, 233–43.

Massey, D. and Meegan, R. (1982). "The anatomy of job loss: the how, where and when of employment decline", Methuen, London.

Meacham, S. (1977). " A life apart: the English working class, 1890–1914", Thames & Hudson, London.

Millward, S. (1977). "Urban harvest: urban renewal in retrospect and prospect", Geographical Publications, Berkhamsted.

Moroney, R. (1976). "The family and the state: considerations for social policy", Longmans, London.

Mumford, L. (1961). "The city in history", Harcourt Brace & World, New York.

Myrdal, A. and Klein, V. (1968). "Women's two roles: home and work", Routledge & Kegan Paul, London.

National Abortion Campaign (1980). Statement of Aims, (mimeo).

National Child Care Campaign (1981). "Nurseries: how and why to fight for them", NCCC, London.

Nichols, T. and Benyon, H. (1977). "Living with capitalism", RKP, London.

Oakley, A. (1976). "Woman's work: the housewife past and present", Vintage, New York.

Olsen, D. J. (1979). "The growth of Victorian London", Penguin, London.

Perin, C. (1977). "Everything in its place: social order and land use in America", University Press, Princeton.

Pinchbeck, I. (1969). "Women workers and the industrial revolution, 1750–1850", Frank Cass, London (originally published in 1930).

Political and Economic Planning (1948). "Population policy in Great Britain", PEP, London.

Pre-school Playgroups Association (1978). "Report on parental involvement in playgroups", PPA, London.

Pre-school Playgroups Association (1980). "PPA coming of age in the eighties", PPA, London.

Reid, A. (1979). The labour aristocracy in British social history, *Our History Journal*, **5** (June) 3–6.

Roberts, R. (1973). "The classic slum: Salford life in the first quarter of the century", Penguin, London.

Rose, D. (1980). Toward a re-evaluation of the political significance of home-ownership in Britain, *in* Conference of Socialist Economists Political Economy of Housing Workshop, "Housing, construction and the state", CSE, London.

Rose, D. (1981a). Accumulation versus reproduction in the inner city: 'the recurrent crisis of London' revisited, *in* M. Dear and A. J. Scott (eds), "Urbanisation and urban planning in capitalist society", Methuen, London/New York.

Rose, D. (1981b). Home-ownership and industrial change: the struggle for a "separate sphere", *University of Sussex Working Papers in Urban and Regional Studies*, No. 25.

Rowbotham, S. (1977). "Hidden from history: 300 years of women's oppression and the fight against it", Pluto, London.

Rowbotham, S., Segal, L. and Wainwright, H. (1979). "Beyond the fragments", Merlin, London.

Saegert, S. (1980). Masculine cities and feminie suburbs: polarised ideas contradictory realities, *Signs*, **5**, 3. Supplement (Spring) 96–111. (Entire supplement republished as C. R. Stimpson (ed.) (1981). "Women and the American city", University Press, Chicago.

Sager, A. (1979). Understanding urban models or understanding cities. *Environment and Planning A*, **11**, 853–862.

Segal, L. (1979). A local experience, *in* S. Rowbotham, L. Segal and H. Wainwright (eds), "Beyond the fragments. Feminism and the making of socialism", Alyson London.

Semmel, B. (1960). "Imperialism and social reform", London.

Shipman, S., McNally, J. and Hill, S. (1981). Pressures on women engaged in factory work, *Employment Gazette*, **89**, 8, 344–349.

Social Planning Council of Metro Toronto (1979). "Metro's suburbs in transition: Part One: evolution and overview", Social Planning Council of Metro Toronto.

Stearns, P. (1975). "Lives of labour", Croom Helm, London.

Stedman Jones, G. (1971). "Outcast London: a study in the relationship between classes in Victorian society", Oxford University Press, London.

Taylor, S. (1977). The effect of marriage on job possibilities for women, and the ideology of the home, Nottingham 1890–1930, *Oral History*, **5**, 2, 46–61.

Tholfsen, T. R. (1976). "Working-class radicalism in Victorian England", Croom Helm, London.

Thompson, E. P. (1966). "The making of the English working class", Vintage, New York.

Tilley, L. and Scott, J. (1978). "Women, work and family", Holt, Rinehart and Winston, New York.

Titmuss, R. (1958). "Essays on the welfare state", Allen and Unwin, London.

Titmuss, R. and Titmuss, K. (1942). "Parents revolt: a study of the declining birth rate in acquisitive societies", Secker and Warburg, London.

Trades Union Congress (1980). "Women workers 1980: Report for 1979–80 of the TUC Women's Advisory Committee and Report of the 50th TUC Women's Conference", TUC, London.

Union Place Publishing and Printing. (1976). "As thing are: women, work and family in South London", Union Place, London.

Walker, R. A. (1978). The transformation of urban structure in the nineteenth century and the beginnings of suburbanisation in the United States, *in* K. Cox (ed.), "Urbanisation and conflict in market societies", 165–212, Maaroufa, Chicago.

Wekerle, G. R. (1979). "A woman's place is in the city", paper prepared for the Lincoln Institute of Land Policy.

Wekerle, G. R. (1980). Women in the urban environment, *Signs*, **5**, 3 Supplement (Spring) 188–214. (Entire supplement republished as C. R. Stimpson (ed.) (1981). "Women and the American city", University Press, Chicago).

Wilson, E. (1977). "Women and the welfare state", Tavistock, London.

Women's Group on Public Welfare, Hygiene Committee (1943). "Our towns: a close-up", OUP, London.

Wright, G. (1975). Sweet and clean: the domestic landscape in the progressive era, *Landscape*, **20**, 7, 38–43.

Young, M. and Willmott, P. (1962). "Family and kinship in East London", Penguin, London.

Zaretsky, E. (1976). "Capitalism, the family and personal life", Harper Colophon, New York.

Notes

1. So, ironically enough, the work of Castells founded a school of "new Marxist urban sociology" dealing with the urban in isolation from the economic, while Marxist studies of industrial change and isolation were (at first) based on the analysis of economic change in isolation from social change.

2. The assumptions made by geographrers about women's social and spatial roles are discussed in Burnett (1973).

3. Labour-power has to be reproduced in *all* societies. However, there are major differences in the ways in which, and the *purposes* for which, it is reproduced, as societies develop from pre-capitalist through transitional to fully-capitalist stages (by which time labour-power is the only commodity the worker has left to sell). As we shall see, such changes have major implications for the domestic economy, home life and women's roles.

4. Much of this work was promulgated as "the geography of women", a new special interest field which itself threatened to reproduce, within the discipline, the ghettoization of women which existed in the city. See Bowlby, Foord and Mackenzie (1981) for geography. Wekerle (1980) raises similar criticisms in the context of urban planning and design.

5. Feminist research which relates "commonsense" social meanings of home life itself explicitly to women's oppression includes Luxton (1980); Markusen (1980); Rose (1980). For a discussion of women and the home as status symbol, see Loyd (1980).

6. In this paper we can provide only the barest outline of these transformations, focussing on their implications for the domestic economy and home life, with particular reference to Britain. There were, in reality, many different . . . processes through which pre-capitalist small-scale and household production became subordinated to capital, leading eventually to the creation of a huge industrial proletariat: see Gregory (1982) and Dobb (1963, pp. 221–254). Both authors also demonstrate the geographical unevenness of capitalist penetration.

7. Marx analysed this process in terms of the transformation from absolute to relative surplus value (Marx, 1976). This is discussed with reference to mid-nineteenth century industrialism in Manchester by Anderson (1977). Evidence presented by power-loom weavers (working for piece rates in Huddersfield) to the *Royal Commission on Labour* Group C, P.P. 1892, XXXV, q.4935) explains the benefits to employers of such a transformation very graphically:

> If a loom weaves faster, is it not in the interests of the workmen that it should do so? – Not if the wages are taken off in proportion to the speed. Suppose a loom is said to run a quarter faster, and you take off a third of the wage, then it is natural that the workmen will get less.

8. Evidence presented to the *Factory and Workshops Acts Commission*, 1875; the *Select Committee on the Sweating system*, 1888; and the *Royal Commission on Labour 1892* provides fascinating case studies of the operation of these processes in different industries. These studies form a basic source for this section.

9. Unpublished Home Office Papers (Home Office 1895, HO45 9859/PRO B12601 99; Fox (1958, 93); Keith Brooker, personal communication (Dec. 1979). The official who made this comment was a former Factory Inspector for an area which included Northampton. Marx (1976, 620–6) discusses the delay in restricting children's employment in the 1860s in similar terms.

10. Evidence given by a group of Edinburgh trade unionists to the *Factory and Workshops Acts Commission* in 1875, and the ensuing discussion (qq.19, 801–7), demonstrated that, by contrast, state agencies were quite prepared to police or supervise common-lodging houses and the like. These, it seemed, were not "respectable", and could thus be legitimately interfered with.

11. There are indications that trade unionists high up in the Trades Union Congress bureaucracy consciously recognized and were prepared to accept such trade-offs in the late nineteenth century. See various speeches by trades union leaders in Davis (1910).

12. This is the title of Meg Luxton's book recounting and analysing the experiences of three generations of women's work in the home in the company town of Flin Flon, Manitoba, where the economic and social transformations outlined in this section were accomplished in less than seventy years (Luxton, 1980).

13. A representative of the Chainmakers' Union, giving evidence to the *Royal Commission on Labour* (Group A, P.P. 1892, XXXIV, q.17, 117), explained the basis of his branch's opposition to the employment of married women:

Everything is being neglected at home, all little domestic duties are neglected, and when the man goes into his little place, his little castle as it should be, there is nothing clean and tidy. It drives him off to the the public house and all that kind of thing in our country, which would not be if the women were better domesticated.

14. Discussions of the critical role of railways and streetcars/trams in suburban development include Jackson (1973); Stedman Jones (1976, 207–210, 221–2); Olsen (1978, 298–324). The involvement of both central and municipal governments in providing inexpensive transportation for the workforce in London marked the beginnings of a recognition of the need to co-ordinate two aspects of the reproduction of labour-power – working-class housing and public transit to and from work – in an overall concept of "planning" (Rose, 1981a, 349–350).

15. Groups of professional women organized *as women* to improve conditions for women. The British Association for Early Childhood Education, founded in 1923, worked for the improved education and welfare of young children in all situations, and especially for the extension of nursery schools and classes. The Society of Women Housing Managers, the Women Public Health Officers Association, the National Federation of Women's Institutes, Women Officers of the National Council of Social Services and an "umbrella" group: the Women's Group on Public Welfare, researched and campaigned for "the needs of the community as a whole", attempting to build a co-ordinated structure of services which leaves no gap" (Women's Group on Public Welfare, Hygiene Committee 1943, vii).

16. By 1930 there were five national birth-control societies, supported by the Women's Co-operative Guild, the National Council of Women and the women's sections of the Labour and Libreral parties. In 1930, the National Birth Control Council was formed to co-ordinate and extend their work of provision and pressure. The struggle to control fertility also included pressing for more liberal abortion laws. The Abortion Law Reform Association was formed in 1936 to press for legal medical abortions.

17. These concerns were heightened by the poor performance of British forces in the South African War, and they significantly accelerated the pace of welfare reforms under the Liberal Government of 1906–11 (see Semmel, 1960), especially those relating to school meals (Wilson, 1977, 106–110). Negligent or incompetent family upbringing, combined with poor housing and low wages, were also deemed responsible for the unfitness of working-class men. A much quoted book of the time was George Haw's *Britain's Homes: the Empire's Heart Disease,* published in 1902. Within the British Trade Union movement the popularity of "social imperialism" reinforced the belief that a woman's place was as the child-bearing guardian angel of the healthy home (Rowbotham, 1977, 73).

18. Simon Duncan and Jane Lewis have helped substantially in writing this section.

19. The quotes are taken from Jane Lewis' Ph.D. research "Industrial restructuring and the development of a new sexual division of labour in the peripheral regions of Britain" Queen Mary College, University of London.

20. These include: the British Pregnancy Advisory Service and the Pregnancy Advisory Service, both set up in 1968 to provide "sympathetic advice and practical help" with medical abortion, contraception and sterilization; the Birth Control

Trust, set up in 1972 to "carry out a program of research and education about contraception and abortion and their demographic effects"; and the Brook Advisory Centres, set up in 1964 to give contraceptive advice to young people. (Quotes from leaflets of the respective organizations.)

21. These include the Association for Improvement in the Maternity Services, the Radical Nurses Group, The Association of Radical Midwives and the recently formed Maternity Alliance, founded by the National Council for One Parent Families, the Spastics Society and the Child Poverty Action Group.

22. The National Childbirth Trust, through its largely autonomous branches, sponsors classes to teach the relaxation and breathing skills necessary for "natural birth". It also co-ordinates breast-feading counselling and post-natal support, the latter in self-run networks of new mothers. The Society to Support Home Confinements pressures for better state services and co-ordinates practical help for women who choose to have their children at home.

23. These include the National Council for One Parent Families and Gingerbread.

EIGHT

Racial conflict, industrial change and social control in post-war Britain

J. DOHERTY

(April 1982)

1. Introduction

The hostility and intimidation experienced by black communities in post-war Britain have taken on an increasingly brutal and vicious character in the past decade. The sporadic attacks of the 1950s and 1960s, peaking in the 1958 disturbances in Nottingham and London's Notting Hill and in the 1969 riots in Leeds, gave way to the more widespread "Paki-bashing" of the early 1970s, and more recently to the numerous murders of black people and widespread physical attacks on black homes, businesses and places of worship. Indicative of this escalation in the level of racist violence has been the rise of neo-fascist and anti-black organizations such as the National Front and its off-shoots, the National Party and the New National Front, as well as the more openly Nazi British Movement (see Edgar, 1977; Walker, 1977).

Racial conflict is now seen as a major part of the so-called inner-city problem, though, as this chapter shows, its extent and certainly its causes in economic and political developments in post-war Britain are by no means confined to inner urban areas.

The Bethnal Green and Stepney Trades Council's report on racial attacks in the East End of London documents the consequences of racist violence for at least one black community:

> ... while the East End is traditionally a high crime area, there is clear evidence that the local Bengalee community has suffered physical attacks and harassment over recent years on a totally different scale from that inflicted on the rest of the community. There is the danger of assuming that this violence is confined to the occasional isolated incident or outburst that finds its way into the headlines; the skin-head 'Paki-bashing' incidents in East London in 1971;

the racialist attacks at the time of the Malawi Asians story; the notorious Kingsley Read speech, and the murder of two coloured students from Mile End in 1976; the racist savagery in Brick Lane, and the deaths of Altab Ali in Whitechapel, Kennith Singh in Newham, and Ishaque Ali in Hackney in the summer of 1978. Behind the headlines is an almost continuous and unrelenting battery of Asian people and their property in the East End of London. The barrage of harassment, insult and intimidation, week in week out, fundamentally determines how the immigrant community here lives and works . . . (Bethnal Green and Stepney Trades Council, 1978, p. 3)

The East End has a long history of racism, from the anti-semitism of the late nineteenth and early twentieth centuries and its revival in the 1930s, to the strong expressions of support for the National Front in the 1978 local elections. Yet as numerous other accounts indicate, even in areas where the history of racism has been less overt, the experiences of black people reflect, to a greater or lesser degree, those of the East End Bengali community.[1]

A recent Home Office survey (1981) of racial violence in selected police areas showed that in comparison with the white population, Asians were 50 times and West Indians 36 times more likely to be the victims of racial attacks (p. 11). The same report suggests that racially motivated attacks could now be running at around 7000 each year (p. 14) and that there has been a "fairly steady rise in the number of attacks reported since 1977 and a marked increase since 1980" (p. 12). Public awareness of this situation also appears to be increasing. A Commission for Racial Equality survey conducted in the early months of 1981 established that 47% of blacks and 33% of whites thought that race relations in Britain were getting worse; six years previously only 13% of the black population and 20% of the white held such a view. Less than 1 in 5 blacks and 1 in 4 whites thought that the situation would improve (reported in *New Society*, 26 November, 1981).

Racist attacks by marauding white youths and neo-fascist sympathizers have been perpetrated in the context of the imposition and tightening of controls on black immigration and settlement; an extension of control legislation which has required a marked increase in the state surveillance of black people. The selective use of stop-and-search procedures,[2] the "swamping operations" conducted in black areas by the SPG and other police units, and the innumerable "fishing raids" of black homes, clubs and workplaces for illegal entrants and overstayers indicate the extent to which surveillance has become part of the direct experience of black people in Britain, young and old, Asian and West Indian.

Paralleling the extension of state surveillance, conflict between black people and the "law and order" agents of the state has become much more overt in the past decade, not only in the frequent street altercations between police and black youths, but also in the more formal "set-piece" confrontations between blacks and police at carnivals (e.g. Notting Hill, 1976) and demonstrations (e.g. Southall, 1979). These trends have recently culminated in the urban riots of the 1980s, beginning in St. Pauls, Bristol in April 1980, and spreading a year later to London, Liverpool, Manchester, Birmingham and many other British cities. Notwithstanding a certain "knock-on" effect, many of these riots were triggered by specific instances of the kind of police activity which has become an established part of their pattern of operation in black communities (Lambeth, 1970; Lambeth Borough, 1980; Institute of Race Relations, 1979).

These riots invite comparison with the disturbances which took place in the northern cities of the USA in the late 1960s (see also Kushnick, 1981). Despite differences in the scale and number of the riots, there are many similarities: in the circumstances leading up to the riots, in the form that they took, and in the reactions of police and government officials. The Kerner Commission (1968) reporting on the 1967 civil disorders in the USA noted that "almost invariably the incident that ignites disorder arises from police action" (p. 206) and that these disorders:

> . . . involve Negroes acting against local symbols of white American society, authority and property in Negro neighbourhoods – rather than against white persons. (p. 6)

Similarly, in St. Paul's, Brixton, Toxteth and Moss Side, it was police action which precipitated the disturbances, and there was no evidence of indiscriminate attacks on white people; indeed whites took part in the rioting alongside blacks. Rather the violence, as in the northern cities of the US, was directed principally at the police as the targets of resentment and symbols of authority (Hytner, 1981; Scarman, 1981).

After the St. Paul's riots and especially after those in London, Liverpool and Manchester, some police chiefs and various politicians attempted to criminalize the events by attributing them to "sheer hooliganism" or, alternatively, characterized them as "orchestrated campaigns" by unidentified outside agitators. The Kerner Commission had to debunk similar charges in relation to the US disturbances. The Scarman inquiry into the April 1981 riots in Brixton has shown that while some criminal activity could be identified, and while a few "outsiders" were involved, such factors are totally inappropriate as explanations for the disturbances (Scarman, 1981, pt. 3).

Britain, however, is not the United States, and while analogies can be useful, any explanation of racial conflict must be based on the analysis of the specific conditions and history of the country in which it occurs. The character of the urban riots of the early 1980s illustrates some of the issues which have to be taken into consideration in examining racial conflict in the British context. First, they illustrate many of the ethnic and generational divisions and differences that exist among Britain's black population. Black participants in the riots were predominantly young and predominantly of West Indian origin. Older blacks have traditionally been more passive in their resistance to white hostility; but the division is not rigid and there is circumstantial evidence, for example in media interviews (e.g. *New Society*, 26 November 1981), to suggest tacit parental approval or, at least, understanding of the behaviour of the young. Asians, partly because of the particular combination of religious and cultural characteristics in their communities (which are themselves extremely variable) have tended to be less demonstrative than West Indians. However, this observation needs to be set against the activities of, for example, the Indian Workers Association which suggests that many Asians have been willing to fight against racism and discrimination through more "acceptable" channels. The participation of at least some Asian youths in the rioting, especially in Leicester, Luton, Southall and Bradford, and the militancy of some Asian groups such as the Southall Youth Movement, indicates that Asian "passivity" may be becoming a thing of the past, at least among second and later generations.

Additionally, the riots have demonstrated what Hall (1978, 26) has called, the "lateral links" between racism on the one hand and the crises of the economy and law and order on the other. The effects of economic recession have cut deep into the fabric of many of Britain's towns and cities, especially in inner city areas where blacks tend to concentrate. Decline in traditional industries has resulted in high rates of unemployment and growing job insecurity among all sections of the population, white as well as black; cuts in public expenditure have meant a reduction in social service provision and a deteriorating environment. The net result is the destruction of traditional ways of life and the creation of a disillusioned and demoralized population; the participation of white youths in the riots suggests that wider issues of youth alienation and the effects of unprecedented levels of unemployment need to be taken into consideration.

Yet racism remains a vitally important ingredient; blacks predominated in the riots and, except for sporadic and relatively trivial outbursts, such as those in Dundee and the Pilton area of Edinburgh, the riots occurred exclusively in areas of black urban settlement (though not all such areas were involved). Clydeside, with relatively few black settlers, yet one of the most deprived of all urban areas in Britain (see Cross, 1978, p. 27) had no riots at this time (although Belfast and rural Northern Ireland provide interesting comparison also). Blacks, discriminated against in times of economic boom, have suffered disproportionately in recession; frustration and resentment have long been smouldering among black people, and it was perhaps to be expected that the first explosions would come from these communities.

This chapter examines how the issues of white hostility, black militancy and state intervention have interrelated with each other and evolved together in the context of the changing economic circumstances of post-war Britain. The late 1960s and early 1970s provide an important benchmark in examining these trends, for during these years, the transition of black people from an immigrant to a settled population – a transition which had been taking

Figure 1. Police officers detaining black youth, Brixton 1981 (courtesy *Socialist Worker*).

place throughout the preceding decade – was essentially completed; additionally at this time the ending of the post-war boom and the downturn in the fortunes of British industry were becoming increasingly clear. Taking the late 1960s as a divide, the first part of this chapter charts the process of black immigration and settlement during the 1950s and 1960s, identifying the social and economic position of black people in British society. While the economy continued to prosper, immigration proceeded freely and the reaction of the white population to black settlers was relatively muted. As the economy began to falter, white hostility grew and state intervention in the immigration process became more pronounced. The second part of the chapter focusses on the 1970s, a period of catastrophic decline for British industry during which black immigration was severely restricted and both white hostility and black militancy considerably increased. These trends have posed an increasingly serious threat to the social order, and have stimulated further state intervention. The concluding section attempts an assessment of these issues and trends, indicating how they provide the essential background for an understanding of the escalation of racial conflict in post-war Britain.

2. From immigrant to settler: The 1950s and 1960s

2·1 The economic and social position of Britain's black population

In their study of migrant workers in post-war Europe, Castles and Kosack (1973) argue that immigrants provide a cheap and flexible source of mainly unskilled labour, especially during periods of economic expansion; that is, they fulfil the function of an "industrial reserve army of labour" contributing to the process of capital accumulation in advanced industrial countries. Such labour has several features which make it particularly attractive to capital. Its reproduction costs tend to be negligible since workers arrive fully developed at least for unskilled employment; dependants are few, in the initial stages; and when no longer needed, these workers often return home thus making little or no demands on the importing country for social security payments.

After the Second World War, as the industries of Britain returned to peace-time production, various immigrant groups performed the function of an industrial reserve. The demand for external sources of labour to relieve domestic shortages was met initially by Irish immigration and the recruitment of European workers (see Tannahill, 1968; Zubrzycki, 1956). However, the demand for labour was such that individual organizations, for example, London Transport, the National Health Service, and the Hotels, Restaurants and Caterers Association, as well as numerous private firms especially in the textile industry, went hunting for workers in the West Indies and in India and Pakistan. The recruitment of a section of "the latent surplus population"[3] of these countries for work in the United Kingdom was facilitated by the introduction of a quota on West Indian immigration to the USA in 1952 and by the upheavals in the Indian sub-continent following partition in 1947.

From 1955 (when statistics became regularly available) to 1968, over a million migrants arrived from the "New (i.e. black) Commonwealth".[4] The majority came from the West Indies and India and Pakistan. In 1966 it was estimated that of the total black population in Britain, that is including British-born children to black immigrant parents, the West Indians comprised the largest group (49%) and Asians from India and Pakistan the second largest (39%), the remainder coming mainly from Ceylon and British West Africa.

Black immigrants to post-war Britain were attracted, principally, not to the older dockland and port areas of former black settlement, but to the new centres of industrial expansion and labour demand in the country's conurbations and cities. They avoided areas with long-standing unemployment problems (e.g. in Scotland and Wales), and also the low urban growth regions of East Anglia and the South West. In 1961 about 70% of all black immigrants had settled in the six major conurbations, particularly in London (47%) and the West Midlands (14%). There were some differences between the various immigrant groups in that the proportion of Pakistanis in the West Yorkshire conurbation was relatively high, while West Indians tended to favour Greater London; additionally, fewer West Indians (20%) than Asian (41%) lived outside the conurbation boundaries. Ten cities in 1961 – London, Birmingham, Liverpool, Manchester, Bristol, Leeds, Coventry, Sheffield, Nottingham and Bradford – accounted for about 50% of all black immigrant settlement. The pattern of settlement in 1966, despite the addition of over 200 000 new arrivals, generally reinforced that of 1961. This was especially the case with regard to the West Indian population. However, rather more Indians moved into the West Midlands and Yorkshire conurbations than would have been expected given the 1961 distributions (Rose *et al.*, 1969, Chapter 10; I.R.R., 1969; Field, 1981).

Within the urban centres which attracted large-scale black immigration, it was the inner areas which were characterized by the highest concentrations. For example, in 1966, all six of the London boroughs with over 5% black populations – Brent, Hackney, Lambeth, Haringey, Islington and Hammersmith – had marked concentrations of black immigrants in their inner city wards. These concentrations were often associated with particular ethnic groups as the West Indian concentrations in Brixton (Lambeth) and Willesden (Brent) suggest. Outside these boroughs other more isolated concentrations occurred. Many of these, as with the Asian settlement in Spitalfields (Tower Hamlets), were located in the inner city; some however, notably the Asian concentration in Northcote (Ealing), were located further out. This association of black people with inner city areas was to be found not only in other large cities (Handsworth and Sparkbrook in Birmingham and Moss Side in Manchester), but also in smaller cities where black people concentrated: in Coventry, Bradford, Leeds, and Leicester (See Doherty, 1969; Jones, 1970; Tommis, 1974; Winchester, 1974; Peach, Winchester, and Woods, 1975; Lee, 1977).   It has been suggested that by returning to their countries of origin on completion of their work contracts, some black immigrants to Britain conformed to the classic circular migration pattern of the international labour reserve described by Castles and Kosack in relation to migrant labour in Western Europe. Most, however, remained and became permanent residents, thus exercising their right, established in the 1948 Nationality Act, to free entry and settlement in the United Kingdom; a right which remained unrestricted until the passing of the 1962 Commonwealth Immigration Act. It has been claimed (Peach, 1968; Rose *et al.*, 1969; Katznelson, 1973; Jones, 1977; Freeman, 1979) that the tendency for black immigrants to shed their migrant status and become permanent settlers can be directly attributed to the 1962 Act. However, there is at least circumstantial evidence to suggest that this merely confirmed a previous trend rather than initiated a new departure. For instance, in the 1950s among West Indians, who formed over half of all black immigrants at that time, there was a high percentage (40%) of economically active females. The propensity for family formation and settlement would thus have been enhanced. Peach (1968, 50) further indicates, using Home Office estimates, that on average only one in seven West Indians who entered Britain between 1956 and 1961 returned home. Additionally, while a cyclical pattern of migration may have been more marked, at least prior to 1962, among Asian immigrants, there was (and is) a great deal of myth associated with the idea of return migration; a myth held in the consciousness of migrants as well as in the observations of outsiders This myth, expressed as a never fulfilled intention to return home after a period of stay in Britain, has been documented with reference to Asian immigrants by both Dahya (1973) and Brooks and Singh (1979); Robinson (1979, 1980) also has some interesting comments to make in this context. A similar phenomenon among the West Indian community has been suggested by Bonhomme (1971), Egbuna (1971), Patterson (1963) and Richmond (1955), (Chapter 5).

However, the 1962 Act, by requiring all primary Commonwealth immigrants to obtain a work voucher before entry to Britain was permitted, certainly encouraged the transition from migrant to settler as is indicated by the "beat-the-ban" immigration rush of 1960–61 (Table I) and the predominance of dependants – between 70% and 80% of the yearly totals – among post 1962 Commonwealth immigrants. The tightening of restrictions on both primary immigrants and dependants during the course of the 1960s further encouraged permanency of settlement.

The permanent settlement of black citizens distinguished New Commonwealth immigration to Britain, along with black settlement in France and Holland, from the recruitment of contract labourers for temporary employ-

TABLE 1. *New Commonwealth and alien immigration 1955–70.*

| | New Commonwealth | | Alien | |
	Net Immigration (primary and dependants)	Voucher holders	Workpermits + Permissions	Admitted for settlement
1955	42 700	–	45 837	–
1956	46 850	–	47 133	–
1957	42 400	–	46 768	–
1958	29 850	–	46 762	–
1959	21 600	–	47 774	–
1960	57 700	–	56 133	–
1961	136 400	–	58 426	–
30 June 1962	94 900	–	55 395	–
1 July	12 435	4 217	–	–
1963	56 071	18 678	52 466	15 347
1964	52 840	13 888	58 338	19 211
1965	53 650	12 125	66 126	20 615
1966	46 602	5 141	66 054	18 948
1967	57 648	4 716	60 627	18 346
1968	50 160	4 353	62 267	20 093
1969	33 942	3 523	67 788	21 862
1970	26 000	3 167	67 654	N.A.

Sources: Institute of Race Relations Fact Papers, 1969; 1970.
Unit for Manpower Studies, 1976: Tables B5, B6(a), B6(b).

ment in other European countries such as West Germany, Sweden and Switzerland. Yet as Castles (1980, 369) stresses, "the function of both groups of immigrants for the capitalist system was the same", namely the provision of a source of cheap labour during a period of rapid industrial expansion.

Among the black immigrants to Britain some obtained relatively secure employment; others, however, obtained only intermittent work and, if they did not return to their countries of origin, effectively joined the British domestic labour reserve, albeit for a short period. Through the 1950s and 60s, black workers were consistently overrepresented in the ranks of the unemployed; their unemployment levels generally indicating a greater rise and a lower fall than the national trend (Rose *et al.*, 1969, 179). Thus in 1958 when national unemployment was around 3%, some 8% of black workers were without jobs; in 1961 the respective figures were 1·9% and 5% (Wright, 1968, 52). The higher unemployment levels of black workers in this time of relative economic prosperity probably reflected, not chronic long-term unemployment, but merely the longer time gap blacks experienced between jobs.

The position of immigrant labour in various sectors of British industry during the 1950s and 1960s has been considered by numerous authors (Butterworth, 1967; Cohen and Jenner, 1968; Wright, 1968; Patterson, 1969; Daniel, 1968, pt. 1; Jones and Smith, 1970; Allen *et al.*, 1977). These studies together with the analysis of the 1961 and 1966 census returns (see Rose *et al.*, 1969, Chapter 13) confirm, in relation to all black immigrant workers, Peach's assessment of West Indian labour, namely that they formed a "replacement" population settling where their labour was most needed and taking jobs which the unemployed British workers were, at that time, unwilling to touch.

Cohen and Jenner's (1968) study of immigrant labour in the wool industry of the West Riding of Yorkshire clearly demonstrates many of these points. In common with other sections of the British economy the wool industry experienced severe labour shortages immediately after the war. Characterized by low wages and poor working conditions, wool firms found it difficult to attract workers in the competitive post-war years. Traditionally wool, like much of the textile industry, had relied on cheap female labour and for certain operations, women continued to predominate after the war. However, profitability and indeed survival in many instances, increasingly came to rely on the recruitment of immigrant workers.

In the mid and late 1940s, European refugees were used in the West Riding wool industry, supplemented by direct recruitment from Ireland, Italy and Yugoslavia; in the 1950s West Indians were also employed; but by the 1960s Pakistani labour predominated among the immigrant workers. It was the availability of these immigrants which allowed the wool firms to find employees for "dead-end, low-paid" labouring jobs. More importantly, though, their availability allowed the introduction of new capital equipment whose profitable operation necessitated shift work for which women, mainly because of legal constraints and commitments to domestic labour, were unavailable.[5] As Cohen and Jenner (1968, 55) conclude, contraction of the wool industry would probably have been much swifter but for the presence of immigrant labour which allowed modernization and the initiation of more efficient production methods.

In their areas of settlement in Britain's conurbations and cities certain immigrant groups were attracted to particular industries, often as the result of the recruiting practices of individual firms and organizations. Asians tended to concentrate in the metal and textile industries of the Northern and Midland cities, while West Indians were strongly represented in the engineering, clothing and transport industries in London and the West Midlands. In all these industries, black workers were predominantly employed in low skilled and manual occupations, working for low wages, in poor conditions and often on shift work (see Hepple, 1970, Chapter 4; Patterson, 1969, Chapter 5).

The economic position of black immigrants in the 1950s and 1960s was reflected in and partly determined the character of their residential environments. The concentration of black people in inner city areas has already been noted, and within these areas, black workers gravitated towards, or were forced into, the private rented sector of the housing market where accommodation was available at relatively low cost. The deteriorating areas of larger Victorian housing in London and the Midlands and the smaller, terraced houses of the Northern cities became the focus of immigrant settlement. Here their accommodation was often overcrowded, shared and lacking in basic amenities (see Burney, 1967; Rex and Moore, 1967; Rose *et al.*, 1969, Chapter 12). The concentration of black people in these poor housing and living environments reflected, in part, the national housing shortage of the early post-war period, a shortage which was particularly marked in the labour-hungry conurbations. But the residential conditions of black workers were exacerbated by their low incomes, their lack of access to council housing, the contraction of the privately rented sector and by discrimination on the part of landlords, estate agents and mortgage companies (see Daniel, 1968, pt. 4).

The economic and social conditions experienced by black immigrants in post-war Britain thus reinforced one another, reflecting the oppressed position of black people in British society as a source of cheap labour for Britain's expanding economy. In their working and living conditions and in their role and function as an immigrant labour force fuelling capitalist expansion, black people in Britain, despite the increasing permanency of their settlement, demonstrated many of the features of migrant labour in West European countries (Castles and Kosack, 1973, Chapters 3 and 7).

2·2 *Racial conflict and black resistance*

In addition to their role as a source of cheap labour, Castles and Kosack have argued that immigrants in advanced capitalist countries facilitate the creation of economic and social divisions within the working class along national and racial lines. Such divisions not only facilitate and contribute to the oppression of immigrants in employment, housing and elsewhere in society, but also inhibit the propensity of labour to battle with capital by inducing a labour aristocracy mentality among sections of the indigenous working class; a mentality which often has a real material basis in relatively privileged working conditions and wages and an ideological basis in the myth of racial or ethnic superiority (Castles and Kosack, 1972; 1973; see also Gorz, 1970).

Part of the basis for such divisions in post-war Britain can be sought in the country's colonial past, for as Segal (1967, 300) has observed:

> the racism so marked in Britain today . . . is recent only in its domestic application. No society but one with an assumption of racial superiority would have conducted and countenanced the slave trade for so long, or have acquired and ruled so vast a coloured empire with such self-assurance.

The racist legacy of empire has been transmitted to the present both through the medium of popular culture in comedy and stereotype and through history and language: the "syntax of racism" (Hall, 1978, 28) has long existed and was readily available for appropriation by anti-black groups and politicians in post-war Britain.

But Segal's observation, as it stands, is an oversimplification. Historical legacy alone cannot account for racism in modern Britain, though it can provide the soil for its roots and some sustenance for growth. The seeds of racism today have to be sought elsewhere – in the present material conditions of society:

> [Racism] may draw on the cultural and ideological traces which are deposited in a society by previous historical phases, [but] it always assumes specific forms which arise out of the present – not the past – conditions and organisation of society. (Hall, 1978, p. 26)

Racism in post-war Britain differs from that of the past in its primarily domestic orientation and, while it has traces of the paternalism and condescension of the "high" colonial period, its increasingly vicious and brutal character is based less on notions of intellectual superiority (though these remain) and more on nationalistic and xenophobic ideas of exclusion.

Britain's post-war economic boom helped lubricate relations between black immigrants and the indigenous society, particularly in the employment market. The boom conditions of the 1950s and early 1960s enabled black immigrants generally, despite low wages and poor housing, to achieve a level of economic prosperity beyond that which they had experienced in their countries of origin (see Desai, 1963; Pixley, 1968). Yet early portents of potential conflict were to be seen in the attacks on blacks by white mobs at Deptford (1949), Liverpool (1948) and Camden Town (1953) (see Hiro, 1971, 36, and Waller, 1981). At another level hostility was apparent in the incidents of discrimination against West Indians and Asians in dance halls, pubs and restaurants as well as in the tacit agreements between managements and white workers with regard to the imposition of quotas and job restrictions in the recruitment of black labour (Hiro, 1971, 250; Wright, 1968).

While immigration responded to the needs of the economy, and social strife associated with black-white conflict was intermittent and relatively low-keyed, there was neither the economic pressure nor the social necessity for legislation. The demands of anti-immigrant politicians and organizations for immigration control were deflected and the campaigns of Fenner Brockway and other Labour M.P.s for legislation against discrimination went unheeded by the governments of the day.

This period of "muted optimism" (Hall, 1978, 27) was abruptly terminated by the race riots in Nottingham and London in 1958. Both of the areas in which the most serious rioting took place, St. Annes and Notting Hill respectively, typified the kind of deprived inner-city district which had absorbed sizeable black settlement. Here the 1957 recession acted as a catalyst to various combinations of urban poverty, youth culture and fascist activity to spark the conflicts (see Hall, 1978; Coates and Silburn, 1971). In the days following these riots tension ran high in many black areas, especially in North London where black homes were petrol-bombed and numerous black people were assaulted (Hiro, 1971, 40). The riots had two major effects. First, they encouraged renewed and vociferous outbursts from politicians, such as the Tory M.P.s Osborne and Pannell, for control of immigration from the Commonwealth and thereby precipitated the passing of the 1962 legislation. Secondly, the riots and their aftermath demonstrated to black people that, in the face of white hostility, a retreat to ethnicity, in an attempt to find support and protection in the culture and religion of their own communities (Desai, 1963; Braithwaite, 1967), was not sufficient; more positive self-defence measures were necessary. Hiro (1971, 40) for instance, reports that the publicity given to West Indian self-defence preparations averted the invasion of Brixton by white youths in the days following the Notting Hill riots. The events of 1958 brought to an end the "age of innocence" for many black settlers in Britain.

Though there was no recurrence of rioting on the 1958 scale; white racism in the early and mid-1960s was vividly demonstrated in the increasing frequency of attacks on black people and their property, especially in 1964 in the months following election at Smethwick of the Tory Peter Griffith on an openly racist platform (Hiro, 1971, 58; Hartley-Brewer, 1965). The activities of anti-black organizations (e.g. the Southall Residents Association) and neo-Nazi groups (e.g. the British National Party) also substantially increased during this period culminating in the formation of the National Front in 1967 (Walker, 1977). More pervasive, though less dramatic forms of racism were demonstrated in the entrenchment, as we have seen, of black immigrants in the lower sections of the job market and in some of the worst housing. The P.E.P. report of 1966 (see Daniel, 1968) indicated the depth and extent of institutional and individual discrimination by employers, landlords, estate agents and local government officials, which operated to ensure that few black people could substantially improve their position in British society.

Inspired in part by civil rights activity in the United States, black reaction to white hostility and discrimination took an increasingly militant form. The early 1960s petitioning of the Home Office for anti-discriminatory legislation gave way in the middle and later years of the decade to the formation of co-ordinating pressure groups such as the Campaign Against Racial Discrimination (CARD) and the Racial Adjustment and Action Society (RAAS). The activities of these organizations, founded after the visit to Britain of Martin Luther King and Malcolm X respectively, reflect the moderate and more militant politics of their patrons. Stokeley Carmichael's tour of the country in 1967 had a less focussed response, but was highly influential in spreading the ideas of "black power"; ideas which were reflected in the determination of blacks to engage in self-defence activities to protect their own communities (see Hiro, 1971, pt. 1, Chapter 8; pt. 2, Chapter 11; Sivanandan, 1981).

The dramatic surfacing of white hostility especially in the street violence of 1958 and the emergence in a muted form of black militancy threatened the economic usefulness of racism. In the interests of capital, the state needed to contain racism within "profitable proportions" (Sivanandan, 1976, 350), and in the interests of its own legitimacy, the state needed to preserve social control. How these objectives were to be obtained was not at all clear, and in the early years of the 1960s was the subject of some dispute between Labour and Tory politicians (Foot, 1965; Katznelson, 1973). During the course of the decade, however, a twofold strategy subscribed to by both main parties evolved; it comprised immigration controls on the one hand and race relations legislation on the other.

2·3 Immigration and race relations legislation

The first faltering step in the development of this strategy was taken with the passing of the 1962 Immigration Act. This Act required all potential immigrants from the Commonwealth to obtain one of three types of work voucher before entry to Britain was permitted: category A vouchers were for those who had been offered definite jobs, category B for those with defined skills and qualifications and category C for unskilled immigrants. Passed by a Tory government, this Act required renewal each year and Labour pledged to repeal it once in power.

Socially and politically, the 1962 Act can be seen as the reluctant response of a Tory government to political pressure from racist individuals and organizations on the one hand, and to the problems of social control created by grass-roots hostility towards black people as displayed in the 1958 riots on the other; the Act was a sop to white racism, an attempt to assuage the "fears" of the anti-immigrant lobby. But the Act also had an economic significance and we can challenge those who recognize its political importance but deny its economic rationale (Rose *et al.*, 1969; Katznelson, 1973; Freeman, 1979).

The predisposition of British capital towards Commonwealth immigration controls was encouraged by certain changes which were taking place in the structure and orientation of the British economy in the late 1950s and early 1960s. First, the anticipated entry of Britain to the EEC, which was being negotiated at this time, inclined British capital towards investment in Europe, and as Friend and Metcalf (1981, 152) suggest, "entry to the EEC and an operative 1948 Nationality Act were incompatible". Secondly, there were several indications, which were to become much clearer by the middle of the 1960s, that Britain was beginning to generate its own internal labour reserve. The major, though brief downturn in the economy from 1957 was the first real suggestion of this trend; the recession was characterized by a then uprecedented doubling of the monthly unemployment figures (Peach, 1979, Table I; see also Wickenden, 1958) from around 230 000 in 1956 to 444 000 in 1959. This development has to be seen in conjunction with the tendency, discussed previously, for Commonwealth citizens to become permanent residents in Britain. The transition from migrant to settler, also involved, for some, a permanent movement from the international labour reserve to Britain's domestic labour reserve. In these circumstances the continuation of the laissez-faire policy towards Commonwealth immigration, a policy which had served British capital admirably through the late 1940s and the most of the 1950s, was seriously questioned, perhaps for the first time, in post-war Britain.

Political and social events may have dominated the public debate and determined the precise timing of the 1962 Act, but changing economic circumstances ensured its acceptance and to a large extent determined its operation through the rest of the decade. Thus in 1964, the issue of category C vouchers was suspended, and in the 1965 White Paper, they were discontinued altogether. This curtailment was related to the increasing numbers of unskilled labourers without work as employment in manufacturing dropped and the British economy entered a period of crisis. Demands for external sources of unskilled labour were consequently reduced, particularly for labour that was likely to become permanently settled. Further, the issue of category A and category B vouchers was also restricted by the 1965 White Paper to 8500 each year, and these vouchers were increasingly directed towards professionals and people with special qualifications (see Deakin, 1970, 51; Counter Information Services, 1976, 13). As a reflection of these restrictions, the 1960s saw a progressive drop in the number of New Commonwealth voucher-holders entering Britain (see Table 1).

From the mid-1960s the much reduced need of the British economy for external sources of unskilled labour was met by the continued immigration of aliens and Irish on the one hand, and by the arrival of a large number of New Commonwealth dependants on the other. Irish immigration averaged around 30 000 per annum in the 1960s, while aliens maintained and indeed slightly increased their pre-1962 annual average to the end of the decade (Table 1). Both groups recorded a return migration rate of around 70% for the 1960s (Unit for Manpower Studies, 1977, Table B; Freeman, 1979, 193). Dependant New Commonwealth immigrants, who were exempt from the voucher controls of the 1962 Act, comprised mostly the wives and children of primary immigrants previously settled in the country (Deakin, 1970, 55). Many of these dependants were already, or were soon to be, in the economically active category; the activity rate for black females, though varying from group to group, was high, 50% in 1971 compared with 43% for the total population.

Throughout the latter part of the 1960s, as a domestic unemployment rate steadily increased, immigration controls even on dependants from the New Commonwealth were made more rigorous. In 1968, dependant children were required to travel to Britain in the company of at least one parent who was a Commonwealth citizen. All dependants were required to obtain an entry certificate from the High Commission in their country of origin which often involved tedious and uncomfortable enquiries as well as long delays. In addition, successive revisions of the Home Office standing regulations to immigration officials not only strengthened health checks on dependants, but also necessitated the production of legal evidence of the relationship between dependant and sponsor, plus medical evidence of age (Moore and Wallace, 1975; Deakin, 1970, Chapter 5).

The overall relationship between the manpower needs of the economy and the operation of the various 1960s Commonwealth immigration control measures has recently been indicated by Peach (1979) and Robinson (1980). Their evidence is suggestive rather than conclusive,[6] but it indicates a direct correlation between the level of unemployment and the size of West Indian and Asian immigration, both primary and dependant, thus continuing the trend of the 1950s. The operation of the 1962 Act and subsequent control legislation, by regulating the supply of external sources of cheap labour, seems to have served the needs of British economy through the 1960s as well as the open door policy did in the 1950s.

However, the control legislation, as is generally recognized even by some who have been enthusiastic supporters (e.g. Deakin, 1970, 390), was not successful in achieving its declared social and political objectives. Though ostensibly designed, by restricting the number of black entrants, to draw the sting of the racist arguments and obviate further racial conflict, it merely served to identify black people as "the problem" (e.g. the "cause" of job and housing shortages), and thus it *encouraged* further demands for curtailment from anti-immigrant and anti-black groups and individuals. As Moore (1971, 3) indicates, the "numbers game" can never be won because "for some, one is too many".

Through the course of the 1960s many of the precepts of the anti-immigrant philosophy were gradually imbibed by former opponents. The retreat, for instance, of Labour from its position of principled opposition to Commonwealth immigration controls in the years following 1962 and especially after the death of Hugh Gaitskell in 1963 has been well documented (see Foot, 1965; Chapter 8). The election of the racist Peter Griffiths at Smethwick was a significant milestone in this retreat, for at Smethwick it was not white youths from deprived urban environments giving vent to racism, but a solid, adult white working class vote in what had been a Labour-held constituency. The tightening of immigration controls in the

1965 White Paper publicly demonstrated Labour's abandonment of its former position of opposition to controls. The significance of this White Paper was not so much, as Katznelson (1973) has argued, that it temporarily depoliticized the immigration issue, but that it symbolically demonstrated the "appropriation of racism into the official policy" of all the major political parties (Hall, 1978, 29); it was the manifestation of a political consensus on immigration that effectively branded blacks as the official scapegoat for the ills of British capitalism. In this period, for black people at least, "dreams of assimilation" were "finally laid low" and the "tide of racism" began to flow (Hall, 1978, 29).

> Publication of the White Paper marked the point at which the racist arguments began to harden, at which anti-black ideas became respectable and at which the final rout of liberals began. Anti-black politics moved into the reputable centre of the main political parties. (Moore, 1975, 26)

The extent of this rout was demonstrated in the 1968 Immigration Act. Passed with unprecedented speed, in direct contrast to the prolonged debate which preceded the 1962 Legislation, this Act introduced the infamous "grandfather clause" (first used in America in the middle of the last century to prevent blacks from getting the vote): British passport-holders without the "substantial connection" of at least one grandparent born in Britain were deprived of the right of entry to the country. The Act was explicitly designed to inhibit the entry of Asians who were being threatened with expulsion from Kenya. In justifying this Act, the spectre of hordes of immigrants invading Britain "placing serious strain on the services of those areas where they decide to settle' and "causing racial disharmony and explosions" (J. Callaghan, *Hansard*, 22 June, 1968, cols 659 and 662) was invoked. The 1968 Act against Kenyan Asians finally removed all pretence of Commonwealth immigration controls being non-racial; most white people in the Commonwealth have at least one grandparent born in Britain, most black UK passport-holders have no such "substantial connection". These distinctions were to be unambiguously extended to all Commonwealth immigrants in the 1971 Immigration Act.

Immigration control legislation in the 1960s was parallelled by a series of race relations initiatives, most prominent of which were the 1965 and 1968 Acts. These two strands of legislative activity – immigration controls on the one hand and race relations legislation on the other – were seen in government circles as two sides of the same coin; a philosophy clearly expressed in Roy Hattersley's comment "integration without limitation is impossible . . . limitation without integration is indesfensible" (quoted in Hill and Issacharoff, 1971, 16).

The 1965 Race Relations Act which outlawed discrimination in public places was but a tentative gesture towards these integration objectives, for it was very limited in scope and the Race Relations Board, established to co-ordinate the legislation lacked any real powers for effective prosecution. The 1968 Race Relations Act extended the provisions of 1965 to discrimination in employment, housing, insurance and credit. But, as Sivanandan (1976, 363) has suggested, the Act remained largely cosmetic, for little was done to improve the weak enforcement powers of the Race Relations Board. The motivation for this legislation has been identified by Macdonald (1971, 5):

> In nearly every speech in support of the 1968 legislation it was stressed that these new race laws were necessary in order to prevent the kinds of civil disorder seen in the U.S.A. They were speaking of Watts, Newark and Detroit . . . M.P.s obviously felt that if the possibility of legal redress for legitimate grievances was not available people would sooner or later take things into their own hands. The 1968 Act was undoubtedly seen as one of the ways of heading off the growing black power movement in Brtain.

If controls on black immigration can be seen as a response to white racism, the race relations legislation of the 1960s can be interpreted as a response to black militancy.

3. Racial Conflict: The 1970s

The economic crises of the 1970s produced entirely different conditions for British capital from those that had prevailed in the boom years of the 1950s and 1960s. Yet black people continued to play the twin roles of cheap labour and scapegoat identified by Castles and Kosack for immigrant labour in advanced industrial countries.

During slump conditions, the demand for cheap labour does not disappear, indeed it can increase. However, capital accumulation requires not only cheap labour but the successful reproduction of the social relations of production and this, particularly while capital operates in a system of nationally defined territories, can be achieved in part by maintaining the loyalty of the native working class to the existing state; immigrant workers and their offspring provide, as Harris (1980, 55) suggests, "the anvil on which this loyalty can be forged". While immigrants continue to provide an element of cheap labour; their socio-political function, which can remain relatively latent in periods of economic expansion, comes very much more apparent in times of recession. In the slump years of the 1970s, race became "the prism through which the British people [were] called upon to live through then understand and then deal with the growing crisis" (Hall, 1978, 30).

3·1 Black workers and industrial change

The 1971 Commonwealth Immigration Act which further restricted the entry of Commonwealth citizens to Britain was passed i⸗ the context of a continued rise in unemployment and downturn in the fortunes of the British economy. It was also passed in the context of rising racist agitation not only by the recently formed National Front but also by several politicians and government ministers of whom Duncan Sandys, Cyril Osborne and, particularly, Enoch Powell were the most notable.

This Act extended the principle of "patriality", first introduced in the 1968 Act, to all potential Commonwealth immigrants. Those Commonwealth citizens without a parent or grandparent born in the United Kingdom, were reduced to the status of aliens. The British citizenship rights of all black Commonwealth peoples were thereby effectively eliminated. Black people from the Commonwealth were to be henceforth admitted to Britain only as migrant workers on a similar basis to that of the European *Gästarbeiter*; the potential settler was turned into a contract labourer.

The 1971 Act not only reduced primary immigration to a trickle, but also imposed further limitations on the entry of dependants with the addition of unreliable x-ray and degrading virginity tests to the list of possible checks on eligibility for admission. As a consequence of these control measures, black settlement in Britain has been considerably reduced. The number of New Commonwealth arrivals has shown an overall downward trend since the late 1960s, as have the numbers of alien immigrants. While the latter have exceeded the former for most of the decade, few have been allowed to settle (Runnymede Trust, 1980, Fig. 1.15). The slight increases in New Commonwealth arrivals in 1975 and 1976 (Figure 1) reflect a speed-up in the processing of the backlog of applications; but these arrival figures, especially after 1973 when the 1971 Act became operational, overstate the number of black people who were actually allowed to settle in the country. The number of New Commonwealth settlers follow the same downward trend as that for arrivals with the major exception of 1972 (Figure 2). The figures for that year were inflated by the influx of 35 000 non-patrial Asians who were expelled by Idi Amin from Uganda (see Knepper *et al.*, 1975). In 1979 only 37 000 New

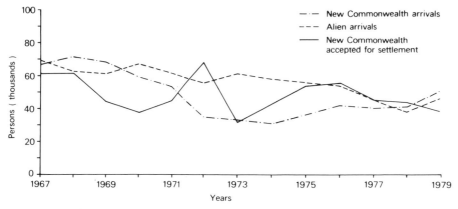

Figure 2. Immigration and settlement in the UK 1967–1979 (from: Runnymede Trust (1980) pp. 17 and 22).

TABLE 2. *Socio-economic distribution of economically active New Commonwealth workers, 1966 and 1971* (%).

| | West Indian | | | | Pakistani | | | | Indian | | | | Total population | | | |
| | 1966 | | 1971 | | 1966 | | 1971 | | 1966 | | 1971 | | 1966 | | 1971 | |
	M	F	M	F	M	F	M	F	M	F	M	F	M	F	M	F
Professional and managerial	2·2	1·2	2·7	0·7	5·9	9·2	7·0	10·3	17·7	7·3	15·9	6·9	15·4	4·9	18·0	6·4
Non-manual	5·8	30·9	7·6	39·7	5·7	53·9	5·1	45·2	19·4	60·8	15·2	43·5	17·5	47·5	18·1	50·3
Total non-manual	8·0	32·1	10·3	40·4	11·6	63·1	12·1	55·5	37·1	68·1	31·1	50·4	32·9	52·4	36·1	56·7
Skilled manual	42·2	9·9	45·1	8·9	22·2	8·2	25·2	12·3	28·3	6·6	32·1	9·5	40·3	10·6	39·7	8·4
Semi-skilled	27·6	49·9	27·2	42·6	34·9	24·2	38·1	29·4	22·9	21·5	23·9	33·9	18·3	29·4	16·0	27·3
Unskilled	22·2	8·3	17·3	8·1	31·3	4·5	24·6	2·8	11·7	3·9	12·9	6·1	8·5	7·6	8·3	7·7
Total manual	92·0	68·1	89·6	59·6	88·4	36·9	87·9	44·5	62·9	32·0	68·9	49·5	67·1	47·6	64·0	43·4

(After: Field *et al.* (1981), Tables 8 and 9).

Commonwealth immigrants were accepted for settlement, 24 000 less than in 1967; 90% of these were dependants (Runnymede Trust, 1980, 16–26). Britain's black population now consists predominantly of settlers who arrived during the 1950s and 1960s plus their children who make up an estimated 40% of the total (Field *et al.*, 1981, 9).

Given the history of other settler populations in Britain and elsewhere in advanced capitalist countries, the movement of black Commonwealth citizens from a migrant to a permanently settled population, from membership of the international labour reserve to membership of Britain's domestic work force should have been reflected in a corresponding improvement in their economic and social position with a discernible movement away from the type of deprivation and degradation which continues to characterize the truly migrant workers in many European countries (see Castles, 1980). Yet as various government reports (Unit for Manpower Studies, 1976), independent surveys (Smith, 1977; Rex and Tomlinson, 1979), and census analyses (Monck and Lomas, 1975) have established, the role and position of black workers in the 1970s remained substantially the same as in the preceding two decades. Despite evidence of token dispersal in jobs and residence (Lomas, 1973; Lee, 1977), black workers continue to be over-represented in unskilled and manual occupations, as they were during the 1960s (Table II) and remain concentrated in the deprived inner areas of Britain's conurbations and cities (Table III).

Today black people in Britain continue to be associated with unpleasant jobs particularly in textiles, rubber, plastics, foundry and rolling mill operations. They also concentrate in the service sector where they are again associated with the lower end of the job market in public transport, the health service and in the hotels and catering trades. In the mid-1970s, 43% of all black workers were employed in plants of 500 or more, which compared with only 29% for the white working-class; almost a third of these were on shift work, more than twice the percentage for whites. A wage differential of

TABLE 3. *Distribution of birthplace groups by urban zone,*
1961 and 1971 (%).

	Urban Core		Metropolitan Ring		Outer Metropolitan Ring	
	1961	1971	1961	1971	1961	1971
West Indians	91·4	90·7	5·9	6·7	2·4	2·3
Asians (Indian and Pakistani)	67·4	77·0	21·8	15·6	8·6	5·6
Total Population	51·8	47·9	27·9	31·1	15·8	16·4

Source: Pinch and Williams, 1977.

8% in favour of white workers, despite the supposedly higher earnings of shift work, further emphasizes the low status of black occupations (Counter Information Services, 1976; Runnymede Trust, 1980, Chapter 3).

The vulnerable position of Britain's black population is also indicated by its residential characteristics. The settlement areas of black immigrants in the 1950s and 1960s, particularly in the large conurbations of the South-East, the West Midlands and the North-West, remain the areas of major concentration today. In 1971 Greater London, Birmingham, Leicester, Bradford and Wolverhampton alone accounted for approximately one third of the entire New Commonwealth born population in Britain (Runnymede Trust, 1980, Table 1·2).

Within these cities again the black population is not evenly distributed, but tends to concentrate in particular boroughs and wards which are often associated with deprived inner city environments. These aspects have been demonstrated in a Department of Environment report which indicates that in 1971, 70% of Britain's New Commonwealth-born population lived in only 10% of all enumeration districts, comprising 20% of the total population in these districts. These same districts also contained three times as many households living in overcrowded conditions: that is, exceeding 1·5 persons per room (see Runnymede Trust, 1980, p. 83).

While some black groups have changed their housing tenure during the late 1960s and 1970s, a trend due partly to the further contraction of a privately rented sector, they still remain disproportionally concentrated in poorer housing (Cross, 1978, Chapter 3). West Indians have moved increasingly into council accommodation (between 1974 and 1978 West Indian council tenancies increased by 19%, from a total of 26%), but they have invariably ended up in dilapidated, hard-to-let estates (Runnymede Trust, 1980, 76; Cross, 1978, 62). Similarly, while Asians have considerably increased their levels of owner-occupation, which now account for over 75% of all Asian tenures, in comparison with their white counterparts, they continue to occupy older and poorly maintained property. Asians are also over-represented among those who share a dwelling, are ten times more likely than white households to share a bath, and six times more likely to be sharing a w.c. As Cross (1978, 29) rather graphically concludes, "the geography of despair tends to coincide with the geography of immigrant settlement and concentration".

Yet it is perhaps in relation to unemployment that the vulnerability of Britain's black population today is most vividly demonstrated. Not only are black people concentrated in unattractive and poorly paid jobs, but they also suffer from a great deal of insecurity of employment. Between 1973 and 1980, a period of severe economic downturn for the British economy, when unemployment for the entire population of the country doubled, for black workers it has quadrupled (Runnymede Trust, 1980, 64–68). However, these figures disguise significant variations within the black communities, variations which reflect generational, ethnic, sex and regional differences. West Indian youths, for instance, tend to experience the highest levels of unemployment. As early as 1971, when unemployment among all young males between 15 and 20 years was 8·6% among West Indian youths it was 14·5% (O'Muircheartaigh and Rees, 1976, 494).

Among Asian youths unemployment tends to be lower, reflecting in part under-registration, but also the apparent ability of some Asian groups to absorb their youth in "formal" and "informal" occupations serving the local community (see Jones, 1977; Robinson, 1979). Yet this situation may be changing; between February 1977 and February 1978 the increase in unemployment in the 16–24 age group accounted for 36% of the total increase in unemployment among Asians. Some of these factors may help to explain other ethnic variations between Asian and West Indian workers. Between February 1979 and February 1980, when total unemployment rose by 2·6%, registered unemployment among West Indians increased by 13·5%, but only by 10·1% among Pakistanis (Runnymede Trust, 1980, 66).

Regional variations in unemployment rates among Britain's black population tend to reflect their pattern of settlement, being highest in those areas where they have settled in numbers. In August 1977 when black workers accounted for 4·0% of total unemployment, in the West Midlands and Greater London, the two conurbation areas with the largest black settlement, they comprised 9·6 and 7·7% respectively (Field *et al.*, 1981, Appendix B). Clearly in certain areas and in certain age groups black workers have borne the brunt of the recession in the British economy during the 1970s.

Though Britain's black population can no longer be regarded as a *migrant* labour force (a role taken on by Spanish, Portugese, Italian and Filipinos workers in recent years; see Migrant Services Unit, 1981), they remain a source of cheap labour for British capital earning, on average, nine-tenths of the wages of their white counterparts (Smith, 1977, 87). They continue to act as a "replacement" population, being disproportionately represented in the ranks of the unemployed and doing some of the worst and least attractive jobs. Black workers are twice as likely (three times in the case of Pakistanis) to be doing shift work as white workers (Smith, 1977, 80, 81). Black people in Britain form a particularly vulnerable section of the working population; they are, as Sivanandan (1980, 295) succinctly puts it, "oppressed in their race, exploited in their class".[7]

Several forces have operated in Britain over the post-war years to explain why today a settled black population continues to occupy essentially the same position and performs the same role in British society as black immigrants of two or three decades ago. First, there has been the ambivalence of trades unions towards the plight of black people, and this despite the high levels of unionization and demonstrations of workplace militancy among black workers (Marsh, 1967; Radin, 1966; Rose *et al.*, 1969, 311–17; Hiro,

1971). Though many trades unions have made principled declarations of intent, few have taken direct action against discrimination. This has been attributed by Miles and Phizacklea (1977; 1978) to the fact that the TUC, until the mid-1970s, at least, did not regard such discrimination as particularly widespread. The major problem in the perspective of the TUC was apparently that of the "integration" of black workers with their white counterparts; the onus for any integration was placed on black workers themselves. Indeed the TUC was opposed for a time to the 1968 Race Relations Act which among other things outlawed job discrimination on the basis of skin colour. TUC argued that such a move would prejudice the employment chances of white workers (see Freeman, 1979). In 1974, however, in an apparent reappraisal of its policy, the TUC began campaigning on the behalf of black people, organizing at least one major demonstration and producing several anti-racist leaflets. This activity, though not sustained through the remainder of the 1970s, was in the estimation of Phizacklea and Miles (1980, 94) a response to the increasing militancy of black workers during the early 1970s (e.g. the Manfield Hosiery and Imperial Typewriters disputes; see Moore, 1975, Chapter 5) and to the alarming successes of the National Front in recruiting white working-class support. This reluctance of trades unions to identify explicitly with the needs and problems of immigrant labour has a long tradition in Britain (see Hiro, 1971; Garrard, 1971) and the words of Ben Tillet, the nineteenth century M.P. and dock workers union organizer, echo down the years typifying trade union attitudes today as much as they did a century ago: "yes, you are our brothers and we will do our duty by you, but we wish you had not come" (quoted in Garrard, 1971, 157). This kind of stance obstructs the development of working-class unity and inhibits the ability of black workers to fight against their lowly position in the employment structure (see CARF/Southall Rights, 1981, Chapter 2).

Freeman and Spencer (1979) in a consideration of the position of black workers in the British economy have noted a second force which may be regarded as helping to confirm the oppressed status of black people. These authors make use of the notion of a "dual labour market" (see Piore, 1979). The "secondary sector" of this labour market, in direct contrast with the "primary sector", has jobs which are unattractive and poorly paid; employers have "little investment in each worker" and therefore "tolerate high turnover rates and in recession can lay-off employees to offset reduced demand" (Freeman and Spencer, 1979, 59). Structural and institutional divisions, supported not only by employers but also by primary sector workers, who form a kind of "labour aristocracy", are seen as operating to severely inhibit the upward movement of secondary sector employees. Freeman and Spencer argue that since black workers tend to concentrate disproportionately in secondary sector employment, structural as well as discriminatory barriers exist to ensure the continued association of black workers with the lower end of the job market and indeed with the domestic labour reserve. This assessment, however, has to be matched against the observation that in some sections of the employment market, particularly in secondary-sector type jobs, black labour, like some immigrant labour elsewhere in Europe (Castells, 1979; Rist, 1978), is becoming structurally irreplaceable. The evidence in Britain is fragmentary, but there are indications of such developments in sections of the textile industry (Allen *et al.*, 1977), public transport (Brooks, 1975) and the National Health Service (Unit for Manpower Studies, 1977, 58–66). These trends, however, are not necessarily contradictory; their relative importance needs to be established by empirical investigation.

A third, and probably the most important force, particularly in the light of the preceding two features, which serves to preserve the oppressed status of black workers, is their legal and political position. The edifice of control over immigration erected during the 1960s and 1970s has progressively eroded the citizenship rights of black Commonwealth immigrants. The 1981 revision of the Nationality Act in establishing a three-tier hierarchy of citizenship continues this erosion, and indirectly calls into question the status of black people in Britain, whether immigrant or not (see Manchester Law Centre, 1981). These developments need to be seen in the context of the attempts by capital at restructuring in the present period of crisis, particularly, as Castles (1980) demonstrates, in the light of the increasing tendency towards investment in underdeveloped countries. This is a feature predominantly of large capital, of the multinational firms, who are attracted to the underdeveloped countries by the carrots of tax holidays and the availability of cheap, non-unionized labour, often controlled by dictatorial regimes (see Coleman and Nixson, 1978); these sections of capital, at least, would prefer immigrant labour to remain in their countries of origin. Against this, however, other sections of capital, which have a less global perspective or are associated with non-moveable and unpleasant jobs in the national economies of advanced industrial countries, continue to demand a cheap and pliable section of the domestic labour force; a demand which is also characteristic of parts of the public service sector of state employment. Immigration controls serve the needs of both sectors of capital not only by restricting the entry to Britain of workers from some underdeveloped countries, but also by helping to assign a politically inferior status to all black people in the country, thus facilitating their continued oppression and scapegoat role in a period of prolonged recession.

3·2   *Racism, black militancy and the State*

Legislation in the 1970s has also been concerned with the control of immigrants once they have gained entry to the country. The establishment of the Illegal Immigrants Intelligence Unit in 1972 and, especially, following the 1978 issue of new regulations to immigration officials, the increasing frequency of "fishing raids" on homes and workplaces in the search for illegal immigrants and overstayers are symptomatic. If suspected of illegal entry or overstaying black people can be arrested without warrant, convicted without trial, and deported without the right of appeal in the United Kingdom (see Macdonald, 1981). These activities are indicative of a marked extension in the level of state surveillance and harassment of blacks during the 1970s (Hall *et al.*, 1978; I.R.R., 1979); they have served to focus attention on blacks as a "problem" and a threat in British society, and thus encouraged an escalation in demands for further controls from the racists, an escalation which could only take the form of repatriation schemes, given that the 1971 Act effectively brought to an end primary immigration from the New Commonwealth. Calls for the repatriation of black immigrants, which have come not only from neo-Nazi groups but also from "respectable" organizations such as the Monday Club (Proctor and Pinniger, 1981 reported in *Guardian*, 28 April, 1981), have so far been resisted, though the voluntary repatriation provisions of the 1971 Act have, in the estimation of one author at least, prepared the ground for the "induced repatriation" of black people (Sivanandan, 1978).

These developments have to be seen and judged alongside the increasingly oppressive and racist interpretations of the rules and regulations concerning entitlement to welfare benefits and access to educational and health services. In the context of massive cuts in public expenditure, the result of the dogmatic pursual of monetarist policies, black people are a relatively easy target. Despite declarations to the contrary by government ministers, black people in Britain are regularly required to produce evidence of legal settlement in the country before access to social services and benefits is conceded; skin colour alone is sufficient to arouse suspicion of non-entitlement (see Gordon, 1981).

State legislation and activity whether designed to prevent the entry of black immigrants or control blacks resident in the country has fostered a climate of hostility in which discrimination and oppression have become part of the everyday experience of black people in Britain. The extent of this discrimination and hostility has been demonstrated nationally in the mid-1970s P.E.P. reports on racial disadvantage in housing and employment (see McIntosh and Smith, 1974; Smith, 1977) and in various local investigations (see C.RE., 1980). The result is manifest in the disadvantaged position of black people in their schools, workplaces and residential areas, as well as in their direct experience of racist abuse and brutality from neo-fascist organizations and their sympathizers.

This is demonstrated in the numerous neo-fascist marches through or near black residential areas and in the increasing number of vicious assaults on black individuals and their property. In 1980 alone, neo-fascists marched in Southwark, Lewisham, Corby, Central London, Blackpool, Brighton, Halifax, Turnbridge Wells, Preston, Glasgow, Nuneaton, Hull, Hoxton,

Dewsbury, Enfield and Welling; while black men, women and children have been attacked and killed in places as far apart as Newham, Southall, Longsight and Leeds.

Oppressive state legislation, gratuitous references by politicians and government ministers to the social and cultural problems apparently posed by the presence of black people, which includes those by the present Prime Minister, Margaret Thatcher, who in a Television interview in January 1978 echoed some of the sentiments of Enoch Powell and the National Front by raising the spectre of the "British way of life" being "swamped by people with a different culture" (see Manchester Law Centre, 1981, 9), plus the vicious propaganda of the neo-Nazis, all serve to identify Britain's black population as a threat: the "cause" of the present (and past) social and economic problems which afflict British society. In a word, racism, assiduously cultivated by anti-black organizations, sections of the news media and opportunist politicians, and promoted by state activity offers to many among the white population a tangible cause for the alienation they increasingly feel in the present period of crisis. Among young whites in particular, experiencing unemployment from the time of leaving school, faced with no prospects for the foreseeable future except the dole queue, and with little education and no skills to offer a dwindling economy, anti-black agitation has become an attractive proposition, offering as it does race hatred and national pride as the basis for a resurgence of individual pride and identity.

The responses of the black communities in the 1970s to the increasing levels of racism and harassment has been to convert, sometimes with the help of white anti-fascists, the informal self-help defence groups of the 1960s into more structured organizations; the Southall Youth Movement and the Coventry-based Committee for Anti-Racist Defence Squads are examples. Exclusively black organizations in the tradition of the Racial Adjustment and Action Society of the late 1960s are few, and tend to be localized, though the Rastafarian movement, to the extent that it has a self-defence component, has a widespread membership among the West Indian population. National organizations like the Anti-Nazi League and the Campaign against Racism and Fascism, established in part for the protection and defence of black people are multi-racial (see Sivanandan, 1981, for a more comprehensive account of these groups).

But the militant behaviour of black people is not entirely or even principally encompassed in their reaction to marauding white youths and the intimidatory activity and physical assaults of the neo-fascist groups. The economic and social conditions which have provided the background for the growth of racism among whites in the 1970s have also given rise to frustration and alienation among blacks who, as we have seen, suffer disproportionately from the effects of recession. Beyond the organization of self-defence, black people have demonstrated a degree of workplace militancy in the 1970s (the disputes at Mansfield Hosiery, Imperial Typewriters and

Grunwick being the most prominent) and now, at the beginning of the 1980s have taken to the streets in violent protest at state oppression and their general condition of degradation.

The usefulness of a particular group as a scapegoat and a source of cheap labour is, as Baran and Sweeny (1968, 260) have indicated, assured only so long as the group plays its role "passively and resignedly", and in an attempt to placate black militancy, the 1970s have seen a series of measures designed to shore up the ineffectual race relations legislation of the 1960s.

The intention of the 1976 Race Relations Act was, according to Sivanandan (1976, 367) not "just to outlaw discrimination, but to carry the fight against discrimination to every area of society", and for the first time "real teeth" were given to the enforcement of anti-discriminatory legislation. However, as the 1979 annual report of the Commission for Racial Equality indicates, these powers of enforcement have been negated in part not only by cuts in the Commission's budget, but also by direct government interference in its day to day operations (CRE, 1979, 8 and 36).

The problems associated with the implementation of the anti-discrimination legislation reflect the difficulties of the British state in reconciling the need to maintain social control by placating black unrest with the need to ensure a profitable level of discrimination so that black people continue to provide a cheap workforce and a convenient scapegoat.

In dealing with potential black protest the inadequacies of the anti-discrimination legislation were partly compensated for by the extension of another strand of official race relations activity, namely the attempt to "integrate" black people and their problems into a wider social context through the agency of community relations. The attempt to co-opt black leaders to what Katznelson (1973, 186) has labelled "buffering institutions" (see also Hill and Issacharoff, 1971) with the establishment of the National Council for Commonwealth Immigrants (NCCI) and its local offshoots, the Voluntary Liaison Committees, in 1965 was the first major move by any government towards this objective. The effect at that time was startingly demonstrated in the collapse of the black-based Campaign Against Racial Discrimination following the defection of two of its leaders, Pitt and Alavi to the NCCI. The 1968 Race Relations Act transformed the NCCI, established as an independent body, into the Community Relations Commission which was made responsible to the Home Office whose principle functions include law and order the internal security (see Bridges, 1975); the Voluntary Liaison Committees were simultaneously replaced by local Community Relations Councils. In 1976 the Community Relations Commission has amalgamated with the Race Relations Board to form the Commission for Racial Equality under the direction of the former Tory M.P. David Lane.

Like the anti-discrimination legislation, the community-relations organizations were designed to create the illusion among black people that their demands could be met through the institutions of the British state. In those few instances where Community Relations Councils (CRCs) appeared to reflect the real interests of the black population, there activities were stifled by the denial of central funds (Mullard, 1971, Chapter 9). The more general experience indicates that the CRCs operated to defuse and accommodate black protest and to co-opt existing and potential independent black leaders

Figure 3. Courtesy Counter Information Services.

to the service of *status quo* organizations (Mullard, 1971, Chapter 10; Hill and Issacharoff, 1971, Chapter 6).[8]

The practice of the CRCs has belied the rhetoric of their initiation and, as the effects of economic recession have borne down with increasing ferocity on black communities, black people, and especially the black young, have been evermore unwilling to be placated by the promises of establishment organizations. As the velvet glove of community relations proved incapable of containing black protest, the iron fist of state coercion has been progressively revealed in order to maintain discipline.

4. Conclusion: Racial conflict, industrial change and social control

The uneven nature of capitalist development is reflected in the differential impact of the present period of crisis. Regionally, the old distressed areas of the inter-war period, Scotland, Northern Ireland, South Wales and parts of Northern England, emerged first as the worst affected. But with the prolongation of the recession traditionally prosperous areas such as the Midlands and the South-East have also experienced a downturn and, though the broad distinctions remain, since the middle of the 1970s there has been a degree of regional convergence with these two areas, the Midlands in particular, experiencing rapid increases in unemployment; between 1975 and 1980 the respective increases for the South-East, the East Midlands and the West Midlands were 43·5%, 45·2% and 48·6%, compared with a UK average of 44·3% (see Friend and Metcalf, 1981, 88).

In all regions, the uneven impact of the recession has also been apparent in that the inner areas of the country's conurbations and cities, in contrast to the outer suburbs, have borne the brunt of the crisis in the form of de-industrialization, mass unemployment, urban decay and declining social service provision. Thus in 1977 when unemployment in the North-West stood at 6·8%, in Merseyside it was 10·7%, while the male unemployment in Liverpool reached 15% and in inner Liverpool, 18% (Friend and Metcalfe, 1981, 89). But again, though the inner areas continue to display some of the worst effects as the recession deepens, its spatial impress becomes more extensive and today working-class areas in the conurbation suburbs, smaller industrial towns, New Towns and rural areas are also characterized by these features.

It was to many of the inner urban areas that black immigrants were first attracted in the more prosperous 1950s and 1960s. Here they acted as a replacement population taking on jobs which were largely unskilled or semi-skilled, and it is these which have proved to be the most dispensable in recession; black workers are among the first to be made unemployed. Unemployment or, at best, temporary and insecure employment, is the present experience of many black workers. Having been recruited from the international reserve army of labour to Britain's domestic work-force, many black settlers and their descendants have now been forced into the domestic labour reserve. Yet other blacks remain in relatively secure employment, albeit on low pay and in poor conditions, doing jobs in catering, transport and the National Health Service that, even today, few whites or indeed second-generation blacks, are willing to touch.

But black people make up only some 4% of the UK population, and in the inner urban areas rarely comprise more, and often less, than 20% of the total. As the recession continues and as successive governments reduce public expenditure, more and more people outside the black community are affected. Mass unemployment, though still disproportionately experienced by black workers, now encompasses other vulnerable sections of the workforce especially among women and school-leavers, white as well as black. Additionally, many adult males working in the traditional industries such as shipbuilding and engineering, have also felt the effects of economic restructuring in the form of lay-offs and redundancies. These groups form a major component of what Marx called the "surplus population": that group in society which is marginal to the requirements of capital in terms of the direct production of surplus value during a long period of recession (Marx, *Capital*, vol. 1, 600-3, 1971 edition).

Politically, the existence of this group has an important role to play in creating divisions within the working class between the "respectable" employed section, the "labour aristocracy" of the "primary sector" of the labour market on the one hand, and the unemployed and semi-employed "surplus population" on the other; divisions which are based on sex, race and generational differences. The "surplus population" also has a breaking effect on the militancy of those workers in employment, and has been used as an effective instrument of wage bargaining, serving to keep wage settlements below the general level of inflation in recent years.

Yet the persistence and growth of the "surplus population", particularly with the addition of many black workers and youths, has posed serious problems of social control for the ruling class in general and for state authorities in particular. Fear of the "marginalized" masses, of the urban poor is not new to British capitalism. Freed from the discipline of wage labour and deprived of resources, the unemployed and casually employed have often engaged in violent activity challenging, albeit often implicitly, the social order and the authority of the state. The latter part of the nineteenth century and the recession years of the 1930s saw many such instances. In 1932 alone there were riots in Liverpool, Tyneside, London, Leeds, Glasgow, Wigan and Stoke; the biggest riot took place in Birkenhead in September, where for three days and nights there were pitched battles between the police and the unemployed (see Stedman-Jones, 1971; Harman, 1981).

In the present recession, the possibility of such disorder has long been apparent, not only in the clashes between police and blacks at carnivals

(Brockwell Park, Notting Hill) and in the violence involving fascists, police and anti-racists at various marches and rallies (Lewisham, Ladywood, Southall), but also, and perhaps more threateningly, in the clashes between police and massed pickets as demonstrated most notably outside the Grunwick film-processing plant in July 1977. The possibility of disorder emanating more specifically from the "surplus population" has also been apparent in recent years, in for instance, the escalation in certain types of crime among the young. In 1977, 51% of all arrests in London involved people under 21, and 44% of all burglary arrests were under 17; youths aged between 17 and 21 accounted for 25% of the prison population (Friend and Metcalf, 1981, 162). The police harassment of the young, black and white, but especially black, apparent in the indiscriminate use of the "sus" law in Manchester, Liverpool and London and in the swamping operations of the SPG (London) and the Tactical Patrol Group (Manchester) must all be seen in this context, as must the coercive nature of police activity in the black communities generally.

Much coercive activity of the police, in the day to day harassment of the young and black people in attempting to control the streets in Britain's towns and cities, and in directly protecting the property and interests of capital, has been legitimized in the eyes of the "respectable" white population by the ideology of racism which helps to link black people with areas of high crime rates – with "mugging" offences and drug abuse in the West Indian communities and with the violation of immigration laws in Asian communities (see Hall *et al.*, 1978) – and by the successful stereotyping of "troublemakers" among the "surplus population" as "scrounger" or "hooligans", and among other sections of the working class as "wreckers" or "mindless militants".

The urban riots of the early 1980s suggest that from among Britain's "surplus population", black people and especially the black young, pose the most immediate threat to social order. State activity relating to black people in the post-war period has increasingly reflected the problems associated with maintaining their economic and political usefulness while negating their disruptive potential. The imposition and tightening of restrictive immigration controls has contributed to attempts to keep the size of the "surplus population" within manageable proportions. The imposition of restrictions on immigrant workers is a familiar pattern of capitalism in crisis. In recent years many European countries have also reduced, often considerably, through expulsion and restricted recruitment, the number of immigrants in their labour markets (OECD, 1979). Repatriation is not (yet) an option that Britain can apply to its *settled* black population, though it does apply (and is applied) to alien workers.

Attempts to contain the potential militancy of the black population in particular and other, growing, sections of the "surplus population" in general, are also apparent in the series of initiatives from successive governments during the late 1960s and 1970s associated with the development of an "urban programme". The urban aid scheme of 1968, the partnership programmes of 1977, even the present Conservative government's urban development corporations and enterprise zones, have all been enacted in the context of actual or threatened social disorder (see Edwards and Batley, 1978; McKay and Cox, 1979). Through the course of the 1970s, the urban programme has increasingly focussed on the inner cities as the areas which have experienced some of the worst effects of economic restructuring and as the areas in which disturbances are most likely to occur, for it is here that the "surplus population" concentrates.

This urban programme needs to be seen alongside other attempts at restraining the disruptive potential of sections of the "surplus population": job creation schemes, youth opportunity programmes and of course the development of race and community relations organizations. The notable lack of success of the urban programme and other initiatives in smoothing the uneven effects of recession suggests that the recommendations of the present Environment Minister, Michael Heseltine, – recommendations which can be characterized as "more of the same" (*Scotsman*, 6 August, 1981) will offer little more than palliatives, particularly in the context of continued cuts in public expenditure.

Increasingly the creation of the conditions for the successful restructuring of capital in the present period of crisis demands the use of the authoritarian and coercive apparatus of the state (Ackroyd *et al.*, 1977; Bunyan, 1981). This is apparent, on the one hand, in the use of repressive legislation (conspiracy and picketing law, public order acts, Criminal Attempts Act, and the Criminal Justice (Scotland) Act) and, on the other hand, in the training of police in riot-control techniques and in the issue of special riot gear, C.S. gas and plastic bullets: techniques and weapons tested and proved in that scene of prolonged social disorder, Northern Ireland.

The need for many of these instruments of "positive policing" is disputed, not only by organizations such as the National Council for Civil Liberties (*Guardian*, 2 September, 1981), but also among government ministers and police officials. The state in Britain maintains and reproduces capitalist social relations principally by promoting popular consent for its own rule and support of the established order, though, in the final analysis, its ability to squash opposition by force is the guarantee of its survival. The ability of the state to deal effectively with outbreaks of public violence which challenge that established order poses a real test of its legitimacy. But in such circumstances, a precipitous resort to force and violence on the part of the state might threaten the popular consent on which the successful pursual of its everyday activities are based. Thus the demands from those agents of the state in the "front-line", from those who have been charged with control of the streets, for the reintroduction of a riot act and enhanced police powers, have to be balanced against pleas for "community policing" and social initiatives designed to win "hearts and minds".[9] This balancing takes place in the context of an assessment not only of the nature of the threat posed by unorganized and largely spontaneous riots by black and white youths, but also of the possibility of their recurrence and even escalation; an escalation which would possibly encompass other sections of the population in places outside the inner cities where, as the recession continues, a combination of declining living standards, rising unemployment, racism and despair create the conditions for further disturbances.

References

Ackroyd, C. *et al.* (1977). "The technology of political control", Penguin, London.

Allen, S. (1970). Immigrants or workers, *in* S. Zubaida (ed.) "Race and racialism", 99–126, Tavistock, London.

Allen, S. (1977). "Work, race and immigration", School of Studies in Social Science, University of Bradford.

Baran, P. and Sweezy, P. (1965). "Monopoly capital", Penguin, London.

Baudouin, T. *et al.* (1978). Women and immigrants: marginal workers?' *in* C. Crouch and A. Pizzorro (eds), "Resurgence of class conflict in Western Europe since 1968, 71–99, Macmillan, London.

Bethnal Green and Stepney Trades Council. (1978). "Blood on the streets", London.

Bonhomme, S. (1971). "Enoch Powell and the West Indian immigrants", Afro-American and West Indian Publishers, London.

Bourne, J. (1980). Cheerleaders and ombudsmen: the sociology of the race relations in Britain, *Race and Class*, **XXI** (4), 331–352.

Braithwaite, E. R. (1967). The coloured immigrant in Britain, *Daedalus*, **96** (2), 456–511.

Bridges, I. (1975). The Ministry of Internal Security: British Urban Social Policy, 1968–74, *Race and Class*, **XVI** (4), 375–86.

Brooks, D. (1975). "Race and labour in London Transport", O. ford University Press, London.

Brooks, D. and Singh, K. (1979). Ethnic commitment versus structural reality: Southern Asian immigrant workers in Britain, *New Community*, 7(1), 9–31.

Bunyan, T. (1981). The police against the people, *Race and Class*, **XXIII** (2/3), 153–170.

Burney, E. (1967). "Housing on trial", Oxford University Press, London.

Butterworth, E. (ed.) (1967). "Immigration in West Yorkshire", I.R.R. Special Series, London.

C.A.R.F./Southall Rights. (1981). "Southall: birth of black community", Institute of Race Relations, London.

Castells, M. (1979). Immigrant workers and class struggles in advanced capitalism, *in* R. Cohen *et al.* (eds), "Peasants and Proletarians", Hutchinson, London.

Castles, S. (1980). The social time-bomb: education of an underclass in West Germany, *Race and Class*, **XXI** (4), 369–387.

Castles, S. and Kosack, G. (1972). The function of labour immigration in Western European capitalism, *New Left Review*, **73**, 3–23.

Castles, S. and Kosack, G. (1973). "Immigrant workers and class structure in Western Europe", Oxford University Press, London.

Coates, K. and Silburn, R. (1971). "Poverty: the forgotten Englishman", Penguin, London.

Cohen, R. G. and Jenner, P. J. (1968). The employment of immigrants: a case study within the wool industry, *Race* **10** (1), 41–56.

Colman, F. and Nixson, D. (1978). "Economics of change in less developed countries", P. Allan, Oxford.

Commission for racial equality. (1979/80). "Annual Reports", HMSO, London.

Counter Information Services. (1976). "Racism, who profits?" Anti-Report, No. 16, London.

Cox, O. (1948). "Caste, class and race", Doubleday & Co., New York.

Cross, C. (1978). "Ethnic minorities in the inner city", C.R.E., London.

Dahya, B. (1973). Pakistanis in Britain: transients or settlers, *Race*, **14**, 246–77.

Daniel, W. W. (1968). "Racial discrimination in England", Penguin, London.

Deakin, N. (1970). "Colour, citizenship and British society", Panther, London.

Desai, R. (1963). "Indian immigrants in Britain", Oxford University Press, London.

Doherty, J. (1969). The distribution and concentration of immigrants in London, *Race Today*, **8**, 227–281.

Egbuna, O. (1971). "Destroy this temple", MacGibbon and Kee, London.

Edgar, D. (1977). Racism, fascism and the politics of the National Front, *Race and Class*, **XIX** (2), 111–131.

Edwards, J. and Batley, R. (1978). "The politics of positive discrimination: an evaluation of the urban programme, 1967–77, Tavistock, London.

Field, S. *et al.* (1981). "Ethnic minorities in Britain", HMSO, London.

Foot, P. (1965). "Immigration and race in British politics", Penguin, London.

Freeman, G. P. (1979). "Immigrant labour and racial conflict in industrial societies: the French and British experience, 1945–75", Princeton University Press, New Jersey.

Freeman, M. D. A. and Spencer, S. (1979). Immigration control, black workers and the economy, *British Journal of Law and Society*, 6 (1), 53–81.

Friend, A. and Metcalf, A. (1981). "Slump city, the politics of mass unemployment" Pluto Press, London.

Garrard, J. A. (1971). "The English and immigration: a comparative study of the Jewish influx, 1880–1910", OUP, London.

Gordon, P. (1981). Pass laws and internal control, *Rights*, **5**(5), 6–7.

Gorz, A. (1970). The role of immigrant labour, *New Left Review*, **61**, 84–92.

Hall, S. (1978). Racism and reaction, *in* Commission for Racial Equality, "Five views of multi-racial Britain", pp. 23–35, London.

Hall, S. *et al.* (1978). "Policing the crisis: mugging, the state and law and order", Macmillan, London.

Hallett, G. (1970). The political economy of immigration control, *in* The Institute of Economic Affairs, "Economic issues in immigration", pp. 123–50, Gresham Press, Surrey.

Harman, C. (1981). The summer of 1981: a post riot analysis, *International Socialism*, **14**, 1–43.

Harris, N. (1980). The new untouchables: the international migration of labour, *International Socialism*, **8**, 37–63.

Hartley-Brewer, M. (1965). Smethwick, *in* N. Deakin (ed.), "Colour and the British electorate, 1964, 54–76, Pall Mall Press, London.

Hepple, B. (1970). "Race, jobs and the law in Britain", Penguin, London.

Hill, M. and Issacharoff, R. (1971). "Community action and race relations", Oxford University Press, London.

Hiro, D. (1971). "Black British, white British", Eyre and Spottiswoode, London.

Home Office. (1965). "Immigration from the Commonwealth", HMSO, London.

Home Office. (1981). "Racial attacks", HMSO, London.

Husbands, C. T. (1979). The National Front: what happens to it now?, *Marxism Today*, September, 18–29.

Hytner, B. (1981). "Report of the Moss Side Enquiry Panel to the Leader of Greater Manchester Council", Manchester.

Institute of Race Relations. (1979). "Police against black people: evidence submitted to the Royal Commission on Criminal Procedures", Institute of Race Relations (IRR), London.

Institute of Race Relations. (1969). "Facts Paper: colour and immigration in the United Kingdom", IRR, London.

Jones, C. (1977). "Immigration and social policy in Britain", Tavistock, London.

Jones, K. and Smith, A. D. (1970). "The economic impact of Commonwealth immigration", Cambridge University Press, Cambridge.

Jones, P. (1981). British unemployment and immigration, *New Community* **IX** (1), 112–16.

Jones, P. N. (1970). Some aspects of the distribution of coloured immigrants in Birmingham, 1961–66, *T.I.B.G.* **50**, 199–219.

Katznelson, I. (1973). "Black men, white cities", Oxford University Press, London.

Kerner, O. (1968). "Report of the National Advisory Commission on Civil Disorders", Bantam Books, New York.

Kindleberger, C. P. (1967). "Europe's post-war growth: the role of labour supply", Harvard University Press, New York.

Knepper, W. *et al.* (1975). "Ugandan Asians in Great Britain", Croom Helm, London.

Kushnick, L. (1981). Parameters of British and North American racism, *Race and Class*, **XXIII** (2/3), 153–172.

Lambeth, J. (1970). "Crime, police and race relations", Oxford University Press, London.

Lambeth, Borough of, (1980). Final Report of the Working Party into Community/Police Relations in Lambeth, Public Relations Division, Lambeth, London.

Lee, T. R. (1977). "Race and residence: the concentration and dispersal of immigrants in London", Oxford University Press, London.

Leech, K. (1966). Migration and the British population, 1955–62, *Race*, **VII** (4), 401–408.

Lomas, G. (1973). "The coloured population of Great Britain", Runnymeade Trust, London.

Lomas, G. (1979). Employment and economic activity, 1971 census data, *New Community*, **VII** (2), 217–224.

Macdonald, I. (1971). "Race relations: the new law", Butterworth, London.

Macdonald, I. (1981). Police raids and searches for immigrant offenders, *New Law Journal*, July 768–770.

McIntosh, N. and Smith, D. (1974). The extent of racial discrimination, *"Population and Economic Planning Report"*, **547**.

MacKay, D. and Cox, A. (1979). "The politics of urban change", Croom Helm, London.

Manchester Law Centre. (1980). The thin edge of the white wedge, *in* "Immigration Handbook", No. 5, Manchester.

Marsh, P. (1967). "The anatomy of a strike: unions, employers and Punjabi workers in a Southall factory", I.R.R. Special Publication, London.

Marx, K. (1971 edition). "Capital", 3 vols. Progress Publishers, Moscow.

Migrant Services Unit. (1981). "Permitted to work: a background report on migrant workers", London Voluntary Service Council Pamphlet, London.

Miles, R. and Phizacklea, A. (1977). The TUC, black workers and new Commonwealth immigration, 1954–73, *Research Unit on Ethnic Relations Working Papers*, No. 6, University of Aston, Birmingham.

Miles, R. and Phizacklea, A. (1978). The TUC and black workers, 1964–76, *British J. of Industrial Relations*, **XVI** (2) 195–207.

Miles, R. and Phizacklea, A. (1979). "Racism and political action in Britain", R.K.P., London.

Monck, E. and Lomas, G. (1975). Employment and socio-economic conditions of the coloured population, Centre for Environmental Studies. Res. Paper 21.

Moore, R. (1971). "Race relations: Britain today", Student Christian Movement Pamphlet, London.

Moore, R. (1975). "Racism and black resistance in Britain", Pluto Press, London.

Moore, R. (1980). Migrants and the class structure of Western Europe, *in* R. Scase (ed.), "Industrial society, class cleavage and control", 136–148, Allen & Unwin, London.

Moore, R. and Wallace, T (1975). "Slamming the door: the administration of immigration control", Martin Robertson, London.

Mullard, C. (1971). "Black Britain", Allen & Unwin, London.

O.E.C.D. (1979). Foreign workers: a current inventory, *Observer*, **79**, 33–34.

O'Muircheartaigh, C. and Rees, T. (1976). Migrant/immigrant labour in Great Britain, France and Germany, *New Community*, **IV** (4), 493–560; and (3), 380–391.

Patterson, S. (1963). "Dark strangers", Penguin, London.

Patterson, S. (1969). "Immigrants in industry", Oxford University Press, London.

Peach, C. (1968). "West Indian migration to Britain", Oxford University Press, London.

Peach, C. (1979). British unemployment cycles and West Indian immigration, 1955–74, *New Community*, **VII** (1), 40–43.

Peach, C., Winchester, S. and Woods, R. (1975). The distribution of coloured immigrants in Britain, *Urban Affairs Quarterly, Annual Review*, No. 9, 394–419.

Phizacklea, A. and Miles, R. (1980). "Labour and racism", Routledge & Kegan Paul, London.

Pinch, S. and Williams, A. (1977). Changes in the distribution of immigrant groups in the British urban system, 1961–71, Paper presented to the Urban Geography group of the IBG May meeting, Kings College, London.

Piore, J. (1979). "Birds of passage: migrant labour, and industrial societies", Cambridge University Press, Cambridge.

Pixley, D. (1968). "The closed question", Chapman, London.

Procter, H. and Pinniger, J. (1981). "Immigration, repatriation and the Commission for Racial Equality", Monday Club, London.

Radin, B. (1966). Coloured workers and British trade unions, *Race*, **VIII** (2), 5–19.

Rex, J. (1980). A working paradigm for race relations research, *Ethnic and Racial Studies*, **4** (1), 1–25.

Rex, J. and Moore, R. (1967). "Race, community and conflict", Oxford University Press, London.

Rex, J. and Tomlinson, S. (1979). "Colonial immigrants in a British city", Routledge and Keegan Paul, London.

Richmond, A. (1955). "The colour problem", Penguin, London.

Rist, R. C. (1978). "Guestworkers in Germany", Praeger, New York.

Robinson, V. (1979). The segregation of Asians within a British city: theory and practice, School of Geography, University of Oxford, Research Paper 22.

Robinson, V. (1980). Correlates of Asian immigration: 1952–72, *New Community*, **VIII** (1/2), 115–123.

Rose, E. J. B. *et al.* (1969). "Colour and citizenship", Oxford University Press, London.

Runnymeade Trust, (1980). "Britain's black population", Heinemann, London.

Scarman, Lord. (1981). "The Brixton disorders, 10–12 April, 1981". HMSO, London.

Segal, R. (1967). "The race war", Penguin, London.

Sivanandan, A. (1976). Race, class and the state: the black experience in Britain, *Race and Class*, **XVII** (4), 347–368.

Sivanandan, A. (1978). From immigration control to induced repatriation, *Race and Class*, **XX** (1), 75–82.

Sivanandan, A. (1980). Fighting Tory racism, *Race and Class*, **XXI**, (3), 291–296.

Sivanandan, A. (1981). From resistance to rebellion: Asians and Afro-Caribbean struggles in Britain, *Race and Class*, **XXIII** (2/3), 111–152.

Smith, D. J. (1977). "Racial disadvantage in Britain", Penguin, London.

Stedman-Jones, G. (1971). "Outcast London: a study in the relationship between classes in Victorian society", Oxford University Press, London.

Tannahill, J. A. (1968). "European volunteer workers in Britain", Manchester University Press, Manchester.

Tommis, S. (1974). Urban residential segregation and an immigrant community, MA thesis, University of Dundee (unpublished).

Unit for Manpower Studies. (1977). "The role of immigrants in the labour market", Department of Employment, London.

Walker, M. (1977). "The National Front", Fontana, London.

Waller, P. (1981). Liverpool: why the clue to violence is economic not racial, *The Times*, July 7.

Wallman, S. (ed.) (1979). "Ethnicity at work", Macmillan, London.

Wickenden, J. (1958). "Colour in Britain", Oxford University Press, London.

Winchester, S. (1974). Immigrant areas in Coventry in 1971, *New Community*, **4** (1), 97–104.

Wright, P. L. (1968). "The coloured worker in British industry", Oxford University Press, London.

Zubrzycki, J. (1956). "Polish immigrants in Britain", Nijhoff, The Hague.

Notes

1. The journals *Race Today* (especially the 1976 issues) and *Searchlight* (e.g., January, 1981) contain many such accounts.

2. In 1977, for example, black youths who make up 2·8% of the total London population accounted for 44% of all "sus" arrests in the city (Institute of Race Relations, 1979, 41)

3. For the derivation of this term and a discussion of the "industrial reserve army", see Marx, *Capital*, Vol. 1, pp. 600–603, 1971 edition.

4. The "New Commonwealth" excludes Australia, New Zealand and Canada.

5. There are, however, important parallels between the position of women and black people in the labour market, and between sexism and racism, which we are unable to pursue here – (see Baudouin *et al.*, 1978).

6. The statistical juggling, particularly by Robinson, to produce significant correlations, and the generally low level of these correlations in both analyses, weakens their arguments (see Jones, 1981).

7. The terms used to characterize the position of black people in British society – "subproletariat" (Sivanandan, 1976), "underclass" (Rex, 1980), "racialized fraction" (Miles and Phizacklea, 1979) – have been the subject of considerable debate and disagreement (see Moore, 1980).

8. The mediating placatory role played by representatives of community organizations in the April 1981 Brixton Riots (Scarman, 1981, pp. 21–32) is a further indication of this tendency.

9. Opposing viewpoints encapsulated in the evidence to the Scarman Inquiry in 1981 by, on the one hand, Assistant Commissioner Gibson of the Metropolitan Police, and, on the other, by John Alderson, Chief Constable of Devon and Cornwall (*Times*, 3 September 1981; *Guardian*, 4 September, 1981).

NINE

Industrial change and Scottish nationalism since 1945

P. B. SMITH and J. BROWN

(February 1982)

1. Introduction

One of the quickest ways of provoking an argument with a Scot would be to talk of Scotland as a *region* of Britain: most Scots have some consciousness of belonging to a *nation*. This consciousness reflects socio-economic developments rooted in the history of Scotland and the country's place in a system of social and international relations. In a short essay such as this, it is not necessary to analyse these developments; rather, it can be asserted that they were determined by changes in the forces and relations of production such as the technological changes underlying the development of capitalism out of feudalism and the social class changes which accompanied them.[1] But the fact of *continuity* of the dimension of "Scottishness" and its effects on the psychological make-up of the Scottish people, acquired over generations, has to be appreciated before one can move on to discuss the post-1945 re-emergence of nationalism as a political movement, and its relationships with industrial change. By way of introducing this theme we will devote some attention to developments in the Scottish, and British, economy as a prerequisite to the resurgence of Scottish nationalism.

In the post-1945 period Scotland has been a "declining urban economy" (see Cameron, 1971). Implicit in this description is the fact that Scotland was once an "ascending urbanizing economy". A detailed description of this "ascent" is beyond the scope of this essay; however we can give a brief outline of its broad pattern (see Hamilton, 1966; Slaven, 1975 for detail).

From the 1830s, and accelerating in the 1870s Scottish economic success came from an industrial sector interconnecting iron and steel, and centred on shipbuilding. Based originally on the distribution of coal and iron, West Central Scotland came to specialize in steel, shipbuilding and heavy engineering, while the East Central region concentrated on lighter industries.

In this period Clydeside was at one corner of a "Golden Triangle" of relative prosperity whose other corners were Belfast and Liverpool. Britain as the "workshop of the world", or, more correctly, Britain as the first and leading imperialist economy, was experiencing a geographical division and specialization of labour and production. An industrial boom area was created which attracted companies seeking the benefits of facilities and skills; for example, Singers (sewing machines) moved to Clydebank in 1870, Babcox and Wilcox (boilers) to Renfrew in the 1890s, and Yarrows (shipbuilders) to Scotstoun, all on the Clyde.

The industries which characterized this area were primarily in heavy engineering, and they altered the social structure through their demands for labour intensiveness and unskilled labour. Cities and towns grew in size as immigrants, mainly from the Highlands and Ireland, were attracted to Central Scotland; social polarization was intense with few middle-class suburbs and little social mobility (see Walter, 1980). It was this pattern which shaped the Scottish economy and society, and population distribution was determined by this pattern of industrial development into the 1960s (Snodgrass, 1966). Thus, Scotland was, and is, a highly urbanized and industrialized country with 75% of its population in the Central Lowlands, and 40% around Glasgow. By 1971, only 5·6% lived in the Highlands and Islands and, overall, less than 5% were engaged in agriculture (see Fig. 1).[3]

However, from the beginning of the 20th century, and particularly after 1918, Scotland lost its position as a relatively prosperous part of Britain, a part which had enjoyed higher wages and lower unemployment than, for example, London. The traditional dependence of Scottish heavy industry on exports led to severe problems as the world economy moved progressively into depression. Specifically, lack of capital investment in new technology caused a deterioration in Scotland's advantages in costs over other countries in the inter-war period.

This decline was halted by the Second World War and the demand by the Government for goods and services. The continued weakness in the structure of the Scottish economy was hidden by the buoyancy of the post-war and early 1950s demand for goods. Thus, although the Scottish economy was in *long-term* decline throughout the period, it was not directly evident because of the post-war boom and the prosperity of the people when compared to the 1930s. It is this post-war period we can now move on to consider.

2. Post-war developments: industrial decline

The return of a Labour Government in 1945 seemed to mark the isolation of the forces of conservatism and privilege, and the development of a radical consensus for qualitative change centred on the organizations of the working class. However, by 1951 the political balance had shifted to the right and

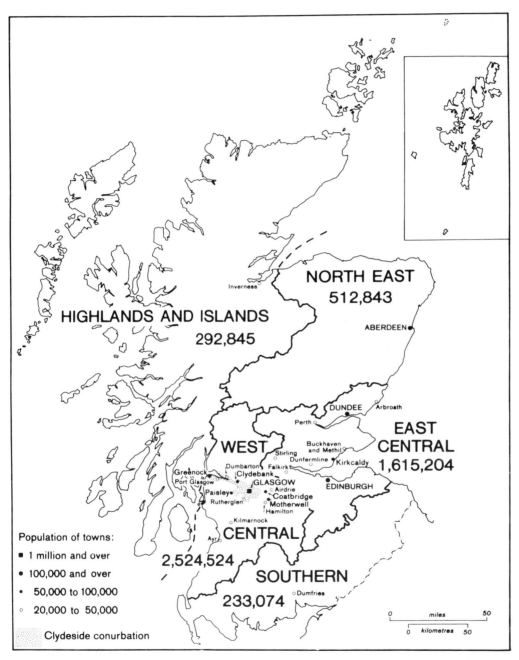

HIGHLANDS AND ISLANDS
292,845

NORTH EAST
512,843

Inverness○

ABERDEEN●

DUNDEE● ○Arbroath

Perth○

WEST

Buckhaven
and Methil○

EAST
CENTRAL
1,615,204

Stirling○

Dunfermline○ ○Kirkcaldy

Dumbarton○ Falkirk○
Greenock● |Clydebank
Port Glasgow   ○GLASGOW
Paisley●   ○Airdrie
        ○Coatbridge
Rutherglen○ ○Motherwell
            |Hamilton

EDINBURGH●

Ayr○

○Kilmarnock

CENTRAL
2,524,524

SOUTHERN
233,074

○Dumfries

Population of towns:
■ 1 million and over
● 100,000 and over
• 50,000 to 100,000
○ 20,000 to 50,000

Clydeside conurbation

0   miles   50
0   kilometres   50

Figure 1. Scotland: population distribution 1971. Source: 1971 census.

the Conservatives under Churchill were back in government reinforcing the
"cold war" political reaction initiated in the later years of Attlee's administration. The trade union movement, with its majority in the grip of so-called
"moderate" forces, participated along with the rightwing in the Labour
Party in the Cold War. This political balance in the unions and Labour Party
did not start to shift away from the right until the late 1960s and early 1970s.
However, no later Labour general election victory generated a popular
enthusiasm to match that shown in 1945. At no time since then has the
Scottish working-class, alone or in unity with its counterparts in England,
Wales and Ireland, effectively threatened, as distinct from challenged, the
existing order of society.

However, the lack of threat to capital in the post-War period does not mean
that British capital could unilaterally define the course of development of the
economy or of society generally. By the 1970s it was obvious that the two
major nations defeated in 1945, Japan and Germany, were the more economically powerful. The two major victors, the USA and Britain, were, relatively
speaking, technologically backward. Within Britain this was particularly
true of Scotland though, and as has been said, this was initially hidden by a
buoyancy of orders in the heavy industrial sector and in its profitability and
employment. Whereas between 1921 and 1931 there had been a fall of 55 615
(22·7%) in the numbers employed in metal working in Scotland, expansion
in the War and post-War years saw employment in this category grow to
257 086 by 1951 (even greater than the 1921 total of 245 000). The Census of
Population of that year could still report that Glasgow "is well in the
forefront of the iron industry, and boilermaking, steel tube making, locomotive building and general engineering . . ." The converse, of course, was that
Clydeside "shows some deficiency in the light industries . . ." (Lesser, 1951).
In the mid-1950s, for example, the Scottish shipbuilding yards employed
27 000, the same number as in 1900, and in the period 1951–54 Scotland's
share of world shipbuilding averaged 12%; railway engineering employed
over 10 000 in the early 1950s, and the North British Locomotive Company
in Springburn, Glasgow, with 5000 employees was a world giant.

Thus, in the 10 years after 1945, as the economy experienced boom
conditions, there were few indicators of discontent from the labour market or
labour force (Marwick, 1964). The old capitalist dynasties of Scottish industry, personified in shipbuilding by Stevens, Yarrows and Lithgows, and
in steel by Colvilles, still held a controlling influence in the direction of the
economy. However, their dominance was being imperceptably undermined,
indeed eroded. This resulted from the intervention of Government ownership in key sectors, such as mining and transport, the growth of new industries under non-Scottish ownership, and the activities of English
capitalists extending ownership over Scottish competitors (e.g. Leyland
took over Albion Motors in Glasgow).

The industrial specialization of Scotland, within British imperialism, was leading to intense contradictions. Despite relatively high prosperity, the Scottish economy was growing slower than the British economy as a whole and there was no replacement of lost export markets.[4] Scotland's contribution to National Income in 1924 was 9·8%. In 1948 it was 8·9%, and by 1960 was down to 8·7% (though it rose to 9·0% in 1976 because of North Sea oil). British imperialism's post-1945 rearguard action in the face of US world expansion, industrial neglect at home and massive capital investment overseas (see Morgan and Sayer this volume), had a disproportionately negative impact on Scotland. The effects of these trends began to be seen after the peaking of employment in Scotland's traditional industries in the 1950s, and the decline thereafter in these industries which had been the basis of prosperity. Employment peaked in textiles and clothing in 1951, in vehicles and marine engineering in 1955, in metal manufacture, shipbuilding and ship repair in 1956, in construction in 1957 and in coal mining in 1958. By 1968 Scotland's share of world shipbuilding was down from an average of 12% in 1951–54 to 1·3%, and only two of the remaining yards were profitable. The North British Locomotive Company was moribund, with only a wagon works at Wishaw, Lanarkshire, and a small locomotive works at Kilmarnock, Ayrshire, together employing less than 1000 workers by 1963. This relative decline in the Scottish economy was made more striking by the "economic miracle" taking place in Japan and some Western European countries from the mid-1950s.

The Clydeside conurbation, with 40% of Scotland's population, displayed in a concentrated way the depth of the problems of the economy, and the underside of the post-war prosperity. Thus, the 1972 local government "Areas of Need" report, in comparing Glasgow with other British cities, found in terms of twenty characteristics that in almost all cases Glasgow was worst. Another report indicated that of the 121 most socially deprived enumeration districts in Britain, the Glasgow area accounted for 115.

Industrial specialization remained the key characteristic and in the 1950s, the Glasgow conurbation remained over-represented in four sectors of manufacture: shipbuilding, engineering, metals and food. These accounted for 57·7% of manufacturing employment compared with 42% for Britain as a whole. The continuing central importance of shipbuilding to the Scottish economy as late as the early 1960s can be seen from the fact that one-sixth to one-seventh of total manufacturing employment still depended upon it. Thus any decline in shipbuilding, and heavy industry as a whole, would have serious economic and social effects (Robertson, 1962). Glasgow alone lost over 85 000 jobs in the 15 years up to 1977. Of these, 65 000 were in manufacturing and 60% of these were in metals, engineering, shipbuilding and marine engineering.

There were two important consequences of this economic decline which affected the social structure. As we shall see, these consequences were to facilitate the rise of the Scottish Nationalist Party (SNP). First, the skilled workers in heavy industry were subject to declining numbers, status, relative wages and industrial power from the late 1950s. Similar changes took place in the coal-mining and railway industries, and these leading sections of the labour movement were forced on to the defensive. In turn this led to changes in the shape of the Scottish labour movement. Working-class communities, socially and politically united over generations by the rigours of existence tied to specific dominant industries, were fragmented and particular political responses lost their meaningful historical context (cf. MacIntyre, 1980).

The second consequence was an influx of foreign capital attracted by low wage-levels, a reserve army of unemployed (Scotland regularly experienced twice the average rate of British unemployment) and the regional policies of successive governments in the 1960s which underwrote foreign investment through various forms of subsidy. (This regional intervention was to some extent the outcome of pressure on governments from the Scottish Trades Union Congress as a response to the obviously deepening economic decline.) Of all the American companies established in Britain after 1945, one-third were sited in Scotland, and in the period 1958–68 overseas companies accounted for 30% of all new employment created by new enterprises. By 1975 only 41% of manufacturing employment was controlled by Scottish owners, while for Clydeside foreign ownership was even higher (see Firn, 1975; Scott and Hughes, 1980).

Two results of this penetration are particularly important in understanding political change. First, the creation of new factories caused organizational problems for the trade-union movement and almost certainly dislocated areas of its operation. This was especially true because of the anti-union stance of many North American employers and their ability, through paying better than local wages, to split the labour force (e.g. IBM in Greenock). A related point is that these foreign-owned plants were mainly branch plants often assembling imported parts. They required semi-skilled labour and low numbers of technical and skilled workers when compared to indigenous employers, and so reinforced de-skilling processes already evident in the economy. These processes led one writer to observe that Scotland was "more working class and its population . . . less skilled, *vis-à-vis* England, than at any time since the First World War" (Payne, 1977). The existing economic and social basis of the labour movement was weakened even further.

Secondly, the influx of foreign capital led to realignments within the capitalist class in Scotland while reinforcing dependence on sources of non-Scottish capital. Also, foreign capital, through employing such a large proportion of the labour force, and by creating a stratum of management not trained by the traditional capitalists, weakened the old networks of social control.[5] The expansion of state employment in government and services had a similar effect. This weakening allowed space for some independent political action by the "new middle class" and led to changes in local politics, especially when "nationalism" came to the fore.

These processes in the economy, altering its balance of industry and employment, and the relative power and organization of different social groups, had important effects on the politics of the labour movement and the Scottish people as a whole. It is these effects that we will look at in the next section through the prism of the economic developments outlined.

3. The politics of nationalism

The form of civil society in Scotland has differences from that of England (e.g. in law and education). However, these differences in *form* should not blind us to the fact that the *content* of the institutions of civil society are almost identical across the two countries; the differences are generally superficial.[6] These institutions function to maintain the class domination of capital, although the differences of form between Scotland and England help sustain the "Scottishness" referred to at the beginning of this essay. However, it is not the differences in civil society which are the key to explaining differences in politics between Scotland and England but rather the evolution of the Scottish economy and the effects this has had on the class configurations in society.

Throughout the post-war period Labour has been the main representative of Scotland in Parliament.

TABLE 1. *Number of Scottish constituencies taken by Labour, 1918–79*
(total number of Scottish constituencies = 71).

1918	'22	'23	'24	'29	'31	'35	'45	'50	'51	'55	'59	'64	'66	'70	'74	'74	'79
9		18	35	26	37	7	24	40	37	35	34	38	43	46	44	40	41	44

Labour could claim to be the *Scottish* party, continuing a tradition of anti-Toryism and representing the aspirations of the majority of the Scottish people (McLean, 1977). The problem of how best to meet the national sentiments of the people could be avoided until the rise of the Scottish National Party pushed it forward. This does not mean it was ignored. Almost every Labour Party Scottish Conference from 1941 to 1959 had resolutions carried calling for a committee of enquiry into the demands for devolution/self-government. However, two points can be made here. First, the Scottish Council of the Labour Party proved itself the "good son" of the British Labour Party by accepting every decision on devolution by the National (i.e. British) Executive Committee. A main factor in the opposition to the concept of devolution was the belief, by the Labour Party in Scotland, that

economic security remains the primary factor for the Scottish people and this cannot be divorced from the economic prospects of the country as a whole . . . inseparable from th..t of England and Wales and cannot be imagined as a self-supporting entity. (Scottish Council Labour Party Conference Report, 1959)

Devolution for Scotland was thus viewed narrowly and so believed to be against the unity of the labour movement in Britain as a totality. As early as 1947, the secretary of the Scottish Council said he had "dropped the desire for devolution immediately [after] they had secured a Socialist government".[7] From this view devolution was a barrier to social and economic progress. According to the secretary, Labour Party members had to make up their minds whether they were "Nationalists or Socialists". Indeed, devolution should be dismissed because there was "no interest among workers in this subject". Support for it came "mostly from the university adolescents and from the professional and middle classes . . ." It is in these statements that one can see an expression of labourist ideology: a consciousness of class which confines the working class to a sectional, subservient position in society, rather than projecting it to head the nation, defining its socio-economic image and the path it should follow.

In actual fact, for most Labour Party members, and for most Scottish people, devolution was not, and is not, a major issue. The major issues were (and are) unemployment, industrial development and housing. It was resolutions on these issues which dominated Conference agendas. Even on the *single-issue* referendum on Scottish devolution in March 1979, only 32·5% of the electorate (or 51·6% of voters) supported devolution. By February 1982, fully 93% of replies to a MORI opinion poll of Scottish voters cited unemployment as the major political issue. Only 8% cited devolution (*The Guardian*, 8 March, 1982).[8]

Yet, the emphasis on industrial and social issues did not lead, as it did in the Scottish Trades Union Congress under the pressures of deteriorating socio-economic conditions, to an adoption of more militant policies; or at least not *until the late 1970s* (see Smith and Brown, 1980). The Scottish Council confined itself to the parameters of British Labour's "planned" restructuring of industry. Thus, the policy document "Signposts for Scotland" (1963) recognized "special needs" in Scotland and identified some of the causes of these needs. It failed, however, to pinpoint the depth of the emerging economic crisis and its probable impact on working-class behaviour in the political and industrial fields. Instead, emphasis was put on increasing the powers and scope of the Scottish Office (the Government's political and administrative centre in Edinburgh). Even as late as 1968, in the wake of a Scottish National Party parliamentary by-election victory at Hamilton (the SNP's first MP since 1950, and in an urban, industrial, working class area at that) and municipal losses to the SNP, the Labour Party referred the question of whether it should support devolution back to its constituency committees. It was not the time, it was argued, for "compromising" or "going on the defensive".[9] Rather, the Scottish people should be told the "facts" of what Labour had done for them. Some Conference delegates had an "implicit faith in the Scottish people; they will once again rally back to the Labour Party . . ." Indeed, the almost instinctive loyalty of the Scottish working-class to Labour has, up until the present, justified this implicit faith of Labour leaders.

However, it should not be thought that support for the Labour Party leads to workers feeling "un-Scottish". Rather, they still identify ethnically, and culturally, with "Scottishness" and define themselves as Scottish. Rather what is meant by being Scottish differs with political identification. Thus, Labour voters, in so far as they choose between Socialism and Nationalism, choose the former without feeling that they have diminished their Scottishness. They believe Labour is Scotland's party and conceive of themselves as Scottish workers giving priority to their "classness" while correlating it with their Scottishness through support for their class organizations (see McLean, 1977; Jaensh, 1976).

This correlation between "class" and "Scottishness" is, however, one which is under almost constant renegotiation within the labour movement under the impact of the present economic crisis. It was one of the factors leading to a splinter from Labour when the Devolution debate was at its most intense in the 1974–79 period. Thus the splinter, the Scottish Labour Party, saw itself explicitly as uniting the socialist and nationalist dimensions. Its initial effect seemed significant because it occurred in Labour's heartland of membership in Ayrshire.[10] However, after an initial surge of support, because of dissatisfaction with Labour's economic failures and the dominance of the right-wing in the Party apparatus, it disintegrated. This was because it failed to win an organizational base, or connect with any significant section of the working class. Once again loyalty kept the majority of working people behind their traditional political organizations. Nevertheless, some of the limits of this loyalty can be seen in the realignments of sections of working people behind the SNP in response to the deep rooted changes in the social structure and the economy. The Labour Party's stress on the unity of Britain for Scotland's prosperity rebounded in the late 1960s and early 1970s when "unity" failed to produce this. At the same time prospects of an oil-rich Scotland, separate from Britain, emerged.

The emergence of nationalism in the form of the SNP is the focal point of a complex range of phenomena connected with a specific historical situation and economic conditions. We can now look at the political impact of the economic events described above. (For histories of Scottish nationalist organizations themselves see Brand, 1978; Webb, 1978.) The attempts by British imperialism to reorientate itself in the face of the post-War dominance of the US and the counter attacks of the EEC, have taken place against the background of a general crisis of capitalism. On the one hand, Britain has been forced to give up its "Empire", and, on the other hand, British capital has withdrawn from the "Celtic fringes" since the 1960s in order to finance the drive into the EEC. This loss of capital engendered local crisis in traditional industries and forced an enlargement of State involvement to provide some new employment and meet the deficits of small capitalists. As discussed above, this weakened the economic power and organizational base of the labour movement, both in industry itself and in working-class communities. This phase of the crisis has also seen a tendency for splits to develop between monopoly capital ("big business") and smaller capitalists located in fringe areas (Greaves, 1968). Simultaneously, the political support for monopoly capital, via the Conservative party, began to fragment as inflation and recession had severe effects on small businessmen, farmers and other sections of the middle class. A reflection of this has been the partial breakup of old relationships between London-based capital, with Scottish connections, and indigenous Scottish capital. This has led to conflicts, contradictions and confusion among the political representatives of capital on how to deal with the Scottish question (of which more below).

These problems for capital, and their effect on its political base, can be seen in the decline in support for the Scottish Conservative and Unionist Party. Its means of influencing and manipulating working people to support it have become less effective. Its share of the vote has declined from 50% in 1955 to 25% in October 1974, although climbing back to 31% in 1979. It has become a party based on the rural and small town areas of Scotland (Joensh, 1976). This can be seen to have led them towards isolation from the centres of electoral power in the urban areas; the figures for population distribution are illuminating in this respect (see Table 2, and also Fig. 1).

TABLE 2. *Distribution of population (1964)*.

Percentage of population living in:	
Cities	35·8
Large towns	17·0
Small towns	18·5
Rural areas	28·7
	100

The Scottish population is predominantly urban. A further, isolating, feature of Conservative rural support can be seen from the regional variations in urban-rural population shares. The electorally crucial industrial areas of Central Scotland are especially urban (Table 3).

Furthermore, as the bases of both Labour and Conservative support weakened, so the chances of electoral success for the SNP increased. A belief developed among a section of the Scottish people that the problems of

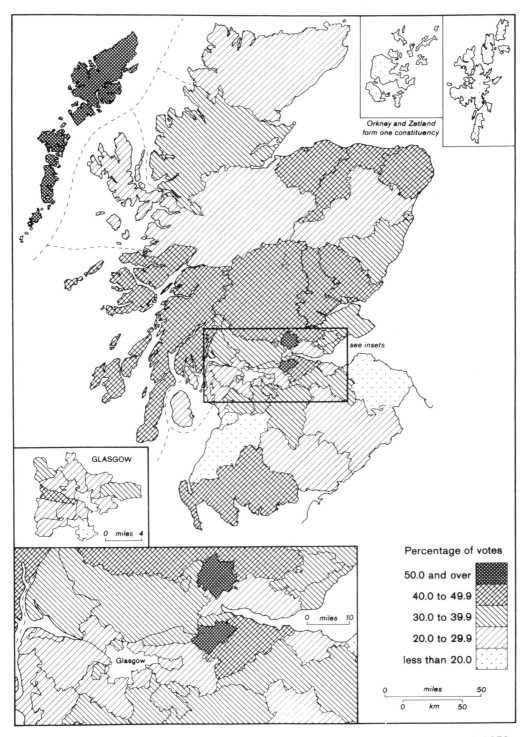

Figure 2. Electoral support for the SNP, October 1974. Source: Butler and Kavanagh 1979.

TABLE 3. *Constituency types by region, 1979 (number of constituencies).*

	Urban	Mixed	Rural	Total
West Central	28	2	2	32
East Central	14	3	1	18
North East	2	–	8	10
Highlands and Islands	–	1	6	7
Southern	–	–	4	4
Total	44	6	21	71

Source: Butler and Kavanagh, 1979, App. 1.

the country could be solved in isolation from the rest of Britain since the "wealth of oil destroys the myth that Scotland is too poor for self-government" (according to the SNP's president, William Wolfe, in 1973). The SNP claimed to "Put Scotland First", and said the choice was between being "poor British" or "rich Scots", since independence would bring "stability and continued prosperity . . ." As a party the SNP combined radical demands with reactionary ideas of national isolation and negation of class struggle. Thus William Wolfe described the SNP as "a genuine movement for social justice . . . which avoided 'left' versus 'right' arguments", and categorized other political parties as "English political forces in Scotland". Margo McDonald, for a few months in 1974, SNP MP for Govan, Glasgow, claimed the SNP was "Scotland's classless and radical party", and Winnie Ewing, SNP MP for Hamilton between 1968 and 1970 and SNP MP for Moray and Nairn between 1974 and 1979, described SNP members as the "good Scots". The rise of support for their party can be seen in Table 4.

The alteration in the social structure gave social and political relevance, and a possibility of success, to the SNP. In voting terms, "nationalists" have always had some local municipal presence, and the occasional good by-election vote which can almost be seen as a localized "protest vote" (e.g. Bridgeton, Glasgow, in 1961 and West Lothian in 1962). Overall, however, the SNP were about as successful, sometimes even less so, as the Communist Party up to 1964. They did not overtake the Liberal party until 1970 (see Table 4). After then the SNP vote began to expand dramatically and even reached second party status by October 1974 (although the increase partly reflected the increase in the number of seats fought).

However, if we compare the votes obtained by the SNP in the 1950s with the period after 1964, things become a little clearer. The Scottish Convention Movement, developing after the Labour Party Conferences of 1948–49 (which in effect killed Labour's commitment to Scottish independence) attracted over a million signatures to a Covenant to "secure for Scotland a

TABLE 4. *% Vote gained by parties in general elections in Scotland.*

Date	Con.	Lab.	Lib.	SNP	Communist
1935	41·6	36·7	14·0	1·3	0·6
1945	36·3	47·3	9·0	1·2	0·4
1950	44·8	46·1	6·6	0·4	1·0
1951	48·6	47·8	2·7	0·3	0·4
1955	50·1	46·7	1·8	0·5	0·5
1959	47·2	46·6	4·0	0·8	0·5
1964	40·6	48·7	7·6	2·4	0·4
1966	37·6	49·9	6·8	5·0	0·6
1970	38·0	44·5	5·5	12·8	0·4
1974 (Feb)	32·9	36·6	8·0	22·7	0·5
1974 (Oct)	24·7	36·3	8·3	30·6	0·3
1979	31·4	41·5	9·0	17·1	0·2

Parliament . . ." This period provided a peak for nationalist (and SNP) political activity, yet the SNP's electoral vote remained tiny. The Covenant did indicate, however, that feelings did exist which could be politically significant in a different context. And this context was created by socio-economic changes reaching a head in the 1970s.

In the 1950s, most people supporting the Convention were unwilling to give expression to their feelings by voting nationalist. They were unwilling to increase their commitment beyond signing a petition, refusing at that stage to move to a qualitatively new attachment to a new political formation. SNP ideology and propaganda lacked credibility while the bases for Labour and Conservative support remained strong.

All who have studied the growth of nationalism in the form of the SNP agree on the importance of economic decline in making it credible (e.g. Marwick 1964, Brand 1978, Maxwell 1978). In previous periods of high unemployment and depression a solution always seemed possible within the framework of *British* capitalism. However, in the post-war period both Conservative and Labour governments have failed to solve the problem of Scotland, while the decline of British imperialism has become obvious. The

TABLE 5. *Average % vote obtained by SNP in seats contested,*
1935–1966.

1935	1945	1950	1955	1959	1964	1966
12·2	9·1	7·4	14·8	11·3	10·6	14·1

failure of Labour, in particular, to improve things in Scotland meant that sections of people who had backed it began to look for alternatives. This coincided with the discovery of oil and gas in the North Sea which gave hope for the future to link with the resentments of the past. As an SNP Member of Parliament, Gordon Wilson, pointed out, there is an "inescapable relationship between self-government and Scotland's North Sea Oil wealth" (reported in Wolfe, 1973, 159).

As has been said, the socio-economic changes caused the break-up of old urban working-class communities, both at home and in the factory. These class communities had built up their social integration over generations, and their break-up led to a fracturing of solidarities and loyalties and resulted in changed attitudes to organizations seeking to represent the interests of the working class. In part this can be illustrated in the decline of "Little Moscows" and Communist votes in seats the Communist Party regularly contested (Table 6).

Any such analysis is complicated by, *inter alia*, boundary changes in (Parliamentary) constituencies, but falls in population show the trend. Thus, in Dundee there was a marked population decline in the city centre and around the docks (e.g. Riverside declined by $34 \cdot 9\%$, Dudhope by $34 \cdot 8\%$ between 1951–61) and this coincided with the decline in the jute processing industry. In Glasgow areas like Cowcaddens, Govan, Hutchisontown and Gorbals lost one third of their populations between 1951 and 1961, with similar losses 1961–71, as sections of the engineering industry closed or moved out of the city.[11] At the same time, and as part of the cause of city-centre "de-industrialization", a number of "new towns" were built around Glasgow (East Kilbride, Cumbernauld) and outside Edinburgh (Livingstone and Glenrothes). These "new towns" had unique class and age compositions. The skilled:unskilled ratio in Glasgow was $2 \cdot 9:1$; in East Kilbride it was $14 \cdot 6:1$ (Henderson, 1974). The average age in the "new towns" was substantially lower than in the older conurbations. It was to these "new towns" that the bulk of foreign factories went, giving rise to a sort of "new middle-class" with little loyalty to the old political dynasties, as well as an industrially and organizationally weaker working-class. And it was in the "new towns" that the SNP made its greatest impact on the Labour vote. Nonetheless, unlike the situation in England, decline in working class occupational and community organization did not lead to an increase in the Conservative vote. From 1959 Scotland's voting behaviour started to deviate from that of England, and Labour dominance became marked by the mid-1960s. It seemed the "natural party of government" in Scotland. However, it *failed* to radically alter the Scottish economy in the period 1964–70, and in the same period it *attacked* working-class aspirations by imposing incomes policy and attacking trade-union rights.

It was from the mid-1960s that membership of the SNP began to grow, from about 2000 in 1959 to between 60 000–100 000 by the mid-1970s. Its

TABLE 6. *Percentage Communist vote in regularly contested seats.*

	1931	1935	1945	1950	1951	1959	1964	1966	1970	1974
Fife West	22·1	37·4	42·1	21·6	10·7	8·4	7·4	3·6	1·7	
Dundee West	5·8				2·7	2·1	2·4	2·4	1·6	1·3
Springburn*	5·8			4·1		4·0	3·7	3·7	1·8	1·4
Gorbals*	7·9			5·9		5·9	5·6	4·1	2·5	
Govan*				2·6		4·9	4·0	4·0	1·5	

* All in Glasgow.

impact on the electorate at large also increased. This made it the largest party in individual membership terms, while in October 1974, it became the second party in voting terms, although falling back in 1979 (and by 1981 membership was down to 40 000.) Important inroads were made into the Labour vote. In 1970 it ran second in 35 of Labour's 44 seats (38 of the 44 were in the Central belt which has 48 of Scotland's 71 seats). In addition, it won 11 seats during the 1970s, three of which had been Labour (Western Isles in 1970, Dundee West and Stirlingshire East in February, 1974) and eight Conservative (Argyll, Aberdeen East, Moray and Nairn, Banff and Galloway in February, 1974, and Dumbartonshire East, South Angus and Perthshire East in October, 1974). In 1979 the SNP fell back to two seats, Western Isles and Dundee West (see Figs 2 and 3 for constituency variations in SNP voting.) While it cut into the Labour vote, the list of seats won by the SNP in 1974 shows that its major impact was in the North East of Scotland and in rural or island areas (although this is overemphasized by the vagaries of the British "first past the post" electoral system). The North-East is particularly interesting in this context. It was there that oil developments had their main impact, and the region has always had a class structure rather different from the rest of Scotland (with a preponderance of small businesses and farms employing labour in small-scale and relatively paternalistic ways, see Carter, 1979).

It is of interest to note that a section of Scottish finance capital was also converted to the SNP. Thus Sir Hugh Fraser, followed by Ronald MacNeil of Dalsuit Merchant Bank, Ian Noble of Seaforth Maritime Investments, Sir William Lithgow and Lord Clydesmuir all publicly backed the SNP. This would be part of a strategy of developing new financial institutions backed by a Scottish government which could utilize oil revenue for foreign investment. This section of finance capital was a minority group and faced the opposition of the dominant sections of Scottish capital, who were better integrated into British capital and found the relationship sufficiently profitable. However, this dominant section was itself somewhat divided over the attitude to take towards independence. Thus, for example, General Accident sought safeguards from the SNP about its actions in an indepedent Scotland, while the CBI came out against devolution. Notwithstanding these conflicting attitudes to the SNP, the support given to it by leading financial personalities such as Lithgow, Noble and MacNeil must have reinforced its influence in the Tory constituencies.

From its success in the North-East and in the "new towns", it can be suggested that the SNP was most successful in the most prosperous parts of Scotland, more specifically those parts of Scotland where peoples' aspirations were greatest, and where any suggestion of regression (as both Labour and Tory governments postulated) would be most resisted. In the most deprived area, Clydeside, it failed to make an electorial break-through of a permanent kind as opposed to winning isolated parliamentary by-elections and some municipal support. This may be related to the base of its support being less specific than Labour and Conservative, both of which are strongly class-based (Jaensh, 1974). The SNP does not seem to be based on distinct social attributes but is cross-sectional in support, as shown in Table 7.

TABLE 7. *O.R.C. Poll, October 1974 by "social class".*

	AB	C1	C2	DE
Labour	9	17	37	44
Liberal	5	9	4	4
Conservative	66	45	24	22
SNP	19	28	33	29
Other	1	1	1	–

Where AB roughly equal "higher professionals"
    C1 roughly equals "managerial/self-employed"
    C2 roughly equals "white collar/skilled workers"
    DE roughly equals "semi-/unskilled workers"

SNP support was thus considerable among each social group, although "skilled workers" gave the highest support, so that it almost reached the level of support given by this group to Labour. The problem for the SNP, given its support by social class, was that the Scottish population tends to be concentrated geographically in such a way as to minimize the SNP's Parliamentary representation. It drew its strength, in Parliamentary terms, from areas which had less class polarization. Thus, it was weak in big cities where the working class were concentrated and stronger in small towns and rural areas (Cornford and Brand, 1969). It is also in these latter areas that the extent of labour movement influence is weakest.

This weaker influence on the ideology of working people may also go some way towards accounting for the strength of SNP support among 18–35-year-olds (McLean, 1977), and its early capturing of local government control in the "new towns" with their below-average age structure. This age group has had little experience of Labour as a *class* party, making an appeal on the basis of class. They were less likely to be involved in traditional factory life but, most important, they grew up under Labour Governments trying to solve problems at the expense of working people. Where socialistic influence was stronger the SNP had less success. Thus William Wolfe felt that the failure among the miners was due to the "anti-SNP propaganda of the Labour Party and Communist Party activists". (1973, 22).

From Table 7 it can be seen that Labour and Conservative Parties have at their core a class-conscious support. Even at times of unpopularity this provides a base for electoral strength. The majority of the working class remained in support of Labour and saw it as representing their interests.[12] This is made clear in Table 8, referring to the 1979 situation.

TABLE 8. *O.R.C. Poll, April 1979 by "social class".*

	AB	C1	C2	DE
Labour	24	30	49	48
Liberal	8	12	8	7
Conservative	54	40	28	27
SNP	13	17	14	17
Other	1	1	–	1

It can be seen that there was a strengthening of working-class support for Labour, while the SNP vote fell across all social groups. Despite the radical elements in the SNP programme, the positive experiences motivating some workers to support it, and disillusionment with Labour's record, the SNP could not attract the core sections of the working class (and compare Figs 2 and 3). For them the "jingoism" of popular nationalism, with its artificial conflict between "Scottishness" and "classness", conflicted with their consciousness of class developed in workplace struggle and urban working-class community cohesion. Only in the far different situation of the Western Isles (although also an early Labour area) has radical opposition and Scottishness more permanently equated with the SNP (see Ennow, 1979).

Thus, at the 1979 election when an extremely rightwing Tory manifesto was sweeping the rest of Britain (although more in the south than the north of England), Scotland remained dominated by Labour, and the SNP lost ground both in terms of votes cast and seats gained (Fig 3; Table 4). Swings were particularly high from the SNP to Labour. William Wolfe, SNP Chairman (who suffered one of the largest electoral swings to Labour) put it very well: "We were not seen as relevant, but there is still a Scottish dimension in terms of votes, although it means that Labour, not the SNP, will represent that mood" (*The Guardian*, 5 May, 1979).

In the aftermath of its parliamentary losses, the SNP (with some of the remnants of the short-lived SLP joining it) seems to have moved "left" but to a "passive resistance"/"civil disobedience" type of strategy rather than one which tries to attach itself to the organized working class. The most recent additional, and for the moment complicating, factor is the emergence of the Social Democratic Party/Liberal Party "alliance". Opinion polls in late 1981 and early 1982 give the alliance over 30% of popular support, only 1 or 2 points behind Labour, with the SNP obtaining only 13% to 14%.

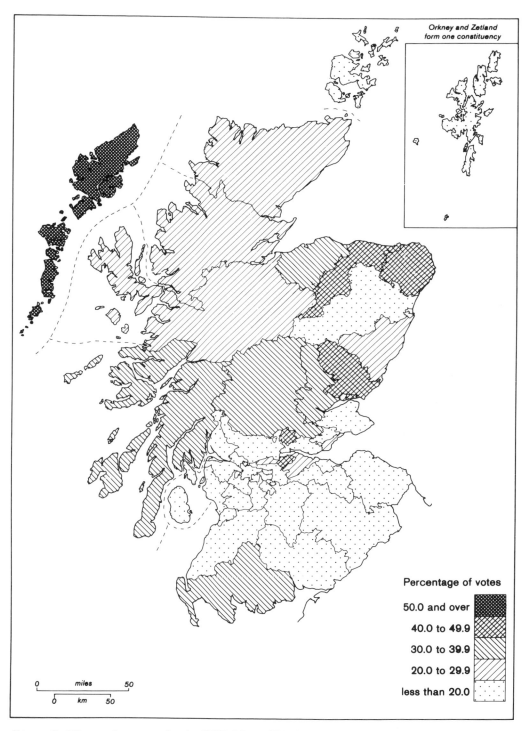

Orkney and Zetland
form one constituency

Percentage of votes

50.0 and over

40.0 to 49.9

30.0 to 39.9

20.0 to 29.9

less than 20.0

Figure 3. Electoral support for the SNP, May 1979. Source: Butler and Kavanagh 198?

From this complex, interesting and, from a left point of view, highly promising situation (in the sense that the parties of the centre and right now vy with each other for popular support) what is likely to emerge? To the extent that the underlying decline of Scotland's economy continues, and to the extent that Labour – with its poor record of leadership in local government administration and its present national conflicts – provides no realistic alternative, then perhaps the other parties can rout and carve up Labour in Scotland. Yet the class loyalty expressed through thick and thin for Labour and based on the organized trade-union movement, expressed at Scottish level by the Scottish TUC, may prove resilient enough to withstand such challenges, to produce new leaders and policies and to maintain the socialist tradition of the Scottish working class.

References

Adams, L. H. (1978). "The making of urban Scotland", Croom Helm, London.

Backel, J. M. and Denvet, D. T. (1972). The decline of the SNP – an alternative view, *Political Studies*, **20**.

Brand, J. (1978). "The national movement in Scotland", RKP, London.

Bull, P. J. (1978). The spatial components of intro-urban manufacturing change – suburbanisation in Clydeside 1958–1968, *Transactions Institute of British Geographers*, **3**, 91–100.

Carter, I. (1979). "Farm life in North East Scotland 1800–1914", John Donald, Edinburgh.

Cornford, J. P. and Brand, J. (1969). "Scottish voting behaviour", Edinburgh.

Dickson, T. (ed.). (1980). "Scottish capitalism", Lawrence & Wishart, London.

Ennew, J. (1980). "The Western Isles today", Cambridge University Press, Cambridge.

Firn, J. (1975). External control & regional policy *in* G. Brown (ed.), "The Red Paper on Scotland", EUSP, Edinburgh.

Greaves, D. (1968). The national problem in Britain. *Marxism Today*, October, 310–312.

Hamilton (1966). "The industrial revolution in Scotland", Cass, London.

Henderson, R. A. (1974). Industrial overspill from Glasgow 1958–1968, *Urban Studies*, **11**, 61–79.

Jaensh, D. (1976). The Scottish vote 1974: a realigning party system, *Political Studies*, **24**, 314–315.

Lenman, B. (1977). "An economic history of modern Scotland", Batsford, London.

Lesser, C. V. (1951). "Some aspects of the industrial structure of Scotland", Glasgow.

MacIntyre, S. (1980). "Little Moscows: communism and working class militancy in interwar Britain", Croom Helm, London.

Marwick, W. H. (1964). "Scotland in modern times", Cass, London.

Maxwell, S. (1978). Politics, *in* "Power and Manouverability", Quarterly Press, Edinburgh.

McCrone, G. (1969). "Scotland's future", Basil Blackwell, Oxford.

McLean, I. (1977). The politics of nationalism and devolution, *Political Studies*, **25**, 425–30.

Mercer, J. (1978). "The devolution of power", Calder, London.

Payne, G. (1977). Occupational transition in advanced industrial societies, *Sociological Review*, **25**, 5–39.

Robertson, J. (1962). Scottish Council report on the Scottish economy, *Scottish Journal of Political Economy*, **9**, 73–77.

Scott, J. and Hughes, M. (1980). "The anatomy of Scottish capital", Croom Helm, London.

Slaven, A. (1975) "The development of the West of Scotland, 1750–1960", Routledge and Kegan Paul, London.

Smith, P. and Brown, J. (1980). Economic crisis, foreign capital and working class response 1945–1970, *in* T. Dickson (ed.), "Scottish Capitalism", Lawrence & Wishart, London.

Snodgrass, C. P. (1966). Scottish conurbations, *in* T. W. Freeman (ed.), "The conurbations of Great Britain", Manchester University Press, Manchester.

Webb, K. (1978). "The growth of nationalism in Scotland", Penguin, London.

Wolfe, W. (1973). "Scotland lives. The quest for independence", *in* G. G. Wright (ed.), Reprographia.

Notes

This chapter is an amended and extended version of an essay which appeared under the title of "Economic crisis, foreign capital and working class response, 1945–1979" in *Scottish Capitalism*, T. Dickson (ed.), Lawrence and Wishart, 1980.

1. See John Foster, "Scottish Nationality and the Origins of Capitalism" and Willie Thomson, "From Reformation to Union" in Dickson (1980) for a class analysis of the development of a Scottish nation and state which takes into account the role of various classes in the formation of the nation.

2. Nineteenth century government reports on the Highland Question speak of the problem of its "surplus population".

3. In 1801, 47% of Scotland's population lived in the Central Belt and 24% in the Highlands, according to Mercer (1978). Adams (1978) points out the differences between Scotland and England's urban development.

4. See, for example, the Toothill Report, Scottish Council (Development and Industry) 1961, Appendix 21.

5. Previous networks of political representation had been dominated by the Liberal Party, by Scottish Conservatives and Unionists and, after 1945, by a coalition of Tory and Labour politicians, the Edinburgh "Scottish civil service", and members of traditional capitalist families.

6. See Marwick (1964), Scott and Hughes (1980). Lenman (1977) points out the concealed English control of Scotland's supposedly separate banks.

7. Report of SCLP Conference, 1947 in *Forum of Scottish Opinion*, December 1947.

8. Brand (1978) gives opinion survey results supporting this view.

9. Report of the British Labour Party Conference, 1968, speech by T. Clarke delegate from Coatbridge and Airdrie, p. 178, and a speech by J. Hamilton, delegate from the CEU.

10. As shown by SCLP Conference Reports on membership. The Scottish Labour Party was formed on 18 January 1976, by Sillars and Robertson, two Scottish Labour MPs.

11. For industrial and population movement see Henderson (1974), Bull (1978).

12. That these interests may not always be class alone, but class interplaced with religion is shown by Brand, 1978, p. 153, where he shows the influence of Roman Catholic voting.

TEN

State planning of spatial change: compromise and contradiction in Peterlee New Town

F. ROBINSON

(May 1982)

1. Introduction

> Let us, therefore, close our eyes on the nineteenth century degradation and squalor, let us look only with unseeing eyes on the sordid excrescence of the first decade of this century, let us blind ourselves to the septic and ugly buildings wens and ribbons perpetuated and planted on us between the wars, but let us open our eyes and look brightly forward and onward to the new town, the new living . . . Peterlee. (C. W. Clarke, "Farewell Squalor", 1947)

The New Towns have tended to evoke strong reactions; they have been both highly praised and violently condemned. Within the planning profession, there has always been much support for these examples of comprehensive, positive planning. The Town and Country Planning Association provides the vanguard of an influential New Towns lobby, and planning textbooks make obligatory reference to this greatest achievement of post-war planning in Britain. On the other hand, the New Towns have had a rather bad press, with reports of "New Towns blues", vandalism and loneliness in an anti-septic, soulless environment. Perhaps in recent years views have become more muted. New Towns have become unfashionable with planners who have rediscovered the inner city and the media also seem to have lost interest in them. Nonetheless, it is still the case that planners (in the widest sense of the term) have a special affection for them (although few live in them), while the public response is generally unenthusiastic, even hostile.

These conflicting attitudes have tended to form the basis for "evaluations" of the New Towns and, by virtue of their superficiality, they have tended to hinder rather than assist analysis. In particular, the New Towns lobby has engaged in defensive and very limited analyses, reducing the complexity of policy evolution and execution to issues of "success" and "failure" in achieving stated physical planning objectives.

This chapter represents an attempt at a more thorough and realistic examination of New Towns policy using a case-study approach. Here, we trace the development of one example, Peterlee in County Durham. Peterlee was not conceived as part of an "overspill" strategy but rather, like Glenrothes and Corby, was built to accommodate and "improve" an existing industrial labour force. In that sense, it is not "typical". It is, however, an example which reveals, particularly well, the link between this type of state intervention and industrial production, remembering that this takes place within a context of *changing* problems and circumstances.

As we shall see, the decision to develop a New Town at Peterlee accords with the conception of the role of the capitalist state in securing the conditions for continued capital accumulation. The provision of social infrastructure to ensure the maintenance and reproduction of a labour force for mining coal can be seen as a necessary adjunct to the reorganization, by nationalization, of a key industry in crisis (Krieger, 1979). The assembly and spatial centralization of a potential source of female labour, which became useful for semi-skilled, low-paid work, and the implantation of consumerism are also a part of this objective of state intervention.

The account begins by discussing the origins of the Peterlee proposal, first as an articulation of local aspirations and, subsequently, as a part of the central state's national reconstruction effort. This illustrates the tensions between local and national interests, and also between the Reithian blueprint for New Towns and the economic imperatives of industry. I will then consider the nature of local interests more fully in relation to housing opportunities in the sub-region and the side-effect of enforced decline of the pit-villages surrounding Peterlee. My discussion of industrial development looks at the initial concerns of the coal industry to maintain production through labour market monopoly, and then at the overthrow of this requirement owing to the contraction of the industry; Peterlee then needed to find a new economic *raison d'être*. Finally, I will focus upon the social components of the Peterlee scheme and the town's social development, concluding with some comments on state intervention.

2. "Farewell Squalor"

2.1 *Labourism and local planning*

The eastern part of County Durham, bounded by Sunderland to the north and Hartlepool to the south, constitutes a significant remnant of what was once the Great Northern Coalfield. To the west, the exposed coalfield has been worked out or abandoned through disinvestment; only open-casting and one or two pits now remain. In east Durham coal measures are overlain by magnesian limestone so development came later, with colliery sinkings in the 1830s, 1860s and in the early 1900s (see Moyes, 1969). The last phase saw the development of large pits close to the coast which exploit undersea reserves; it is these which have (so far) survived (see Fig. 1).

The mining development of east Durham, from the 1830s onwards, transformed this rather isolated, primarily agricultural area. The population increased dramatically with migration to the new pits. Pit villages, "the barracks of the industry", were hastily developed by the colliery companies alongside the new sinkings. Colliery companies exercised powerful control over labour both as employers and housing landlords. Labour organized its own mutual support at the local level, with co-operative stores, the methodist chapels and the Union. Finally the Labour Party emerged and gained control over local government after the First World War.

The local authority, Easington Rural District Council, reflected this local basis of the labour movement, and its influence on local government. In the inter-war period it made significant efforts to try to initiate improvements in living conditions: sanitation was improved, 100 slum clearance schemes were designated and the Council built 4500 houses. Even so, overcrowding remained a serious problem: a local survey conducted in 1935 showed that 2882 out of about 20 000 houses in the Rural District were overcrowded.[1] Not only were housing conditions poor and in some cases desperate; the area also suffered the effects of defeats in two major strikes (1921, 1926), depression, and large-scale unemployment. However, from the late 1930s, rearmament temporarily reversed the fortunes of the coalfield. Collieries were worked to capacity for the first time since the First World War, and the coal industry was recognized as vital to the nation's war effort.

The Second World War substantially altered the political agenda because the national emergency made radical policies both necessary and acceptable and, in addition, it was politically necessary to hold out the prospect of a rather different post-war Britain (Miliband, 1973; see Backwell and Dickens, 1978, for the effects on planning legislation). Production and consumption were centrally planned and labour resources used fully and judiciously. During the last two years of the war, reconstruction (where urban planning was a central part) became a major, much-debated issue.

Early in 1943, the Ministry of Health requested local authorities to review their post-war housing needs.[2] Easington R.D.C. considered their housing requirements in some detail and came to the view that sporadic building in all the pit villages was not desirable. Where the pit had a short life, or had already been closed, new building was not justified. And some villages did not possess the environmental conditions or social amenities to warrant redevelopment or expansion. At first it was suggested that several new, large-scale estates should be built, but gradually the scheme was redefined and the Council agreed to centralize virtually all future development at one site. The Clerk to the Council said that such a scheme

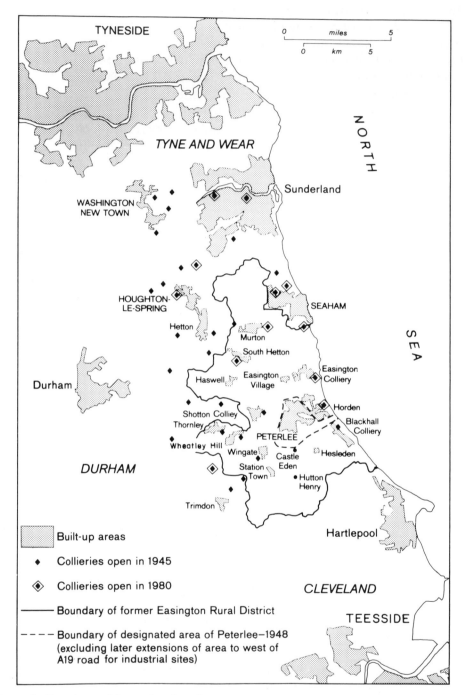

Figure 1. Peterlee and its regional setting.

would prove the solution to the whole of the Council's post-war programme and, drastic though it may seem at the outset, particularly in what would appear to be the elimination of parochial ideas, he was convinced that if (it) was launched and brought to an accomplished fact . . . then those who were fortunate enough to reap its benefits would look back and shower blessings upon their benefactors, who had the foresight and courage to take such a step in the interests of housing progress".[3]

The idea of centralized development thus emerged directly from the 1943 review of post-war housing needs. It was conceived and then developed into the form of a most ambitious project by the Council's architect-planner, C. W. Clarke, himself strongly influenced by ideas about reconstruction (including New Towns) which were being widely discussed at that time. Clarke was an idealist who was later to renounce secular life and join the priesthood. He worked enthusiastically on the initial proposal, added refinements and detail, finally producing a pamphlet entitled "Farewell Squalor" which explained the scheme and was eventually published by the Council in March 1947. In addition to new housing, Clarke argued that the scheme should provide new industry and thus diversify the local economy. For those with lesser ideals, the centralization of development was seen as helpful in making the area an attractive propostion for incoming industry. Although it was essentially a proposal for a New Town for miners, Clarke (and the Council) recognized that the single-industry economy had been seriously vulnerable in the past and that reductions in the mining labour force were inevitable.[4] As the proposal originated at the local level to meet local needs, Clarke suggested that the New Town be named after one of the area's best-known personalities, the miners' leader and politician, Peter Lee.

2.2 Central Government involvement

Easington R.D.C.'s proposal was formulated at the same time as the Government was preparing policies for the establishment of New Towns. The Reith Committee had been appointed, shortly after the Labour election victory, to consider the issues involved in setting up New Towns, "self-contained and balanced communities for work and living", as part of the programme for post-war reconstruction. The Committee produced three reports in 1946, and in August of that year the New Towns Act was passed. Under the provisions of the Act, New Towns were to be designated by the Minister of Town and Country Planning in accordance with the "national interest", and were to be developed and managed by Development Corporations, appointed by and acting for the Minister. New Towns were part of the wider reconstruction effort but had a special role as an important social experiment. There were strong overtones of Ebeneezer Howard and an element of utopianism as well:

The aim must be to combine in the New Town the friendly spirit of the . . . slum . . . with the vastly improved health conditions of the new estate but it must be a broadened spirit embracing all classes of society.[5]

Residents should be given:

the means for a happy and gracious way of life.[6]

But the New Towns were also part and parcel of growing state intervention in both housing provision and in industry: they were to combine public sector rented housing with serviced industrial sites developed along similar lines to the Trading Estates of the 1930s.

While preparing his plan, Clarke was in contact with the Ministry and received some assistance from their Regional Office. But the Council did expect to undertake the scheme themselves or, at least, have a large degree of control over it.

However, the Ministry became increasingly interested in carrying out the development themselves under the New Towns Act, and in removing development from the local government, electoral orbit. This desire was strengthened by the experience of strong local opposition at Stevenage (Orlans, 1952) and in the context of serious production problems in the coal industry. The Ministry wanted to use the Act in circumstances where a New Town was welcomed and to show commitment to the improvement of miners' living conditions in an effort to placate and stabilize the labour force. In March 1947, Easington R.D.C. agreed to the New Town being built under the Provisions of the Act. It appears that the Council was not fully aware of the implications of this; it has been suggested that members anticipated a close involvement and "jobs for the boys" on the Corporation, while Clarke expected to become architect-planner for the scheme.[7]

The Minister, Lewis Silkin, met the Council in August 1947. He repeated Clarke's arguments for centralized development and against village redevelopment. Silkin also agreed with Clarke's choice of site, his plan for an ultimate population of 30 000, and his suggestion that it be named "Peterlee". It would provide housing mainly for people from the Rural District, it would provide a recreational and shopping centre to serve the area, and it would bring industrial employment for women and "any male labour not employed in coal mining". This last issue was very important. Clarke had envisaged substantial diversification for male employment in addition to many new opportunities for women. However, Silkin was not forthcoming on this issue; he talked vaguely of the need for miners to have the "opportunity of mixing with people of other occupations and income levels", but did not relate this to employment provision.[8]

Peterlee, initiated by local politicians apparently sincere in their desire to improve local conditions, thus became part of a Central Government programme justified as being in the "national interest". Development was to be controlled by the central state, where local government would only have, at best, a consultative role. The New Town was formally designated on 10 March 1948, but three years of disagreements and delays were to elapse before the first tenants moved in.

3. The policy in practice

3.1 *Conflict and disenchantment, 1948–50*

At first, the prospects for Peterlee appeared very favourable. The local authority supported the scheme. The site (a greenfield site containing only about 200 people at designation) could be made available without much difficulty by purchase from the two main landlords: the Burdon family estate (which was to be dispersed following the death of the last surviving member of the family) and the National Coal Board (NCB). And Clarke had already done much of the necessary survey work in a diligent and comprehensive manner. However, these advantages were soon to be overshadowed by two apparently intractable issues: the composition and character of the Development Corporation and the coal extraction problem.

Development Corporation board members are appointed directly by the Minister to whom they are also responsible, (cf. the present Urban Development Corporations; see Anderson, this volume). Silkin's choice of members for Peterlee clearly offended the Easington R.D.C., since the Council had (perhaps naively) anticipated substantial involvement. Only one of the Council's nominees (a councillor) was appointed, and, of the eight board members, only two were local people. The Chairman was Dr Monica Felton, former member of London County Council and of the Reith Committee. Subsequent appointments during the 1950s conformed to this pattern of choosing outsiders,[9] and this continued to be a source of annoyance to the R.D.C. The Corporation chose Shotton Hall, a country house on the edge of the designated area, for its headquarters and this contributed to the view of the Corporation as remote, aloof and out of touch with the locality. By adopting an increasingly secretive style of administration, the Corporation did nothing to dispel this view. In addition, C. W. Clarke was not appointed to the technical staff. Instead, an internationally-known architect, Berthold Lubetkin was brought in to lead a team of "experts", again without local roots. Relations between the Corporation and the Council deteriorated and were marked by hostility and suspicion, especially since the Corporation tended to regard much of its planning proposals and policy deliberations as confidential, so providing little direct information to the Council. Relations remained poor until the early 1970s.

Local people also became hostile to the New Town scheme in the months following designation. They urgently needed new housing to relieve the severe shortage, but wrangles over the coal problem continued to delay construction. Certainly they could exert no direct electoral or political influence over New Town corporation policy. Furthermore Dr Felton, the Corporation's Chairman, attracted considerable criticism from local people who saw her as temperamental and dogmatic. She was committed and progressive, but people resented the interference of an outsider, especially since she and the Corporation tended to justify Peterlee by disparaging the villages. And, in addition, Dr Felton attracted unpopularity as a woman in a masculine preserve; here was a direct clash with the traditional, reactionary aspect of the mining community.

Secondly, the Peterlee site was underlain by usable coal measures, much of which still awaited extraction. Before designation, Clarke had discussed this aspect with the NCB and had reached agreement on a low-density programme of construction, phased with mining operations, which would minimize the subsidence risk. But Lubetkin wanted a high-rise town centre, which would necessarily entail the sterilization of millions of tons of coal and refused to work to constraints imposed by mining. Consequently, a heated argument developed between the Corporation and the NCB (see Steele, 1962). The latter had previously supported the Peterlee scheme as a means to improve living conditions for miners and thus help to retain their labour force. Now it became strongly opposed to it, as did the mining unions, who were concerned for employment levels. This acrimonious dispute was finally settled by the intervention of the Lord President's Committee of the Cabinet, which largely supported the NCB's position. Local planning issues had reached the highest body of the central state.

Lubetkin, his plans thrown back in his face, left Peterlee in 1950. Dr Felton had left some months earlier. The Corporation had managed to dispel support for the New Town, to prepare plans which were rendered impracticable, and had not yet built any houses.

Work on the preparation of a Master Plan was now handed over to consultants, who worked with the NCB to provide a development programme in phase with mining activities. The plan, for low-rise, relatively low-density development, represented a major compromise; not only did it differ fundamentally from Lubetkin's intentions, it also went against contemporary planning practice, for it meant that the town would develop in piecemeal fashion as each section was mined (Dobson et al., 1959). The Master Plan was published in 1952, but initial agreement between the Corporation and NCB was reached during 1950, allowing the Corporation to start house-building. Peterlee's first tenants moved in, at last, in February 1951. Production had won out against architectural ideology. How would it go with people's housing and employment needs?

3.2 Housing development and settlement policy

Housing development at Peterlee has been a relatively slow process. About 300 houses have been completed each year; only twice, in the early 1950s, did annual completions reach 600 houses. The construction programme slackened in the 1970s and, by the end of that decade, Peterlee finally attained its 30 000 population target.

The need to work within the severe constraints of the phasing programme had a considerable effect on the pace of development, but it was also restrained by the difficulties which seemed to bedevil some of its building contractors. All contracts were awarded to private builders since the Corporation did not have a Direct Labour Organization.

The first phases of the programme comprised traditional designs: there was little to distinguish Peterlee from the average 1950s Council estate. It was not immediately identifiable as a New Town, as part of an idealistic experiment in housing and social policy, nor was it receiving accolades in the architectural press. The Corporation's General Manager, dissatisfied with this obscurity, thus engaged Victor Passmore, a modern artist, to provide a new housing "aesthetic". The result was flat-roofed, black and white boxes, some with cantilever structures forming overhanging rooms. These were started in the late 1950s, but completion was held back by the spectacular bankruptcy of the contractor. They are notoriously badly-designed and badly built, and have been a liability ever since. Shortly after completion there were major problems of raining-in, and the flat roofs, in particular, have brought repeated problems as well as expensive maintenance. Nonetheless, the Passmore houses did attract much favourable comment in the architectural press and, in that sense, put Peterlee "on the map". Architectural ideology had a second bite at the cherry or, as *The Observer* inaccurately headlined "New Town miners are at home with Cubism" (26 February 1961).[10]

Subsequently, during the 1960s, the Corporation experimented with industrialized construction which, at that time, was being very actively promoted by the Ministry who regarded it as a way of reducing costs and speeding-up housing programmes. These estates again comprise flat-roofed boxes, made of concrete sections manufactured on site and assembled in terraces. These have also had maintenance problems; in fact, generally speaking, only the early traditional designs have not had serious structural problems. Under the provisions of the 1976 New Towns (Amendment) Act, Corporation housing (90% of the stock of 8000 houses) was transferred to the local authority in 1977, as was the massive repair bill for housing defects. The Council itself has built very few houses in Peterlee, completing only one significant project in the mid-1970s when it became clear that the housing transfer would take place.

It is important to set Peterlee's housing development and tenancy allocation within a sub-regional context, since the New Town's objectives were sub-regional and the impact of Peterlee has been strongly felt in the surrounding villages. In "Farewell Squalor", Clarke had anticipated that all of Easington R.D.'s housing needs (from both new household formation and slum clearance) would be met at Peterlee. This conception was repeated, in a looser form, in the Designation Order for Peterlee, and was carried through to the County Durham Development Plan (1951). The latter established a settlement policy whereby some settlements were to expand and serve to regroup population at the expense of others which were to be subject to benign neglect: the notorious "category D" village policy (see also Byrne and Parson, this volume). Within this framework, Peterlee would grow while surrounding villages would decline in terms of population, housing stock and other infrastructure.

During the first few years of development, Peterlee provided housing for families "living in" with relatives in the villages, and in general, those unable to obtain housing in the overcrowded villages. Peterlee's function was to relieve immediate local housing stress. Rents were, however, much higher in Peterlee.[11] This was a source of much difficulty for tenants who were said to be "starving in luxury" at "hungry hill". It also was a major factor behind Peterlee's high turnover and its label as "a transit camp".

In the late 1950s it became clear that Peterlee was not only supposed to take "excess" housing demand, but also cater for slum clearance. In other words, people displaced by slum clearance in the villages would have to accept being rehoused in Peterlee. This was strongly opposed. Established residents of the villages were attached to them and did not want to move; they did not want to pay high rents, and they appreciated living close to the local pit where they worked. The issue was fiercely debated at the 1960 Public Inquiry on the Easington Town Map (an adjunct to the County Development Plan) which vividly demonstrated the opposition to Peterlee. Easington R.D.C. now sought full replacement of slum clearance within the villages, thus revoking their earlier commitment to the whole notion of centralized development (MHLG, 1960). Villagers made many representations against forced movement to the New Town; one village group referred to Farewell Squalor as "an infamous document" and "the author's Mein Kampf".[12] The villages, possibly informally supported by the Development Corporation's unwillingness to take slum clearance families (Robinson, 1978, pp. 123–4), won major concessions; replacement housing was allowed in many of the villages, except those closest to the New Town. Peterlee's initial planning objective was substantially compromised. Local public and political opposition had, apparently, a bit more bite than architectural ideology.

Movement into Peterlee continued however, as the town could supply houses for newly-formed households when the villages could not. The villages, at best, were only building for rehousing; at worst, villages close to Peterlee were building virtually nothing and the housing stock (much of it colliery housing) was steadily falling into disrepair. In general, young people would almost inevitably move to Peterlee when they married, for there was little or no chance of a house in the villages where they had been brought up. Even so, in the mid 1960s there was a housing surplus in Peterlee, resulting partly from rent increases in unpopular houses leading to increased turnover, at a time of pit closures and migration from the area. At this time people from outside the area moved in to take short-term advantage of this supply of rented housing; more than half the tenancies were allocated to people from outside Easington R.D.: a situation which clearly conflicted with Peterlee's initial objectives. By contrast, in recent years, Peterlee has experienced a housing shortage, so that, with the exception of some key-worker intake, housing has been allocated almost exclusively to newly formed households, an increasing number of which are second-generation Peterlee residents.

The impact of Peterlee's development on the villages has been very significant. Over the period 1951–71, the number of houses in the pit-villages of Easington R.D. remained virtually stable at around 22 000, while Peterlee built over 6500 houses. Village population fell, from 81 872 to 63 584, while Peterlee's rose from 298 to 21 846. Underlying these changes is a powerful process of age–specific migration to the New Town which meant, for example, that in 1961 only 17.2% of Peterlee's population was aged 40 and over, compared with 44.2% in England and Wales. Housing policy thus led to the rapid ageing of the population structure of the villages, making them increasingly moribund, while creating a New Town which certainly could not be described as a "balanced community" in terms of age structure. The continued allocation of Peterlee houses to new households, together with the tenancy termination of relatively older households, has slowed adjustment to a more normal age-structure.

The physical impact on the villages has also been considerable. Many had to wait until the mid-1960s before gaining new housing to replace slum clearance under the Town Map provisions, while those closest to Peterlee, notably Shotton Colliery, had to wait a further decade for new housing. With Peterlee approaching its target population, and with the decision to transfer Corporation housing to the local authority following the creation of the new Easington District, housing policy was relaxed in the mid-1970s and, at last, substantial redevelopment of the villages became possible.[13] But the villages had clearly suffered years of neglect to ensure Peterlee's growth, contrary to the assurances of Clarke and Silkin.[14] In some cases the change in policy may have come too late to bring about a complete revival; some of the more blighted villages have lost many of their shops and services, and these are unlikely to be regained.

3.3 Industry and employment

C. W. Clarke had regarded the provision of new industry, providing employment both for men and women, as an integral part of his proposal. Traditionally, there were few job opportunities for women in the area and, consequently the female economic activity rate was well below the national level. For men there were few alternatives to the pit; a survey conducted in the villages in 1948 showed that 71% of economically active men worked in mining. Clarke estimated that mechanization and the exhaustion of seams would lead to a significant reduction in mining employment at pits in the Rural District. He felt that employment for women and new, alternative employment for men was essential and accordingly included an industrial estate in his plan for Peterlee.

However, in contrast, Silkin and the Ministry saw Peterlee as basically a New Town for miners which would also include some employment for their wives. At this time, the newly-nationalized coal industry was striving hard to produce coal "at any price" to serve the reconstruction effort, and was having some difficulty retaining its labour force in the face of competition from other industries where conditions were usually far better. Consequently, while supporting the New Town as a means to improve miners' living conditions, the National Coal Board (NCB) was strongly opposed to the introduction of industry which might attract miners away from the pits. It seems clear that the Ministry of Town and Country Planning was prepared to accede to the requirements of the Ministry of Fuel and Power and the NCB and thus exclude the introduction of male-employing alternative industry in its plans for Peterlee. The concern not to weaken the NCB's monopoly of employment can be traced in the 1949 Pepler-MacFarlane Plan for the North East:

> In areas of stable mining where little diminution of employment is anticipated (particularly in East Durham and South East Northumberland) male employment should be concentrated on mining, and other industry that would compete with mining for available labour should not be introduced. Hence in the main, such industry should be restricted to predominantly female-employing concerns. (p. 295, Principal Recommendations)

This was a view which seems very much to have been shared by the Board of Trade. Following designation, the Corporation, keen to develop industry at Peterlee, drew up plans for an industrial estate. These plans were agreed in 1950, but the basis for the agreement was that the estate should be managed by North-East Trading Estates, an agency of the Board of Trade. The Corporation was strongly committed to providing male and female employment; the 1952 Master Plan stated (p. 28) that:

> Today, mining is prosperous and likely to remain so for a considerable time, but the combined effects of mechanisation and the running out of seams cannot be ignored. Nor can the incidence of disablement. In spite of the importance of providing jobs for women the employment of men surplus to mining is therefore of greater import.

Lubetkin's team had received estimates of future manpower requirements from the NCB, suggesting a reduction of 3400 mining jobs in the R.D. by

1971, but these were felt to be inaccurate (Peterlee Development Corporation, 1950, p. 129). The Corporation suggested an unofficial estimate of 7000; in the event, the figure was about 10 000. In the Corporation's view a substantial number of alternative jobs would be required, later if not sooner.

But the Board of Trade did not share the Corporation's concern and, in the view of the latter, accorded Peterlee low priority for investment to attract new industry[15]. Only two factories of significant size were established in Peterlee in the 1950s, one in the textile and the other in the clothing industry, which provided only 100 male jobs and 600 jobs for women by 1960. In the case of employment strategy, the short-term interests of production easily won out over the longer term interests of people living in Peterlee.

However by the end of the 1950s, it was becoming clear that Clarke's and the Corporation's view, stressing the need for new industrial development, would be justified. With the widespread switch to the use of oil, demand for coal was falling, and in 1959, the NCB responded with a plan for capacity reductions (NCB, 1959). A reduction of 4000 mining jobs in Easington R.D. between 1958 and 1978 was anticipated. In fact, the loss was to be twice this figure. The NCB carried out a massive closure programme during the 1960s and early 1970s (see Krieger, 1979) involving five of the ten pits in the R.D. Clearly, one of the implications of this, aside from increasing unemployment, was that Peterlee could no longer be seen as a "New Town for Miners". The short-term production considerations had changed.

Slowly the Corporation established new capabilities and functions in the sphere of industrial development. In 1958, the Ministry at last allowed the Corporation to build factories to rent (but, until 1966 only for a specified tenant, not in advance of demand) and so provided a degree of freedom from the Board of Trade. But little progress was made. Then, in 1963, came the publication of the Hailsham Report on the economic problems of the North-East. This marked something of a watershed, since Central Government at last recognized Peterlee as a potential centre for new industry, envisaging the New Town within a Tyne-Tees "growth zone" strategy. Peterlee was promised more industrial land and improved communications, – but, at the same time, Hailsham also created another New Town, at Washington, which proved to be a powerful counter-attraction to mobile industry. Washington and Peterlee are now in the absurd position of spending considerable sums in advertising their respective, competing, attractions to private firms.

The provision of more land and improved communications to serve Peterlee took several years to materialize. In the meantime, throughout the 1960s, Peterlee gained only a little new industry. But it was a period noted for grand schemes as attempts were made to modernize the Region and shed its "Andy Capp image". At Peterlee, the Region's most prominent politician, T. Dan Smith, was appointed Chairman of Peterlee Development Corporation in 1968. For some years his public relations consultancy had been engaged by the Corporation to promote the town and he was now brought in to realize his dream of a Science Centre at Peterlee (see Smith, 1970, ch. 13). This was to be modelled on the American science-park concept, to include high-technology research units and industry. Peterlee, the New Town for miners, was now to accommodate a "colony of top boffins". The scheme attracted much publicity, but nothing very much ever happened. Smith left the Corporation in 1970 and a few years later the Corporation, perhaps anxious to sever connections with the discredited Smith (gaoled for corruption) said that the project had been nothing more than "a public relations gimmick and an unrealistic proposition".

After Smith's departure, the Corporation settled down to more "realistic" methods of industrial promotion in an effort to attract mobile industry (methods which, in recent years, have become less realistic as industrial mobility has markedly declined). Further additions of industrial land, larger-scale factory building and grander promotional campaigns have helped to secure some progress and, by 1980, Peterlee's industrial estates provided employment for about 5400 workers. However, this employment and that provided by the service sector, has certainly not been adequate to meet local job demand and counter job losses. In the South-East Durham area (comprising Peterlee and Wingate employment offices), 3897 people were registered unemployed in March 1981. The male unemployment rate stood at 15·3% and the female rate at 14·3%. However, the position of South-East Durham relative to the Northern Region and the nation has improved in recent years because of the effects of recession elsewhere, although the combined unemployment rate of 14·3% is still above that of the Region (13·6%) and, of course, Great Britain as a whole (10·1%; March 1981 figures). On balance, production concerns have dominated over the long-term needs for both housing and jobs felt by people in Peterlee and the surrounding area.

3.4 Social objectives: a "happy and gracious way of life"?

The Reith Committee laid down detailed "guiding principles" for the development of New Towns. These principles were very much derived from a conception of how the New Towns were to develop as a social experiment, and this conception was generally shared by Lewis Silkin, the Minister.

As "self-contained communities", they should offer an adequate and broad range of opportunities for employment, shopping, recreation and social life; they should not be like the dormitory suburbs which proliferated between the wars. As "balanced communities", they should have a mix of social classes and occupational groups, without residential or social segregation. Social facilities should be abundant; the Committee made reference to societies, clubs, the churches, theatres and so on. There was a good deal of moralizing in the Committee's reports. There was, for example, much concern about the "delicate, contentious and vital issue" of licenced premises and the "evil of drinking to excess"; it was necessary to "keep New Towns free of this, as of other, degrading influences".

These objectives for the programme as a whole were not particularly relevant to the Peterlee proposal; once again a compromise had to be reached, first at the planning stage and, subsequently, during the course of development. Peterlee was first and foremost to accommodate miners, and other, competing industry was not to be introduced (except, possibly, in the long term). Physical development itself was to be phased in with the demands of coal mining. Hence, the town could not be "balanced" in terms of social and occupational class. Nor could it be "self-contained": employment was provided at pits in the surrounding villages, and the New Town was supposed to provide recreational and shopping facilities for the whole Rural District. However, despite this divergence from the Reithian model, there was still a concern to embark on a social experiment:

> It is essential that [Peterlee] should retain the active comradeship and friendliness of the colliery villages, which stems from the local tradition and common occupation, but avoid perpetuating the narrow cramping life of the villages within the New Town.[16]

The New Town was seen as part of both physical and social reconstruction. Within this, the role of women is particularly interesting. The Corporation was unhappy about the "male solidarity that now opposes the introduction of new ideas and ways in the area" (Peterlee Development Corporation, 1950, p. 50), while Dr Felton declared that women in the pit villages lived lives of "sheer drudgery". On the one hand, the Corporation argued that women should be enabled to work outside the home, not least so that people could afford Peterlee's high rents (Peterlee Development Corporation, 1952, p. 39). But, the family unit must be safeguarded:

> The wife must be enabled to bring up a family of four or more children without forfeiting the right to exist as an independent person. The high birthrate of the mining areas must be preserved, while the position both of mothers and children must be vastly improved.[17]

There was much concern that the family should be safeguarded as a functioning reproductive unit and that the social cohesion of the area be maintained; the family and community were seen as stabilizing elements which would discourage migration and so prevent "a consequent shortage of miners at a time when coal is vital".[18]

These various strands of the Peterlee proposal were woven together by the Lubetkin team, but received little mention after Lubetkin's departure over the coal extraction issue. The 1952 Master Plan, drawn up by consultants, is a bland land-use document, which introduced the concept of relatively self-sufficient neighbourhood units but also laid stress, in a somewhat contradictory manner, on the need for a well-served town centre. However, because of the risk of subsidence, some facilities would be dispersed; in particular, land seriously prone to subsidence would form Peterlee's open spaces while subsidence-free areas would have to be fully used for building and thus be deficient in open space. Again, specific circumstances led to a departure from planning principles.

The actual process of development was fraught with difficulties and delays. At first, a strong pioneering spirit was sufficient to overcome the frustrations of minimal facilities and services, but by the mid-1950s, the high level of tenancy turnover, largely a reaction to high rents, and the increasing size of Peterlee served to disperse initial enthusiasm for formal social activities. Conflicts developed over the running of the newly-provided Community Centre, and many residents hardly involved themselves in activities outside the home. The TV set was, of course, becoming ubiquitous.

The town centre developed very slowly; ten years after the arrival of the first tenants it remained "virtually as much of a planner's dream as ever" (*Sunderland Echo*, 10 February 1961). An Anglican Church was completed in 1957, and a Methodist Church in 1958, but the public library was built only in 1962, and a youth centre was not provided until 1965. The lack of youth facilities meant that the New Town was "not much better than a housing estate . . . at the moment there is not even a juke box, let alone something more ambitious like a snack bar" (*Durham County Advertiser*, 8 September 1961). Many people, including both youths and young families, continued to rely heavily on social contacts and activities in the villages from which they had moved.

By the late 1960s, as Peterlee reached 20 000 population, the town centre was starting to provide sufficient shops and services to cater for the Peterlee population, but it was a long way from becoming substantial enough to serve the villages as well. However, two elements helped to secure its eventual, if partial, success by enabling its continued growth. First, the underprovision of neighbourhood shops in the later housing developments generated growth in the town centre. Secondly, the continuing (and planned) decline of the villages, coupled with a widespread trend towards larger scale retailing, resulted in an increasing centralization of functions at Peterlee. As shops and other services closed down in villages no longer able to support them, people in the villages came to depend more and more on the New Town. By the late 1970s, following the construction of a department store and leisure centre, Peterlee town centre undoubtedly had developed a sub-regional role. Even so, low car-ownership (in 1971, 35% of households in the villages had a car, compared with 43% in Peterlee and 62% in England and Wales), together with high bus fares, necessarily place constraints on Peterlee's function as the sub-regional centre.

Certainly an important issue, common to many New Towns, is the difficulty of providing various facilities (ranging from public telephones to sports centres) in advance of full demand (MHLG, 1967; Wirtz, 1975).

Private-sector developers have been very reluctant to undertake development, particularly for non-retail uses, in Peterlee. This is partly because of the high degree of uncertainty in a New Town which has not been a great success and which suffers high unemployment, but also because Peterlee will not have a large enough population to support substantial social facilities. The response of the local authorities has also been poor, stemming mainly from the unhappy relationship between Easington R.D. (now District) Council and the Corporation. Easington, suspicious of the Corporation and heavily committed to the villages, has fulfilled its statutory duties, but has been slow to do more – until recently, when agreement was reached for the transfer of Corporation housing to the Council, thus allowing the Council to win back its lost territory. In circumstances where other private and public sector agencies are reluctant to develop, a New Town experiences inescapable difficulties because the Corporation themselves have very limited funds for amenity provision. At Peterlee, the situation has been exacerbated by the location of the New Town on a greenfield site without existing services.

Finally, we must consider the wider issues of social and community development, aside from the provision of facilities. As we have seen, the Reithian notion of "balance" (undoubtedly a suspect concept) had to be seriously modified to take account of Peterlee's specific function as a New Town for miners. Since the mid-1960s, only about one-in-eight of incoming tenants were miners; in 1971 only 12% of male workers resident in Peterlee were miners, compared with almost 50% in the villages. Hence, this obstacle to the achievement of balance has gone and, in terms of occupation, Peterlee is more "balanced" than was first anticipated. However, it remains considerably different from both the R.D. and the County, with an over-representation, in 1971, of skilled workers and lower proportions of both the unskilled and employers and managers. Its age structure was also still heavily skewed, especially in comparison with the ageing villages from which it has taken population.

Perhaps more significant, however, is the distribution of socio-economic characteristics within Peterlee itself. Even within the majority rented sector there are large differences, broadly between the older and newer estates. Deprivation is particularly concentrated in one older estate; here, some 1971 enumeration districts contained levels of unemployment up to three times the level for Peterlee as a whole, and household car ownership was well below 30%. It is certain that some estates have become heavily stigmatized and that this has been reinforced by insensitive housing management. As the Corporation puts it: "A problem with some of the older areas, and with others, is that they contain a high proportion of 'bad' tenants".[19]

Peterlee had been intended to represent the "modern" way of life in contrast to the "traditional" pit villages, and it was justified in these terms. The early planning documents laid stress on the need to preserve certain (selected and romanticized) characteristics of the pit community. But this was self-evidently contradictory. First of all, the move to the New Town meant high rents and an orientation to consumerism. In addition, the age-specific process of migration deriving from housing allocation policy, not only creates an unbalanced age structure, it also removes immediate contact with kin. Thus, the young nuclear families, without the support of the extended kin, have had new difficulties to overcome, and have required the support of secondary agencies outside the family. The New Town has thus provided new housing, but in so doing, has produced social problems of isolation and family stress. Moreover, the villages have also been weakened by the loss of their younger members and there, too, older people are cut off from their extended kin.

4. Overview: the New Town experience of Peterlee

Perhaps the most obvious lesson to be learnt from the Peterlee saga is that both the formulation and the execution of public policy is a complex affair. Policies have to be tailored to meet local conditions and altered in the light of experience and events. Objectives are revised and plans lose their relevance. And, in carrying out a policy, there are conflicts between the agencies involved. In addition, a policy such as that of New Town development produces intended and unintended side-effects.

Peterlee was first proposed by the local Council which, following well-established Labourist tradition, sought to improve local housing and economic conditions for its supporters. Once it was taken out of local hands, it became a tarnished vision as well as a proposal cast in terms of the "national interest". Relations between the two local state institutions – local government on the one hand and a local agency of central state on the other – soured. The Council's commitment waned to the extent that it later sought a major compromise on the re-housing issue and was slow to provide amenities which might have helped Peterlee to become a sub-regional centre, while the Corporation's plans became dominated by short term production concerns.

It is often supposed that New Town Development Corporations are in a privileged position. They have extensive powers and thus are able to pursue, single-mindedly, comprehensive development. Since they are not subject to democratic control they do not have to canvass support; but, as a result, they do lose this source of legitimacy. As we have seen, their powers are limited in a number of very important ways. This is clearly shown in the conflict with the NCB which led to a radically revised plan for development and also prevented the pursuit of strong industrial policies. Here it is clear that the "national interest" was the interest of the NCB, not the Corporation, still less the need for rational, planned social development. Similarly, the Corporation's later attempts to secure new industry were frustrated by the fact that neither the Corporation, nor Government, were able to effectively control industrial movement. This remains very much in private hands (see Morgan and Sayer, this volume). Also, in much the same way, the Corporation had no control over the provision of social facilities and infrastructure where it was dependent upon the decisions of other private and public sector agencies. The Corporation was thus placed in a contradictory position, charged with planning an entire New Town but unable to control vital elements.

The saga also has ironic overtones in the sense that a plan initially intended to revitalize the area has had a detrimental effect on the villages which, through the Rural District Council, originally proposed it. Migration, much of it resulting from artificial restraint on housing development in the villages, has served to distort the demographic and social structure of both the villages and the New Town. And, even judged on the basis of a limited objective – housing provision – Peterlee has not been a great success. Rents were very high owing to an unhelpful Government policy, and some housing is structurally unsound and expensive to maintain, owing to the Corporation's attempts to follow architectural fashion (and, subsequently, accepting the Ministry's concern to promote industrialized building) rather than simply meet well-known needs.

The Corporation itself deserves specific criticism for its failure to exercise its powers, notably as planning agency and landlord, in a judicious manner. It has been excessively secretive, prone to serious misjudgement, and has tended to mislead and exaggerate (as with the Science Centre proposal, for example). Two former members of the Corporation's Policy Research Unit (now disbanded) argued that the best policy that it could pursue would be its dissolution; it could not be reformed so as to serve the area rather than subjugate it:

> The Corporation is so narrowly preoccupied with houses, industry and landscaping that it is positively destructive of the quality of people's lives, of their simple wishes and desires and thus their humanity. As tenants they are offered bad housing, little control and no dignity. As worker, merely a statistic in the case for more industrial land. As mother and child, offered aesthetic landscaping frustrating the most simple desires. As citizens, offered public relations information. As people with special needs, silence.[20]

In much the same vein, a Community Development Officer commented that channels of communication between the Corporation and residents are "so defective . . . that most information about the Corporation's activities are wild rumour."[21] The Corporation's lack of interest in Peterlee's residents is further underlined by the fact that it was not until 1977 that it embarked on a social survey of the town; this was the *first* such survey it had conducted since the 1948 survey of the villages. As a housing landlord it continued to take a remarkably small-minded attitude; even as recently as 1975, the Corporation announced that "routine inspections" had shown that some tenants had removed an unwanted storage cupboard in their kitchens but the

Corporation, reacting liberally, was prepared to grant an "amnesty" for this severe transgression![22] The New Town experience provides a somewhat twisted memorial to the miners' leader, Peter Lee.

5. Concluding remarks

We do not doubt that this sketch of Peterlee's development will strike a familiar note with those who have examined public policy elsewhere. It does demonstrate that state intervention is, in practice, a complex affair; this poses considerable problems for the development and application of adequate analytical concepts.

A prime conclusion is that "The State" is clearly not an indifferentiated whole; rather there are tensions and contraditions between its branches, between national and subnational levels, and between and within its policies. However, the overriding importance of production imperatives in State intervention are shown by the fact that it was the NCB's concerns, rather than Reithian visions, which were dominant in establishing Peterlee's objectives. The Corporation's attempts to create something other than a New Town for miners were unsuccessful. The social and political demands of the local Council and then the Development Corporation could not be reconciled with the economic imperatives of the production system. This was the case, not just over the question of industrial diversification, but also on the issue of the provision of "loss-making" social infrastructure.

Such a formulation goes part of the way towards understanding Peterlee's development, but it is also necessary to point to the chaotic nature of state intervention, arising both from its internal tensions and its contradictions with the production system. To cite one example: Government fuel policies led to pit closures, and therefore the need for Peterlee to acquire a new industrial role. This role was recognized by Government but then compromised by the designation of a competing New Town at Washington.

State intervention generates crises which are incapable of resolution because of the inherently limited nature of intervention in the production system.

These conceptualizations of state intervention are helpful in identifying underlying structural elements, but the details of actions, policies, bureaucratic and individual behaviour both enrich the study of public policy and pose problems for analysis.

References

Backwell, J. and Dickens, P. (1978). Town planning, mass loyalty and the restructuring of capital: the 1947 Planning Act revisited, *University of Sussex Working Papers in Urban and Regional Studies.* **11.**
Clarke, C. W. (1947). "Farewell squalor", Easington R.D.C.
Dobson, W. D., Potts, E. L. J., Roberts, R. G. S. and Wilson, K. (1959). The

co-ordination of surface and underground development at Peterlee, Co. Durham, *Inst. Mining Engineers, Transactions*, **119**, 5, 279–300.

Durham County Council. (1958). Easington Town Map, written analysis (draft).

Easington Rural District Council. (1943). "Council Minutes and Housing Committee minutes", Durham County Records Office.

Fraser, D. (1976). "Urban Politics in Victorian England", Leicester University Press.

Krieger, J. (1979). British Colliery Closure Programmes in the North East: from paradox to contradiction, *London Papers in Regional Science*, **9**, Pion, London.

Miliband, R. (1973). "Parliamentary Socialism: a study in the politics of labour", Merlin Press, London.

Ministry of Housing and Local Government (n.d.) Easington Town Map, Inquiry into Objections, *Report* (mimeo) by H. F. Yeomans, M.H.L.G. file 662/40101 A15.

Ministry of Town and Country Planning. (1946). Reports of the New Towns (Reith) Committee. (First) Interim Report, Cmd. 6876, HMSO, London.

Morgan, R. and Robinson, D. (1976). Institutions for Man: the dismissal of Peterlee Development Corporation, *Forma*, **4**, 1, March 1976.

Moyes, W. A. (1969). "Mostly mining – a study of the development of Easington Rural District since earliest times", Frank Graham, Newcastle.

National Coal Board. (1959). "Revised Plan for Coal", N.C.B.

Pepler, Sir G. and MacFarlane, P. W. (1949). "North East Area Development Plan (Interim Confidential Edition)", Ministry of Town and Country Planning.

Peterlee Development Corporation. (1950). Peterlee – social and economic research (confidential), April 1950, P.D.C.

Peterlee Development Corporation. (1952). "Peterlee Master Plan, Report", Produced by consultants Grenfell Baines and Hargreaves, P.D.C.

Robinson, J. F. F. (1978). Peterlee: a study of New Town Development, Ph.D thesis, University of Durham, (unpublished).

Secretary of State for Industry, Trade and Regional Development. (1963). "The North-East: a programme for regional development and growth", (Hailsham Report).

Smith, T. D. (1970). "Dan Smith: an autobiography", Oriel Press, Newcastle.

Steele, D. B. (1962). The origin of Peterlee New Town and some features of its subsequent development, M.A. thesis, University of Durham, (unpublished).

Wirtz, H. M. (1975). "Social aspects of planning in New Towns", Saxon House, Gower, Aldershot.

Notes

1. Easington R.D.C., Housing Committee minutes, September 1935.
2. Ministry of Health Circular 2778, March 1943.
3. Easington R.D.C., Housing Committee minutes, August 1943.
4. See Clarke, 1947, Ch. IX: "The Case for New Industry".
5. Lewis Silkin in the Commons debate on the New Towns Bill; *Hansard*, v. 422, col. 1091.
6. Reith Committee, Interim Report, para. 1 (7).
7. Interview with a senior local government officer, 21 January 1976.

8. See verbatim report of the Minister's meeting with local authorities at Easington, 27 August 1947 in Easington R.D.C. minutes, 1947.

9. Biographical details of board members are given in Robinson, 1978.

10. The Chairman of Easington R.D.C. Housing Committee commented "we are pulling down condemned pit houses which are better than these wooden shambles" (*Daily Express*, 20 November 1959). More recently, residents challenged Passmore to "leave his villa in Malta and spend a winter in one of these houses" and suggested that he should try being "put into a pram and tipped up on end to get into the house" "Showpiece homes 'slumway'," *Peterlee Chronicle* 7 May 1976). For further details see Robinson, 1978, ch. III.

11. Peterlee rents were, at first, nearly double those charged to tenants of Council housing in the villages because Corporation rents directly reflected current costs, while the Council could "pool" rents, thus subsidizing new stock with rents paid on older, pre-war stock. This differential was finally overcome as a result of the "fair rent" procedure in the 1972 Housing Finance Act. In addition to this differential, there also existed another substantial stock of housing, owned by the NCB, which was rent-free to miners.

12. *Sunderland Echo*, 21 September 1960. See also "Go to Peterlee? We Might as Well Emigrate, say S. Hetton Folk", *Sunderland Echo*, 17 April, 1959.

13. Shotton failed on several occasions to secure new housing: "Rats Appear as Shotton Fights to Live" (*Northern Echo*, 21 November, 1963) and "Shotton's Appeal is for a Way of Life", Inquiry Told" (*Sunderland Echo*, 3 December, 1964). Shotton at last secured redevelopment in 1976.

14. "The policy of centralised development does not mean the abandonment of existing places, far from it. Vast improvements can be carried out by the clearance of sites of slum clearance houses, the liberal planting of trees and provision of permanent open spaces, the making up of unmade streets, the levelling of redundant spoil heaps and the provision of community halls and other amenities. Further development should, however, be limited." C. W. Clarke, 1947, p. 64.

15. The Corporation's General Manager commented that it has "been difficult to persuade the Board of Trade that Peterlee is not just a miners' town and even within the region it has never received the priority to which it was entitled" (*Sunderland Echo*, 15 August, 1962).

16. General Manager's report to the Corporation Board on Social Development, 16 October 1950 in PDC File AS22. Note the close similarity between this and Silkin's comment in the Commons debate.

17. Report on Social Development at Peterlee presented to the Corporation by Charles Madge and J. R. James, 31 March 1948 in PDC File RS2/1. This report was intended to be preparatory to a research study by Madge and James which appears not to have gone ahead. Similar thoughts on social development pervade the subsequent work of Lubetkin's team but are stated more subtly.

18. *Ibid*, pp. 2–3.

19. *Housing Policy in Peterlee*, a report by the Corporation's Acting Chief Estates Officer, 9 August 1973; para. 8.7. See also Robinson, 1978, pp. 162–174.

20. Press release by R. Morgan and D. Robinson, 13.6.75. These two former Corporation officers expounded their views fully in Robinson and Morgan, 1976.

21. Report to the Corporation on the social problems of the Edenhill estate, 20 August 1974.

22. Report in *Peterlee Scene* (a local news-sheet sponsored by the Corporation), August 1976.

ELEVEN

Local economic policies:
trying to drain an ocean with a teaspoon

A. COCHRANE

(April 1982)

1. Introduction: the re-emergence of local government

In the last decade local government has become an important area of interest
for socialist and radical intellectuals in Britain. This is a remarkable change
of fortune. In the 1960s the study of local government had a wholly justified
reputation for stultifying boredom, and this was apparently confirmed in the
resounding apathy which greeted the debate about local government reorganization leading up to the 1972 Local Government Act. The change is
still more remarkable since almost everyone appears agreed that the powers
of local government to influence events have actually declined over the last
decade, with the balance of power shifting markedly towards central government.

Several reasons can, however, he adduced for this increased interest. The
same period has seen a growth in locally based community politics as action
groups have been prepared to fight for changes in their local environments
and for imporvements in service provision. This has inevitably focussed
their attention on to local government institutions which could be expected
to respond to pressure. Meanwhile, within the professions of local government there has been an increased desire to involve people in participation
exercises, whether to genuinely extend democracy, to shift the weight of
activity to voluntary groups, or to absorb potential sources of opposition and
conflict effectively. It has begun to appear possible for relatively disadvantaged groups and radical councillors to influence and to gain access to the
local levers of power. At national level, central government's obsession with
the Public Sector Borrowing Requirement has encouraged a conflict over
the allocation and distribution of resources, bringing local government into
the centre of the political stage for the first time in many years. Local

government, alone of Britain's governmental institutions, appeared in the late 1970s to have the potential for resisting pressures to reduce public spending and service provision.

Whatever the particular reasons, there can be little doubt about the new level of interest. Already by the mid 1970s, Benington (1976) was complaining that the techniques of business efficiency and corporate management were removing council activity from effective control by councillors, and therefore taking it still further away from any control by local communities. Cockburn (1977) develops similar themes, but places local government firmly in its place as part of a national hierarchy and as a local expression of the capitalist state. She argues that local government helped to direct attention away from divisions along lines of class and gender, allowing the local state to absorb and deal with locally generated pressures. Dearlove (1979), in an analysis of local government reorganization, maintains that the 1972 Act was intended to take power away from working-class representatives on councils and to encourage the development of more "efficient" technical approaches, supervised by middle-class councillors. It was thus intended to make it more difficult for working-class communities to use councils as a focus for action and debate and to ensure that most council activity was effectively depoliticized. Councils could also be more easily controlled from the centre.

But it could be argued that the attempts to remove powers and working-class involvement from local government are taking place precisely because conflicts over the provision of services or what Castells (1977) calls "collective consumption" are growing. Thus, Castells (1978) argues that in France it has been possible to develop broad campaigns to take over political power at local authority level, partly as a prelude to national electoral victory but also to begin to implement local programmes. Dunleavy (1980) similarly argues for the potential significance of such campaigns in Britain. Saunders (1982, S.4.2) suggests that while it may be appropriate to see national government as corporate, dominated by bureaucracies representing major class-interests, local government can best be analysed in competitive or pluralist terms, allowing for a significant input from rather smaller and not necessarily class-based interest groups.

All these approaches are concerned with the central issue concerning the state in capitalist society, namely the extent to which and the ways in which the state is relatively autonomous as it appears to stand above society. Two issues in particular are raised at the local level: first, whether local government is locked into a heirarchy of levels, so that it simply represents the local administration of the state, with certain more or less clearly stated functions to perform; secondly, whether local government is in some way responsive to the needs of local rather than national capital, or is by its very nature more responsive to pressures from working-class residents. Clearly these issues are not only of theoretical importance. Saunders (1979) study of Croydon indicates how the balance between local elites and externally generated pressures have changed the face of the town. The extent to which local government can escape from either national political constraints or from ultimately reflecting capitalist interests will determine the extent to which it can be viewed as a serious arena of political struggle. It has become increasingly accepted by the left, even outside the Labour Party, that it is necessary to undertake action within or directed towards local government, even if this may sometimes involve unpleasant compromise.

In this chapter these themes will be approached by looking at a relatively new aspect of local authority activity, and one which appears to offer real scope for new initiatives: that is the development of local authority economic policy. The discussion is divided into two parts. The first of these explains how the policy area grew as a non-controversial one, and describes what, despite their apparent novelty, can be seen as the traditional policies of economic development. The second looks at more radical (and more recent) proposals and programmes and assesses the extent of their break from tradition.

This exercise of comparison has an additional value since legal advice has tended to be more cautious in the wake of the Law Lord's ruling in December 1981 against the Greater London Council's cheap fares scheme on London Transport. The Labour Party nationally is now committed to extending local economic powers, while Conservative plans are to restrict them. There is a danger that any failings in local economic policy will be blamed on legal restrictions rather than the value of the policies themselves.

2. The growth of local economic policy-making

The effects of Britain's mounting economic problems are not just to be seen in sets of national statistics; they are experienced by us all, and they are felt more strongly in some locations than in others. The regional problem has been officially acknowledged since the 1930s and Britain's continued economic decline has hit the traditionally depressed regions particularly hard. Between 1975 and 1980 unemployment in Scotland, Wales, the North of England, and Yorkshire and Humberside rose faster than the national average. But cities all over Britain have suffered, too, particularly the core areas or inner cities. Their economic decay has been recorded so widely (e.g. CDP 1977; DoE 1977(b); Friend and Metcalf, 1981) that the notion of an inner-city economic crisis is commonplace. Even in the more prosperous South-East and the once prosperous West Midlands, unemployment has risen dramatically, and the increases have been concentrated in the major cities.

Since economic decline is experienced differently in different places it has presented itself as more of a problem for some local authorities than for others. As locally accessible and electoral bodies, whose members are influenced by the experience of their friends and neighbours and possibly by their own experiences of unemployment, it is not surprising that authorities with economic problems have sought to diminish them. Such a concern by councillors, particularly in the second half of the 1970s, coincided with a growing view within the professions of local government, encouraged by reports such as the Bains Report (1972), that they should be concerned not just with the provision of services but with the overall management of the authority area in the best interests of its inhabitants. This view was particularly strong within County planning-departments (since it fitted in well with notions of strategic planning and added some possibilities of implementation) but it was relatively widespread. Local government reorganization encouraged local authority officers to stray outside their traditional areas of competence, and one of the areas into which they strayed was economic development.

All over the country and particularly in urban areas, councils have begun to develop some sort of local economic policy. Both Conservative and Labour councils have done so and, until recently at least, there has been little party political controversy about the issue. Policy has often been developed from within the officer structure, and been endorsed with little dissent. Almost every urban council now has some officer, department or group responsible for economic affairs or industrial development and many also have specialist council committees or sub-committees. Following the pattern of other local government officers, industrial development officers (IDOs) have set up their own professional organization (the Association of Industrial Development Officers) with its own journal and its own conferences.

In fact, most of the policies being pursued are not new. As early as 1907 the Borough of West Ham was advertising itself as "the factory centre of the south of England" (quoted in Buck, 1981 p. 157).

But it was in the 1930s that the familiar pattern of advertising, advice to industry, and the construction of industrial estates was established. Both Liverpool (1936) and Jarrow (1939) had private act powers to make such activity easier, and elsewhere small-scale activity was being undertaken. Bristol had a separate council-sponsored Bristol Development Board which also involved representatives of local industry. Local authorities and industry also co-operated in the Northern Industrial Board. This fitted in well with the self-help ethic of the National Government. The Commissioner for the Special Areas called for more local authority initiatives in his Report 1934–5, and criticized the view that "the future of the Areas must be left to the Government" (quoted in Camina 1974, p. 88).

Since the war, local authority economic activity has generally been limited to small-scale advertising and the construction of small industrial estates. Estates have been built by authorities such as Abingdon (Vale of White Horse), as well as more likely ones such as Newcastle, but the extent of construction has always been greater in the North-East and other areas of high unemployment. There can be little doubt that the scale of financial and manpower commitment has increased significantly in the last ten years, although it is not possible to produce precise figures since this activity is not a statutory responsibility and the position of a council's industrial development officer within the departmental hierarchy is often idiosyncratic. A survey undertaken by Falk (1979) indicates that 64% of authorities with Industrial Development Officers first appointed them between 1971 and 1978, and 41% did so between 1975 and 1978.

3. The "traditional" approach

There are four main traditional forms of local authority economic activity (Young *et al.*, 1980; Lawless, 1980; Boddy and Barrett, 1980; Johnson and Cochrane, 1981):

3·1 Publicity

The newspapers and specialist magazines are gradually filling up with more and more advertisements extolling the virtues of one area over another. Some authorities appear to be better at it than others, using more sophisticated techniques, identifying potential target firms, sending delegations to foreign countries, and taking or supporting stands at trade and industrial fairs. Some have larger budgets than others (approaching £100 000 in some cases). Everywhere publicity budgets are the first to grow as economic problems are seen to be important. Promotional activity is one of the easiest and least controversial of policies to be initiated. It shows concern and commitment, even if its potential for success is questionable.

By its very nature, the value of advertising and publicity is difficult to assess. Only in a limited number of cases can a direct link be drawn between a campaign and a particular development. One publicity officer has graphically described the process as: "casting bread upon the water and hoping it comes back as buttered toast" (Cochrane, 1980, p. 8). Fundamentally, of course, this policy does little, if anything, to create new industry even if it does produce "buttered toast". Rather it redistributes what already exists, and local authorities are effectively spending money to fight one another.

3·2. Advice, information and assistance

Local authorities have in the past been blamed for acting harshly in restricting industrial growth. Their policies (planning policies, in particular) are said to have stopped firms from expanding in urban areas. This view was expressed by the Department of the Environment in a circular to local authorities under the last Labour government (DoE, 1977a) and is one of the bases of the Conservative government's commitment to Enterprise Zones (see Anderson, this volume)

This seems to have encouraged councils and their officers to try to change their images. They want to help. They refer developers to the areas appropriate for development; they pass them on to relevant estate agents; they help with advice on housing, education, planning, finance and even on potential government grants. Libraries provide technical information; careers officers, colleges and schools, help to produce suitable labour.

Planners have been most affected by the changes in attitude, however. They all want to be nice to potential private developers, particularly in inner urban areas, despite criticisms from some local residents who do not always find the proposed developments particularly attractive. Most planners now emphasize that they are prepared to allow industrial or commercial development in areas which are primarily residential as long as jobs are provided (or protected) and, in principle at least, as long as the nature of the area is not significantly affected. Planners are often directly involved in promotional and other industrial development work.

Nor is their concern to apply plans "flexibly" restricted to the inner cities. In many cases they negotiate to achieve the package which the developers want. Nottinghamshire's planners, for example, helped Kodak through a long drawn out process of planning consultation in the mid-1970s in order to ensure that the company was able to develop a 93-hectare site on good agricultural land within the Sketch Green Belt, because the development is expected to provide employment for 4000 people in the 1990s (Johnson and Cochrane, 1981, p. 52). Again, this seems primarily competetive with other authorities, affecting the distribution of industry rather than its creation or expansion.

3·3. Provision of land and premises

Some local authorities are becoming quite effective developers and estate agents in their own right. Most retain lists of suitable local sites for development, acting as central points of contact for developers. But a large number also prepare land for development and construct or improve premises for use by small firms or branches of larger concerns. In some cases, funds have been attracted from the private sector in order to fund authority-backed development companies. These latter projects have usually been shopping centres or other commercial developments (such as the National Exhibition Centre, just outside Birmingham (see Minns and Thornley, 1979b pp. 121–2), while the provision of premises for industry and warehousing, which is less profitable, has almost always been wholly funded by local authorities. The latest local government fashion in conjunction with universities and polytechnics, is for the construction of science parks where it is hoped innovators will develop high technology firms.

Levels of commitment vary, but active authorities provide parcels of land for development and advance factories of various types, generally towards the smaller end of the market, and in some cases for one or two-person firms as a replacement for firms which traditionally operated under the railway arches, or without planning permission in lock-up garages. The wheel of planning policy now seems to have turned full circle, and in Nottingham, the city council is helping to subsidize a co-operative providing garages for industrial use in a council estate (Waind, 1982).

Although most of these units are not heavily subsidized and are expected to break even in the long run, such has been the expansion of local government activity that commercial rates cannot be estimated with any confidence. There is very little privately funded construction of small factory units (below 2500 ft^2) in Britain's urban areas, because of the relatively high initial capital outlay and the instability and insecurity of most of the firms which would use them.

If local government had not entered this market it is not clear where small firms would find new premises. In that sense, therefore, subsidies are being provided. Councils are prepared to accept slightly less-secure tenants. Local authority IDOs generally use the same model of rebates and rent-free periods as private developers to let the units which they construct, but this disguises the fact that they are providing property for a diferent section of the market. Such is the gap in the market that most authorities have had little difficulty in letting property, at least until recently, and there has been little pressure for more direct subsidy. This activity may do a little more than just shifting industry around. In lowering constraints on the supply of land and premises some developments may occur which would otherwise have been precluded through the normal operations of the property and land markets.

But councils have little control over the nature of employment which is provided in the units they build. Where attempts have been made to specify that units should only be occupied by manufacturing industry (which employs more people per square foot of floor space than warehousing), units have sometimes been left empty for long periods and authorities have been forced to relax their restrictions. In some cases, large manufacturing companies have taken over units as extra storage space.

3·4. *Subsidies and loans*

Some authorities have offered subsidies to firms to encourage development, but these have generally been on a relatively small scale and not competitive with central government Regional Development Grants. In some cases rate subsidy has been offered, but usually on a whole clearly identifiable category such as empty office property. A more common commitment has been to offer mortgages to developers on council land and elsewhere if legally possible. These grants and mortgages have rarely been taken up very enthusiastically. Most small firms are content with rented premises, and the allowances for mortgages in many local authority budgets have generally been left unused for many years. Local authority mortgages have not been significantly more attractive than loans from banks or building societies.

In the past, most authorities have been reluctant to become involved heavily in long term and heavy financial commitments or in large-scale subsidy. So, although subsidies can assist firms to survive or grow, and can therefore do more than merely shift plants around, local authority activity has generally been marginal in this respect. This is in some contrast to the high level of subsidies often available from central government, either directly or in disguised form (e.g. regional policy). Furthermore, and this crucial point applies to all the strategies discussed in this section, assisting firms does *not* necessarily mean creating jobs. Indeed, "jobless growth" is now the norm for those firms which are still expanding, both in Britain and the EEC (see Morgan and Sayer, this volume).

4. Constraints and limitations to local government economic policy

Why is it that these essentially peripheral policies and proposals have dominated local government action in the economic policy field? The similarity of policies followed by widely different local authorities (in terms of size, economic structure, politics etc.) seems to suggest some overall, and rather severe, limitations on their action. Alternatively there may be a remarkable agreement on the causes, consequences and amelioration of locally-felt economic problems. In fact we can determine at least two sets of overriding constraints: first, the position of local government *vis-à-vis* an international economic system which is dominated by large, multinational firms and, secondly, the political and ideological position of local authorities themselves.

4·1 The power of the market

The most significant aspect of local government economic activity, at least of this more traditional form, is its clear dependence on the market; on the decisions and requirements of individual firms, particularly small firms. And, even if local authorities were successful in influencing small firms, these are least important in terms of employment and economic effect. Local authorities give little attention to changing central government policy, and even less priority to the preservation or expansion of their own employment except by using centrally supported Manpower Services Commission schemes.

The attempt throughout has been to make some contribution to the rebuilding, or the regeneration, of a healthy economy. In practice at local level this transforms all activities into begging or pleading as private actors have to be prodded or persuaded into action. In some cases there is a vague hope that the right atmosphere in the provision of "starter-units" will somehow call forth hidden entrepreneurial spirit to build up success from below again.

The acceptance by most local authorities that they cannot expect to seriously influence the policy decisions of those firms which are most important in terms of employment (such as Ford or ICI) has not stopped them trying to do so by offering assistance and generating publicity, but it has led to an emphasis on smaller concerns. The main component of employment decline, however, is not in the small firms sector. In Saltley in Birmingham between 1971 and 1975, 4000 jobs were lost in the reorganization of British Leyland's light commercial vehicle division – far more than the total employed by small firms in the area. Similar figures could be produced for most of Britain's inner urban areas (Cochrane and Dicker, 1979, p. 6; CDP 1977, p. 41). In the GLC area and the South-East Region, in the manufacturing sector the share of small firm employment rose in the early 1970s, but this reflected a greater decline in employment in large firms rather than any *growth* in employment along small firms (Brimson *et al.*, 1981, s.1.2). Certainly, in some parts of some of our cities the decline in small-firm employment has been the major source of job loss, but this is a reflection of the overall weakness of their economies rather than the significance of small firms (Brimson, 1979, Part 2). In such areas, the large firms sector is underdeveloped, and in them have been concentrated the weak, marginal firms moving easily in and out of business.

These firms are not the shining examples of entrepreneurial initiative they are sometimes believed to be. Green *et al.* (1979) graphically describe them as the new sweat shops and Brimson (1979) catalogues the experience of several firms in Islington which were receiving assistance from the council. Training was negligible, wage rates low (often below £41 per week), and firms tended to move to another site if better offers of financial assistance were available.

Britain's small firms have been squeezed out of existence by the growth of larger firms as they have attempted to rationalize and fully develop economies of scale. This has been encouraged by government assistance to large firms and by the lending policies of Britain's major financial institutions. However successful the rationalization process has been, it cannot be expected to create new jobs, since the emphasis is on raising productivity and in practice, production has been rationalized away from the urban cores (CDP, 1977; Massey and Meegan, 1978). Most small firms are not in recent growth areas such as electronics, but are in more backward sectors and struggling to survive on the scraps from the bigger firms. They can rarely afford to be major innovators since capital costs for research and development are high, but they are instead often used by large firms as sub-contractors, able to cut costs to the bone because of the lack of union organization. Their decline has not been caused by unsympathetic town-planning policies.

Despite the enthusiasm of some supporters (e.g. Falk, 1978b) small firms can never be expected to rival the large firms sector in terms of employment. Small firms are difficult to influence and still more difficult to create and keep in business. The local authority is only a part and usually a very small part, of the business environment within which the small firm has to operate. It is also far more dramatically affected by changes in national government policy, for example, on interest rates or even VAT. At best local authorities are likely to be competing for the location of a pool of small firms at a regional level, often within a 25-mile radius.

Recent local authority economic policy can best be described as opportunistic. It is not in any sense planned, but depends on the expressed or perceived demands of potential employers and developers. IDOs are expected to identify firms which may be interested and to grab them quickly, offering whatever may be necessary in the process. They are negotiating from a position of weakness.

4·2 Political and ideological constraints

Local authorities are also pushed into the weak direction outlined in section 3 by a tight mesh of political and ideological constraints. It is difficult to put precise weight on the different aspects of political determination, but it seems clear that neither central government edict nor direct interference by local business interests can completely explain the framework and pattern of local authority economic activity. Both may have a more indirect influence. Local authority activity takes place within a fairly clearly understood political and ideological framework which is the product of its past development, its position within British political culture, as well as the statutory basis for its existence. To some extent this relates to the functions it has been expected to perform, and to some extent, it simply reflects ideas which are dominant at all levels of the political system.

In general action cannot be taken by local authorities except as allowed specific national legislation (the notion of *ultra vires*). For most economic expenditure there is little need to search for special justification. It is there in Local Government Acts, Housing Acts, Planning Acts and the Inner Urban Areas Act. There have been no attempts by irate ratepayers to challenge the construction of advance factories or the organization of publicity programmes. But it is argued that spending to set up co-operatives or invest directly in industry is only possible under Section 137 of the 1972 Local Government Act which permits the spending of the product of a 2p rate on any activity held to be in the interests of the area or its residents. It could be argued that such a limit is quite strict, but for the GLC it amounts to some £40m, and in other urban areas and most counties it allows for far more spending than would be usual.

The return of legalism to local authority debates since the Law Lords ruling on London's fares is difficult to exaggerate. Local authority legal officers have traditionally used concerns about legal powers to ensure that new policy departures have been restricted. Local authority economic activity seemed just such a departure, but one which was widely accepted. Now there are threats that ratepayers will challenge the GLC's economic proposals, and a group of large local employers is contemplating court action to challenge the legality of using rate revenue to fund the West Midlands Enterprise Board. Finally, Tom King, the minister at the Department of the Environment with responsibility for local government, has announced legal changes which he hopes will reduce local authority economic activity. Only authorities designated under the Inner Areas Act 1978 will be able to spend the product of a 2p rate on economic promotion. Others, the large majority, will face a limit of ½p, and will only be able to assist small firms (up to 25 employees). It is unclear whether these limits apply to indirect assistance, but whatever the precise legal position, there is a renewed atmosphere of caution in town halls up and down the country. Perhaps this is a major aim of such legislation.[1]

Few authorities have attempted to challenge or significantly extend legal norms. In general the statutory framework of local government has operated as a back-cloth encouraging care and responsibility but rarely challenged. Even the GLC did not *deliberately* challenge legal convention on the fares issue. The legal battle ground was chosen by Bromley's political leaders rather than those of the GLC.

It has frequently been observed (e.g. Saunders, 1982; Minns and Thornley, 1979) that local government has increasingly lost its productive functions. In the post-war period, most of the large-scale productive activities have been nationalized: e.g. gas and electricity provision. Many basic service activities (especially those which have become politically contentious at the local level) have also been removed to other agencies, such as the National Health Service and the Department of Health and Social Security. As a result, local authorities have been left with a service orientation, concerned to identify problems and associated client groups. Thus, housing is provided for those in need of homes; social services are provided directly to those identified as being in social need or being social problems. In the case of economic policy the links are less clear. In most cases the identification of unemployment as a problem has not led to the provision of services to the unemployed, except on a limited scale, but rather to the identification of small firms or other businessmen and developers as clients.

The service orientation actually encourages local authorities to direct their attention towards the provision of assistance to industry, and has helped to create a profession whose principal loyalty is towards businessmen rather than the local authority itself – still less its inhabitants. Johnson and Cochrane (1981, p. 80) comment that the goals of IDOs "tend to be defined

The legislators do like to keep busy. Particularly when it comes to imposing centralised control on local affairs.

In 1979 they put the Local Government Planning and Land Bill before Parliament.

Parliament didn't care for it. And the Bill was withdrawn.

Swiftly Whitehall put together some new proposals, imaginatively entitled the Local Government Planning and Land (No.2) Bill. It became law, transforming the financial framework within which Local Authorities work.

Within a year Whitehall was back with the punitive Local Government Finance Bill.

So many M.P.s doubted the constitutional wisdom of the referendum clause, the Bill was withdrawn within a month.

Now, for the fourth time in two years, the legislators are back. With (wait for it) the Local Government Finance (No.2) Bill.

And even as this Bill is about to become fixed in law, there is already in existence a Government Green Paper outlining radical changes to the financing of Local Government.

The conclusion is that Whitehall is in too much of a hurry.

We believe this latest Bill should at least have a time limit imposed on it.

So that it can be replaced or abandoned once all parties are agreed on the proper relationship between Central and Local Government. And upon a new rating system.

To quote G.W. Jones and J.D. Stewart (Professors of Government, and Local Government respectively),

Whitehall's "record is amazing: four bills in two years; two bills withdrawn; three major changes in intention; and a grant system that is not merely complex beyond belief but contradictory in purposes."

Is this the right way to legislate?

If you think not, write to your M.P. Ask him to voice the demand for a time limit on the Bill.

KEEP IT local

Figure 1. Courtesy *New Statesman* and *AMA.*

in the terms used by their clients, that is local firms and potential new arrivals".

This orientation is reinforced by the fact that officers and councillors want to do things and to be seen to be doing things. They are practical men and women who want to see positive action being taken. They rarely have any effective way of measuring success, for example in terms of jobs created or not lost, but the provision of premises, advertising and meeting businessmen provide the necessary stamps of activity. Since local government is generally about the detailed running of particular departments (particularly housing and education), any new activity has to show that actions are being taken and can be discussed. In this case it encourages action oriented towards the attraction of business and developers. It encourages, too, the opportunist approach described above, that is the desire to take any employer, however small and whatever the problems.

Although the notion of local government as non-political even-handed administration is fading out, it still retains a significant hold. In the field of economic policy it has been very important. Attempts have been made to set up special committees involving trade unions and chambers of commerce. And controversy has usually been minimal although there have sometimes been differences of degree. This has been reinforced by and has itself reinforced the view that the task of local government is to revitalize the local economy by helping existing firms and attracting new ones.

In some cases and in some places, evidence can be found of successful pressure by business interests resulting in particular development policies at local level, but such evidence is rare. In most councils, lawyers, estate agents and builders are well represented but industrial managers or small business-men are not. The interest of most chambers of commerce and regional CBIs seems to be restricted to calls for rate reductions and less restrictive planning policies.

But it is not necessary to view local government as basically corrupt to understand that business interests are likely to have their views sympathetic-ally considered. Local authority member's and officers generally see the local economy as something else – outside, over there – which they *may* be able to influence but cannot direct. The main group to be influenced must be local businessmen. This means that business influences the council rather more than the council influences business since an opportunist approach is adopted: that is the council responds to the particular requirements of the developer.

The local authority tries to assess what businessmen will want and to provide it, even if there are few formal consultative channels. It is influenced by the demands of individual firms with whom it is involved in detailed negotiations. In practice most authorities are proud if they have good rela-tions with local firms.

The very existence of *local* government implies a high degree of localism among councillors and officers. For most of them local government bound-aries, which often bear little relationship to economic structures, are para-mount. They provide the framework within which they operate. This tends to reinforce the emphasis on small firms since they are quintessentially local, and often not part of some non-local concern. It also reinforces the view that some sort of solution is possible at local level. This may be hard to sustain in other areas of policy, but it is remarkably unconvincing here. It sometimes encourages competition between neighbouring authorities for firms, although most people are usually prepared to cross local authority boundaries to go to work.

The pressures and constraints within which local authorities operate, therefore, have produced a tight net from which it is difficult to escape. Until recently at local level the main distinction on party political lines has probably been the extent to which the parties have been prepared to spend money on the same sorts of things. In the past this has been true of more radical authorities, but in the local elections of 1981 a number of Labour manifestos argued for a distinct break, making economic issues a central plank and maintaining that some new approach was possible; this was particularly the case in Greater London, the West Midlands and in Sheffield. At last, it seems, some new and more fundamental initiatives are being undertaken.

5. Socialist initiatives[2]

5·1 Municipal socialism and Enterprise Boards

Much of the argument for the new approaches is exciting. They are not supposed to provide just another activity which local government can add to its present responsibilities and carry on much as before. Rather they are seen as an essential part of the Labour Party's attempt to construct a convincing alternative economic strategy to that of Thatcher's government and, indeed, to the Callaghan government before that. One clearly stated aim is to show at local level how the failures of the past can be overcome, for example, by negotiating a series of successful local planning agreements with companies receiving assistance from the authorities. But more than this is also expected. The development of specifically *local* initiatives is supposed to encourage the development of decentralized political power, directly involving community and trade union organizations. It is thus intended to offer an alternative to the bureaucratic and unresponsive decision-making associated with the nationalized industries, the civil service and the town hall.

Centralized planning, it is argued, has been discredited, because it has failed to involve workers in its decision-making. Decisions have always come from above. National state agencies have shown their inability to alter capitalism fundamentally; the National Enterprise Board of the 1974–79 Labour government is held up as a prime example. Rather, it is now necessary to develop "planning from below", by encouraging the local development of workers' plans, based on industrial sectors and supported by local councils. Even if these local initiatives can only relatively increase the involvement of previously unrepresented groups, it is suggested that they offer the prospects of significant political change (see Wintour, 1982, pp. 10–12; Massey, 1982, pp. 38–41).

Geoff Edge (Chairman of the West Midlands County Council Economic

Development Committee) has said that he hopes the West Midlands Enterprise Board "will provide a model for the next Labour Government" (Graves, 1982, p. 6); and that the County Council "are advocates and missionaries of new Socialist ideas" (Brown, 1981, p. 27). Michael Ward (now chairman of the GLC Industry and Employment Committee) acknowledges that in the past, local government has been dominated by capitalist values, and that local authorities ought to respond to the needs and demands of working people. However, he maintains:

> The task is to reverse those trends . . . Industrial policy need not necessarily be an activity carried out on behalf of and in the interests of private capital. National policy at the moment is dominated by a reliance on market forces, and an extremely limited role for public intervention. The alternative commitment is to democratic planning and use of resources in order to create new jobs. There is a need to demonstrate that that alternative can work, and local democratic institutions form one base for putting it into practice. Local government can be used in order to create alternative institutions and alternative sources of power in the economy. (Ward, 1980, pp. 14–15)

The gap between the old and the new, the traditional and the left alternative, can be seen clearly from the two advertisements shown below. Bexley's IDO is to be more traditional, emphasizing the needs of local businesses. Sheffield on the other hand is attempting to create a new department with explicitly radical ideas, with links to trade unions and community organizations as well as employers.

The new-style posts are not even seen as industrial development officers, but as economic advisors or as having more direct investment responsibilities. Applicants for the Sheffield posts received not only the usual job descriptions, but quite detailed outlines of policy options being discussed. In the case of the GLC they received a copy of the relevant extract from the 1981 Labour Party Manifesto "A Socialist Policy for the GLC".

For the first time in many years it seems appropriate to talk of a revival of the traditions of "municipal socialism". In its earliest, most Fabian years, "municipal socialism" was associated with the local provision of public utilities such as gas, water and electricity. Local authorities municipalized and rationalized the privately organized provision of these services both for domestic and industrial users. Probably the most famous of the municipal "socialists" in this sense was Joseph Chamberlain the Tory mayor of Birmingham. These activities "benefited capital as a whole and assisted in the process of capital accumulation" (Minns and Thornley, 1978, p. 41), and had little to do with challenging the system, or indeed providing employment. The new municipal socialists clearly want to do more than this.

While Chamberlain was making Birmingham fit for capitalism, other local authorities led by the LCC fought for and won the right to undertake certain public works largely in order to provide employment, as an alternative to the provision of poor relief. They also had powers under the

Figure 2. Sunday Times, January 1982.

same Act – the Unemployed Workmen Act 1905 – to train workers for migration and emigration and to set up local Labour Exchanges (Minns and Thornley, 1978, p. 42). Already in the 1890s, West Ham Borough Council was offering relief work to the unemployed and, partly at least in order to provide a more permanent solution, had set up a direct labour organization for building construction (Buck, 1981; pp. 520–30). It was on the issues of poor relief and payment for public works that some of the major local socialist initiatives and battles took place in the 1920s and 1930s. Poplar is famous for the conflicts between both its Council and Board of Guardians and the authorities of central government over the levels of relief which it was prepared to pay to the able-bodied unemployed (Branson, 1979). But similar conflicts took place with a number of other Labour and Communist-controlled councils (see, for example, Macintyre, 1980). Indeed, "Poplarism" threatened to become a locally based socialist movement – or so the Cabinet of the time believed (Deacon and Briggs, 1974). The issue on which the left, led by the National Unemployed Workers' Movement, was concerned to fight was the level of maintenance for the unemployed. They were not interested in providing financial assistance to employers; indeed

City of Sheffield
Employment Department

Join a team developing
Radical Strategic Action Against Unemployment

Sheffield is one of the first local authorities to set up an Employment Committee and Department. Its aim is to co-ordinate everything the City Council can do (alongside trade unions, employers, and community organisations), (ii) to prevent further loss of jobs in the City, (iii) to alleviate the worst effects of unemployment and to encourage the development of new skills, (iii) to stimulate new investment, to create new kinds of employment, and to diversify job opportunities, (iv) to explore new forms of industrial democracy and co-operative control over work.

The Council has agreed five broad areas of work for the new Department and initial staffing of 30. Two programmes are already in operation: industrial development (the promotion of trade, inward investment, industrial land and premises) and Sheffield Enterprises (financial assistance and specialist advice to workers' co-operatives, small firms and new job creation initiatives). We now need staff to head up three major new programmes, and further specialists to join those already transferred from other Departments in small project teams which are being formed for each of the five programme areas.

3 PRINCIPAL DEVELOPMENT OFFICERS (PO2 RANGE £11,220-£13,884)
to pioneer the following new programmes, and co-ordinate small project teams:

(i) ECONOMIC DEVELOPMENT AND MAJOR INVESTMENTS (2 year contract in first instance)
to explore the opportunities for directing larger scale investment in the local economy, through co-financing arrangements with banks, pension funds, local enterprise board, planning agreements etc.

(ii) EMPLOYMENT RESEARCH AND RESOURCE UNIT
to monitor Sheffield's economy, industry and firms; to disseminate information about employment trends to councillors, trade unions, employers and community organisations; to assist groups trying to prevent further loss of jobs by carrying out social audits on firms threatened with closure or redundancy and by preparing alternative community plans for local industries.

(iii) NEW TECHNOLOGY
to investigate the impact of micro electronic technology upon existing employment, to identify and generate opportunities for diversification into new skills and jobs, to stimulate constructive debate, policy and action in response to new technology.

12 SPECIALIST OFFICERS to be deployed between the 5 project teams, but available as a pool of skills for the Department as a whole to draw upon.

6 of these posts at PO1 e/f — £9,528-£11,517

(i) AIDS TO INDUSTRY: to provide applicants at initial interview with detailed advice about the various financial and other incentives for job creation or preservation available from Central Government, the EEC, the financial institutions, and the local authority.

(ii) PRODUCT DEVELOPMENT: to provide new enterprises with technical and marketing expertise in the development of viable socially useful products.

(iii) EQUAL OPPORTUNITIES: to investigate the employment situation and needs of women, ethnic groups and the disabled, and to develop positive action and job creation proposals.

(iv) MUNICIPAL ENTERPRISE: to explore opportunities for the local authority to generate jobs by an expansion of its own role as a local investor, trader and provider of services.

(v) ACCOUNTANT: This post will be on the staff of the City Treasury but the successful applicant will be required to work with the minimum of supervision as part of a small multi-disciplinary team led by the Council's Employment Co-ordinator. He/she will also be responsible for providing advice and assistance on new job creation initiatives to small firms and workers co-operatives in developing their proposals and in obtaining finance from other sources which will involve liaison and discussions with banks and Government departments.

Applicants must be members of a recognised accountancy body. Experience and knowledge of commercial practices in a wide range of companies would be an advantage.

Applications for the above post by letter, giving full details of qualifications, background and experience, together with the name and address of one referee, should be sent to the City Treasurer, Town Hall, Sheffield S1 1UL by 19 January.

(vi) SOLICITOR: this officer will be on the staff of the Administration and Legal Department but will be outposted to the Employment Department to work as part of a multi-disciplinary team offering advice on job-creating and job preserving initiatives. This may involve advice regarding small firms' legal structures, the legal rights of groups of workers, planning agreements, covenants, patents and licensing agreements.

Applicants must be solicitors, preferably with experience of work on employment issues, in industry, the trade unions, the public or voluntary sector.

Applications for the above post by letter, giving full details of qualifications, background and experience, and a brief outline of your approach to resolving the employment problems outlined, together with the name and address of one referee, should be sent to the Head of Administration and Legal Department, Town Hall, Sheffield S1 2HH by 19 January

6 further posts at the salaries shown

(vii) EMPLOYMENT RESEARCH ASSISTANT (SO1/2 £8,190-£9,528): to build up a bank of statistical and financial information on the local economy, industries and firms, for publication in regular bulletins and briefings.

(viii) GROUP AND ORGANISATIONAL DEVELOPMENT (AP5/SO2 £7,371-£9,528): to help new employment projects to develop the best forms of organisation to maintain workers' control, and to explore new methods of production

(ix) ENTERPRISE WORKSHOP MANAGER (£7,371 pa — 2 year contract in first instance) to manage a small 'nursery' factory unit equipped with basic machinery and other facilities, and to support the new enterprises which are fostered there

(x) FINANCIAL AND ADMINISTRATIVE ASSISTANT (AP4/5 £6,501-£7,875): to establish and run financial and administrative systems to help the Department work efficiently, quickly and non bureaucratically.

(xi) ADMINISTRATIVE ASSISTANT (AP4 £6,501-£7,137): to do the same job as (x) above, but within the Sheffield Enterprises Team

(xii) SHORTHAND/TYPIST (Scale 1/2 £2,445-£4,926): to join several other secretarial staff working as integral members of the project teams

Applicants for all posts must be committed to working energetically as part of a multi-disciplinary team, trying to mobilise the resources of the local authority and other agencies in developing radical effective measures for tackling the employment problem.

Assistance towards the cost of relocation expenses up to a maximum of £750, together with temporary lodging allowance, will be given in appropriate cases.
Further details and application forms (except where stated) from John Benington, Employment Co-ordinator, Employment Department, Town Hall, Sheffield S1 2HH.
For informal discussion, telephone (0742) 734118
Applications to be returned by 19 January
It is the policy of the Sheffield City Council to provide equal employment opportunities and consideration will be given to all suitably experienced and qualified applicants regardless of handicap, sex or race. Proposals will be welcomed from applicants who are interested in job sharing.

—— CITY OF SHEFFIELD ——

Figure 3. New Statesman, 7 January 1982.

much of the argument between left and right centred on the degree to which employers could afford to pay sufficient rates to meet the needs of the unemployed.

Socialist authorities then, in this field at least, operated more clearly within the service traditions of local government. They had identified a group – the unemployed – which needed assistance, and they provided it directly. Their powers to do so, or rather the responsibility to do so, have long since been removed and reside instead in the hands of the Department of Health and Social Security. This shift in responsibility also helped to shift the concerns of local government away from such controversial policies. Now, it appears that they are beginning to move into them again, through the back door of local economic policy.

But the new policies are being developed in a new context. Even the most left-wing authorities have been dragged into a discussion of local authority powers. So in an agitational pamphlet, Ward (1981) can spend some time explaining how Section 137 of the Local Government Act could be used. Similarly the GLC Labour Manifesto (GLRLP, 1981) explains to bemused electors which funds will be listed in the budget as coming under S. 137 conditions, which can be used under the Inner Urban Areas Act, and which action will require resources from the GLC Pension Fund.

The discussion of powers shows the extent to which the new ideas have to be located within traditional local government approaches. Here, too, the new activity is explained in terms of working the local authority system rather than in terms of new political principles.

Nevertheless there are a series of central proposals which appear to represent a significant change from the "normal" economic activity by local authorities. The most important of these for London is probably the suggestion of setting up a Greater London Enterprise Board (GLEB) – (GLRCLP, 1981b, S.13, Recommendation 13), but the proposed London Industrial Strategy includes other elements too. A similar enterprise board has been set up in the West Midlands. It now seems unlikely that GLEB will get off the ground in quite the way envisaged in the Manifesto or earlier documents, partly because of newly discovered legal constraints and partly because of limited finance. But it is important to discuss the proposals here since they do appear to present a carefully considered programme.

A great deal of the proposed work of GLEB will be familiar. One of its three main functions is to "develop" – that is to acquire sites, build and refurbish factories. If this were to become its dominant activity then it would be little different from other authorities and could be criticized on the same basis. The other two main functions are different. Under the heading "investment to promote strategic or structural change", funds are to be channelled to industrial co-operatives, new public enterprise and municipal enterprise; under "general investment", they are to be available to any public or private enterprise operating in Greater London (priority going to new

firms, firms under threat of closure, and firms operating in high unemployment areas or in trades with high unemployment levels).

Investment to promote strategic or structural change will tend to be
funded from GLC funds, but it is hoped that resources from Pension Funds
(above all, in the first instance, the GLCs own Pension Fund) will be
invested under the other two headings. Investment of any sort will depend on
a local planning agreement between GLEB, the enterprise and the unions
involved. GLEB, following the example of national policy on the National
Enterprise Board (NEB), is not to be part of the GLC, but to be made up of
members appointed by a council committee.

The enterprise boards are intended to go beyond traditional local authority
limits. Such independent agencies are needed to ensure that it is legally
possible to have extensive share holdings in various enterprises. The intention of the enterprise boards is to make it possible to have some longer-term
input into the decision-making of private industry. Geoff Edge maintains
"What we are anxious to do is to get money into companies, and into
companies long term, for actual production purposes". He emphasizes the
value of equity shareholding over loans from the company point of view: "It
is far more sensible to put money in the form of equity because you are
increasing the capital of a company but not increasing the floating charges
arising from the loan" (Graves, 1982). In other words, equity shareholding
through the Municipal Enterprise Boards (MEBs) is also a way of providing
cheap capital to private industry. In that sense, of course, despite the novelty
of the method, in fact the Boards will be carrying on the traditional state role
of subsidizing commerce and industry, albeit this time from the rates rather
than general taxation, and at more modest levels (around £3m in the West
Midlands 1982–3). But it can still be claimed that potential for radical
change remains in the *way* such subsidies are used: to direct production or to
change working practices for example. It may be possible to produce more
for "local needs", allow workers greater control over their working lives or
improve their pay and conditions. Some of these claims will be evaluated
below.

5·2 *Planning agreements*

The radical echoes of the failed National Enterprise Board are more clearly
to be heard in the importance accorded to planning agreements. Even at
national level the notion is a problematic one. In principle one might expect
it to imply that the state would draw up an economic plan on the basis of full
and complete information from Britain's largest companies (what Holland
(1975) calls the "mesoeconomic sector") and then expect the corporate plans
of individual firms to fit into that overall plan. But this, of course, would not
fit very well with the concerns for decentralization implicit in local strategies;
nor would it fit very well with the dominant notion that state economic

planning should not be directive. Indeed, with the present British state and political structure, it is arguable that it cannot (Jessop, 1980). Within the Labour Party, the tension between alternative approaches remains. Holland (1975) argues for a systematic bargaining process between government and the giant corporations, while retaining the basic mechanism of the market. Meacher, on the other hand, emphasizes that planning agreements should be achieved on the basis of bargaining between management and workers at company or plant level over issues such as "investment, manpower planning, product development, buying and selling of industrial assets" (Meacher, 1982, p. 21). Whatever the overall differences of approach, it is clear that for neither author is there any intention of drawing up some overall national plan of production; such a plan could only be produced after the event by stitching together the myriad of detailed "plans" which had been drawn up at different levels.

At local level the element of planning is still more difficult to identify. At best local authorities are in a position to bargain for certain commitments from those companies they assist. Thus Brimson suggests that local authorities should attempt "to conclude long term agreements with firms which guarantee numbers of employees and guarantee union rates of pay" (Brimson, 1979, p. 21). In the West Midlands agreements have already been signed with several firms in return for cheap loans (5% below market rates). These agreements include: a commitment to stay in the area; to create a specified number of jobs; to allow workers to join trade unions; to fully recognize equal opportunity legislation; and to pay reasonable wages. The full enterprise board agreements are expected to be more detailed and comprehensive, but it is not clear how much more can be included.

This is clearly an advance on the policies of the past, which involved subsidies, hidden and overt, and merely the hope of success and job creation without any specification of the type or security of jobs possibly created. But it remains unclear why firms should be more committed to sticking to agreements of this sort (common enough under the Industry Act, both for industrial and regional policy) with local authorities than they are with central government. The councils will still depend on firms to express interest, even to face financial problems, before they approach the enterprise board. Large firms are likely to be still less dependent on local than national assistance, and whatever promises they make will be amended in the light of commercial experience. In other words, if hoped for markets disappear, or rationalization is unsuccessful, or better offers come from elsewhere, it will be difficult to enforce agreements. Meanwhile the ability of small firms to predict the future and implement agreements is likely to be severely restricted; they very often depend on the unpredictable demands of large concerns.

With the best will in the world, these agreements will only work if predictions about markets, technical change and competition come true. There is not even any need to postulate high levels of mendacity by the companies receiving the money to see that the agreements must be rather flimsy documents. For instance, local enterprise boards and planning agreements imply the possibility of planning multi-plant companies or small firms on the basis of plant by plant, small-firm by small-firm bargains. But this simply ignores the unplanned intrusion of competitors and the overall national or transnational plans of the parent company.

One could even reach a situation in which different local authorities had *conflicting* agreements with different parts of the same multi-plant company. In the bus industry, the possibility of such conflicts can already be seen. In the West Midlands, Metro-Cammell (part of the Laird group) is demanding guaranteed orders from the local Passenger Transport Executive, and in the past (when the Park Royal Plant was open), similar demands were made of London Transport by Leyland (Birmingham CDP, 1977a). Labour's 1981 Manifesto for the GLC includes a call for London Transport to establish its own bus-manufacturing plant in London, which would generate still more inter-authority competition. Traditionally, bus manufacture has been a rather chaotic area with recurring shortages and over-capacity. It would seem to be a prime candidate for some sort of national planning. Most of the purchasers are public bodies (National Bus, local authorities and Passenger Transport Executives), and one of the biggest suppliers is quasi-nationalized. If planning were extended to the national level, then the logic of the system would become clearer, although it would be less clear why such carefully planned producers remained in private ownership.

5·3 The Pension Funds

The vision of extra finance available from Pension Funds as a way out of the dead end of economic decline seems to be little more than a mirage. The orientation towards such funds is based on the view that somehow their investment priorities are wrong. The GLC Labour Party Discussion Paper which fed into the 1981 Manifesto wished to emphasize the advantages of long-term investment which it is believed Pension Funds with their city advisers tend to ignore.

> The aim of long-term capital investment in firms, from the pension fund point of view is to benefit from the growth of the firms by being able either to sell the investment at a capital gain or to benefit from the long-term increased income. (GLRCLP, 1981, p. 18)

Minns, (1981b) argues that there is a clear split between financial and industrial capital, and that if the advice of the financiers could be overridden, more productive industrial investment would take place. The ideology of the financiers is held to be one encouraging short-term returns while industry requires long-term investment and provides long-term returns. This ideology is also held to encourage investment abroad, where returns are better, rather than in the UK (Minns, 1980). The arguments are a sort of radical version of the Wilson Committee on Britain's financial institutions (HMSO, 1980).

There may be some truth in this, and there certainly are real conflicts between different sections of capital. But as a radical strategy designed to help revitalize industry and provide employment, it seems to have limited value. The differences in time-scale are not as significant as such a view implies. After all, this has been the basis of the bulk of national state spending on industry, at least since the early 1960s. The Industrial Reorganization Corporation, the Industry Act 1972, and the NEB have all been intended to provide investment to rationalize and raise productivity, providing a profitable return in the long term. There have been two main problems associated with this focus on providing assistance (however guaranteed) to individual firms or industries. First it must be clear to anybody who has looked at Britain's post-war economic history that the returns from state-backed investment by private firms have been a long time coming. Indeed, it would take an optimist to predict when some of them will arrive at all. Yet this is how the local policies are justified: both pensioners and ratepayers will benefit in the long run if a healthy economy is created, even if present returns are low. Minns argues that "prevailing investment ideology is no more than an ideology with its own (pessimistic) beliefs about the future of production in Britain" (Minns, 1980, p. 162). But little evidence is provided to justify a more optimistic view of British capitalism. The real issue then is how long is the long run? In the long run, as it has frequently been stated, even the sprightliest of pensioners is likely to be dead.

Secondly, the main effect of new investment on employment appears to have been negative, since rationalization has actually meant the gradual collapse of employment. Industrialists are no more committed to the creation of long-term employment than are financiers. As Brimson (1979, p. 22) puts it: "expanding firms sustain themselves primarily by capital investment; not taking on more labour". The enterprise boards are certainly not *intended* to encourage this sort of rationalization. But health to individual firms need not mean full employment or anything like it (see also Morgan and Sayer, this volume). It is unlikely that the boards will be able to pick and choose between firms in quite the way they hope. Just like the NEB which attempted to regenerate British industry, that is a "mixed economy" dominated by private ownership, so GLEB and its counterparts in the West Midlands and Sheffield will be doing the same at a local level. But this means that they will remain dependent on, rather than able to escape from, the priorities of private industry. The appointment of the former head of the Northern Ireland Development Agency as senior executive of the West Midlands enterprise board seems to confirm that this is the direction in which we can expect the enterprise boards to move.

5·4 Co-operatives

In order to escape from these ties to private enterprise there has also been an emphasis on co-operative agencies and local co-operatives. But this emphasis has its own problems. the belief that it will be possible to call co-operatives into existence on any significant scale seems rather optimistic. Certainly the experience of Wandsworth (O'Malley, 1979) suggests that there will be major problems in getting anything off the ground. There are not necessarily a whole lot of "good" ideas for economically viable small enterprises just lying around waiting for cash to turn up. More often there are good reasons for cash not having turned up.

In Wandsworth, the most successful co-operative initiative in the wake of the council's proposals (Wandsworth, 1976) was a wholefoods retail co-operative. Many of the co-operatives which succeed will be based on particular political or idealistic approaches, and their members are likely to be prepared to make financial sacrifices to ensure that their wider hopes can be realized. Such co-operatives often provide goods which would otherwise not be available, and encourage experiments in democratic working arrangements which may be useful to others. Thus the wholefoods co-operative in Wandsworth has no doubt had a valuable effect on eating habits in South London, and the GLC has been courageous in supporting the co-operative which publishes "City Limits". But these co-operatives are rather special.

They can hardly be expected to make much of a contribution to the regeneration of London's economy, yet the renewed emphasis on co-operative enterprise in local authority programmes seems to imply that they can. In many respects, although not all, the same criticisms which have been levied at small firms by the left can equally be applied to small co-operatives. In practice, however, the evidence for the greater longevity of co-operatives is rather mixed, since the numbers involved are still small and there is often a stronger ideological motive for survival. At the Triumph, Meriden plant, for example, such was the commitment to the success of the scheme that workers were prepared to take reduced wages, accept changed work practices, and accept redundancies in a way which no privately owned firm could have expected.

The numbers involved in local authority-sponsored co-operatives are likely to be small. They are going to be launched into a sea of other small firms, and are going to have to compete with them and face the same problems they do, unless they are guaranteed long-term subsidy which seems unlikely. In the West Midlands, advice will be easily available from council-backed agencies, but only £250 000 per annum is likely to be available to back co-operative schemes. Most small co-operatives operate in the same areas as other small firms (for example, textiles and the building trade). Like them, they will tend to enter fields where little initial capital is required. Sheffield has already noticed that the creation of building co-operatives is also likely to conflict with its commitment to the expansion of its Direct Labour Organization. Instead it is suggested that such co-operatives might operate as "satellites" or "prime sub-contractors" to the DLO (Sheffield, 1982, p. 23). So just as small firms are often, in effect, just sub-contracting adjuncts to large firms, so may co-operatives become equally vulnerable to local authority changes.

If small firms are facing economic problems, so will the new co-operatives, but for them there is a danger that collapse or steady decline will also mean demoralization for the workforce and even the rest of the trade union movement. The workers will democratically discipline themselves and declare themselves redundant. Even the sympathetic authorities are finding it difficult to provide the support required. One of London's longest standing co-operatives (Metropolitan Motor Cabs Co-operatives) with nearly 100 drivers, was forced to close in February 1982 after the GLC refused to provide a £50 000 grant and a £50 000 loan.

6. Some conclusions

The proposed socialist local economic policies are not the break from tradition which they sometimes appear. Many of the policies are intended to strengthen the policies of the past, by explicitly striking bargains with firms and developers. But the local authorities, their officers and members still face many of the constraints outlined earlier in the paper.

The local authority tradition pushes them back to local solutions in the desire to identify some local client group(s) to help. The new radical Labour authorities differ from their more staid colleagues only in their desire to involve local community and trade union activists in planning agreements. They are searching for local solutions and local solutions which will *avoid* the need for confrontation with Central Government. They want to prove that they can do things on their own. Unfortunately, the area they have chosen in which to expand is one which has many pitfalls, and it will commit them to the sorts of economic priorities – those of the market – which they are trying so hard to avoid.

Finally, the contrast with the socialist authorities of the past is striking. It could be argued that contemporary radical policies are more a continuation in a different age of the sort of "municipal socialism" developed by Chamberlain in the nineteenth century with the intention of sustaining the private sector. Certainly they have little in common with the policies of Poplar. There has been no discussion of public works programmes or of unemployment relief, except rather obliquely in pledges that there will be no redundancies among local government staff and in attempts to maintain direct labour construction organizations, or proposals for a quasi-independent London Community Builders in the case of the GLC. But such policies are oriented more towards conditions of employment rather than the *creation* of employment. At the level of general policy there is an awareness that Britain's cities are in need of major programmes of house-building and renewal, road building and improvement and an overhaul of the Victorian legacy of sewers, water pipes and gas mains. And there is an explicit understanding that programmes of this sort could provide useful employment (see for example, AMA, 1976), but the main emphasis of local authority propaganda has not been on the need for new programmes which would require national support, as well. It has instead been on the need to maintain local democracy, to keep central government out of local decision-making (for example, in the Association of Metropolitan Authorities "keep it local" advertising campaign).

It is one of the ironies of history that the decisions of central government and the judiciary to make local authority economic activity more difficult may give it just the radical cachet needed to ensure its survival in Labour Party policy documents. It will be seen as socialist more because the Conservatives in government do not want it, rather than as a result of enthusiastic support for the policy itself. Already Labour's Draft Manifesto (1980) wants to extend the powers of local government "to engage in industrial and commercial activities" while the Conservative government seems equally keen to prevent this sort of local activity. Perhaps, indeed, these "socialist" local economic policies are in fact more about political organization and political challenge than their ostensible purpose – and hence the need for opponents to stamp so hard.

References

Brimson, P. (1979). "Islington multinationals and small firms: magic or myth?", Islington Political Economy Group, London.

Brimson, P., Massey, D., Meegan, R., Minns, R. and Whitfield, S. (1981). "Small firms. The solution to unemployment? An examination of employment in small firms in the South East of England", South-East Regional Council.

Brown, M. (1981). Socialist self-help key to recovery say the enterprising Midlanders, *Guardian*, October 6, p. 27.

Buck, N. (1981). The analysis of state intervention in nineteenth century cities: the case of municipal labour policy in East London 1886–1914, *in* M. Dear and A. Scott (eds), "Urbanisation and urban planning in capitalist society", Methuen, London.

Bush, H. J. (1900). Unemployment in Bristol. The search for a local solution, (unpublished thesis).

Camina, M. M. (1974). Local authorities and the attraction of industry, "Progress in Planning", Vol. 3, Part 2, Pergamon, Oxford.

Castells, M. (1977). "The urban question", Edward Arnold, London.

Castells, M. (1978). "City, class and power", Macmillan, London.

Cochrane, A. (1980). Economic policy-making by local authorities in Britain and the federal republic of Germany: a comparative study. Paper presented to the Political Studies Association Conference 1980, Exeter.

Cochrane, A. and Dicker, R. (1979). The regeneration of British industry. Jobs and the inner city, *in* CDPPEC, 1979, *op. cit.*

Cockburn, C. (1977). "The local state: management of cities and people", Pluto, London.

Community Development Project. (1977). "The Costs of industrial change", London. (Available from 85–87 Adelaide Terrace, Benwell, Newcastle upon Tyne).

Community Development Project Political Economy Collective. (1979). "The state and the local economy", Bankside, Seaton Burn, Newcastle upon Tyne.

Deacon, A. and Briggs, J. (1974). Local democracy and central policy. The issue of pauper votes in the 1920's, *Policy and Politics*, **2**,4, 347–364.

Dearlove, J. (1979). "The reorganisation of local government. Old orthodoxies and a political perspective", Cambridge University Press, Cambridge.

Department of the Environment. (1977a). Circular 71/77 on the Industrial strategy, Department of Environment, London.

Department of the Environment (1977b). "Inner area studies. Liverpool, Birmingham and Lambeth. Summaries of consultants final reports", Department of Environment, HMSO, London.

Dunleavy, P. (1980). "Urban political analysis", Macmillan, London.

Falk, N. (1978a). "Local authorities and industrial development: results of a survey", Urbed, London.

Falk, N. (1978b). Think small, enterprise and the economy, *Fabian Tract*, **453**, Fabian Society, London.

Flynn, T. (1981). Local politics and local government, *Capital and Class*, **13**, 114–127.

Friend, A. and Metcalf, A. (1981). "Slump city: the politics of mass unemployment", Pluto, London.

GLRCLP. (1981a). "A socialist policy for the GLC. Discussion paper on Labour's GLC election policy", Greater London Regional Council of the Labour Party, The Labour Party, London.

GLRCLP. (1981b). "A socialist policy for the GLC", Greater London Regional Council of the Labour Party, The Labour Party, London.

Graves, K. (1982). Enterprise Board starts creating jobs, *Labour Weekly*, February 26, 6.

Green J., Murray, U. and Davis, R. (1979). The new sweatshops, *in* "Community development project political economy collective, The state and the local economy".

HMSO. (1980). "Committee to review the functioning of financial institutions", Report and appendices Cmnd 7937. HMSO, London.

Holland, S. (1975). "The Socialist challenge", Quartet, London.

Jessop, B. (1980). The transformation of the state in post-war Britain, *in* R. Scase (ed.), "The state in Western Europe", Croom Helm, London.

Johnson, N. and Cochrane, A. (1981). "Economic policy-making by local authorities in Britain and West Germany", George Allen and Unwin, London.

Labour Party. (1980). "Draft manifesto", The Labour Party, London.

Lawless, P. (1980). New approaches to local authority economic intervention, *Local Government Studies*, **6**, 1, 17–31.

Macintyre, S. (1980). "Little Moscows: communism and working class militancy in inter-war Britain", Croom Helm, London.

Massey, D. (1982). Going to town on the jobs crisis, *New Socialist*, **4**, 38.

Massey, D. and Meegan, R. (1978). Industrial restructuring versus the cities, *Urban Studies*, **15**, 3, 278–88.

Meacher, M. (1982). Socialism with a human face, *New Socialist*, **4**, 18–21.

Minns, R. (1981b). A comment on "Finance capital and the crisis in Britain", *Capital and Class*, **14**, 98–110.

Minns, R. and Thornley, J. (1979). "State shareholding. The role of local and regional authorities", Macmillan, London.

O'Malley, J. J. (1979). Local authority intervention: the Wandsworth experience, *in* CDPPEC, 1979, *op. cit.*

Saunders, P. (1979). "Urban politics", Hutchinson, London.

Saunders, P. (1982). The state as investor, Unit 25 of "D202 Urban Change and Conflict", Open University Press, Milton Keynes.

Sheffield. (1982). "Employment Department: initial outline", City of Sheffield, Sheffield.

Waind, A. (1982). The concrete elephant, *New Society*, February 18, 274.

Wandsworth. (1976). "Prosperity or slump? The future of Wandsworth's economy", London Borough of Wandsworth, London.

Ward, M. (1981). Job creation by the council, local government and the struggle for full employment, *Institute for Workers' Control Pamphlet*, **78**.

Wintour, P. (1982). Out of the drainpipes, *New Statesman*, March 15, 10–12.

Young, K., Mason, C. and Mills, F. (1980). Urban governments and economic change, *The inner city in context*, **11**, Social Science Research Council, London.

Notes

1. This legislation, originally scheduled for summer 1982, has now been postponed, following the opposition from Conservative as well as Labour councils and the local authority associations.

2. There has been some considerable development around this issue since the chapter was written.

TWELVE

Geography as ideology and the politics of crisis: the Enterprise Zones experiment

J. ANDERSON
(April 1982)

It would be designed to go further and more swiftly than the general policy changes that we have been proposing to liberate enterprise throughout the country . . . the idea would be to set up test market areas or laboratories in which to enable fresh policies to prime the pump of prosperity, and to establish their potential for doing so elsewhere . . . If . . . we . . . find communities queuing up for Enterprise Zone status . . . we shall have gone a long way towards winning the debate. (Sir Geoffrey Howe MP, 1978)

1. Introduction: the enterprise zones as a political experiment?

The Enterprise Zones experiment was officially introduced as Conservative Government policy by Sir Geoffrey Howe in his March 1980 Budget. Eleven Enterprise Zones (EZs) have been designated under the Local Government, Planning and Land Act 1980, and although it is a Conservative policy, over half the EZs were allocated to Labour-controlled local authority areas (Fig. 1), and the majority of the unsuccessful contenders were also Labour-controlled.[1]

In the "neutral" language of the Department of the Environment:

The idea is to see how far industrial and commercial activity can be encouraged by the removal of certain tax burdens, and by relaxing or speeding up the application of certain statutory or administrative controls. (DoE, 1981)

These incentives, of which the most important is exemption from paying rates, are to remain in force for a period of ten years.

The technical details of these incentives and their likely impact on the ground are analysed in the second half of this chapter, but first it is necessary

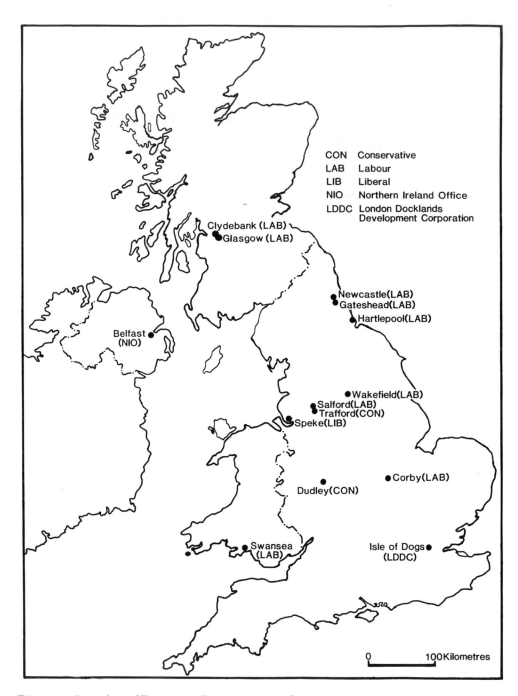

CON   Conservative
LAB   Labour
LIB   Liberal
NIO   Northern Ireland Office
LDDC London Docklands
      Development Corporation

Clydebank (LAB)
Glasgow (LAB)

Newcastle(LAB)
Gateshead(LAB)
Hartlepool(LAB)

Belfast
(NIO)

Wakefield(LAB)
Salford(LAB)
Trafford(CON)
Speke(LIB)

Corby(LAB)

Dudley(CON)

Swansea
(LAB)

Isle of Dogs
(LDDC)

0   100 Kilometres

Figure 1. Location of Enterprise Zones, April 1982.

to set the experiment in its wider economic and political context: its main objectives are political and ideological rather than narrowly economic, as Sir Geoffrey Howe indicated when he first proposed the idea in 1978 (see quote above). It is too early to say with any degree of certainty what its overall impact on the ground will be or whether it will succeed or fail. Indeed it is by no means obvious just what would constitute "success" or "failure", and a proper assessment of the experiment involves much more than the technical measurement of new activity in the zones, even if its *negative* effects outside the zones were accurately measured. The policy is already having some impact on the local geography of the eleven zones and further afield, but its impact on politics, at a national as well as a local level, was considerable even before the zones were designated. Its long-term political significance is potentially out of all proportion to its possible impact on local economies.

It is indeed an unusual policy experiment. This, combined with considerable modifications to the scheme and its use as a short-term political expedient, has led to confusions over what its objectives really are, thus further complicating the assessment of it. For example, it has been widely seen as an answer to unemployment, particularly by some Labour Councils, and it was announced as such by the Prime Minister, yet even enthusiastic supporters of the scheme admit that it may not create new jobs as distinct from changing the geographical location of existing ones. Again, it was hailed as the salvation of small firms, and its birth coincided with a growing emphasis on their importance in economic regeneration, yet small firms have perhaps least to gain and most to lose from the scheme, and organizations representing them are now among its severest critics. Some of these confusions undoubtedly stem from technical changes to the scheme since 1978, but more fundamentally they stem from its basic ideological nature and the political motives surrounding it.

In this initial assessment of the experiment it is therefore necessary to trace how the idea arose and developed in the context of Britain's industrial decline and the national and international changes in the location of industry since the 1960s. This in turn will throw light on issues of wider significance such as the relationship between technical and political aspects of policy, and the effectiveness of state responses in general and of small-area based policies in particular.

When he proposed "free enterprise zones" in 1978, Sir Geoffrey Howe noted that to deal with Britain's economic decline "two distinct philosophies are on offer": the "Socialist alternative" involving "state direction of our resources" and public investment, and his own "liberation approach". The EZs would demonstrate in practice the advantages of "liberating" private enterprise, on the diagnosis that "over-regulation is a major part of Britain's present disease" (Howe, 1978, 4–5).

However, and here the confusions begin, he insisted that the experiment was not politically partisan, and he expressed delight that "a distinguished

Socialist, Professor Peter Hall, was beginning to reach for the same prescription as myself" (Howe, 1978, p. 11). Professor of Geography at the University of Reading, Peter Hall was also a former Chairman of the Labour Party's Fabian Society, and in his March 1980 Budget speech Sir Geoffrey again paid tribute to him, saying that his own thinking "had taken place in parallel with that of the distinguished Fabian . . ." (Howe, 1980). In 1977 Peter Hall had proposed Hong Kong-style "freeports" as an "extremely drastic last-ditch solution to urban problems" (Hall, 1977), and indeed as far back as 1969 he had co-authored a similar area-based "experiment in freedom" (Banham *et al.,* 1969). Yet despite an alledgedly socialist parentage, Sir Geoffrey's package came securely gift-wrapped in the slogans of the Tory monetarist Right, and it was later denounced by the Labour Party National Executive Committee (1980) and by Labour Front-Bench spokesmen. However, by then Labour-controlled local authorities were vying for the limited number of EZs on offer; and immediately after the 1980 Budget, Peter Hall had supported Sir Geoffrey's contention that the experiment was "not politically partisan", claiming "there is political convergence in the thinking of both Left and Right, and a feeling that the old ideas have run out" (*Observer*, 30 March 1980).

To understand this we have to see it in terms of the comparative ineffectualness of the British state in dealing with Britain's economic decline, and the strength of anti-state ideology which has increased as depression deepened. EZs encapsulate this ideology.[2] Although not very significant in strictly economic terms, they are important in the continuing debate over the role of the state in the economy, and over related issues such as the role of local authority planning and local–central government relationships. And they are of particular interest to geographers, not simply because of Peter Hall's contribution, but because they exemplify the use of geography as ideology.

They also highlight in a particularly dramatic way some of the difficulties of social experiments and policies based on small geographical areas. Sir Geoffrey Howe referred to EZs as "laboratories", but in fact they are not and cannot be isolated from their surrounding areas, from local labour markets or the rest of the economy. There are problems of geographical boundaries, of negative effects on areas outside the zones, and of generalizing from eleven zones (total area less than 6000 acres) to the national economy as a whole. The EZs are being subsidized from the rest of the economy, and clearly there are limits to the generalizability of the experiment, at least as far as the financial incentives are concerned. Thus even if the incentives do encourage significant activity within the zones, it is not immediately obvious what this should imply for economic policy and state planning in general. And although the experiment has already brought political gains for the sort of *laissez-faire* approach favoured by Sir Geoffrey Howe, it could ultimately "backfire", providing evidence *against* his "liberation approach" if the zones do not generate significant new economic activity *and* the negative effects outside the zones are properly taken into account.

The next section traces the history of the idea of enterprise zones. It sets it in the context of economic decline, "de-industrialization" and changes in the international distribution of industry, and relates it to the post-war development of mainstream politics in Britain and to small-area policies and the recent emphasis on small firms. Then, having established the ideological and political implications of the idea, the second section deals with the EZs as formulated in official policy. It outlines the initial responses to the experiment, its modifications and the confusions surrounding its objectives, and some of its political effects. Its likely impact on the ground is analysed, and the official monitoring procedures are assessed to see what sorts of evidence can be delivered.

On the basis of this history and analysis, the concluding section discusses the implications likely to be drawn from "successes" and "failures" in the on-going debate over the role of the state in the economy. It focusses on differences between rhetoric and reality, to see what the ideology of *laissez-faire* really means in present-day Britain, and just what "generalization" of the experiment would be likely to mean in practice.

2. A short history of a bad idea[3]

2·1 Hong Kong "freedoms" and the bright lights of "non-plan"

Peter Hall presented his extremely drastic "freeport solution . . . an essay in non-plan" to the Royal Town Planning Institute Annual Conference in 1977. Arguing that the extraordinary economic growth of places like Hong Kong and Singapore was based on low taxes and freedom from controls, he proposed that to help inner cities in Britain these conditions should be recreated in selected small areas. These areas would be:

> free of United Kingdom taxes, social services, industrial and other regulations. Bureaucracy would be kept to an absolute minimum. So would personal and corporate taxation. Trades' unions would be allowed, as in Hong Kong, but there would be no closed shops. Wages would find their own level. (Hall, 1977)

In something of an understatement he noted that "Such an area would not conform at all to modern British notions of the welfare state".

The Hong Kong economy is administered as a Colony of the Crown and is based on a large supply of cheap labour sometimes working in often appalling "sweatshop" conditions. However, in wanting to "recreate the Hong Kong of the 1950s and 1960s inside inner Liverpool or inner Glasgow", Peter Hall does not appear to have considered seriously the question of wages and labour supply, or the implications of the fact that his small inner city areas would remain part of larger labour markets. He talked of attracting small businessmen to set up small workshop industries (including "Third World" businessmen with capital), and of a tourist industry like Hong Kong's based on rock-bottom competitive prices. But how would they get labour at wage levels even remotely comparable to those on which Hong Kong's type of labour-intensive economy is based, or even at a level substantially reduced below the existing relatively low British levels? Would even the chronically unemployed of Liverpool and Glasgow want to work in his "Hong Kongs" if they had any other means of staying alive?

In the 1880s and 1890s, the Fabians were enthusiastic advocates of forcing the chronically unemployed into "labour colonies", partly by denying them unemployment relief.⁴ But while Hall's "Hong Kongs" were to have reduced social security benefits as well as taxes, and would be administered as Crown Colonies, as derelict areas, they would have few existing residents. Also, as UK passport-holders, these would be free to leave (though those who stayed might not subsequently be allowed to transfer from the "Colony" to the UK proper until their social security contributions were made up). It would follow, therefore, that the bulk of the "Colonies" labour supply would have to be attracted, or coerced, from *outside* these small areas. But how? The lower personal taxes would certainly help, but not if wage levels in these areas were substantially lower than wage levels outside, and particularly if they fell below the level of outside unemployment benefits, unless, of course, these benefits and the welfare state in the UK proper were also drastically reduced. Peter Hall himself was concerned with the "inner city problem", a concern which typically involved a rather narrow technocratic approach which isolated "the problem" from the society of which it is part. But it was the wider political and ideological implications of his idea which were to be seized on by Sir Geoffrey Howe.

Hall's 1977 proposal reflected a long-standing disenchantment with postwar British town planning, and this stemmed as much from a boyish enthusiasm for the neon glitter and spontaneity of unplanned strip development in North America as from a coherent political philosophy. Britain's more controlled environment seemed to him dreary in comparison. Nevertheless, the logic of his enthusiasm for a more *laissez-faire* environment, and of the way he explained some of the very real shortcomings of British planning, led inexorably to a political perspective (and even a terminology) very similar to the philosophy which was to be popularized by Sir Geoffrey Howe and the Tory Right. Thus Hall's earlier advocacy of "non-plan" both exemplifies and reflects the general growth of the anti-state ideology which was to result in, among other things, the EZs experiment.

The "Open Group" of which he was a member published a manifesto in *New Society* in 1969 which included a call for planning to be "modified as to multiply choice":

> We think that on an experimental basis, in limited areas of the country, it
> would be thoroughly healthy to let *laissez-faire* rip, in order to see what results.
> (Open Group, 1969)

Six months earlier, he and several other imaginative technocrats of leftish
hue had published such a scheme, also in *New Society*: "Non-Plan: An
Experiment in Freedom" (Banham *et al.*, 1969). They thought that "the
whole concept of planning (the town-and-country kind at least)" had "gone
cockeyed" in a tangle of negative bureaucratic controls, and a tendancy "to
lurch from one fashion to another" such as high-rise flats.

However, while they pointed towards some real problems in planning,
their (largely implicit) explanation of these problems was superficial and
their solution naïve. For instance, they implied that high-rise flats had been
"in fashion" because architects and planners dreamt up the bizarre idea of
"vertical streets". In fact the main reason they were "fashionable" was
because Conservative and then Labour Governments had considered them a
cheaper way of providing housing where industrialized building methods
might be used, an idea upported by *large* construction firms who had a
monopoly of the requisite technology, and by local authorities who had been
given financial inducements to build them. High-rise flats were built *in spite*
of the well-known fact that most Council tenants preferred houses, and that
these houses were actually cheaper to build (Dunleavy, 1982). Nor did the
"non-planners" analyse *why* planning tends to be "bureaucratic" because of
the general lack of public resources for investment and a more "positive"
approach. They did not consider who actually controls "the planner", either
in terms of the elected authorities, or the unequal partnerships they are often
under pressure to form with property developers who own the land and do
have the financial resources to initiate development (see Colenutt, 1981).

Instead, inspired by the thought that Las Vegas and Sunset Strip represented "the living architecture of our age", they illustrated their article with
the neon advertising signs which were allowed in Britain, and declared:

> The notion that the planner has the right to say what is 'right' is really an
> extraordinary hangover from the days of collectivism in left-wing thought,
> which has long ago been abandoned elsewhere . . . We seem so afraid of
> freedom. (Banham *et al.*, 1969)

The similarities with the rhetoric of the Tory Right are indeed striking.

> The right approach (even that phrase now has a familiar ring!) is . . . to seize on
> a few appropriate zones of the country, and use them as launch pads for
> Non-Plan. At least, one would find out what people want. (Banham *et al.*,
> 1969)

Or perhaps only what *some* people want? They asked what would people
prefer to do "if there was no plan . . . if their choice were untrammelled?" But
in fact *most* people's choices are more trammelled by such things as income

and education and by what more powerful people such as developers, financiers and industrialists decide to do, than they are by plans and planners. "Non-plan" was an experiment where "freedom" would in practice vary even more widely depending on wealth, social position and power than was already the case. The criteria of "the market" were to operate with even greater freedom from the already-weak planning controls whose criteria, however imperfect, are at least in theory supposed to express the democratic wishes of the majority of the electorate.

Thus the objection to "non-plan" is not that the planning system is basically alright, but rather that the cure is worse than the disease and the disease is inadequately diagnosed. When, in support of Sir Geoffrey Howe, Peter Hall said there was "political convergence in the thinking of both Left and Right" (*Observer*, 30 March 1980), one can only reply that it is his "Left" which has done the "converging".

2·2 The weak state and the "converging Left"

The high point of state intervention in modern Britain came in the 1940s during the Second World War and immediately after it when a Labour Government nationalized some basic industries and finally established the "welfare state", the first New Towns and modern town and country planning. But by the relatively prosperous 1950s, with the Conservatives in government, Labour was already firmly wedded to the "consensus politics" of the "mixed economy". In the post-war boom it was assumed that Keynesian policies had overcome the main contradictions and crisis tendencies of capitalism, direct state intervention could be largely confined to the field of social welfare, and there was a minimal commitment to direct intervention in industry,[6] a position most coherently stated by Anthony Crosland (1957). So when Britain's relative industrial decline became evident in the 1960s, the Labour Government had a seriously weakened ideological and practical commitment to state investment and planning. Compared to France, for example, the role of the British state in modernizing British industry was characteristically fragmentary and largely ineffective in stemming a deepening crisis. Attempts were made, but the withdrawal of a National Plan after just nine months in the mid-1960s was symptomatic of their limitations, and anti-state ideology was in turn strengthened by these limitations.

The underlying reasons lie in the balance and nature of class forces in Britain, and while we cannot analyse them in detail here, it is important to note a few points. Britain had a relatively strong trade union movement, and the Labour Party, organizationally linked to it and nominally "socialist", had provided either the government or the official opposition since the 1920s. On the other hand, British capital has disproportionately large overseas interests (partly a legacy from the days of the Empire); and this politically powerful "international" section of British capital – the City and industrial corporations with overseas interests – has generally opposed any concerted attempt by the state to modernize Britain's domestic economy. There are basically two main reasons. First, because of Labour's electoral strength and trade-union links, it was feared that successful state investment and planning of the sort carried out by *non*-socialist governments in countries like France or Japan would, in the British context, give much wider credence to socialist ideas and aspirations. Second, and perhaps more important, any concerted state attempt to modernize the domestic economy would entail increased control over private capital and especially over the freedom of the "international" section of British capital to export capital overseas.

Labour in government has thus curtailed, or been forced to curtail, any attempts at a more interventionist solution to Britain's decline. However, the deepening and apparent intractability of the crisis led to a weakening of the "mixed economy" concensus, and to polarization. By 1978 Sir Geoffrey Howe could talk, quite realistically, of there being basically "two distinct philosophies on offer": either greatly increased state direction of resources, or the further "liberation" of economic activity from state ownership or regulation. In opposition in the early 1970s, Labour had developed a more radically interventionist strategy to revive British capitalism; but the Labour Governments of Harold Wilson and James Callaghan, (1974–79) retreated from this "state capitalist" strategy back to a more "consensus" approach. It was based on a "social contract" with the leadership of the trade movement to try to keep pay increases *below* the rate of inflation. But in its anti-inflationary monetarist policy (and acquiesence to the International Monetary Fund), and in its emphasis on the role of small firms in economic revival, Callaghan's Labour Government anticipated some elements of the strategy which was to be pursued much more vigorously by Mrs Thatcher's Conservative Government from 1979. In this sense there had indeed been considerable "convergence".[7]

However, "Thatcherism" is a radical break from the consensus politics of the "middle ground". Through further tightening control of the money supply and reducing state involvement in the economy, it is an attempt to force private enterprise to increase its efficiency and labour productivity, in response to market forces and the threat of bankruptcy. The resulting rise in unemployment is (as intended) forcing those still in work to accept lower pay and new work-practices. A frontal assault on the power of the trade unions (already weakened by the years of "social contract"), on the ability of workers to influence how they work, and on institutions which are sometimes more open to their influence (e.g. local government), is intended to further weaken their ability to resist. It was to help "win the debate" for this general strategy that Sir Geoffrey Howe pushed through the EZs experiment, and its future, in turn, ultimately depends on the future success or failure of the general strategy.

In opposition, the Labour Party again advocated the radical interventionist strategy, the left-wing of the Party associated with Tony Benn blaming electoral defeat in 1979 on the previous retreat from this. But the deepening of the crisis since the early 1970s meant that the "state capitalist" strategy, popularly known as "Bennism", would now have to be even more radical to have any chance of success, while the depth of the crisis meant there was potentially widespread popular support for it. Fear of it by capital was thus correspondingly greater, even though the labour movement at grass roots level had been significantly weakened. Many employers seem to have appreciated that the economic situation now called for a radical break from the consensus approach of the previous decades, and would have agreed with Sir Geoffrey Howe that there were only two basic ways of reviving capitalism in Britain. They may not like the harsh medicine of "Thatcherism" which was causing closures and bankruptcies; but it was also weakening the power of workers and was certainly preferable to the other radical alternative which would both increase controls on private capital and increase workers' self-confidence, initially at least and possibly to the extent that they would press beyond the comparatively mild reforms that people like Tony Benn were likely to implement. Fear of this helps to explain what on the surface appeared to be a disproportionately vicious, even rather hysterical, personal attack by sections of the media on Benn and on the left-wing of Labour generally.

These were the circumstances in which some right-wing Labour MPs split off to form the Social Democratic Party and "break the mould" of British politics. In fact this was more a reassertion of the consensus politics of the "middle ground", against both "Bennism" and "Thatcherism"; and because of its electoral implications, it forced the Labour Party leadership to attempt a similar reassertion. Significantly, some of the SDPs leading figures had been closely identified with Anthony Crosland's minimalist position on intervention in industry ever since the 1950s; they can justifiably be called "yesterday's men" (and women), though by the late 1970s the "middle ground" had shifted significantly to the right. This is what underlay the "convergence" of some of the "Left" with the "Right", and it is perhaps not surprising that Peter Hall is among those who moved from Labour to the SDP.

2·3 Small areas and small firms

Two particular aspects of this general ideological and political context are particularly important in explaining how the EZ experiment arose: the fragmentary nature of the state response to crisis already included the *geographical* fragmentation of policies and experiments limited to small areas and not connected to each other in a coherent fashion; and secondly, the policy emphasis on small firms had already given wide currency to an ideology of "blame the planners" for industrial decline. Both types of policy were initiated by Labour Governments.

Small-area policies, such as Education Priority Areas and General Improvement Areas in housing, mushroomed from the mid-1960s onwards. A response to what were seen as small pockets of "urban deprivation", they defined economic and social problems in narrowly geographical terms. Initially confined to the realm of social policy, they were aptly summed up as "gilding the ghetto" by the Community Development Project, itself a "neighbourhood-based experiment" one element of which was the intention of developing a cheap form of social control for "inner cities"[8]. However, with unemployment rising in the 1970s, attention increasingly focussed on the need to attract industry back to "inner city areas", and the narrowly geographical small-area approach was extended to the realm of economic policy. "Partnership Schemes" were established between central government and a small number of local authorities; industry was provided with rent-free premises for an initial period in "Industrial Improvement Areas" (see CDP-PEC, 1979).

Another small-area policy proposal was an even more direct ancestor of EZs although it never actually became official policy. This was the idea of "free trade zones" or "freeports" which Peter Hall incorporated in his 1977 proposal. From the mid-1970s, some declining areas pressed for special treatment for themselves in the form of "freeports", initially on the lines of those at the port of Hamburg and Shannon Airport and without the "Hong Kong" embellishments.[9] Such "free trade zones" allow goods to be imported duty-free if they are being re-exported or processed for export; they can free capital from being tied up in customs bonds, simplify customs documentation, and may enable goods sold to the "freeport" from surrounding areas to qualify for export incentives. HM Customs and Excise, however, opposed the idea, preferring the traditional British system of bonded warehousing as more flexible than territorially delimited "freeports" (*Press Notice* 500, 13 January 1978).

Yet precisely because they are area-specific and give special advantages to the chosen areas, pressure for "freeports" continued, most notably from the decaying dockland areas of London and Liverpool. It was officially supported by Liverpool City Council, and by the Labour as well as the Tory group on the Greater London Council.[10] Pressure came from private business interests and, like the parallel "small-firms" campaign (see below), it took on a strong anti-planning flavour. For example, in June 1978 the Greater London Council in co-operation with Taylor Woodrow Ltd established a working party to investigate the possibilities of "a free trade zone which has the customs, planning and other obstacles minimized . . . (GLC, 1978).[11] And in October 1979 Taylor Woodrow announced that it would develop a £400 million shopping, hotel and "freeport" complex on 199 acres in London's Surrey Docks, but only if it was granted all planning permissions in advance in a "special development charter". It was accused of "holding the planning authorities to ransom" (*Planning*, 340 and 342, 19 October 1979 and 2 November 1979)[12], but the idea of advance planning permission prefigured the "deemed planning permission" of the EZ experiment.

So complaints about planning being an "obstacle" were not all by, or on behalf of, the small businessman. But the small-firms policy launched by Labour in 1977 (with a senior Cabinet Minister, Harold Lever promoting small businesses as the solution to mounting unemployment) helped to give the "blame the planners" ideology a more general currency (see Davis and Green, 1979, pp. 43–50). This was achieved partly because this policy, unlike "freeports", was not area-specific; and it could plausibly be argued that small firms everywhere did not have the resources to meet various government requirements and regulations, and were at a comparative disadvantage compared to larger companies. But it was also achieved by linking the policy with "inner city" revival and by presenting an image of small firms which was only remotely connected with the reality.[13] Inner city decline, particularly with respect to small firms, was blamed conveniently but superficially on "the planners" (who already had a "bad press" from the controversy over high-rise flats, and conflicts over office developments), and on the widely-accepted but basically mistaken notion that it was mainly due to regional planning policy luring firms away from inner cities to peripheral regions (see Hudson, 1978)[14], and to Industrial and Office Development Certificates preventing redevelopment.

A dominant image of small firms was of technological innovators being choked by "red tape". The micro-processor firms of "Silicon Valley", California, provided one favourite model of "small is beautiful". Remove the red tape and small firms would provide the basis for solving unemployment. In fact, a government report in 1971 had showed that small firms had been declining in relative importance since the 1920s, a trend it expected would continue (*Report of Committee on Small Firms*, 1971). There is no evidence that the *quantity* of jobs likely to be generated by small firms can match the number being lost in large-scale redundancies from large companies (or perhaps even the number lost from the collapse of small firms, for they have a high "death rate" as well as a relatively high "birth rate"). Yet most of the current local job-creation strategies involving local authorities rest, somewhat forlornly, on the small-firms sector (as the previous chapter indicated), and to the extent that it relies on small firms, the EZ experiment is another addition to an already-overcrowded but barely-moving "bandwaggon".

The divergence between "image" and "reality" is also marked in the *quality* of jobs. There is considerable evidence that the small firms being established in declining areas are in many cases "sweatshops" or "backstreet factories", characterized by cheap premises, a non-unionized labour-force, poor working conditions, low pay, and minimal training opportunities (Brimson 1979, pp. 17–27; Morris 1979, and 1980; Green *et al.*, 1979). In some cases "Hong Kong" has already arrived and small is "sweaty" rather than "beautiful".

Six days before Sir Geoffrey Howe proposed his free enterprise zones in 1978, a Conservative Party committee published a policy statement on urban matters which advocated giving small business "a clear run" in inner city areas by abolishing Industrial and Office Development Certificates and reducing other planning controls (Conservative Central Office, 1978).

2·4 *"Free enterprise zones", 1978 variety*

The "convergence" of the "left", the growth of anti-planning ideology and the tradition of small-area experiments set the stage for Sir Geoffrey Howe's "free enterprise zones" in 1978. His proposal incorporated elements of existing policies and proposals, but broke new ground in several respects. Although presented as "non-partisan" and more "modest" than Peter Hall's "mini Hong Kongs" (a little too "dramatic" for Sir Geoffrey "at this stage"), it is clear that, far from converging towards the left, Sir Geoffrey's experiment was intended to further undermine Labour opposition to Tory policies and shift British politics even further to the right. In contrast to previous small-area experiments dealing (however inadequately) with social deprivation problems in inner-city areas, the "inner-city problem" and the specific problems of areas of high unemployment were almost incidental in Sir Geoffrey's scheme – something to be used rather than solved except in so far as any activity generated in these areas could be taken as "proof" that some of the EZ incentives and the philosophy embodied in the experiment should be generalized to the whole country.

He declared that while the "much-maligned multi-nationals" could still do "more for economic progress than all the meditations of Karl Marx", new, small enterprises had a "vital role to play" (Howe, 1978, p. 9). Four or five zones should be set up in Clydeside, Merseyside, the West Midlands and East London in which "planning control of any detailed kind would cease to apply"; only "very basic anti-pollution, health and safety standards" would be enforced; price control and pay policy would not operate, nor would "some or all of the provisions of the Employment Protection Act"; the Community Land Act would be "reversed", forcing local authorities to auction off their land-holdings to private bidders; new developments would be free from rent control, Development Land Tax, and "perhaps . . . from rates, in whole or in part". Businesses would be guaranteed against any future nationalization, but they would not be eligible for normal government grants or subsidies. Because of "the difficulty in securing a common view between overlapping or adjacent local authorities", the zones would be administered by something like a New Town Corporation (Howe, 1978, pp. 13–15) – something, in fact, like the Urban Development Corporations which were later to be imposed on the London and Liverpool docklands.

Some of these provisions were overtaken by general policy changes (e.g. in pay policy and the Community Land Act) when the Tories came to power in 1979, but others, as we shall see, were withdrawn because of opposition to them, and it was a less extreme version of Howe's 1978 scheme which was actually implemented in 1980, just as the 1978 scheme was more modest than Hall's 1977 version. But are these earlier versions a harbinger of what might be tried if the crisis continues to worsen? Because of some of the confusions surrounding the objectives of the present experiment, these earlier versions certainly indicate more clearly the basic ideology underlying it.

Sir Geoffrey pinned his colours to the mast with his enthusiasms for nineteenth century British private enterprise and the late twentieth century "freedoms" of such countries as Hong Kong and South Korea. *Back to the Nineteenth Century* could have been his slogan (Anderson, 1980). His argument was absurdly simplistic. He cited the speed and standards to which private enterprise had housed the newly urbanized working class. Subsequent decline in the twentieth century was due to "state interference". From this rewriting of history – the state started "interferring", after all, precisely because appalling housing conditions had amply demonstrated some of the inadequacies of *laissez-faire* private enterprise (see Wohl, 1977; Foster, 1979) – he concluded that reversing the historical trend towards greater state involvement would bring economic success.

This argument was reinforced by contemporary examples of countries with fast growth rates:

> . . . those whose economic policies are still nearest to our ideal. We find surprising – but convincing – examples in Taiwan, South Korea, Hong Kong and Singapore. (Howe, 1978, 5)

Peter Hall had seen Hong Kong as "fairly shameless free enterprise", and while Sir Geoffrey ticked him off for his "Fabian reserve" (freedom was nothing to be ashamed of), both of them implied that the reason for fast growth was freedom from state intervention, Hall suggesting that along with low taxes it allowed innovative small businesses to flourish in Hong Kong and Singapore (Hall, 1977).[7] But this is another example of superficial explanation: more "ideology" than "science".

This rhetoric of "freedom" sounds fine if we forget the reality: the freedom to employ child labour in Hong Kong,[15] or to force Korean textile workers to work a seven-day week, or the simple freedoms of Singapore where newspapers critical of that great defender of the "free world", Lee Kuan Yew, are closed down and the correspondents of such subversive publications as *The Economist* and *The Financial Times* are locked up (Wheen, 1979). Moreover, a detailed analysis of the four "Asian boom economies" by Nigel Harris (1978) shows that their extraordinary growth rates were largely due to very *active* intervention by the state and its *tight* control over the economy. Hong Kong *is* the nearest approximation to the "free economy" of *laissez-faire* ideology: the state just ensures low labour costs and high levels of infrastructure for private enterprise. But in Singapore, South Korea and Taiwan, the state plays the leading role in publicly financing and guiding private investment to the major growth sectors, and these (unlike Hong Kong's) are in *heavy* industry (e.g. petrochemicals, steel, vehicles, and shipbuilding, including giant "supertankers").[16] Hardly the realm of small businesses, innovative or otherwise, and indeed this model of "state-directed economies" is in *some* respects less like Sir Geoffrey's "liberation approach" and more like the other "distinct philosophy on offer" which he referred to as the "Socialist alternative" (Howe, 1978, 4). It shows there is nothing necessarily or inherently "socialist" about thorough-going state intervention *per se*, but what particularly appealed to the *laissez-faire* enthusiasts were the freedoms these economies gave to employers of labour, and though they might be loath to talk about it, the *lack* of freedoms for employees. These dictatorial regimes make effective trade union action very difficult where it is not outright illegal, and wages range from a third to a tenth of European levels. As Harris concludes, these "boom economies" rest on:

> dictatorship, the butchery of all opposition, the subordination of consumption to the maintenance of very high levels of profit, profits far above those prevailing in the world market and sustained only by the scale of exploitation. (Harris, 1978)

As in nineteenth century private enterprise Britain, labour is cheap and life is cheap, and in many ways for capital these countries are indeed "ideal".

Some of the "much-maligned multi-nationals" certainly seem to think so. They have been relocating some of their investment and production in such cheap-labour countries as one way of countering falling rates of profit in western Europe and North America, in the process contributing to the "de-industrialization" to which the EZs are one response. Another way of countering a decline in profits is, of course, to create similar conditions for profitability back in Britain, and such is the logic of the "new international division of labour" (Fröebel *et al.*, 1980; Perrons, 1981) that it makes *capitalist* sense to attempt to bring Asian labour conditions to Britain, even if at first it has to be done gradually in small zones of around 500 acres.[17]

Sir Geoffrey's proposal was denounced by some Labour MPs. Just as he had referred to the ideas of "a distinguished Socialist" for political effect, so Michael Foot replied with a quote from the Tory MP Peter Walker who, on this evidence at least, was politically to the "left" of Peter Hall (*Guardian*, 6 June, 1978). Walker had attacked the monetarist guru of the Tory Right, Professor Milton Friedman, for the idea that inner city problems could be solved by market forces:

Mr Milton Friedman has only to take a short cab ride from his University of Chicago to see what free market forces have done to some districts of that city . . . The free market condemns the weak and therefore becomes a powerful source for social disorder. (*Weekly Hansard*, 1095, 9 February 1978)

A *Guardian* editorial (30 June 1978) argued that "making a bonfire of controls is not the answer", and it echoed a criticism made by the *Financial Times* columnist, Peter Riddell:

If there is a case for removing these controls and obligations then the changes should apply to the whole country and not just certain zones which are, in practice, inseparable from the rest of the UK. (*Financial Times*, 29 June 1978)

But, as we have seen, Sir Geoffrey's objective in 1978 was precisely that of establishing the potential of "remedies that need to be applied generally". His critics generally proceeded from the assumption that his proposal was yet another experiment to deal with the "inner-city problem" when its objectives were in fact significantly different. He had said explicitly that his proposal was "*not* based on considerations of regional policy (. . . an entirely distinct subject . . .)" [his emphasis], and he had expressed sympathy with people who thought that his "free enterprise" remedies should be "applied through the economy, forthwith". But he cautioned that "in the present state of political argument" it was better to first demonstrate their potential in a few derelict areas, and he promised the impatient that when local communities started "queuing up for Enterprise zone status . . . we shall have gone a long way towards winning the debate" (Howe, 1978, 15).

Sir Geoffrey thus had the specifically ideological objective of *changing* the "state of political argument". He was in all probability aware that many derelict areas of high and rising unemployment were under Labour Councils, that they were increasingly desperate to attract any job-creating investment, and that the geographically-devisive idea of special treatment and "special pleading" for such areas was already firmly implanted (e.g. by previous "small-area" policies and demands for "freeports"). We have already outlined the erosion of Labour's opposition and alternative to "free enterprise" solutions at a national level since the late 1940s, but these local areas of dereliction and mounting unemployment were particularly vulnerable. Enticing their Labour Councils to "queue up" for the opportunity to implement right-wing Tory policies would further weaken Labour's alternative "philosophy" of state investment and regulation, and would help to undermine its national level opposition to EZs.

That, in any case, is effectively what happened. When Sir Geoffrey introduced the modified version of his idea in his March 1980 Budget, Labour Councils in hard-hit areas were already beginning to compete with each other for the limited number of zones on offer. In his Budget speech he was able to claim:

Even before this proposal had any official status at all, there has been no lack of interest in the idea. (Howe, 1980)

As it turned out, the great majority of competing Councils were Labour-controlled.[1] To mix metaphors, it was a case of the thin end of the wedge being applied to the weakest links in an already-weakened chain.

3. The idea becomes policy

3·1 Policy measures

The modified version of the scheme announced as official policy in March 1980 provided eight different incentives to existing and new industrial and commercial enterprises within the EZs (DoE, 1981). Four are incentives to *develop sites* within the zones:

(1) complete exemption from Development Land Tax;
(2) 100% allowances for Corporation and Income Tax purposes for capital expenditure on industrial and commercial buildings;
(3) the complete abolition of the need for Industrial Development Certificates; and
(4) a "greatly simplified planning regime".

(Meaning that developments conforming to the published outline plan for each zone would be given "deemed planning permission", and would no longer be required to apply individually to the local authority planning department.)

The other four incentives apply to *operating businesses* in the EZs:

(5) a reduction in official requests for statistical information;
(6) exemption from industrial training levies and from the requirement to supply information to Industrial Training Boards;
(7) accelerated processing of applications for customs-free warehousing; and, last but not least,
(8) exemption from paying rates on industrial and commercial property (the Treasury reimbursing the local authorities for their loss of rate revenues).

As incentives to private enterprise, some of these inducements (e.g. the reduction in requests for information) are of almost purely symbolic or ideological significance, but the financial savings for firms in the zones are real enough. This section assesses their likely impact both inside and outside the zones, and their varying attractiveness to different types of enterprise, to gauge to what extent the policy is geared to reducing unemployment. This will also show why the small firms sector, on whose behalf the scheme was ostensibly launched, has become severely critical of it. But first we need to outline the political responses as the idea was modified to become official policy; we need to clarify some of the confusions surrounding its objectives and its use as a short-term political expedient. It has already scored several political successes for the Government in terms of dividing the Labour Party and weakening local democracy.

3·2 *Responses and confusions*

Sir Geoffrey Howe forced a hasty formulation of the EZ experiment, according to Taylor (1981), so that he could announce it in March 1980 as "sweetening on an expectedly bitter budget pill". In pressing ahead he reportedly went "against all the advice of his officials" (*Observer*, 30 March 1980). This helps explain some of the technical flaws and modifications to the scheme. In January 1980, the *Financial Times* reported that it had "*surprisingly*, gained a considerable amount of support among Ministers" (emphasis added), though it was not "likely to be of much relevance to the immediate problems of Britain's declining base". For the officials involved, the problem was how to make the zones sufficiently different and atractive to industry while at the same time keeping them "socially acceptable and protecting them from property speculators" (*Financial Times*, 24 January 1980).

The scheme was formalized by the Industrial Policy Group at the Treasury in consultation with other government departments. The Health and Safety Executive ruled out any exemptions from its requirements, the Department of Employment objected to exemptions from the Employment Act, and, rather than create new bodies to run the EZs (at the time the Government was abolishing "quangos"), responsibility for them was to be given to the local authorities under the direction of the Department of the Environment. To "compensate" for the retention of health, safety and employment protection requirements, firms in the EZs would retain their eligibility for normal government grants as well as getting additional tax concessions and full rates exemption, all of which meant much greater public expenditure than Sir Geoffrey had originally envisaged.

Just before the March 1980 Budget the *Financial Weekly* (7 March 1980) reported:

> As was expected the original idea of hell for leather business ghettos has been emasculated by the Whitehall machine.

In addition, Tory MPs and Councillors at a Conservative Local Government Conference were reportedly worried that the *laissez-faire* element in the scheme had:

> been so watered down by Whitehall civil servants as to be worse than useless as a testing ground for Tories' theories that a hands-off policy for the inner cities would do more good than hand-outs. (*Sunday Telegraph*, 30 March 1980)

Clearly they would draw quite different implications from any "failures" within the zones than would people opposed to the philosophy underlying the experiment.

Initial reactions after the Budget were very mixed. Some Tory MPs wondered whether the experiment as now modified would work at all; local government officers in some of the areas likely to get an EZ were reportedly enthusiastic (*Sunday Telegraph*, 30 March 1980); the response from industry was generally favourable, but one sceptical businessman on Tyneside noted that in Budget week, Vickers alone had announced 350 redundancies:

> To absorb just those people you would need 35 small firms. The government just wants to be seen to be doing something . . . (*Sunday Times*, 30 March 1980)

There were fears that the zones might "encourage simply anti-social businessmen as well as good entrepreneurs" (*Financial Times*, 27 March 1980); and that:

> . . . firms just outside the zone will be understandably sore about unfair competition . . . so should they move? That just shuffles businesses around again. There is no escape from that one – until the whole country becomes an enterprise zone. (*Economist*, 29 March 1980)

However, the response from the Labour Party and trade unions was patchy and split on geographical as well as "right-left" lines. Just after the Budget, the Labour Chairman of Sheffield's Planning Committee remarked of Attercliffe, one of the short-listed areas:

> It was unrestricted free enterprise that put Attercliffe in its present mess in the first place, shoving up lousy factories, lousy housing developments, every thing that we've had to spend 50 years putting right with public money. We don't want to have to do the same again. (*Daily Telegraph*, 29 March 1980)

And some weeks later the Scottish Trades Union Congress condemned the experiment as:

> providing the Government with the maximum propaganda value for the least possible effort and commitment to industrial regeneration. (STUC, 1980)

But most of the local Councils competing for an EZ were, as we have seen, Labour-controlled and increasingly desperate to attract any job-creating investment. In a well-publicized statement the Labour Provost of Clydebank had joined the shop stewards from Clydebank's doomed Singer factory in welcoming the scheme (*Sunday Telegraph*, 30 March 1980).

With this response from some local Labour authorities Labour's national response was understandably muted. However, the lack of a clear lead earlier at national level had contributed to this situation, and it reflected the right-ward "convergence" of dominant sections of the Labour Party at national and local leadership levels which we have already discussed. This can be contrasted with the response from the Royal Town Planning Institute which as early as November 1979 had tried to pre-empt the scheme in a strongly-worded policy statement (RTPI, 1979). It condemned what it called "planning free zones" and challenged the Government to produce proper evidence that planning controls had prevented industrial development. Planners, it pointed out, helped entrepreneurs (e.g. to find sites), and removing controls would at best give them marginal gains but at a high cost to local communities:

> Industry is primarily concerned to make a financial profit; it can only satisfy social, environmental and community considerations where these are coincidental to its main aim, or when it is required by law to do so. The regulation implied by the latter kind of legislation is precisely what it is intended that 'Planning Free Zones' would remove. (RTPI, 1979)

Two months after the March Budget there was reportedly growing opposition among Labour MPs (*Guardian*, 21 May 1980) and in June 1980 David Hill (adviser to Roy Hattersley, Shadow Secretary for the Environment) rather belatedly warned that support for the experiment could not be squared with Labour's belief in the need for substantial public investment and planning to deal with industrial decline (Hill 1980). But in a parliamentary debate some Labour MPs from short-listed areas (e.g. Patrick Duffy, MP for Sheffield Attercliffe) spoke in favour of EZs, and against their own Front Bench, much to the delight of Conservative MPs; another Sheffield MP, Frank Hooley, spoke strongly agaisnt the policy, and the local Labour Party in Sheffield was also split on the issue (*Weekly Hansard*, 1174, 4 June 1980; and *Financial Times*, 5 June 1980).

It was not till August 1980 that the Labour Party National Executive Committee issued an official policy statement condemning the experiment as a "gimmick" which would cause dereliction in surrounding areas and was already weakening local democratic control and public consultation (Labour Party NEC, 1980). But by then the Labour Provost of Clydebank had already publicly declared that the Clydebank EZ was "the ideal solution – a real boost" (*Financial Times*, 30 July 1980); and of all the Labour Councils in short-listed areas, the one covering Telford New Town in the West Midlands was quite exceptional in its outright rejection of the scheme as likely merely to attract "cowboy developers" (*Guardian*, 13 August 1980).

There were similar if less publicly-expressed divisions within the trade unions. The main TUC followed behind the Scottish TUC in opposing the scheme, arguing instead the need for more public investment (TUC, 1980), but many individual unions did not have a policy on the issue, and the scheme was supported by some trade union representatives at a local level (e.g. in Clydebank).[19] The ambivalence of the response and its geographical fragmentation was neatly exemplified by the Welsh TUC. After condemning the scheme, saying it was "based more upon political ideology than on economic criteria", it nevertheless decided that:

we would, on balance, not wish to oppose or obstruct the establishment of an Enterprise Zone in Wales. (Wales TUC, 1980)

These partly geographical divisions were to some extent due to confusions over the main objectives of EZs. Some people completely missed its central ideological objective, seeing it as simply another in a long line of small-area based policies to help "inner cities"[20] and create jobs in areas of industrial decline. This idea was indeed fostered by the opportunistic way the scheme was launched and some of the zones selected.

For example, it was in replying to an Opposition Censure motion on 29 July 1980 on the Government's record on unemployment (then officially approaching two million), that Mrs Thatcher chose to announce officially the selection of seven of the EZ sites (Taylor, 1981, p. 430), and they were widely publicized as part of the Government's "attack" on unemployment. Some of the zones were clearly chosen to give this impression. Corby, where over 5000 steel workers had been made redundant in 1980 was not on the original list of possible EZ sites, but it was one of the sites chosen. Clydebank, a town of some 50 000 people had lost over 11 000 jobs in thirteen major redundancies, 5000 of them being due to the rundown of the Singer factory between 1977 and 1980 (Clydebank Task Force, 1980). The Liverpool EZ is in an area where British Leyland and Dunlop had closed down plants, while the Belfast EZ is adjacent to areas where unemployment levels reached 50%.

By September 1980 a writer in *The Economist* was concluding:

There is no escaping the muddle at the heart of the government's eleven enterprise zones . . . (*Economist*, 19 September 1980)

What had started as an experiment to demonstrate the advantages of "liberating private enterprise" was being used as a short-term expedient to head-off political pressure from areas where unemployment was particularly dramatic.

However, as we shall see, some of the EZ sites were chosen because they had *already* received considerable public investment and development was *already* taking place. Perhaps this development could later be credited to the *laissez-faire* ideology symbolized by the EZs. Certainly there does not appear to have been a consistent set of criteria for selecting the eleven sites and they vary widely in character, location and size (see Fig. 2). Although all consist in large part of vacant or under-used land, much of it owned by the local authorities or other public bodies, it ranges from derelict land through reclaimed industrial land to greenfield sites.

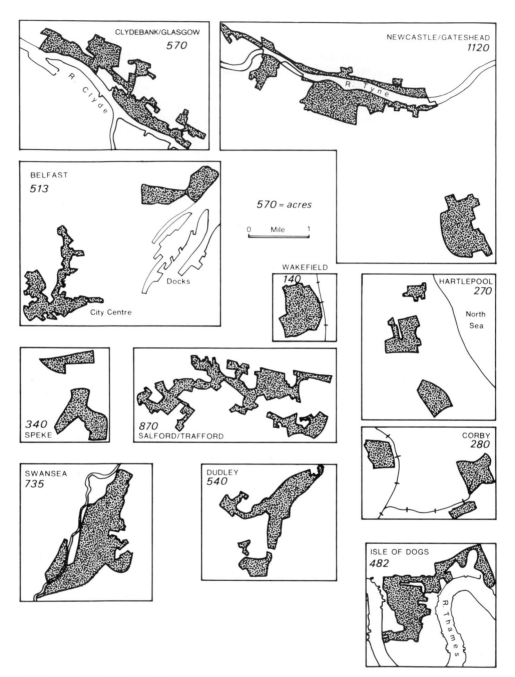

Figure 2. Size and shape of Enterprise Zones, (April 1982).

3·3 Weakening local democracy

Political factors were clearly important in site selection. In this and in the subsequent administration of the zones, the EZ experiment represents part of the general weakening of local government and public consultation, and the strengthening of central political control referred to in the last chapter.

Sir Keith Joseph had set the tone in March 1980:

> If local authorities are going to insist on rigid town planning punctilio, they won't show themselves very suitable for enterprise zones. (*Financial Times*, 28 March 1980)

The speed required in applying for an EZ given the way the competition for them was set up, and the lack of public inquiry procedures when the zones were established, both meant that there was very little local consultation. In effect the central authorities (the DoE, the Scottish and Welsh Offices) dictated the selection of sites and their outline plans. They resisted local pressures to control certain types of development, the limits imposed on large retailing development in some zones being only a partial exception. For instance, Sheffield presented an analysis of the harmful effects which a hypermarket in its proposed EZ would have on existing investment elsewhere in Sheffield (City of Sheffield, 1980), and its insistence that hypermarkets be excluded contributed to its application for an EZ being turned down. Also, while local authorities supplied local knowledge, the boundaries of the zones were for the Secretary of State for the Environment alone to decide.[21]

After the zones are designated, the Secretary of State can modify or change the original plan, but the local authorities have no such powers. The Secretary of State suggested that "representatives of the local business community" (as distinct from elected representatives of the local electorate) should play a direct role in the actual running of the EZs (*New Society*, 16 April 1981). In March 1982 a special feature on EZs in *The Times* (9 March 1982) reported:

> At local authority level, too, new thinking is apparent. Power is being delegated to enterprise zone officers on an unprecedented scale to negotiate deals with developers and tenants.

The balance of power had significantly shifted away from local electorates and elected Labour councillors towards local business interests as well as towards central government.

3·4 The impact in the zones

Despite the modifications to his original conception, Sir Geoffrey Howe appears to be "winning the debate". But will he, in the final analysis, win the war? Ultimately this depends on the general fortunes of the Conservative

Government, but more immediately it depends on the impact of the incentives inside and outside the zones, and perhaps particularly their effects on employment.

The attractiveness of the main financial incentives differs greatly for different types of enterprise, depending on their development and operating costs, and on what tax and other concessions are already available to them outside the zones. Basically, retailing, warehousing, offices and hotels have most to gain from an EZ location; manufacturing industry has least to gain, and *small* manufacturing firms gain least of all. On the development side, for example, from March 1981 for a three-year period, small workshops of less than 2500 ft^2 get 100% capital allowance for tax purposes anywhere in the country, while larger industrial developments get a 50% allowance. In contrast, there was no capital allowance for office development outside the zones, and only a 20% allowance for hotel development, so the 100% allowance for *all* commercial and industrial developments in the zones make office and hotel developments comparatively more attractive as far as the tax concession is concerned. Such developments might also be expected to gain most from the Development Land Tax concession, with industry gaining little as most of the EZ land is already classed as "industrial". However, most of the zones are not attractive environments for hotels, or even for offices. And the present ten-year period which the incentives last is quite short in relation to the time-scale over which the important institutional investors (e.g. pension funds) calculate their returns from property development so they may not find the zones as attractive as shorter-term investors.

On the operating side, rates are generally a low proportion of total manufacturing costs, and significantly more for offices, hotels and warehouses so their relative gain is again much greater. And for firms which do not own their own premises (often the case with small firms), the rates exemption may be largely cancelled out by the higher rents charged, so it is the developer or landlord who benefits.

Evidence is still sketchy, but there are reports that property values have been inflated by 30% or more in some cases (*Economist*, 19 September 1981), while in one case in Newcastle the rents charged were 50% higher inside the zone than for comparable rented premises outside it (*Sunday Times*, 5 July 1981). Such higher rents would act as a brake on the expansion of business within the zones, and property developers and owners could be the main beneficiaries of the rates exemption.

There may well be some spectacular "success stories" in some of the better placed zones (e.g. with improved transport links with the City of London the Isle of Dogs might attract a large complex with hotel and office development), but the amount of activity generated will probably vary greatly from zone to zone. Given the orientation of the incentives towards retailing and warehousing, which are not labour-intensive, rather than to manufacturing and small workshops, and the absence of any discrimination in favour of *newly*-created firms, the scheme appears to have only limited job-creation potential. Indeed it is not specifically geared to that objective. Job targets, against which the actual generation of jobs could be compared, have not been officially published, and now less emphasis appears to be given to the job-creation potential of the EZs by the officials directly concerned. Thus in March 1982 it was said of the Newcastle EZ:

> Our aim is not so much to create jobs as to safeguard them for the future.
> (*Times*, 9 March 1982)

The relative advantage of the incentives inside the zones, compared to those available outside, could of course change in the future. But if the balance stays more or less the same, the most noticeable effect of the incentives may be to stimulate the building of new premises on previously vacant land. This will look good in a series of "before" and "after" publicity photographs, but the use of public money to encourage or participate directly in this sort of investment can be questioned on a number of grounds. It will divert some investment that would otherwise have gone to comparable or better locations elsewhere. Similarly, the use of considerable amounts of public money in reclaiming some zone sites, will effectively merely divert investment to higher-cost sites from lower-cost ones (McDonald and Howick, 1981). Such is the logic of a *laissez-faire* experiment applied to small areas! Individual firms constrained by inadequate sites or premises will benefit, but in fact there is a large amount of industrial and commercial premises already vacant or under-used in Britain, as firms have closed down or retracted in the crisis, and as advance factories built by local authorities to attract industry to their areas have remained empty (e.g. in Hartlepool). So rather than reflecting priorities for economic recovery in Britain, the experiment's orientation towards property development may have more to do with the political influence of developers and property interests. The depressed Isle of Dogs was the symbolic location from which Sir Geoffrey Howe launched his EZ proposal in 1978; ironically, the Exhibition launching the eleven zones in September 1981 was in Centrepoint, the office block which by accumulating asset value through remaining empty had ten years earlier been a national symbol of wasteful property speculation and "the unacceptable face of capitalism".

3.5 Outside the zones

Activity generated in the zones will, at least partly, be *at the expense of* areas, firms and jobs outside them. There will be some positive "spill over" effects to adjacent areas, but most of the available, though as yet inadequate, evidence points towards *negative* effects predominating.

There are the detrimental effects of "unfair" competition on outside firms, and of firms and jobs moving into an EZ leaving dereliction behind them; and new development which would have taken place elsewhere may be located in one of the zones instead – even though, as discussed above, this new development will have cost *more* to achieve in an EZ than outside.

Businessmen outside the zones, and the local authorities, have expressed worries that existing firms, and other schemes to attract industry and commerce to their areas, could be jeopardized by "unfair competition" from the EZs. A major worry was that established or newly-developed shopping centres will be adversely effected: the EZs are attractive to retailing and competition in retailing is highly localized. Because of this the local authorities involved have to varying degrees persuaded the central authorities that there should be limits on the size of retailing development given "deemed planning permission" in order to exclude hypermarkets and regional shopping centres. For example, in Swansea the upper limit was set at 65 000 ft^2; any retail developments over the limit (and hypermarkets generally need an area of at least 100 000 ft^2 to be viable) have to apply for planning permission in the normal way and can be refused (*New Society*, 19 February 1981). In the Clydebank EZ retailing was excluded after the Secretary of State for Scotland intervened, because a shopping centre was in the process of being developed close to the zone (*Guardian*, 26 June 1981). However, the central authorities have generally insisted on keeping such conditions to a minimum, and localized "unfair" competition will apply to other activities besides retailing.

For instance, outside firms see themselves as subsidizing their competitors inside the zones by paying rates, higher taxes, and Training Board levies. Their property values (and hence company assets) may also be reduced. While some property values in the EZs have been inflated by 30%, some of those outside have been depressed by 25% (*Economist*, 19 September 1981).

Much of the criticism focused on the allegedly "illogical" drawing of zone boundaries as firms just outside lobbied to be included. Thus in Newcastle, for example, the boundary was drawn between two steel stockholding companies, and this brought complaints from both the local Engineering Industries Association and the Northern Region Confederation of British Industry on behalf of the excluded firm (*Journal*, Newcastle, 19 May 1981). Some of the zone boundaries (see Fig. 2) are indeed extremely tortuous. The logic here seems to be that of maximizing the proportion of vacant land and of excluding established businesses as far as possible, in order to minimize the Treasury's rates bill to the local authorities. As a complicating exception, however, there appears to have been a conscious attempt to *include* some established plants: the Newcastle boundary was reportedly drawn to include Vickers "as a carrot, to keep it going" (*Financial Times*, 8 September 1981).

Excluded firms can, in some cases at least, relocate within a zone. But this may not result in any *additional* activity or jobs; indeed it could lead to a *reduction* in jobs if the process of relocation is taken as an opportunity to shed labour, or the EZ financial incentives are used to finance job-replacing machinery. Also the adverse effects on their areas of origin could well be felt by other firms and their workforces: a *negative* "multiplier effect" would operate to some extent.

The euphoria in business circles died down as the problems of EZs became more apparent to them. Enthusiasts became critics, and none more so than the small-firms sector. Not only do small firms generally have least to gain from an EZ location, as we have seen, but they are also the most vulnerable to "unfair competition" if in the vicinity of an EZ. The National Federation of the Self-Employed and Small Businesses has opposed the experiment, and the Association of Independent Businesses, while supporting "the spirit of the initiative", now sees it as simply favouring property developers and shifting existing firms around. They called for a prohibition on *re*locations and for the incentives to apply *only* to genuinely *new* economic developments (*Guardian*, 20 June 1980), but that, of course, would be contrary to the "spirit" of the experiment. It would reduce the amount of property development and activity in the zones.

Mr Walter Goldsmith of the Institute of Directors (and a strong supporter of Conservative economic policy in general) bitterly attacked the "arbitrary" nature of the boundaries as meaning death to firms just outside the EZs (and he blamed those familiar "whipping boys", the town hall planners, despite the fact that, as we have seen, the boundaries were for the Secretary of State alone to decide). Goldsmith even suggested that there should be public compensation for such disadvantaged firms outside the zones (*Times*, 2 June 1981).

But how far outside? Boundary anomalies are inherent in the EZ concept, but the firms and areas disadvantaged by "unfair competition" are not just in the immediate vicinity of the EZs. Some rivals of firms in the EZ may be located a long way away, even in a different city. As for the negative effects of industry shifting to an EZ, that too could be "long distance". For example, the Vickers company is relocating its subsidiary company from Tewkesbury, Gloucestershire, to the Newcastle EZ. Ironically, one of the workers in the Tewkesbury subsidiary had uprooted his family and moved there from Newcastle to get a job (*Guardian*, 9 November 1981).

The conclusion from all this is that while the experiment will produce an increase in industrial and commercial premises, and in economic activity within the zones, it could well destroy as many firms, jobs and areas as it creates or revives. Overall, it could even lead to a *net loss* in jobs, but will it be possible to tell?

3.6 *Monitoring the experiment*

It will be difficult if not impossible accurately to measure the overall economic impact of the experiment. Early statements by politicians and officials suggested that the investigation of negative effects outside the zones would be minimal, and this impression was reinforced by the incentive of requiring *less* statistical information from firms in the zones, when one might have expected an *experiment* to require *more* information. On the important question of whether activity in the zones is genuinely *new*, the director of the Swansea zone said in 1981 that he was anxious to avoid re-extending bureaucracy to find out such information as this would be against the very spirit of the experiment! And *The Times* feature in March 1982 concluded that:

> nobody will know how many are new jobs, or merely jobs shuffled from one place to another, or jobs which will vanish when the fiscal benefits dry up. (*Times*, 9 March 1982)

However, the local authorities involved and the Association of Metropolitan Authorities expressed concern about inadequate monitoring outside the zones (*New Society*, 16 April 1981), and the monitoring being planned is now actually more thorough than originally expected (another modification by "the Whitehall machine"?).

The Department of the Environment has commissioned Roger Tym and Partners, an urban economic consultancy firm, to monitor the experiment over a three-year period. Starting in February 1981, they have so far established the state of the zones – land uses, quality of vacant land, existing firms and employment, and premises – at or around the time of designation, and they have designed how the impact of the incentives is to be monitored (DoE, 1982; McDonald and Howick, 1981). They hope to get a total record of all physical development and additional economic activity in the zones, and to sample survey sixty firms in the zones, and forty matched firms outside the boundaries to gauge the advantages of an EZ location and the effects outside of "unfair competition". There are plans for a small number of detailed case studies: of different types of physical development; of the property market in several areas; of the financial operations of some zone businesses; and of the continuing investment and promotion by the public sector.[23]

Clearly from all this information it should be possible to assess how much of the additional activity in the zones is genuinely new, how the relaxation of planning controls is affecting economic and environmental conditions, and from where existing firms and proposed investments have been relocated. The relative importance of the different incentives should also be clarified, as should at least some of the negative effects on outside areas. However, the negative "multiplier effect" of "unfair competition" and geographical relocation will not be accurately measured, particularly in areas (such as Tewkesbury) which are not close to a zone, and which will not be officially covered by even small sample surveys or case studies.

4. Rhetoric and reality: some conclusions

4.1 Economic gains, political gains?

The total negative impact of the incentives *outside* the zones, unlike the total additional activity inside them, will not be monitored, but it may cancel out most, or even all, of the gains in the zones themselves. And these economic "gains" in the zones will often be short-term or narrow. A considerable amount of information about them will be collected, but it remains to be seen how it will be used politically.

We have seen some of the short-term *political* gains which the policy has already brought the Conservative Government. It divided the Labour Party and the trade union movement, partly along geographical lines, as some Labour Councils scrambled for the chance to purvey a Tory policy. It has helped to weaken local democracy, especially in Labour areas. Although not specifically geared to the creation of jobs nor likely to create many, it provided a "fig-leaf" to cover the Government's nakedness on the question of attempting to "solve" the problem of rising unemployment. In so using it, Mrs Thatcher was at least consistent for we saw that creating *more* unemployment is an integral part of her medicine for the economy.

In this context, and remembering Sir Geoffrey Howe's ideological objectives, it seems likely that additional activity in the zones, and particularly any spectacular "success stories", will be hailed as "proof" of the *laissez-faire* ideology that "liberating" private enterprise from "state interference" is the road to national recovery. Certainly the reduction of state controls, particularly those exercised by locally-elected Councils and their planning departments, would be easier and cheaper to generalize to the rest of the country than the financial incentives. These incentives the Treasury certainly could not afford to generalize to the whole economy. But the impact of the rates exemption could be used to bolster the on-going argument that industrial and commercial rates should generally be reduced, to push more of the rate burden on to the general residential population and/or lead to further "cuts" in local authority services.

Ironically, the more the EZ incentives were generalized to the rest of the country, the less would be the comparative advantage of an EZ location. If they are seen as generating significant activity on previously vacant land, there could also be political pressures to designate more zones and enlarge existing ones (*The Times*, 9 March 1982). However, it does not necessarily follow that such success would be replicated in larger zones, never mind in the country as a whole. The potential for success in the zones (as well as the viability of publicly financing the incentives from the rest of the economy) lies precisely in their *smallness*: in the fact that the firms and investment which can be transferred from elsewhere are spatially concentrated in small areas, and in the fact that these small areas give many firms a competitive edge over *local* rivals which do not get the financial concessions. To the extent that larger zones were successful their negative effects on surrounding areas would also be greater and probably to a disproportionally greater extent (see also McDonald and Howick, 1981, p. 37).

There will also probably be pressure to prolong the period of benefits beyond the present ten years. It may, for instance, be argued that a longer period is necessary to attract more long-term institutional investors. The Treasury will be loath to commit yet more public expenditure in advance to a scheme whose potential is inherently limited and as yet unproven, though some modifications to the scheme can be expected, probably when the three-year monitoring exercise is completed.

What sorts of modifications? Whatever the technical evidence the policy implications drawn from it will be essentially political, depending on prior assumptions about the "proper" role of the state in the economy.

4.2 *Where is* laissez-faire?

The reality of the present scheme is a long way from the *laissez-faire* rhetoric which launched it: from Sir Geoffrey's simplistic "model" of nineteenth century private enterprise and from Peter Hall's "Hong Kong". Successes cannot validly be claimed as a victory for *laissez-faire*, nor will failure prove that it "doesn't work". Indeed fear of failure has already prompted calls for changes to the scheme which would bring its reality closer to the rhetoric. But even in its present form, the experiment raises the question of what *laissez-faire* really means in late twentieth century Britain.

There is actually *more* state involvement in the zones than in the economy generally. There are increased financial subsidies to private enterprise, and prior to designation there had been very substantial public expenditure in some zone areas (e.g. Clydebank, Corby, Hartlepool, Swansea). For instance, Swansea did not ask for an EZ but it got one, in an area already prepared for redevelopment at public expense, which suggested to one commentator that the Government "rigged the choice of zones by putting money on horses half-way down the course" (*New Society*, 19 February 1981). Half of the unused land in the chosen areas was owned by local authorities and other public bodies, and continuing capital expenditure and promotion by the public sector is "a crucial factor in the success of all but a few Enterprise Zones"; the experiment is yet another of the small area policies seeking to attract industry to problem localities (McDonald and Howick, 1981, pp. 35, 36). As such, it faces many of the problems discussed in the last chapter.

However, it still retains distinctive features: more central government help and more publicity; publicity which emphasizes "de-regulation", though here again the reality differs from the rhetoric. As an official of the Clydebank EZ pointed out, the accelerated planning procedures are not a major attraction (*The Times*, 9 March 1982), basically because planning is not a serious obstacle to development elsewhere and certainly not in the many areas desperately trying to attract investment. On the other hand, the EZs are by no means the "planning-free zones" originally feared by the RTPI (1979), and fears that they would simply be havens for small "cowboy firms", scrap merchants and the like, have certainly turned out to be exaggerated. Some of the "cowboys" may be quite large. And they like planning – on their terms.

Each zone has an outline plan and additional retained powers (e.g. to refuse planning permission to large hypermarkets), and there are further controls in the leasing arrangements for publicly-owned land. Planning controls are essential for attracting medium- and long-term investment to the zones: they reduce the risks to investors (e.g. by ensuring against "bad neighbours"). Clearly, then, such investors do not want a "free-for-all"; if they support "de-regulation", their conception of it is much more selective than the rhetoric of *laissez-faire* suggests.

The selective reality of modern-day *laissez-faire* is even more apparent in the sorts of changes wanted by those who fear the scheme may fail. Peter Hall now concludes that:

> . . . there is nothing very radical about the Enterprise Zones. The worry is that in practice they will not achieve very much, and what they do achieve will be counter-productive. (Hall, 1981, p. 7)

He compared them unfavourably with their American counterparts which *are* geared to small business creation because "new jobs are created disproportionately by new, small firms". That was why in 1977 he had proposed EZs which would:

> . . . replicate, as far as possible, the conditions of successful entrepreneurship in the innovative countries of the new industrial world. (Hall, 1981, p. 10)

However, we saw that the success of the Asian "boom economies" was largely due to very *active* state intervention (Hall now recognizes its importance for innovation) and, above all, to dictatorial regimes which ensure freedom for employers in the form of low wages and pliable workforces – by denying their employees basic freedoms. And we saw that with the continuing crisis of profitability, and the highly integrated and competitive nature of the world market, it makes *capitalist* sense to attempt to replicate Asian labour conditions in Britain or North America, even if it has to be done gradually, and initially in small geographical areas.

And so Peter Hall now advocates the suspension of minimum wage laws in the American EZs as "an interesting socio-economic experiment" (Hall, 1981, 12),[24] while in Britain there are calls to weaken trade union organization in the zones.[25] The earlier versions of the EZ idea may indeed be a harbinger of future changes to the scheme if the present version does not achieve very much and the crisis continues to worsen.[26] Continuing pressure to reduce public expenditure would militate against any significant increase in state "handouts" to private enterprise, but freedom for employers could be extended by further "de-regulating" the health, safety and employment conditions of their workers.

That is what *laissez-faire* really means in late twentieth century Britain: continued and substantial state help for private capital and the scrapping of regulations which directly benefit labour. Less the "classical" *laissez-faire* of Hong Kong, closer to the "model" of Singapore, Taiwan and South Korea.

Of course it may not happen. Opponents of the EZ scheme will see its failures in terms of the failure of private capital to invest in Britain even when given all sorts of financial incentives. And its failures will further confirm the belief of the Labour Left and others in the labour movement that direct state investment and national planning are necessary to deal with the obsolescence of British industry and restore its international competitiveness.

A social base for this "state capitalist" strategy exists in sections of the British trade union movement, and a future Labour Government might attempt to implement it. This could initially increase workers' self-confidence, as we have seen, *possibly* to the extent that they would push beyond the relatively mild reforms and nationalistic "solutions" (e.g. import controls supported by sections of domestic capital) which are all that can realistically be expected of a Labour Government. Even comparatively mild reforms will only be achieved with considerable "pressure from below" in the labour movement, but mild reforms are not enough. As Nigel Harris (1980, p. 80) points out: "the scale of obsolescence (is) so gigantic that much more than a reformist government will be required to change it". However, in the longer term, a movement to reform capitalism in Britain could under force of circumstances be converted into a movement which attempts to reorganize society on *socialist* lines, with production organized according to human needs rather than being determined by profitability criteria whether these are imposed by private or state capital.[27] Industry in Britain is being strangled by a profitability crisis of world capitalism, and so long as production continues to be governed by profitability criteria there will be continuing pressure to push down workers' wages, working conditions and living standards to levels which capital finds more competitive with places like Singapore and South Korea.

Meanwhile, in the shorter term, Britain remains one of the "weak links" in world capitalism, and *neither* of the "two distinct philosophies" currently on offer looks likely to alter that fact. The political conflict over the role of the state in the economy is likely to intensify, and the immediate prospect is that enterprise zones and their "liberation" ideology will feature prominently in the debate for the foreseeable future. EZs cannot solve the problems of capital in Britain, but they have helped to pre-empt reforms which have support from, and the potential to mobilize, the labour movement, and it is possible that they will continue to do so. That is the measure of their significance.[28]

References

Anderson, J. (1973). Ideology in Geography, *Antipode*, **5**, 3, 1–6.

Anderson, J. (1980). Back to the nineteenth century, *New Statesman*, 11 July.

Banham, R., Barker, P., Hall, P. and Price, C. (1969). Non-plan: an experiment in freedom, *New Society*, 20 March.

Barker, C. and Weber, C. (1982). Solidarnosč: from Gdansk to military repression, special issue of *International Socialism*, **15**.

Brimson, P. (1979). "Islington's multinationals and small firms: magic or myth?", Islington Political Economy Group, London.

Butler, S. M. (1981). "Supply side" in the inner city Enterprise Zones in America, *Built Environment*, **7**, 1, 42–49.

City of Sheffield. (1980). Joint report to Policy Committee, (submitted to the Secretary of State), Department of Planning and Design, May.

Clydebank Task Force. (1980). "Historical summary and situation report", November.

Colenutt, B. (1981). Planning and the property market: conflict or co-operation?, *in* D. Potter *et al.* (eds), "Society and the Social Sciences: an introduction", Routledge and Kegan Paul in association with the Open University Press.

Community Development Project Inter-Project Editorial Team. (1977). "Gilding the Ghetto: the state and the poverty experiments", London (available from 85–87 Adelaide Terrace, Benwell, Newcastle-upon-Tyne).

Community Development Project Political Economy Collective (CDP-PEC). (1979). "The state and the local economy", Brookside, Seaton Burn, Newcatle upon Tyne.

Conservative Central Office. (1978). "Urban Challenge – 10 point Tory Declaration for Towns and Cities", 824/78, 20 June.

Crosland, C. A. R. (1957). "The future of socialism", Macmillan, New York.

Davis, B. and Green, J. (1979). "The political framework: a Marxist view", *in* M. Loney and M. Allan (eds), "The crisis of the Inner City", Macmillan, London.

Department of the Environment. (1981). "Enterprise zones", HMSO, April.

Department of the Environment. (1982). Monitoring enterprise zones: year one report, Vol. 1, "Main report"; and Vol. 2, "State of the zones", London, March.

Dunleavy, P. (1982). "The politics of mass housing", Clarendon Press, Oxford.

Foster, J. (1979). How imperial London preserved its slums, *International Journal of Urban and Regional Research*, **3**, 1, 93–114.

Fröebel, F., Heinrichs, J. and Kreye, O. (1980). "The New International Division of Labour", Cambridge University Press, Cambridge.

Goldsmith, W. (1981). "Enterprise zones in the United States: lessons from international experience", Annual Conference of the Association of Collegiate Schools of Planning, Washington DC, October.

Greater London Council. (1978). Planning and Communications Policy Committee, P. C. 251, 8 June.

Green, J., Murray, U. and Davis, B. (1979). The new sweatshops, *in* CDP-PEC "The state and the local economy", Brookside, Seaton Burn, Newcastle upon Tyne.

Hall, P. (1977). "Green fields and grey areas", Royal Town Planning Institute, Annual Conference, 15 June.

Hall, P. (1981). Enterprise zones: British origins and American adaptations, *Built Environment*, 7, 1, 5–12.

Harris, N. (1978). The Asian boom economies and the "impossibility" of national economic development, *International Socialism*, 3, 1–16.

Harris, N. (1980). Deindustrialisation, *International Socialism*, 7, 72–81.

Hill, D. (1980). Enterprise zones, *Local Government Chronicle*, 13 June.

Howe, G. (1978). "Liberating free enterprise: a new experiment", Speech to the Bow Group, Isle of Dogs, London, 26 June, 1978 (Text: Conservative Central Office, News Service, 856/78) (Also reprinted in G. Sternlieb, and D. Listakin (eds), 1981.

Howe, G. (1980). Budget speech. 26 March (reproduced in *The Times*, 27 March 1980).

Hudson, R. (1978). Spatial policy in Britain: regional or urban. *Area*, 10, 2, 121–22.

Jessop, B. (1980). The transformation of the state in post-war Britain, *in* R. Scase (ed.), "The State in Western Europe", Croom Helm, London.

Keeble, D. (1977). Spatial policy in Britain: regional or urban, *Area*, 9, 1, 3–8.

Labour Party National Executive Committee. (1980). "Enterprise zones policy statement", Home Policy Committee, August.

McDonald, I. and Howick, C. (1981). Monitoring the enterprise zones, *Built Environment*, 7, 31–7.

Morris, P. (1979). Race, community and marginality: siralynx, *in* G. Craig, M. Mayo and N. Sherman (eds), "Jobs and Community Action", Routledge & Kegan Paul, London.

Morris, P. (1980). "Back street factory", CDP-PEC, Brookside, Seaton Burn, Newcastle upon Tyne.

Open Group, (1969). Social reform in the centrifugal society, *New Society*, 11 September.

"Report of Committee on Small Firms", (Bolton Report) (1971). Cmnd. 4811, HMSO, London.

Royal Town Planning Institute. (1979). "Planning free zones: a policy statement", London, 28 November.

Scottish Trades Union Congress. (1980). "Enterprise zones: a response to the Government's policy proposals", 9 April.

Skinner, I. (1978). "Free ports and related facilities", Greater London Council Research Library, London Topics No. 29, August.

Stedman Jones, G. (1971). "Outcast London: a study of the relationship between classes in Victorian Society", Oxford University Press, Oxford.

Sternlieb, G. (1981). Kemp-Garcia Act: an initial evaluation *in* G. Sternlieb and D. Listokin (eds), "New tools for economic development", Center for Urban Policy Research, Rutgers University, New Jersey.

Taylor, S. (1981). The politics of enterprise zones, *Public Administration*, **59**, 421–39.

Trades Union Congress. (1980). "Enterprise zones", 23 April.

Wales Trades Union Congress. (1980). "Response to the Government's enterprise zones" (undated).

Wheen, F. (1979). The economics of Sir Fu Manchu, *New Statesman*, 19 January.

Wohl, A. S. (1977). "The eternal slum: housing and social policy in Victorian London, Arnold, London.

Notes

1. The unsuccessful contenders included: North Tyneside, South Tyneside, Sunderland, Middlesborough and Stockton in the North-East; Sheffield; Wolverhampton; Bristol and Kerrier in the South-West; and in London the Boroughs of Islington, Hammersmith, Newham, Hackney and Wandsworth (*Local Government Chronicle*, 18 July 1980).

2. At its simplest the term "ideology" refers to systems of ideas which give distorted and partial accounts of reality, with the objective (and not necessarily intended) effect of serving the partial interests of a particular social group or class; it is not just ideas, but can be reified in particular policies, institutions, physical structures, etc. (see Anderson 1973).

3. This section is based on a paper with the same title written just after the March 1980 introduction of EZs as official policy. It was not published but was distributed privately, parts of it even finding their way into the Labour Party NEC policy statement on EZs (August, 1980). The paper was updated for the Annual Conference of the British Sociological Association/Political Studies Association Political Sociology Group, University of Sheffield, January 1982, and this chapter benefitted from the discussion there, as it did from later comments, including those of Doreen Massey and Simon Duncan.

4. The Fabians, along with other middle-class intellectuals such as William Beveridge and Alfred Marshall, saw the chronically unemployed in Social Darwinist terms: they advocated sterilization as well as labour colonies for this biologically "unfit" stratum of society (see Stedman Jones 1971, 330–334).

5. The "Open Group" comprised: Paul Barker, Peter Hall, Brian MacArthur, John Maddox, Peter Marris, Della Nevitt, L. J. Sharpe, Peter Willmott and Michael Young (*New Society* 11 September 1969).

6. This is *not* to imply that there was a golden "socialist" age in the Labour Party until the 1950s. For example, the Fabian Society, which pre-dates the Labour Party (see note 4, above) has been influential in the Party since it was founded in 1906, and its elitist conception of "socialism" has, despite variations, always been quite compatible with a private enterprise economy.

7. This "convergence" helps explain why some current Labour policies at local level which are now widely seen as very radical do not seem quite so radical when compared to their historical forerunners, as was pointed out in the previous chapter by Allan Cochrane. A detailed analysis of state intervention in post-war Britain is provided by Jessop (1980).

8. A Home Office Chief Inspector said of the CDP that there was "an element of looking for a new method of social control ... Gilding the ghetto or buying time ..." (CDP, 1977, 46). (This is *not* an argument against the principle of policies for particularly needy areas, only against the content and disconnectedness of some of the policies implemented.)

9. There are about thirty "freeports" in Europe. Hamburg's can be traced back to the medieval Hanseatic League, but in Britain, partly because the unitary national territory was consolidated relatively early, the bonded warehouse' system has been used instead (see Skinner 1978).

10. In October 1979 Liverpool Conservative MP Anthony Steen proposed a Parliamentary Bill to set up "tax-free zones in inner-city areas" in which planning controls would be reduced and "UK taxation, customs and excise duties would not apply" (*Hansard* 1147, 31 October 1979). In addition, the Deputy Leader of the GLC Labour Opposition, Illtyd Harrington advocated "Why London should have its own freeport" in *The Times*, 9 August 1978.

11. According to a correspondent in *The Sunday Telegraph* ('Duty-free from the Isle of Dogs", 18 June 1978) the idea had been "engendered" by Mr Peter Drew, Chairman of the Taylor Woodrow subsidiary, St Katherine-by-the Tower Ltd. In the London docklands, Taylor Woodrow "owns bits and pieces . . . and may very well hope to participate in the co-ordination of these zones . . . as a construction company it will be interested in tendering for any factory developments".

12. Judy Hillman, ex-Planning Correspondent of *The Guardian* and now Communications Executive of St Katherine-by-the Tower Ltd, indignantly replied that the "development charter" was essential to attract Pension Fund financing, though she did not explain why (*Planning* **342**, 2 November 1979).

13. The *Financial Times*, 29 March 1977, had encouraged the Government to "let capital rip" in the inner cities; the Conservative Party published *Small Business: Big Future*, London, 1977; Nigel Mobbs (Chairman of Slough Estates Ltd, later involved with Sir Geoffrey Howe in developing the EZ idea – see note 22, below) stressed the importance of small firms and of the Government restoring business confidence in "How to attract industry to the inner city", *Municipal Review*, May, 1978; and Harold Lever likewise saw small firms as "vital to our economy . . . never more so than now . . . and never more so than in deprived and dejected inner-city areas" (quoted in Davis and Green, 1979, 44).

14. Hudson was replying to Keeble (1977); their debate continued in *Area* **10**, Nos 2 and 5, 1978.

15. Hong Kong's 1971 *Census* showed that over 35 000 children of between ten and fourteen were employed, mainly in textiles, construction and mining; schooling is neither compulsory nor free for children over twelve (Wheen, 1979).

16. These export-oriented economies also rely heavily on foreign investment and are in effect off-shore extensions of the Japanese and, to a lesser extent, the United States economies (Harris, 1978).

17. This logic now also appeals to the Reagan administration though the American EZ policies are rather different from the British case (see Goldsmith, 1981; Hall, 1981; Butler, 1981; Sternlieb, 1981).

18. Useful information on the internal decision-making processes in the formulation of the official policy is provided by Taylor (1981).

19. An official of the Amalgamated Union of Engineering Workers noted the dangers "that in their desperation, Labour Councils will become purveyors of the worst kind of Tory economic policy", and "that if the measures are unsuccessful, the demand for stronger medicine will grow, leading to lower standards of health and safety, pollution control and building requirements"; however, the AUEW policy making body had not yet discussed the matter by July 1980 (correspondence from the General Secretary, 17 July 1980). Two of the largest unions, the General and Municipal Workers Union (which had members at Singers in Clydebank) and the Transport and General Workers Union still had no policy a year later (correspondence dated 20 July 1981 and 27 July 1981, respectively).

20. Despite the statement in the "Treasury Press Release on Enterprise Zones", 26 March 1980, that the EZs had "no direct connection with . . . inner city policy".

21. Correspondence from Mr H. W. D. Sculthorpe, Chief Executive, Borough of Trafford, Manchester, 16 July 1981.

22. For example, firms such as Taylor Woodrow and Slough Estates collaborated directly with public authorities and politicians in preparing the way for the EZ experiment (see notes 11 and 13 above). In February 1981, the British Property Federation held a joint conference on EZs with the National Association of Pension Funds and one of the main speakers was Nigel Mobbs, Chairman of Slough Estates, who mentioned in his paper that he had "actively collaborated with the Chancellor in developing his embryo ideas". Nigel Broakes, Chairman of Trafalgar House which has major interests in property and construction, was appointed Chairman of the London Docklands Development Corporation which controls the Isle of Dogs EZ.

23. I am grateful to Cristina Howick of Roger Tym and Partners for information on monitoring procedures.

24. He qualified this by suggesting it should apply only in a limited number of small areas and only to young workers who are most prone to unemployment and least likely to have family responsibilities (Hall, 1981, 12). In practice, however, it would be difficult to ensure against young workers displacing older ones who do have such responsibilities, even if one accepted Peter Hall's proposition (and would it remain limited to small EZs?).

25. For example, Nigel Mobbs (1981 – note 22 above) proposed that the Dock Labour Scheme, which replaced the casual labour system in the docks and gave the unions joint-control of the deployment of dock workers, should be abolished in EZs close to ports, – something the Conservative Government would like to do for docks in general.

26. In 1978 Sir Geoffrey Howe did say of Peter Hall's Hong Kong proposal: "I should not *at this stage* support an experiment as dramatic as this; but the idea should be kept at the back of one's mind – if only as a yardstick against which to judge more modest proposals" (Howe, 1978, 13 – emphasis added).

27. In arguing for an internationalist socialist approach which fully recognizes the dominance of the *world* capitalist system over national economies, Harris (1980, 80) quotes a Cambridge Economic Policy Group estimate: to restore capitalism in Britain to a competitive position in the world market would require a 50% increase in manufacturing investment over the past trend rate, sustained for at

least 10 years (see also Singh, 1979, 208–214). Harris comments that an investment programme of this magnitude would necessitate the complete destruction or incorporation of the trade union movement, a radical reduction in state welfare services and a sharp cut in real wages: "For that, the nationalist Left would need a police State".

The current plight of Polish workers in a "workers' state" which is in hock to the international banking system, provides a grim reminder of what state capitalism can mean in crisis conditions (see Barker and Weber, 1982).

28. Since this chapter was written, a debate on Enterprise Zones has appeared in *International Journal of Urban and Regional Research* 1, 1982. More Enterprise Zones have been established, and legislation is available to set up Freeports.

Index